ROMANS AND BLACKS

Oklahoma Series in Classical Culture

ROMANS AND BLACKS

LLOYD A. THOMPSON

Professor of Classics
University of Ibadan

University of Oklahoma Press:
Norman and London

Library of Congress Cataloging-in-Publication Data

Thompson, Lloyd A.
Romans and Blacks/Lloyd A. Thompson. — 1st University of
Oklahoma Press ed.
p. cm. — (Oklahoma series in classical culture ; v. 2)
Bibliography: p.
Includes index.
ISBN 0–8061–2201–3
1. Blacks–Rome. I. Title. II. Series: Oklahoma series in
classical culture: #2.
DG190.T48 1989
305.8′96′037–dc19
88–40549 CIP

Romans and Blacks is Volume 2 in the Oklahoma Series in Classical Culture.

CONTENTS

v

CONTENTS

VXORI FILIISQVE

PREFACE

This work had its beginnings in a number of notes which I made on F.M. Snowden's *Blacks in Antiquity* during my first reading of that book in 1971, but which were left to gather dust throughout the rest of that decade owing to my heavy administrative responsibilities at the University of Ibadan. A preliminary draft of the second chapter, completed in 1982, had perforce to be extensively rewritten to take account of more recent literature, and most of the work was done in the course of a sabbatical in 1986–87, thanks to which I was eventually able to complete the manuscript in the autumn of 1987. I take this opportunity to express my gratitude to Professor John Ferguson, who for several years regularly drew my attention to items of classical art depicting blacks; to Professor Paul MacKendrick of the University of Wisconsin and his wife Dorothy for the kind and invaluable assistance which they gave me during my visit to Madison in the autumn of 1986; to the anonymous referee who kindly offered some helpful suggestions and references; and to Professor John Crook of St John's College, Cambridge, who read through the entire manuscript and made invaluable comments. Needless to say, he is not to be held responsible for any deficiencies that remain.

L.A.T.
Ibadan, March 1988

ABBREVIATIONS

ABSA	*Annual of the British School at Athens*
Acta Cl.	*Acta Classica*
Afr.Hist.St.	*African Historical Studies*
AHR	*American Historical Review*
AJA	*American Journal of Archaeology*
AJP	*American Journal of Philology*
AM	*Mitteilungen des Deutschen Archäologischen Instituts: Athenische Abteilung*
Anc.Soc.	*Ancient Society*
André, *Étude*	J. André, *Étude sur les termes de couleur dans la langue latine* (Paris 1949)
ANRW	*Aufstieg und Niedergang der römischen Welt: Geschichte und Kultur Roms im Spiegel der neueren Forschung,* ed. H. Temporini and W. Haase
Ant.Cl.	*L'Antiquité Classique*
Anth.Gr.	*Anthologia Graeca,* ed. W.R.Paton (Loeb Classical Library)
Anth.Lat.	*Anthologia Latina,* ed. F. Buecheler, E. Lommatzsch, and A. Riese
Brit.J.Psych.	*British Journal of Psychology*
Brit.J.Soc.	*British Journal of Sociology*
CCL	*Corpus christianorum: series Latina*
CIL	*Corpus inscriptionum Latinarum*
CLE	*Carmina Latina epigraphica,* ed. F. Buecheler
Cl.et Med.	*Classica et Mediaevalia*
CQ	*Classical Quarterly*
CR	*Classical Review*

Cracco Ruggini, 1974	L. Cracco Ruggini, 'Leggenda e realtà degli Etiopi nella cultura tardoimperiale', in *Atti del IV° congresso internazionale di studi etiopici*, (Rome 1974) I, 141-93.
Cracco Ruggini, 1979	L. Cracco Ruggini, 'Il negro buono e il negro malvagio nel mondo antico', in Marta Sordi (ed.), *Conoscenze etniche e rapporti di convivenza nell' antichità* (Milan 1979) 108-133
CSEL	*Corpus scriptorum ecclesiasticorum Latinorum*
Desanges, Catalogue	J. Desanges, *Catalogue des tribus africaines de l'antiquité classique à l'ouest du Nil* (Dakar 1962)
Desanges, Recherches	J. Desanges, *Recherches sur l'activité des méditerranéens aux confins de l'Afrique: VIe siècle avant J.-C. – IVe siècle après J.-C.* (Paris 1978)
EAA	*Enciclopedia dell' arte antica classica e orientale*
Et.Cl.	*Les Etudes Classiques*
GGM	*Geographi Graeci Minores*, ed. C. Müller
HSCP	*Harvard Studies in Classical Philology*
HTR	*Harvard Theological Review*
ILS	*Inscriptiones Latinae selectae*, ed. H. Dessau
Image	*The Image of the Black in Western Art*, I (New York 1976), II (Cambridge, Mass. 1979): contributions by J. Vercoutter, F.M. Snowden, and others.
J.Afr.H.	*Journal of African History*
JbAC	*Jahrbuch für Antike und Christentum*
JEA	*Journal of Egyptian Archaeology*
JOAI	*Jahreshefte des Oesterreichischen Archäologischen Instituts*
JRS	*Journal of Roman Studies*
MEFRA	*Mélanges de l'École Française de Rome: Antiquité*
Mem.Am.Ac.	*Memoirs of the American Academy in Rome*
Mnem.	*Mnemosyne*
Mon.Germ.Hist.	*Monumenta Germaniae historica: auctores antiquissimi*
Mon.Piot.	*Monuments et mémoires publiés par l'Académie des Inscriptions et Belles-Lettres: Fondation Eugène Piot*
PACA	*Proceedings of the African Classical Associations*
PBSR	*Papers of the British School at Rome*
PG	*Patrologiae cursus completus: series Graeca*, ed. J.P. Migne

P.Giess.	O. Eger, E. Kornemann, and P.M. Meyer, *Griechische Papyri im Museum des oberhessischen Geschichtsvereins zu Giessen* (Leipzig/Berlin 1910-1912)
PL	*Patrologiae cursus completus: series Latina.* ed. J.P. Migne
P.Lond.	*Greek Papyri in the British Museum*, ed. F.G. Kenyon and H.I. Bell (London 1893-1917)
P.Oxy.	*The Oxyrhynchus Papyri*, ed. B.B. Grenfell, A.S. Hunt *et al.* (London 1898-)
Proc.Brit.Ac.	*Proceedings of the British Academy*
PSI	*Papiri greci e latini* (Pubblicazioni della Società italiana per la ricerca dei papiri greci e latini in Egitto), ed. G. Vitelli and M. Norsa (Florence 1912-)
P.Yale	*Yale Papyri in the Meineke Rare Book and Manuscript Library*, ed. J.F. Oates, A.E. Samuel, and C.B. Welles (New Haven 1967)
P.Zen	*Zenon Papyri: Business Papers of the third century BC dealing with Palestine and Egypt.* I, ed. W.L. Westermann *et al.* (New York 1940)
RE	*Realencyclopädie der classischen Altertumswissenschaft* ed. A. Pauly, G. Wissowa and others.
REA	*Revue des études anciennes*
Rec.Bodin	*Recueils de la Société Jean Bodin*
REL	*Revue des études Latines*
RFHOM	*Revue Française d'histoire d'outre-Mer*
Rh.M.	*Rheinisches Museum für Philologie*
RM	*Mitteilungen des Deutschen Archäologischen Instituts: Römische Abteilung*
SEG	*Supplementum epigraphicum Graecum*
Snowden, *Blacks*	F.M. Snowden, *Blacks in Antiquity: Ethiopians in the Greco-Roman Experience* (Cambridge, Mass. 1970)
TAPA	*Transactions of the American Philological Association*
TLL	*Thesaurus linguae Latinae*
ZPE	*Zeitschrift für Papyrologie und Epigraphik*

INTRODUCTION

'Fools rush in where angels fear to tread', wrote Alexander Pope, encapsulating in a memorable *sententia* a universal perception. In the wake of recent scholarship on the theme of blacks in ancient Roman society,[1] the undertaking of another study of this narrow subject may well be widely regarded as a superfluous and pointless enterprise[2] – a feeling probably shared even by those who have (not unjustifiably) reacted with impatience to treatments of the subject which have seemed designed to serve 'a spurious cultural nationalism of colour and form' by attempting to 'isolate the negro' (in the highly artificial and particularistic modern American sense of the term) in the societies of classical antiquity.[3] Be that as it may, I see the question of Roman attitudes and behaviour towards blacks as one that is very much open to new discussion. To be sure, practically all the ancient evidence at my disposal has featured in earlier discussions, and in the very rare cases where I know of no earlier consideration of a piece of evidence, that evidence indicates nothing about Roman society that is not already indicated by some item of the frequently discussed data. What is required is a discussion of this data on the basis of a perspective more appropriate to the assumptions of Roman antiquity than those hitherto adopted.[4] The subject is one in which fundamental importance must be given to the framework of concepts and assumptions underlying the investigation. The present study (which is mainly concerned with the period from the first century BC to the third century AD) rests on the conviction that some of the matters which are integral to any inquiry into the way or ways in which Romans thought, felt, and acted towards somatically distant persons, such as blacks (*Aethiopes*), transcend the themes discussed

1

(adequately or not) in the existing literature.

For the most part, that literature seeks to explain Roman attitudes towards blacks (and black–white social relations in Roman society) in terms of 'race', but without presenting any justification for such an approach; the authors make free use of terms like 'racial prejudice' and 'racism' without attempting to define these concepts or to distinguish from other kinds of social–psychological situations the phenomena designated in modern sociological theory by the term 'racism' and its cognates. This terminology, by definition, presupposes a systematic exploitation of one social segment by another group in the same society, in an ideological system that ascribes membership of the oppressed underclass to all descendants of members of that group *sub specie aeternitatis*.[5] But, as employed in the literature on blacks in Roman antiquity, these terms amount to little more than a set of nebulous notions which tend to give substance to the sarcastic observation of a well known anthropologist to the effect that too many people wrongly believe that they know, and are only too eager to say, what 'race' is.[6] One would perhaps be better served by a recollection of the confession made by Norman Baynes some forty years ago: 'as soon as the word 'race' is introduced into any discussion I realize that my only safe course lies in a resolute silence, for I have never been able to understand the precise significance of that ambiguous term.'[7] On the basis of the concept of 'race' in sociological theory it is certainly not legitimate to presume (as almost all earlier discussions have done)[8] that the issue of blacks in Roman antiquity is a question of 'race relations'. Engagement of the sociological concept 'race' in relation to the structures of Roman society is an obvious precondition for any confident and meaningful conclusion that Roman society was either 'racist' or 'non-racist' with regard to blacks or 'Ethiopians' or 'negroes', and even for any satisfactory explanation, for a modern reader, of Roman attitudes and behaviour towards blacks, or of black–white social relations in the Roman world.

For these reasons I shall explain in the final pages of this introduction the definitions of such terms as 'race', 'racisim', 'colour prejudice', and 'race relations' which find general acceptance among modern sociologists, and I make these definitions the foundation of much of my discussion for two reasons. First, the sociological theorists to whom their formulation is due have perceived some quite essential distinctions (for example, between 'racism' and 'ethnocentrism') which it is imperative to observe if we are to avoid confusion and distortion in our interpretation of Roman attitudes; furthermore, the definitions are correct in the sense that, once stated, they can be seen to stand to reason. Second, it is vital to the present subject that those who study it should agree on some definitions of commonly utilized terminology. If, as has hitherto been the case, the same terms are used (albeit for the most part unconsciously) to mean different things, the result can only be misconception, inconsistency, lack of clarity, profound (though often unjustifiable) differences of opinion, and much unnecessary polemic. Nor is it accceptable to attempt to analyse the social and psychological impact of perceived somatic distance (in popular parlance, physical 'race' differences) without first giving serious consideration to the *Roman* concept 'black person' (*Aethiops*) and to *Roman* perceptions of somatic distance.[9] An examination of the degrees of somatic distance which, in the perceptions of ancient Romans, separated the *Aethiops* type and certain other types of physiognomy from the Roman norm is a second precondition for a meaningful study of the theme of blacks in Roman society. But again, this prerequisite has been either altogether ignored, or inadequately met, in earlier discussions

Failure to satisfy these two preconditions explains why one scholar, for whom 'colour prejudice' (in the context of black–white social relations) is quite rightly a synonym of 'racial prejudice', has nonetheless been able to conclude that Roman society was not racist, while at the same time appearing to admit that blacks in that society encountered some degree of 'colour prejudice', albeit milder and less widespread than the 'intense' modern variety.[10] Similarly, another scholar, in the misguided belief that 'racism' and 'racist ideology' are independent and separable phenomena, arrived at an inherently inconsistent conclusion about the Christian society of the Roman world, to which he attributed at one and the same time an absence of anti-black racism 'on the ideological level', a lack of 'marked antipathy toward blackness itself and, as a consequence, toward black people', a stratification system that allowed blacks upward social mobility on the basis of the normal criteria for such mobility, and a *de facto* racial inequality 'at the level of daily life and concrete social relationships' which 'bred prejudice and raised barriers' against blacks.[11] Quite obviously, if the system did in fact permit the social mobility envisaged by this scholar, there can have been no *racial* inequality, unless we are to suppose that the social mobility related, not to the same system of stratification that applied to non-blacks, but only to an internal stratification within a degraded segment of the population to which all blacks were perforce consigned; and that would attest to the very racism ('on the ideological level') denied by this scholar. Others, again, speak of certain items of Roman literature as *'pamphlets franchement racistes'* or allude to *'la violence de certaines charges racistes'* in Roman writing, or envisage the Romans as 'the master race', driven by a superiority complex to impose 'racial inequality' upon others.[12] And such pronouncements are always made without reference to the structures of Roman society or reflection on the psychological processes which shaped Roman perceptions of human otherness and merit.[13] What is more, no one has been able to produce a convincing contradiction of Brunt's observation (on possessors of Roman citizenship) that 'if by culture and sentiment men were Romans, Romans they were', or of the argument that the concepts 'wog' and 'nigger' cannot be translated into Latin or Greek.[14] There are, accordingly, considerable grounds for dissatisfaction with the present state of the question on blacks (or on so-called 'race relations') in Roman society and with all the various attempts to interpret the issue of black–white social relations as one of *race* – even if some eminent scholars have expressed satisfaction with the general position.[15]

THE QUESTION OF PERSPECTIVE

In recent decades much has been written about the attitudes of Romans towards peoples whom they perceived as significantly different from themselves. But this literature has been devoted for the most part to the themes of 'barbarians' and 'antisemitism', and there has been comparatively little interest among scholars in ancient social relations specifically involving individuals and groups of the sort nowadays described as 'non-white'.[16] Yet learned people have at various times expressed a firm conviction that physical 'race' differences have always played a role in history and have always had some social implications; and the question of ancient attitudes towards blacks appears to have generated considerable popular interest and speculation in countries like the United States

4

since the early nineteenth century.[17] It would seem that, among scholars, interest in this subject has been deterred more by the scantiness of the ancient evidence than by appreciation of the problematic nature of that evidence. For in a study of blacks in Roman antiquity, the objects of which comprise social relations and attitudes (the opinions, feelings, and strivings of people, and the degrees of closeness or distance which marked the interactions of blacks and non-blacks living in the same social space),[18] investigators are forced to content themselves with reading a few bits of Latin and Greek and studying representations of blacks and other 'aliens' in Roman iconography, endeavouring never to forget that they are hearing voices and receiving signals from a great distance in terms of cultural context as well as time, and that they are therefore likely to be couched in an unfamiliar code. One premise of the discussion, moreover, has to be that collective behaviour cannot be fully understood in isolation from the social forces that shape it, and the search for indications of Roman attitudes and behaviour must go beyond the occasional instances of highly articulated and 'philosophical' ideas so as to embrace all Roman notions and beliefs about blacks (to the extent that these are recoverable), and all indications of Roman reactions to blacks as social beings, including remarks of the casual and tangential kind which, in many societies, are often the most important sources of information on attitudes.[19] The background for the interpretation of the written and iconographic material must accordingly include the structures of Roman society and the Roman value system. What Romans thought about their own place in the universal scheme of things naturally influenced their perceptions of aliens, and so an understanding of the Roman ideological, social, and economic system is essential to the discussion of Roman attitudes towards blacks and of the positions of blacks in Roman society.[20] But these attitudes are most profitably studied in the context of Roman attitudes towards aliens in general,[21] even if that involves some repetition of much that is already common knowledge among professional students of Roman antiquity.

In his essay on Roman attitudes suggested by the references to blacks and blackness in Christian patristic literature, J.M. Courtès commendably took care to explain the nature of those references, pointing out their coincidental and 'dependent' character, drawing attention to the fact that they are practically silent on concrete examples of blacks, and noting that they are mostly metaphorical allusions to blackness in the context either of exegetical interpretations of the scriptures or of anecdotes on the theme of demons (envisaged as black in colour) – in both cases symbolically 'marking the opposition between good and evil, between the graced and the ungraced'.[22] The pagan texts are also limited in scope and mostly coincidental. In the first place, they all represent the voices of men whose status distanced them socially from the great majority of such blacks as happened to be within their reach. We have no first-hand record of the observations of men of the humbler classes, some of whom obviously had extensive and intensive social relations with blacks. In the second place, the available texts (apart from ethno-geographical writing about 'Aethiopians' in remote and often nebulous African habitats) for the most part speak coincidentally and from a remote standpoint about 'a black person' (*Aethiops*), 'two Aethiopians', and the like, very often with the purpose of voicing a stereotype or echoing the negative symbolism of the colour black. Only very rarely do such references offer concrete information as limited even as 'a black soldier'; references to blacks with personal names are rarer still. Again, there are no texts in which blacks speak directly for themselves. Thus the few texts in which a writer directly addresses a particular black in praise or disparagement assume much importance as the only items in which the themes of blacks and blackness, and the writer's interest in the black, are other than coincidental to some other purpose.

By its very nature, therefore, the written material on the whole suggests the absence (among the educated and leisured classes of Roman society) of a preoccupation with blacks as social objects. Nor does the substance of this material indicate any special interest in the lives and fortunes of blacks *qua* blacks among these classes. It would seem that interest in blacks on the part of such persons depended on some personal connection with a given black (as personal servant or dependant), or was otherwise aroused only by some glamorous activity such as the achievements of a successful black performer in the circus or arena, or scandalous reports about the relations of black gigolos and prostitutes with sexual partners of high rank. Some texts (as also some iconographic depictions of macrophallic blacks) certainly imply an upper-class curiosity in the sexual sphere, and this is even attested to in some of the Christian material.[23] But the interest of the educated classes seems otherwise to have been directed towards the remote 'Aethiopians' of the Nilotic kingdom of Meroe, who clearly aroused considerable curiosity and even kindly interest. On the other hand, among the silent ranks of the Roman lower orders (and especially among the slave population) interest in the lives of blacks must have been quite extensive and intensive, for blacks, being evidently individuals of humble rank and status for the most part, must on the whole have had closer social interactions with whites of humble station than they had with members of the leisure classes. Despite the limitations of the sort of material on which we perforce depend, it would be over-pessimistic to adopt the view that this material can tell us practically nothing about feelings and attitudes towards blacks among the lower classes of Roman society.[24] For one thing, the voices of the educated occasionally transcend narrowly upper-class points of view to indicate popular ideas, interests, and attitudes. For another, many of the artists responsible for the iconography relating to blacks must have been quite ordinary plebeians of the sort described by Lucian as 'earning a small wage, a man of low esteem, neither courted by friends, feared by enemies, nor envied by fellow-citizens, but just a common workman, a face in a crowd, one who makes his living with his hands.'[25] And their depictions of blacks offer signals of their own attitudes and of the outlook of people of their own humble station. The relevant iconography contains an element of caricature of blacks, but in general the representations of blacks (found mostly on small utilitarian objects like earrings and terracotta lamps) suggest an absence of anti-black xenophobia and a tendency on the part of the owners and users of these objects to take blacks for granted, at least in those localities where blacks were actually a familiar part of the social scene (in other localities the dominant suggestion would be a vogue for the exotic).[26]

Some of the modern literature has discussed certain aspects of the Roman ideological system in relation to the theme of blacks – notably the notion of the geographical environment as a key to the explanation of ethnic diversity, colour symbolism, and popular beliefs in biological atavism and 'maternal impression', according to which a white couple could produce a black baby if either of the partners had a black ascendant, however distant, or if a black person observed by the woman made a deep impression on her mind.[27] But the antique simplicity of Roman perceptions of somatic distance has continued to elude the grasp of scholars. No serious attempt has so far been made to grasp this Roman perceptual context and to relate it to the framework of assumptions inherent in the structures of Roman society. For instance, the various discussions have not recognized the necessity of distinguishing between, on the one hand, the kind of reactions to black somatic characteristics that are nurtured by a racist system (reactions which have nothing to do with the strangeness of blacks and unfamiliarity with their appearance in the society concerned), and, on the other hand, ethnocentric reactions to a strange and unfamiliar somatic appearance. Unlike the latter (a natural and universally evidenced human response), the former are essentially reactions to an ideologically ascribed, and so almost infallibly predictable, social significance of a given set of somatic characteristics.[28] This important distinction is perhaps fully comprehended only if (as is the principle followed in the present work) the discussion is allowed to dwell almost as extensively on the perceptual context of certain modern societies as on that of the ancient Romans. Unlike kinship, nationality, and cultural or religious identity, skin colour in itself has no more meaning than height or weight. It is the mind of the observer that, drawing on past experience, renders pigmentation and other physical traits a repository of messages about personal beliefs, cultural habits, and social status, and makes these traits a focus of passionate sentiments transcending the merely aesthetic.[29] And, of course, the notion of a collective mind precisely and exclusively linked at any given point in time with a particular skin colour (let alone the idea of an eternally fixed 'white' or 'black' or 'yellow' mentality) is an utter absurdity. Hence the importance of an *appropriate* model for the study of the present subject.

To be sure, all interpretation of ancient evidence necessarily rests on some kind of model: explicit and consciously used, or implicit and sometimes unconsciously used. But the implicit model involves an undue reliance on so-called common sense, which in turn always depends upon a set of assumptions and unconscious prejudices arising from one's own social conditioning.[30] A distinguished French historian some time ago deplored the use of implicit models by members of his confraternity, remarking that these scholars tended to react with surprise at 'discovering in the past what they themselves have put there' by drawing too heavily on familiar assumptions.[31] Oddly enough, no surprise has been evident in the work of any of the scholars who have discovered 'racism' or 'racial prejudice' in Roman society. The sole indications of surprise in this matter have appeared in the work of scholars who, while maintaining that 'race prejudice' was unknown among the ancient Romans, have adjudged the *absence* of that phenomenon to be a 'remarkable' fact, and indeed one demanding explanation – as though the *presence* of racism were what was naturally to be expected.[32] Yet in the perspective of world history racism is evidently the aberration demanding explanation, and surprise at discovering that this phenomenon *did* exist in Roman society would be appropriate in so far as nothing that is known about the anatomy, physiology, pathology, and psychology of that society suggests any parallel with what sociologists call a 'race relations situation' (that is, racist social structures with or without overt discriminatory legislation).

Quite evidently the study of blacks in Roman society involves a certain amount of combat with the tyranny of modern habits of mind. But some assistance can be obtained from an attempt to compare the Roman situation with, for instance, that of fifteenth-century Europe, where the term 'black man' did not designate the same concept or the same social object that it currently designates, and where the modern notion of the 'sociological black' would have been unintelligible.[33] It was not until the eighteenth century that Europeans (whether at home or in their colonies) began to attach greater significance to somatic distance than to the religious and other cultural differences between themselves and other peoples. In earlier times non-Europeans were not perceived as *essentially* different: there was always a belief in the possibility of the passage of people of all ethnic categories from one socio-cultural category to another, as was undoubtedly also the case among the Romans.[34] The transition in the European outlook began when people became highly conscious of the distance in culture and in technological and material power that had, by the eighteenth century, come to separate some parts of the world (which happened to be 'white') from the rest (which happened to be 'non-white'). Reinforced by another historically peculiar situation, the institution of an all-black chattel-slavery, and by European imperialism in other continents, this hyperconsciousness resulted in a peculiar ecumenical configuration of rich/'white' and poor/'coloured' peoples, separated by previously unimaginable differences in gross national product *per caput*. That went hand in hand with a peculiar pattern of power-distribution, easily correlated in the imagination with degrees of human pigmentation (or lack of pigmentation), to the advantage of 'whites'. Europeans, hitherto born 'to a status, to a cultural world', were thereafter born 'to an appearance, to a physical condition, as well'.[35] The major race relations situations of the past two hundred years or so have their roots in the psychological urge felt by the dominant groups in those conditions to justify the historically peculiar configuration of 'white' master/conqueror set against 'coloured' slave/subject.[36]

It is important (even if often difficult) to avoid the unwarranted assumption that the constraints of this historically peculiar situation are somehow natural, and that somatic distance (what is popularly called 'race') is by nature as powerful a determinant of social distance as are differences in cultural habits, and in quality and scale of material goods. In our world, to be sure, terms like 'European', 'whites', 'blacks', and 'the third world' easily serve as symbols of a particular cultural situation, group experience, and level of technological development and material power. Differences in somatic appearance have long symbolized 'differences between present wealth and power and present poverty and weakness, between present fame and present obscurity, between present eminence in intellectual creativity and present intellectual unproductiveness.'[37] But the assumptions fostered by this modern symbolism can hardly be relevant to the society of the ancient Romans, whose *Weltanschauung* included a perception of the majority of the world's *white* inhabitants as 'savages' and benighted 'barbarians'.[38] By the same token – and against the background of the Graeco-Roman view of the geographical environment as an explanation of the somatic and temperamental diversity of human groups, with its clear distinction between the 'developed' world of pale-brown (*albus*) Mediterranean people, the barbarian 'under-developed' world, and another barbarian but 'cultivated' world –[39] no concept of 'white' people as a meaningful socio-cultural category could arise in Roman society. Nor could the prevailing mentality link superiority to an ascending scale of whiteness as has been the case in modern times, since that mode of ranking has become, in some areas, a dominant ideological principle.[40] For if the 'developed world' of the Roman world view was definitely the world of pale-brown Mediterraneans, both the 'underdeveloped world' and the intermediate 'cultivated world' of that *Weltanschauung* always embraced populations of different somatic types, including blacks and pale-white northern and central Europeans.[41]

This again points to the necessity of erecting a *Roman* model, however difficult the exercise. The eighteenth-century poet, William Blake, shares with the author of a third-century Romano-Egyptian epitaph the urge to describe a black man as possessor of a white soul despite his somatic blackness. Similarly, in nineteenth-century France, Victor Hugo sought to console a black man with the sentiment that all souls are white in God's sight, while a black poet of the seventh-century Arab world contrasted the 'black garment' of his own body with his 'lustrous' inner whiteness.[42] If, on the surface, these messages appear identical, it cannot be legitimate to assume that the social-psychological conditions of the blacks concerned were also identical or nearly so. Each of these contrasts between somatic blackness and spiritual whiteness takes its sociological significance from its own social-psychological context. That is the major axiom on which the present work is anchored.

The discussion and definitions of terminology and concepts which follow are designed to eliminate certain misconceptions that have marred much of the existing literature on so-called 'race relations' in classical antiquity. Chapter 1 is devoted to a critique of the modern literature on blacks in Roman society in the light of the ancient evidence and of modern sociological theory. In Chapter 2 I discuss the perception of somatic distance in Roman society, with particular reference to the anthropological type described in Roman antiquity by the term *Aethiops* ('black African'). That discussion attempts to throw some light on the collective mentality that formed the general background of assumptions behind Roman comments on blacks in literature and in iconography, and here I demonstrate in a decisive manner that Roman attitudes in no way merit the labels 'race prejudice', 'colour prejudice', and 'racism'. Some emphasis is also given to the extent to which an appreciation of the true nature of Roman attitudes depends upon a prior and serious questioning of certain familiar modern assumptions which have been allowed to pass unquestioned in earlier discussions of the subject. With the purpose of throwing further light on the Roman situation, the discussion in chapter 3 centres on certain values and cognitive structures that shaped attitudes of appreciation or disparagement of somatic and cultural traits as well as conceptions of deference-worthiness and of inferiority in the Roman socio-cultural system. In the course of this discussion attempts are made to relate the ancient evidence on blacks in Roman society to the emerging picture of the Roman ideological system. Finally, I set out a summary of the conclusions reached in the various chapters regarding the attitudes, behavioural patterns, and social-psychological situations that marked interpersonal relations between blacks and whites as signalled by the meagre and problematic ancient evidence on the subject.

THE CONCEPTS 'RACE', 'RACISM', AND 'COLOUR PREJUDICE'

In biological science the term 'race' has connoted 'a large population which differs from another population in the frequency distribution of given hereditary characteristics' – a genetic reality which (according to biologists) has no sociological implications and can contribute nothing towards elucidation of phenomena like racism or the social and power-political roles of popular ideas, myths, and fantasies about 'race'.[43] On the other hand, historians have observed that 'race', in a certain sense, must have been historically 'the first determinant of inter-group social relations' and that (again, 'in a certain sense') 'race difference has always played a role in history'.[44] In such a context 'race' is presumably intended as a synonym of 'somatic type' or 'somatic distance between human groups'; but social scientists mean something different again when they speak of 'the problems of race that perplex the moral conscience of the world' or when they say that 'race' has had a significant role in 'moulding the parameters' of modern society.[45] Impatience with this ambiguity has induced some scientists to pray for the disappearance of the word 'race' from our vocabulary, and in scientific usage there has been a general tendency to replace the word with 'anthropological type' or 'somatic type'.[46] But, for all its ambiguity, the term 'race' is hardly likely to disappear; even if it were to disappear, we should still be left with the sociological reality that it currently designates.

Scholars in the human sciences should accordingly content themselves with emphasizing the fact that, in their fields of study, 'race' is meaningful only as a complex sociological phenomenon, and that data from the natural sciences can serve (and have served) only as a symbol of this sociological reality.[47]

Arnold Toynbee, writing at a time when a notion of 'race' as *moteur* of human history was much in vogue, explained that particular concept (which he personally treated with the scorn that it deserved) as a congeries of 'distinctive psychic or spiritual qualities' innate in a given people and precisely correlated with the somatic type represented by that people.[48] That was one of the faces assumed by the racism of the grand era of European colonialism, when learned men could shamelessly indulge in postures like that to which Bruce Trigger recently drew attention: stressing the 'whiteness' of ancient Nubians when contrasting them and their achievements with blacks and black achievements, but denigrating them as Africans or 'blacks' in contexts of contrast with paler-hued peoples and their achievements.[49] The particular concept of 'race' to which Toynbee alluded has long since been in recession, yielding to newer ideological bases for the persisting phenomenon of racism.[50] But the ambiguity surrounding the term 'race' and its cognates persists, largely owing to the persistent popularity of some of the oldest usages of these terms.

In these old and ever-popular usages, 'race' bears two sometimes overlapping connotations: on the one hand, an ethnic group, a people, or a nation; and, on the other hand, a somatic type defined in terms of perceived skin colour, hair type, and morphology – a concept of 'race' that dates from the latter part of the seventeenth century.[51] As recently as thirty years ago even serious writers on 'race relations' could define 'race' in this popular manner, as 'a group of people who believe themselves to be, or are thought to be, distinguished from others by physical differences'.[52] But this popular concept has no necessary connection with racist ideology and the sociological phenomenon known as race prejudice; it acquires such a connection only as a consequence of a particular kind of structure of social relations. In Churchillian descriptions of Britons as 'this island *race*', the concept has the simple and popular meaning of 'people', and the conceptual overlap with 'somatic type' is often evident in journalistic usages of the single term '*race* riots' to cover violent conflicts between citizens of a

European country and their white 'guestworkers' as well as similar conflicts between whites and blacks, or whites and 'Asians'.[53] In Roman literature the Latin word *genus* and its Greek equivalent are used in much the same ways.[54] The notion of somatic type is sometimes prominent, and sometimes even dominant. It is given prominence in Martial's reference to 'the irresponsible *genus* of blond-haired Usipi' and in Synesius' allusion to Germanic 'palefaces' in his complaint that 'the same blond barbarians who in private life fill the role of domestic servants, give us orders in public life' and that the empire was defended by 'armies composed of men of the same stock as our slaves'.[55] It is dominant in the description of a slave as 'a woman of the [black] African *genus*', whose physiognomy proclaims her membership of the *genus*.[56] But *genus* and its Greek equivalent usually have the simple meaning of 'people' or 'ethnic group', without reference to physiognomy.[57]

These popular concepts, ancient and modern, make it easy to use terms like 'racial prejudice' and 'race relations': if, after all, a 'race' is an ethnic group or national group or one defined in terms of somatic type, 'race prejudice' can by a certain logic readily be defined as any kind of prejudice against such a group or against a member of the group *qua* member. That notion indeed rests at the basis of practically all discussions on 'race relations' in classical antiquity, and it also informs a considerable amount of writing on modern social history.[58] But it leads to confusion and erroneous equations between essentially different *kinds* of social phenomena; for instance, attitudes that are explainable simply in terms of personality, on the one hand, and those, on the other hand, that can be explained only in terms of a particular structure of social relations. Finley highlighted this risk of confusion in his remark that it is very difficult to devise a reliable yardstick to distinguish 'prejudice, a bad thing' from 'rational and "unprejudicial" likings and dislikings'.[59] This distinction between rational and irrational is expressed by G.W. Allport as a distinction between 'sufficiently warranted' and 'insufficiently warranted' attitudes: a feeling of favour or disfavour is a prejudice only if it is both insufficiently warranted and inflexible, while sensory aversions to particular somatic traits (or to particular mannerisms, foods, and so on) 'are not themselves prejudices', though often 'they provide a ready rationalization for prejudice.' But a negative prejudice may be a mere reflex of a given society's value system, so Allport defines a negative prejudice as an attitude of disfavour 'based upon a faulty and inflexible generalization' and directed towards a group or an individual *qua* member of the group, but not merited by any misconduct on the part of that individual.[60] However, even this does not eliminate the risk of wrongly equating examples of 'prejudice' which, though displaying the common denominator of 'insufficient warrant', actually differ in *kind* and not merely in degree. Prejudice as a reflex of the dominant values in the South African apartheid system (or of the values of the dominant group in any other 'race relations situation') differs in kind from the prejudices that arise in a society whose value system is dominated by the meritocratic ideology: the difference is a difference in kind because the social-psychological effects and contexts are different in kind. In a race relations situation (as defined in sociological theory) a prejudice which is a reflex of the dominant value system is inevitably part and parcel of an exploitation and oppression of one socially defined group by another, and it also reflects a deterministic ideological perception of the situation of the oppressed group.[61]

In every society individuals respond to other persons with appreciation or derogation of the worth of those other individuals, estimating that worth against a background of their own images of themselves in terms of certain acknowledged deference-entitling properties. These properties may vary in nature from society to society, but they are always the basis on which people 'are granted deference, grant it to themselves, claim it from others', and 'regulate their conduct towards others.'[62] In the kind of social system exemplified by apartheid (or any other modern race relations situation) or by the ascribed social roles and rights of groups like the Helots of classical Lacedaemonia and the ex-Jewish *Conversos* of the Iberian peninsula in the sixteenth and seventeenth centuries, the most salient criteria of deference and the primary determinants of status in the society at large are biological stock or ethno-cultural identity, as judged by the prejudices of the dominant group. In such societies all other deference-entitling properties are of secondary importance and have validity for members of the inferiorized group or groups only in relation to an internal stratification within their own socially defined ethno-cultural group. In the society as a whole, the meanest possessor of the primary deference-entitling property ('purity' of white or Christian

15

'blood', or Spartiate stock, and so on) is, *qua* possessor, the social superior of the ablest and greatest non-possessor (non-white person, Iberian *Converso* of Jewish lineage, Helot, and so on). Moreover, the inferior social roles and rights ascribed by the system to individual non-possessors of this primary deference-entitling property are inherited by their descendants *qua* descendants, irrespective of their personal somatic appearance and personal qualities, or actual cultural identity.[63] If we accept 'racism' as the proper label for this kind of social phenomenon, some other designation or designations must be found for other kinds in order to avoid confusing racial prejudice or racial discrimination (which are manifestations of racism) with the sort of prejudice that can be explained simply in terms of an individual personality, or with the (also essentially different) phenomena of cultural prejudice (ethnocentrism) and class prejudice, which amount merely to an unquestioning adherence to a set of values to which *all* members of a given society or social class subscribe to some degree. Ethnocentrism is defined as the common human characteristic of classifying and evaluating out-groups, their cultures, and their individual members by the standards of one's own group, and of placing the in-group and its values and assumptions at the centre of everything, presuming the superiority of all those who conform to these values over all those who do not.[64]

The visions of a Roman 'racism' that have occurred to some scholars are to be explained precisely by the false notion that racism and ethnocentrism, if they differ at all, are different only in degree.[65] This false notion also accounts for the vague and meaningless references to different degrees of 'racial prejudice' or 'colour prejudice' that are to be found in some comparisons between ancient and modern attitudes and situations,[66] as well as comments to the effect that, until the nineteenth century, there was 'little or no colour prejudice in England *in the modern sense of the expression*', or that there was a degree of race prejudice in Elizabethan England, though not the extreme, institutionalized variety found in South Africa or the United States.[67] But a somewhat different form of confusion is evident in arguments which seek to cast the concept of 'racial prejudice' itself into scientific disrepute on the ground that, among the groups which have been victims of the sociological phenomenon known by that term, 'Jews are not a race' and 'mulattoes are as much Caucasian as Negro.'[68] Here the confusion stems from an intrusion of the popular notion of 'race' as somatic type, for in some European societies in modern times Jews certainly have been a (sociological) race, and 'mulattoes' are a race in South Africa, and have been part of the 'black race' in the United States since the eighteenth century, these races being socially defined creations of the dominant group in each of the societies concerned, as is always the case when what is called a 'race' has any real connection with the sociological concept 'racism'.

As I have remarked elsewhere,[69] it is idle to suppose that (for instance) the so-called immigrant problem in contemporary Britain, the antisemitism of the Third Reich, the *Gastarbeiter* 'problem' in Germany or Sweden, and the Jewish 'problem' in nineteenth-century England are all simple variants (at different degrees of intensity) of one and the same sociological phenomenon; and to group these situations under a single terminological banner ('race relations' or 'racial prejudice') would be to engage in pretence and deception.[70] To be sure, the four situations are all marked by prejudice and group antipathy. But two factors place the first and second of these examples of prejudice and antipathy in a special category distinct from the other two: first, the existence of social structures in which inferior and unalterable roles and rights are ascribed to a socially defined minority group (which may or may not also be a numerical minority in addition to being a degraded sociological minority), and in which it is impossible (or practically so) for individuals of the inferiorized group or their descendants to make a transition to the superior roles and rights enjoyed by the dominant group in the society; and second, the existence of a deterministic belief-system or ideology supporting these social structures. These two factors constitute the typology of social situations (called 'race relations situations' by sociologists) for which the term 'race' and its cognates must be reserved. It is a type of social situation with a particular pattern of distribution of power and privilege, characterized by social inequalities and differentiation 'related to physical and cultural criteria of an ascriptive kind' and 'rationalized in terms of deterministic belief-systems.'[71] Whatever the justificatory ideology in such a system, a race is therefore a *social* category, created by human design. The racization of groups by a dominant group in the same society *socially* defines the groups on the basis of supposedly distinct identities founded upon biological descent and prejudiced perceptions of somatic or cultural 'identity', and on that basis all the 'race'-groups in the society concerned are ascribed particular (inferior or superior) roles and rights in society.[72] In other words, the mere fact of visibly distinct somatic characteristics does not create a *race*. Where physical characteristics (or cultural identity) are not socially significant, where they do not function as symbols of ascribed social roles and rights, the society is a non-racial one, however ethnically or somatically diverse it may actually be; where those characteristics do function in that manner, the society is racist (marked by racial prejudice, racial discrimination, and the group conflict predicated by that discrimination).

The term 'racial prejudice', then, properly describes the attitudes that underlie the practice of discrimination inherent in a race relations situation as defined above. It is a kind of prejudice that rests on an ideological perception of the individual as necessarily possessing particular desirable or undesirable qualities by virtue of his or her membership of a given socially defined group, in a social context in which the individual can do nothing to alter the basic situation 'either for himself or for his descendants'.[73] As for the term 'colour prejudice', since it has no value as a sociological concept except as a synonym of 'racial prejudice' in those race relations situations in which the races are marked by differences of colour, it too must be restricted to the typology of race relations situations. Significantly, no one ever thinks of applying it as a label for an irrational distaste on the part of a white person for red hair or grey eyes or extreme pallor, so there is no good reason to apply it to the same kind of distaste (what social psychologists call a 'sensory aversion') when the object of the aversion happens to be blackness of skin. Indeed, as has already been noted, social psychologists maintain that a sensory aversion is not in itself a prejudice.[74] The readiness with which the term 'colour prejudice' is applied to sensory aversions is but a consequence of the enormous effect that the history of relations between whites and non-whites in recent centuries continues to exert on the modern mind. That psychological influence, and that alone, explains the bogus distinction between a given white person's irrational distaste for red hair and the same kind of personality-conditioned aversion to black skin.

On the basis of this sociological conceptualization, the situation of the Jewish minority in the Third Reich belongs to the typology of racism because it was one of unalterable abasement and inferiority established and sustained by a deterministic ideology, but that of Jews in nineteenth-century England does not, since English xenophobia and antisemitism did not extend to anglicized apostates from Judaism and their descendants.[75] This is the perspective from which we must consider Roman references to 'purity of blood' and Roman disparagement of black and 'nordic' characteristics (or those of the Huns, who, according to a perception attributed to the Romans by a modern scholar, were little *yellow* men),[76] and also the various Roman expressions of antipathy to the cultural and political dispositions of Jews and northern European barbarians.[77] From this perspective it must be said that most works on blacks and on 'race relations' in classical antiquity display three unwarranted convictions held by scholars with varying degrees of firmness and fervour: first, that where a society's population is divisible into groups distinguished by somatic type or ethnicity, the emotional reactions of members of one group to the somatic or cultural traits of members of another group (or, at any rate, the public and unabashed expression of such reactions) must be an index of something properly describable as the state of 'race relations' in that society; second, that in such a society praise or disparagement of the qualities of blacks (or Jews and the like) necessarily relate to the issue of racial attitudes; and third, that open disparagement of black somatic features (or those of any other group) is *ipso facto* racist, or constitutes racial prejudice.[78] But unless it can be shown that the structures of Roman society and their justificatory ideology were racist (according to the concept outlined above), the instances of Roman disparagement of nigritude must be seen as mere ethnocentric reactions to black otherness and mere expressions of conformism to the dominant aesthetic values. Similar ethnocentric reactions occur in Roman disparagement of Jews and in references to Germans as less than human and as little removed from dumb animals.[79] Unlike such contemptuous stereo-types, racism ideologically negates, and in practice precludes, even the most limited mobility in the established system of stratification on the part of members of the racized group or groups and their descendants.[80] The essential difference between the psychological condition of the victim of

19

ethnocentric attitudes, on the one hand, and that of the victim of racism on the other hand, is emphasized by social scientists who point out that the everyday realities of the world of a racized sociological minority call upon every member of that group, *qua* member, to battle against an imposed and unalterable inferiority which places his ego 'under constant assault from all the conditions of his social life.'[81] In the case of blacks in Roman society, unless evidence to the contrary can be found, the appropriate assumption must be that any feelings of 'self-hate' or 'mortification' that may have arisen from hyperconsciousness of personal distance from the Roman somatic norm image (whether the blacks concerned were indigent illiterates or educated and well-to-do people)[82] were not of the kind that arise under pressure of 'constant assault from *all* the conditions' of one's daily life *qua* black, but were of the fundamentally different kind noted by researchers in 'nordic' adolescents in Puerto Rico,[83] and in many a modern society, in people who are driven by the dominant values of their milieu into an almost constant mood of low self-esteem on the grounds of size of breasts, shape of nose, deficiency in height, remarkably massive and uncontrollable weight, and the like.

Chapter One

REVIEW OF THE MODERN LITERATURE

In the late nineteenth century and in the early years of the twentieth, archaeologists presented several reports on finds of Graeco-Roman iconographic items which they considered to be representations of negroes. Comments on these objects often mirrored contemporary racist attitudes, implicitly attributing to the ancient Greeks and Romans habits of mind similar to those which characterized the colonialist and racist ecumenical order of the time. For instance, anachronistic descriptions of some of the 'models' of the ancient artists as 'mulatto' or 'quadroon' indicated an unconscious assumption that these distinctly modern concepts had also been part of the social psychology of the world of classical antiquity.[1] Many of the early archaeological reports and discussions also showed a tendency to label as both 'negro' and 'slave' all portraits perceived by the commentators as portraits of 'persons of colour', implying that in classical antiquity all 'persons of colour' (that is, non-whites, in the perceptions of Europeans of that era) were not only perceived in that same light but were also categorized as 'blacks' (*Aethiopes*), and were, in addition, slaves.[2] Some scholars of that era even assumed that the Graeco-Roman use of the term *Aethiopes* ('black person') involved the same contemptuous intention as the word 'nigger' conveyed in their own social environment.[3] The same era, it is true, witnessed a few explicit observations on Graeco-Roman attitudes to the effect that the curse of colour prejudice or 'the colour bar' (a familiar aspect of the writers' own society) had been unknown in the Graeco-Roman world.[4] But these views were little more than general impressions, unsupported by compelling arguments and documentation. No thorough study of the available ancient material had as

21

yet been undertaken, and, in the absence of such a study, some scholars outside the field of classical studies could assert with unfettered confidence that the then familiar 'attitude of the Caucasian toward intermixture with the Negro' had been a constant and unchanged fact throughout recorded history.[5]

The first attempt at an authoritative study of blacks in Roman (and Greek) antiquity was the work of the American scholar, Grace Beardsley.[6] That work set a pattern of investigation that was to be followed in its essentials by practically all subsequent discussions of the subject.[7] Along with Beardsley's work, all later studies have constituted a debate on the question of whether blacks encountered 'racial prejudice', or 'racism', or 'colour prejudice' in the Roman world; the various discussions have also attempted to explain black–white social relations in that world in terms of 'race'. But the commonly adopted approach has been one of balancing positive against negative signals about blacks in the literary texts and iconography (especially indications of Roman reactions to the physiognomy of blacks), without appropriate consideration of the structures of Roman society, and with inadequate reference to the ideological system of that society. Because of the inadequate attention devoted to the social–psychological setting of the ancient source material, these discussions share in some measure the defect of misunderstanding the *forma mentis* associated with the various Roman comments on blacks, and (in consequence) the misinterpretations of the data. This failing is heightened by a general tendency to begin the inquiry with the wrong question, explicitly or implicitly: namely, what was the *status* (or 'the position') of the black 'race' (or 'the black man') in Roman society? That question betrays a presupposition, however unconscious, that a particular group status must have been ascribed to blacks as such; and it ensures from the very start of the exercise that the aim of the study will merely be to discover the facts of the presumed group status. What is more, the question ignores the fact that the reality of such a group status would in itself be an indication of racism, for, as has been indicated in the earlier definitions of sociological concepts, it is only in a racist society that a status is ascribed to a *group* definable in terms of somatic type or ethnicity or cultural identity.[8]

No doubt this notion of an ascribed group status comes easily to the modern mind. It has, after all, been a characteristic of several modern societies. Thirty years ago, for instance, it was noted that blacks in Britain were ascribed a degraded group status entirely outside the system of social stratification that applied to whites: in the dominant ideology, not only were blacks denied the possibility of upward social mobility, but even 'a wealthy black in a Savile Row suit, with polished manners and Oxford accent' had no place at all in that system. Similarly, more recent investigations have emphasized the persistence of this situation, showing that the white community at large refuses to recognize assimilation of the black minority as legitimate, and persists in an ideology which not only judges black characteristics unfavourably, but sees them as incapable of being socialized away in the foreseeable future.[9] But if scholars have (for the most part unconsciously) assumed that this kind of situation and perceptual context is relevant to Roman society, they have not attempted any demonstration of the relevance, let alone offered a convincing defence of the validity, of their assumption.

On the basis of the defective methodology outlined above, Beardsley discovered a Roman anti-black 'racism',[10] and her conclusion has been endorsed by a number of other scholars,[11] while also receiving some (perhaps often involuntary) support from those who have drawn attention to so-called evidence of 'colour prejudice',[12] or a 'color line',[13] or 'un début de racisme', or 'a certain racism',[14] or a situation similar to that in the United States some decades ago,[15] or a low (or 'negative') evaluation of black people,[16] or a de facto 'racial inequality',[17] or 'a little color prejudice',[18] or a lack of 'intense color prejudice'.[19] On the other hand, some have maintained that Roman society neither made colour 'the focus of irrational sentiments' nor erected social barriers on the basis of colour, but 'counted black peoples in', the social–psychological ambience being one in which doctrines of 'white supremacy' and the ideology of white 'racial purity' were unknown, and in which 'colour prejudice' (at any rate, 'widespread' and 'intense' colour prejudice) was absent.[20] Despite the generally shared vision of blacks in Roman society as a race, this literature is thus sometimes apt to give the impression of a polarization of opinion between those who argue for, and those who argue against, a Roman racism. That impression is supported by the element of polemic that marks some of the literature,[21] and by the fact that the frame of reference of some of the contributors to the debate (notably Beardsley and Wiesen) reflects rather crudely some of the racist assumptions of their own social–psychological milieu,[22] while in opposing discussions the argument sometimes appears to suggest that the Roman world was some kind of social paradise-on-earth for blacks.[23] But there is in fact considerable common ground in these various conclusions. For instance, Wiesen's notion of a sort of grassroots 'racism', described by him as 'something akin to modern racism' but unsupported by institutions and less virulent than the modern variety,[24] is in reality rather close to Snowden's idea of an absence of 'marked antipathy' and of 'intense color prejudice' towards blacks in Roman society.[25] These two notions, in turn, hardly differ from the view that the Roman situation was marked by a 'prejudice towards black-skinned people' which sometimes came quite close to an antipathy of the racist kind,[26] or from the idea of a 'quite widespread color prejudice' which, though not 'highly articulated', was not 'overly subtle or subliminal' either.[27] This glimmer of unwitting consensus beneath an apparent polarization of opinion is a clear index of the misconceptions about 'race' that underlie these various discussions. None of the arguments in favour of racism or colour prejudice rests on anything more substantial than negative references to blacks, such as indications of a distaste for black somatic characteristics, and, in the light of the foregoing definitions of sociological concepts, it is necessary to emphasize the fact that nothing in the ancient evidence (written or archaeological) entitles us to see Roman society as one in which skin colour or somatic type functioned as a deference-relevant property, either positive (like wealth, noble birth, power, or high educational attainments) or negative (like poverty, illiteracy, or servile birth), as distinct from a mere appreciated quality like kindness or femininity or a *vitium* like obesity, alcoholism, or emaciation.[28] For this reason alone, all the various interpretations of ancient data as evidence of racial prejudice or colour prejudice must be dismissed as misconceptions. With this dismissal, the way becomes open for a meaningful examination of the true social–psychological significance of the various negative and positive references to blacks in Roman material.

INTERPRETATIONS OF THE SOURCE MATERIAL

The iconography depicting blacks is very much open to subjective interpretation,[29] but, on any reasonable interpretation, it will be found to contain both positive and negative signals. Beardsley saw evidence of a contemptuous attitude towards blacks *qua* blacks in the Roman tendency to decorate mere utilitarian objects with depictions of blacks. Most of those depictions are indeed found on ordinary household objects (tableware and lamps, for instance) and trinkets (earrings, perfume jars, ring-bezels, amulets, scarabs), and the examples even include a child's rattle.[30] But where this does not merely reflect 'an artificial taste for the exotic', it rather suggests (contrary to Beardsley's negative interpretation) 'a certain anecdotal familiarity' with blacks and a relaxed disposition towards blacks on the part of the users of these objects, or popular beliefs in the apotropaic charm of blacks.[31] Snowden emphasized the positive messages, such as the indications that a number of blacks held positions of some esteem in Roman society, from the standpoint of the broad mass of plebeians, at any rate. While the terracotta and bronze figures generally relate to the lives of humble blacks in a variety of low social positions, a number of portraits in marble are undoubtedly portraits of black individuals in well-to-do socio-economic strata, like Memnon, the pupil and protégé of the wealthy and distinguished sophist and Roman senator, Herodes Atticus.[32] But the iconographic record also contains clear evidence of mocking attitudes towards the black physiognomy. These attitudes are reflected, not only in grotesque caricatures of 'Nilotic' pygmies (which are balanced by equally grotesque caricatures of white dwarfs) but also in artists' use of 'thick lips, flat nose and exaggerated prognathism', even without blackness of colour, as 'a conventional vocabulary for the alien, barbaric and brutish, in contrast with nobility of spirit or the quality of feminine grace.'[33] The element of mockery and caricature evidently implies that some Romans (including some of the artists and craftsmen who created these objects) felt a sensory aversion to nigritude, at any rate in its 'barbarian' manifestations, and to other forms of extreme distance from the Roman somatic norm image. But if some portraits of blacks convey the pejorative image of the 'barbarian' black, others convey the positive image of the Romanized and integrated black.[34] What is indicated, then, is not 'the status' of blacks, but the fact that blacks possessed a variety of statuses; not a particular attitude, but a variety of attitudes.

In assessing the written material Beardsley, Wiesen, and others of the 'race prejudice' school tended to stress the seemingly unfavourable, while Snowden emphasized the seemingly favourable and played down the negative. This approach is one that offers excessive scope for criticism and counter-criticism, and it is not particularly surprising, therefore, that some critics have either dismissed Snowden's entire case for the absence of race prejudice (a reception far from deserved) or pointed to traces of Roman 'prejudice' overlooked or played down by him.[35] The written material in which negative references to blacks occurs includes some satirical texts on the theme of adultery between ladies of the leisured classes and humble black men, for instance, an epigram of Martial which paints a picture of such a lady's adultery with several of her own servants and dependants, including a 'Moor' and a black:

> pater ex Marulla, Cinna, factus es septem
> non liberorum: namque nec tuus quisquam
> nec est amici filiusve vicini,
> sed in grabatis tegetibusque concepti
> materna produnt capitibus suis furta.
> hic qui retorto crine Maurus incedit
> subolem fatetur esse se coci Santrae.
> at ille sima nare, turgidis labris
> ipsa est imago Pannychi palaestritae.

Cinna, your wife Marulla has made you a father of seven – I
can't say *children*; for not a single one of them is a son of yours, or
even the child of a friend or neighbour, but they are all brats
conceived on truckle-beds and mats, and they betray by their
features their mother's sexual cheatings. The crinkly-haired
Moor who struts about is obviously the offspring of your cook,
Santra. But that other one with the flat nose and turgid lips is
the very spit and image of Pannychus the wrestler.[36]

Texts of this kind do not, as some have argued,[37] offer any indication of 'a special stigma' attached to 'interracial adultery', not even when they refer to the resulting 'brats' by a term like *decolor heres* ('an heir of the wrong colour').[38] In terms of the

26

concept 'race' in sociological theory, inter-*racial* adultery can, in any case, occur only in a context of racist structures.[39] In other kinds of social context, such as must be assumed for Roman society in the absence of evidence to the contrary, one must be content to speak of 'adultery between persons of different somatic types'; and that immediately suggests a reading of these texts very different from those advocated in most earlier discussions. Snowden rightly interpreted such texts as voices expressing disapproval, not of 'miscegenation' or black–white sexual relations *per se*, but of a recognized urge among aristocratic women of a certain type for extramarital sexual relations with humble men, some of whom happened to be black.[40] However, Snowden rather perversely regarded these and other negative references to blacks as devoid of sociological relevance. In the epigram cited above, for instance, the descriptions of black somatic traits are not value-free, as Snowden maintained.[41] They are mocking and derogatory comments. So too are the terms 'off-colour' (*decolor*) and 'discoloured' (*discolor*) when used with negative tones in descriptions of imaginary 'bastards' fathered upon upper-class women by humble blacks.[42] Although the attitudes conveyed by such comments have nothing to do with race prejudice, they obviously have some relevance to the issue of social relations and Roman perceptions of blacks. The object of the satire in texts of this kind is evidently the threat which the adultery of these women poses to the social hierarchy and the maintenance of the established boundaries of rank because of the potential of that adultery for legitimizing as aristocratic heirs children who, *qua* 'bastards' of humble paternal extraction, can be seen as deserving the status of slaves, or at best that of free plebeians. Particularly significant of this concern with the social hierarchy is the suggestion in the epigram that the 'bastard brats', who do not deserve the name 'children', would have merited that appellation if their natural fathers had been men of appropriate social status ('friends or neighbours' of the cuckolded husband).[43] On the other hand, the satirical picture painted in this epigram is one in which a *de facto* bastard of black African or 'Moorish' appearance can feel free to 'strut about' with aristocratic *hauteur*, and commands the deference due to an aristocratic youth, however much this angers the poetic persona.[44] That is not, of course, to suggest that the epigram accurately records a real-life situation. It merely presents an exaggerated picture of the sort of situation which, in the author's view, might occur if the natural consequences of adultery among upper-class women were not obviated by contraception, abortion, infanticide, and the practice of abandoning unwanted infants.

In the very similar picture presented by Juvenal, in which an aristocratic 'heir of the wrong colour' results from a lady's adultery with some humble black man, it is even suggested that a high incidence of such *de facto* bastards was prevented only by the prevalence of abortion and other means of getting rid of unwanted infants:

> *gaude, infelix, atque ipse bibendum*
> *porrige quidquid erit; nam si distendere vellet*
> *et vexare uterum pueris salientibus, esses*
> *Aethiopis fortasse pater, mox decolor heres*
> *impleret tabulas numquam tibi mane videndus.*

Cheer up, you poor fellow, and personally offer your wife the dose of abortifacient she wants to take; for if she should choose to remain pregnant and bother her womb with jumping baby-boys, you would probably be the father of a black child, and soon that heir of the wrong colour, never to be seen by you in the morning light, would be inheriting your estate.[45]

But here too there is an element of derogation of nigritude: the text reflects both the popular belief that the first thing seen in the morning influenced one's luck on that day and the superstition which associated black strangers with the ominous and unlucky.

In a similar text of the fourth-century court poet Claudian, in which some have wrongly seen evidence of a special stigma on adultery with black men, a personified Roman Africa laments

> *nec damna pudoris*
> *turpia sufficiunt; Mauris clarissima quaeque*
> *fastidita datur. media Carthagine ductae*
> *barbara Sidoniae subeunt conubia matres;*
> *Aethiopem nobis generum, Nasamona maritum*
> *ingerit; exterret cunabula discolor infans.*
> *his fretus sociis ipso iam principe maior*
> *incedit.*

Nor does the disgraceful loss of their good name satisfy Gildo: all the most noble ladies are given to Moors when Gildo himself has grown tired of them. In the middle of Carthage Sidonian ladies, already married and already mothers, are forced to submit to wedlock with barbarians. Gildo thrusts upon us black African sons-in-law, Nasamonian husbands. The discoloured infant arising from such a union absolutely terrifies the cradle. Relying on allies of this kind, Gildo struts about with arrogant posturing, feeling already greater than our emperor.[46]

Here the reference is to distant and barbarian 'blacks', not blacks who are an integral part of the Roman social scene, and the text exudes the xenophobia that prevailed in the ranks of the Roman upper classes in the face of the relentless barbarian military menace after the middle of the third century AD, when the barbarization of the Roman world became a pressing problem, and when Romans were no longer sure of their military superiority over the 'beastly primitives' of the barbarian world.[47] Also illustrated here is the 'anthropological law' according to which the alien becomes more alien, and his negative stereotype more unrealistic, when he comes to represent a real threat to the in-group's livelihood and values, as Gildo and his 'black' barbarians have done by their seizure of Rome's African granary (in actual fact) and by their numerous outrages against Roman values (in Claudian's poetic imagination).[48] In the poet's imagination these intolerable outrages include a violent imposition of black and lowly barbarian husbands upon aristocratic Roman women in the province of Africa in arrogant defiance of Roman law, in the eyes of which such a marriage did not count as a proper marriage. The consequent stigma suffered by the women is regarded as even worse than the disgrace previously arising from Gildo's own treatment of them as sexual playthings, for Gildo, despite his crimes, is a Roman official and a man of status, connected by marriage with the imperial family itself. The stigma arises not from the blackness of the violently imposed husbands, but from their lowly and non-Roman status, and their barbarian cultural identity. But the picture is heavily influenced by the negative symbolism of blackness, by contemporary physiognomonic lore (which prompted the drawing of inferences about character from certain physical traits), and by the aesthetics of the Roman somatic norm image. The imagery of 'discoloured' infants accordingly has a strong moral flavour, proclaiming the moral and cultural distance of these infants from their noble Roman mothers; the infants, like Juvenal's 'heir of the wrong colour', are *de facto* bastards of humble paternal extraction (and, what is more, barbarian extraction), and so their alien faces terrify cradles that are accustomed only to genuinely Roman and aristocratic infants, just as black faces were known (in real life situations) to terrify children unfamiliar with the sight of blacks.[49] But although Claudian's contemptuously used terms *Aethiopem* and *Nasamona* refer to barbarians from beyond the bounds of Roman society, the tone of his *Aethiopem nobis generum ingerit*('he imposes upon us *Aethiopian* sons-in-law') suggests a contemporary Roman habit of mentally associating blacks with low status – a natural consequence of an objective situation in which blacks in Roman society (as distinct from progeny and descendants of blacks, who were not themselves necessarily blacks) generally occupied humble positions.[50]

A number of texts present descriptions of the *Aethiops* physiognomy or comment on some of its details. Even when the descriptions are realistic, they contain an element of mockery or at least suggest a distaste for the black physiognomy. The *public and unashamed* character of this mockery is much in conflict with modern tastes and habits. For that reason scholars have been inclined to see such expressions of aversion as 'brutal' or 'unkind',[51] and it is that frame of mind which has induced some to misinterpret the sociological significance of such texts and to see them as indications of so-called racism. Wiesen, for instance, insisted that these derogatory expressions (and iconographic caricatures offering similar messages) are expressions of hostility towards blacks *qua* blacks, since the disparagement (as he saw it) is directed at blacks irrespective of their personal non-somatic qualities and attributes.[52] One such text describes the physical appearance of a black woman, the slave and sole house-companion of a simple peasant:

> erat unica custos,
> *Afra genus, tota patriam testante figura,*
> *torta comam, labro tumens et fusca colore,*
> *pectore lata, iacens mammis, compressior alvo,*
> *cruribus exilis, spatiosa prodiga planta.*

She was his only help. She was African in stock, and all her physical features gave testimony of her land of origin: tightly-curled hair, swollen lips, dusky complexion, broad chest with low-swinging breasts, belly rather pinched, thin legs, broad and ample feet.[53]

J. Desanges called attention to the possibly derogatory significance of this black woman's appellation, Scybale, which suggests 'rubbish', 'shit', or 'riff-raff'.[54] He accordingly interpreted the text as evidence of 'prejudice' against blacks in Roman antiquity – admittedly, 'a prejudice that was certainly less widespread in antiquity than in modern times', but nonetheless one wrongly envisaged as a negative attitude of the same *kind* as that which he associates with 'modern times'. The 'prejudice' is in fact nothing more than an aesthetic evaluation, based on ethnocentric canons of beauty, and expressed as an attitude of open distaste on the part of some, many or most Romans for what they would have described as the somatic appearance of the 'typical' *Aethiops*. Indeed, Desanges suggests much the same elsewhere when he associates the phenomenon with Roman aesthetic values.[55] Precisely the same message is conveyed by Petronius' description of the 'typical' black slave as possessing 'dreadfully swollen lips' (*labra tumore taeterrima*), crinkly hair, 'scarred forehead', bow legs, and sagging ankles.[56] Such comments give free and unabashed expression to the general Roman preference for the Mediterranean type of physical appearance[57] (what the sociologist Hoetink calls 'the somatic norm image').[58]

The prominence of this worship of the somatic norm image in the culture of the Roman educated classes explains the tone and language of many of the references to blacks. For example, an epigram by the sixth-century poet Luxorius extols Olympius, a black hero of the contemporary arena in Carthage.[59]

> nil tibi forma nocet nigro fuscata colore.
> sic ebenum pretiosum atrum natura creavit;
> purpura sic parvo depressa in murice fulget;
> sic nigrae violae per mollia gramina vernant;
> sic tetras quaedam commendat gratia gemmas;
> sic placet obscuros elephans immanis ad artus;
> sic turis piperisque Indi nigredo placessit;
> postremum tanto populi pulcrescis amore,
> foedior est quantum pulcher sine viribus alter.

Your black-coloured physiognomy does you no harm at all. So did nature create priceless ebony black. So does the purple

31

deeply set in the tiny murex gleam; so do dark violets bloom amidst the soft grass; so does a certain grace set off gems of sombre hue; so does the huge elephant please in respect of its dark limbs; so does the blackness of Indian incense and pepper give pleasure. Finally, because of the people's great love for you, you are as handsome as another man who lacks strength is ugly, despite his handsome appearance.[60]

This black hero's physique is that of a Hercules carved in priceless ebony; but his 'handsomeness' arises from the glamour and charisma surrounding his prowess in the occupational role of *venator*. The strength of his society's aesthetic values constrains Luxorius to contrast his hero's 'handsomeness' with the 'ugliness' of the conventionally handsome man (*pulcher*) who lacks the Herculean build and physical power of this black man, and to liken the black's 'handsomeness' to the charm of priceless ebony and the like, just as the dictates of traditional values and contemporary fashion had inspired apologetic references to swarthy beauty in earlier Roman poetry.[61] It is a case of a particular black man rendered handsome not by the actual shape and colour of his face, but by his combination of Herculean build, glamorous occupation, and, in particular, outstanding success in that occupational role. As Garson has observed, if the encomium conveys a notion of 'black *and* beautiful', the beauty is of a kind that transcends the purely physical.[62] This black man is perceived as a Hercules *despite* his nigritude. For, as Luxorius himself demonstrates elsewhere, among the leisured classes of his society there was a widespread disposition (which he himself shared) to equate nigritude with the ugly and to see 'whiteness' as an essential component of beauty, particularly in relation to the female sex.[63]

Particularly notable, however, is Luxorius' statement 'your black physiognomy does you no harm at all' (*nil tibi forma nocet nigro fuscata colore*). The implicit notion of blackness as a potential handicap of some kind suggests a social–psychological situation similar to that of the Arab world in the seventh and eighth centuries, where the black poets Suhaym and Nusayb could represent nigritude as a quality that, more often than not, 'harmed' or 'marred' or 'diminished' its possessor.[64] Raoul Lonis rightly drew a similar inference from a text of Heliodorus,[65] who represents his fictional 'Aethiopian' princess, Chariclea, as white (indeed, golden blonde) rather than black, despite her entirely black parentage.[66] That representation obeyed a literary convention which demanded beauty in heroines while also upholding ethnocentric canons and contemporary fashions of beauty, enshrining the legend of a white or merely 'swarthy' Aethiopian Andromeda, whose beauty could be attributed to the 'genetic' principles of 'maternal impression' and biological atavism. The potential handicap of blackness was, of course, not the handicap of racism, as Lonis supposed.[67] Some blacks, like Luxorius' Olympius, were exempt from this handicap. Whatever its precise nature (and this clearly calls for serious examination), the handicap undoubtedly had a connection with the mocking of blacks to which Juvenal alludes:

> 'ego te ceventem, Sexte, verebor?'
> infamis Varillus ait: 'quo deterior te?
> loripedem rectus derideat, Aethiopem albus.'
> quis tulerit Gracchos de seditione querentes?
> quis caelum terris non misceat et mare caelo,
> si fur displiceat Verri, homicida Miloni,
> Clodius accuset moechos, Catilina Cethegum,
> in tabulam Sullae si dicant discipuli tres?

Says the notorious 'queen' Varillus, 'You expect *me* to respect *you*, Sextus – a faggot like myself? What makes me worse than you? A straight-legged man may mock a cripple, or a white a black.' Quite right too. Who would put up with an apostle of the extreme left, like one of the Gracchi brothers, complaining about revolution? Who wouldn't confound heaven with earth and sea with sky if a privileged thief like Verres started condemning thieves of his own ilk, or a murderer like Milo piously berating murder, or a Clodius condemning adultery in others, or a Catilina lashing out at fellow terrorists, or Sulla's three disciples denouncing the evil of proscriptions?[68]

This text (especially the sentence specifically alluding to mockery of blacks and cripples) has attracted considerable comment. Peter Green translated the last part of this sentence (*derideat Aethiopem albus*) as 'you can't bait niggers when you're tarred with the same brush'.[69] But that translation perversely sets the Roman satirist in a racist social and psychological context with its imagery of the *taint* of so-called black blood in a situation in which whites and blacks are socially defined categories, and in which blacks (*qua* blacks) are open to cruel disparagement by a usage of the term *Aethiops* possessing the present-day import of the word 'nigger'. Snowden, on the other hand, interpreted this part of the text as merely an example of proverbial black–white contrasts with a force similar to that of the English adage that warns against 'the pot calling the kettle black',[70] an interpretation which implies the overly 'irenic' or 'optimistic' view that the text has no relevance to the issue of social relations. Wiesen, who took the opposing view suggested by Green's translation and earlier advanced by Beardsley, detected in this text as a whole 'a low estimate of *the Negro*' in Roman society, and a Roman perception of the *Aethiops* somatic type as 'a kind of parody upon nature' or 'insult to nature and natures proper product – *the white man*.' He accordingly concluded that, in the Roman mind (or at least in the minds of many Romans), the negro was the natural inferior of the white man.[71] But that will certainly not do.

The theme of the passage is hypocrisy – the habit of criticizing or ridiculing in others flaws that are also present in oneself. The immediate issue is the hypocrisy of fully adult catamites who seek to screen their homosexuality behind grand moral–philosophical stances, and an honest 'queen' is represented as attacking the hypocrisy of a fellow homosexual. But this attack does not, as Wiesen held, associate *the black man* with 'the greatest criminals and revolutionaries of Roman history.'[72] The association exists only in the banal sense that black, criminal and revolutionary are mentioned in one and the same general argument. The various examples employed to illustrate the argument that 'the pot should not call the kettle black' fall into two distinct categories: embodiments of somatic defects (the cripple and the *Aethiops*, both exemplifying some form of 'deviation' from the somatic norm), and examples of moral and behavioural defects. Juvenal does not attempt here (as he does elsewhere)[73] to subcategorize somatic deviation into the classes of absolute abnormality (the cripple) and relative abnormality or *commune vitium* (the black person). But he clearly demarcates the moral–behavioural from the merely somatic, emphasizing on the one hand the absurdity of one *Aethiops* ridiculing the black African colour and morphology in another, and on the other hand the hypocrisy of a moral deviant criticizing another for a deviance that they both share. The text makes it clear that (as Seneca puts it)[74] the *Aethiops* physiognomy was often perceived as a 'defect' – at least among Romans of the leisured classes and albeit as an 'ethnic' defect, and that in certain circumstances cripples were apt to be mocked by people of sound physique, and blacks by people whose somatic characteristics conformed or approximated to the Roman somatic norm image.[75] Notable is the way in which Juvenal's presentation differs from the presentation of embodiments of the non-normal in a passage from a modern novel, in which a character, who dreads becoming 'a fat bemedalled pillar of society', is 'subconsciously attracted to the unconventional, by those who lived on the fringes of society – gypsies, prostitutes, drunkards, thieves', and feels 'sympathy for the poor, for invalids, pacifists, divorced women, Negroes, Jews, communists, socialists.'[76] In this presentation there is an undoubted association of blacks with a variety of socially (and sometimes also morally) disfavoured categories, including 'the poor', and the negro's blackness is an outward and visible symbol of the social marginality that he shares with all the other categories. By contrast, the disfavour attaching to blacks and cripples in Juvenal's presentation relates only to their physical 'defects'. There is no suggestion that this disfavour *socially* marginalizes these two categories, or that it is any different in kind from the disfavour shown to other physical 'defects' such as emaciation, gross corpulence, red hair, or blue eyes.[77]

According to a widely held Roman view, the somatic 'defects' of the *Aethiops* somatic type comprised colour, hair, facial shape, and over-large breasts in the female of the *genus*. But the blue eyes, blond hair (in the male sex, at any rate), and pale whiteness regarded as 'typical' of the central and northern European were also perceived with some disfavour; so too were redness of skin and hair, and dark or bronzed complexions in women of the 'Caucasian' type.[78] For these reasons it is important to avoid emphasizing Roman disparagement of black somatic traits while glossing over similar disparagement of those of other types like the 'nordic', as some have done.[79] Wiesen, for instance, though rightly noting (as the message of two Latin texts) that 'a huge-breasted African woman nursing her fat child would have been an amazing, perhaps disgusting, sight to a Roman viewer, like the Alpine goiter and the blue eyes and twisted blond hair of a German',[80] made no attempt to balance his view of the Roman perception of *Aethiops* somatic 'deviance' ('an insult to nature') by a similar allusion to Roman perceptions of the 'nordic' physique as another (if less extreme) aberration of nature. Such a balance, logically required by Wiesen's argument, clearly precludes the view advanced by him that equates the Roman notion of 'nature's proper product' with the modern taxonomic concept 'the white man'.

Among the texts which refer in disparaging terms to the black physiognomy are two Romano-African epigrams, apparently by the same author:

> *faex Garamantarum nostrum processit ad axem*
> *et piceo gaudet corpore verna niger,*
> *quem nisi vox hominem labris emissa sonaret,*
> *terreret visu horrida larva viros.*
> *dira, Harumeta, tuum rapiant sibi Tartara monstrum:*
> *custodem hunc Ditis debet habere domus.*

The riff-raff of the Garamantians came up to our part of the world, and a black slave rejoices in his pitch-coloured body; a frightful spook who would scare even grown men by his appearance were it not that the sounds issuing from his lips proclaim him human. Hadrumeta, let the fearsome regions of the dead carry off for their own use this weird creature of yours. He ought to be standing guard at the home of the god of the nether world.[81]

> *ex orientis die noctis processit alumnus,*
> *sub radiis Phoebi solus habet tenebras.*
> *corvus carbo cinis concordant cuncta colori.*
> *quod legeris nomen, convenit: Aethiopis.*

From the region of the rising sun came Night's foster-son who alone keeps his blackness in broad daylight. The crow, the carbon, the cinders are completely congruent with his colour. The name by which you are called is the appropriate one – that of Blackface.[82]

These two texts undoubtedly convey an attitude of distaste for the *Aethiops* somatic appearance as well as open mockery of one or more persons of that somatic type.[83] The first text has a decidedly abusive and hostile tone, notably in its use of an expression like 'riff-raff' (or 'shit', or 'filthy black'): the Latin word *faex*[84] and in the description of a black as 'a frightful spook' (*horrida larva*) whose sole qualification for membership of the human species is his human speech, and who is in any case more of a freak (*monstrum*) than a human being. The comments also echo the clichés of the popular colour symbolism which associated blackness with death. But the violence of the language suggests something more than simple sensory aversion to nigritude, mockery of an alien and unfamiliar somatic appearance, or a concern with voicing a stereotype of the *Aethiops*. Desanges suggested that the whole attitude displayed here might be of interest to psychologists.[85] It is best seen as a xenophobic attitude relating to a situation of armed conflict with Saharan barbarians (as quite often occurred in the post-Severan era to which the epigram seems to belong),[86] and reflecting a fear of marauding Saharan warriors and an associated hatred and contempt for those swarthy desert barbarians.[87] It has generally been supposed that the mockery is directed at a single black person – a Saharan marauder who became a slave after his capture in combat. But the idea of a prisoner-of-war in his new life as a slave at Hadrumetum '*rejoicing* in his pitch-black body' (as is stressed in this epigram) seems distinctly odd. The word *verna* (translated above simply as 'slave') may well be used here in its strict sense of 'slave born in the household', referring not to the riff-raff who literally came up from the Sahara to Roman territory, but to a black slave at Hadrumetum (the modern Sousse in Tunisia) for whom the arrival of 'the shit of the Garamantians' (a collective term for a troop of marauders) has in some sense been an occasion for rejoicing, even though he is a locally born and bred black. In other words, we may have here an imputation which presumes sympathy and collaboration with barbarian marauders from the Sahara on the part of one or more local blacks at Hadrumetum, and the hostility reflected by the epigram would thus also possess a scapegoating dimension. Although the mocking tone of the second epigram is less violent (merely stressing the black's ugly colour and its unpleasant permanence, and mocking him as 'Blackface' and as 'Night's foster-son'), the studied repetition of the Latin *c* sound throughout the third verse (*corvus carbo cinis concordant cuncta colori*: 'the crow, the carbon, the cinders are completely congruent with his colour') may be intended to match the *faex* ('shit') of the first epigram by evoking an imagery of *caca-* (excrement), like the image seen by Desanges in the name Scybale, borne by the black slave

37

woman of the poem *Moretum*.[88] It may well be that the dirt and filth symbolism of blackness even suggested to some Romans a likeness between the complexion of blacks and the colour of dirt and excrement, just as a contemporary of the medieval Arab poet Nusayb (a black man) mockingly suggested that the latter was less than human and likened his colour to that of 'cattle' and (symbolically) to 'the dark face of the oppressor'.[89]

Another often discussed text which requires close examination is the well known passage where Juvenal contrasts an expensive 'Ganymede' with another slave in the same household, described as a 'Saharan groom' (*cursor Gaetulus*).[90] The groom (who has the temporary duty of waiting at table on some despised hangers-on of his master's, while the services of the 'Ganymede' are reserved for the master and his favoured guests) is 'a black Moor with hard hands' (*nigri manus ossea Mauri*),[91] a description which emphasizes both the incongruous presence of a muscular stable-hand on dining-room duty and the contrast with the pale complexion and girlish build of the Ganymede type, who is regarded by fashionable society as the dining-room servant *par excellence*, and whose service makes the food and wine taste better (as would be the case for the average modern man if served by a beautiful and charming waitress in contrast with a grim-looking and muscle-bound waiter).[92] Scholars of what may be called 'the race prejudice school' have unwarrantedly drawn from this contrast between the two servants the inference that black slaves in Juvenal's time were (*qua* black slaves) inexpensive and also occupied a low position in the hierarchy of domestic slaves.[93] On the sole basis of this same satirical picture, in which the minor guests are subjected to discriminatory treatment in terms of both menu and service, Wiesen even generalized that Romans regarded it as a grave insult 'to receive one's cup from the hand of *a black man*.'[94] Slipping into a too facile parallel with America, that same scholar also imagined that the alliterative oxymoron 'Gaetulian Ganymede' (*Gaetulum Ganymedem*) applied to the black slave in this picture must have had for Romans the same social–psychological significance as 'African Adonis' would have had for an American of the nineteenth-century South, and that the Roman satirist is here presenting a picture of the 'uppity black' and expressing an attitude according to which 'the assumption of airs by *a black man* is the ultimate symbol of a society turned upon its head' when, as in this satirical picture, that 'uppity' behaviour could go unpunished.[95]

These interpretations ignore certain important points in the satirical picture. The description of the favoured 'Ganymede' as *flos Asiae* ('flower of Asia Minor') sharpens the image evoked by the term 'Ganymede' itself: that of the mythical 'pansy' of Asia Minor, cup-bearer of the god Zeus, and prototype of the 'Ganymedes' of wealthy and fashionable Roman dining rooms. In fashionable circles this type of girlishly beautiful slave-boy was a very expensive and *à la mode* status-symbol. But fashion also demanded a battalion of dining-room servants of a variety of national origins, ages, colours, and hair-types.[96] In Juvenal's picture the black groom, in contrast with the young and beautiful catamite, is a fully grown man, aggressively masculine, and showing the ugliness of the ruffian 'whom one would not care to meet late at night as one drives past the tombs on the Latin Way.'[97] His temporary transfer from the stables to wait on the inferior guests is part of his master's calculated insult to these hangers-on, and this is underscored by the bizarre oxymoron 'Gaetulian Ganymede'. But the main reason for the black groom's appearance is the host's desire to protect his Ganymede from the sexual advances of the hangers-on.[98] Comments by other Roman writers on this type of dinner-party help us to place Juvenal's picture in proper focus.[99] The inferior guests tend to get drunk easily and, if left unchecked, they make sexual advances to the host's wife or daughter or Ganymede, for Ganymedes are young catamites 'with complexions more dazzlingly white than snow, eyes vying with the stars, and soft long hair tumbling over their necks', and they rival beautiful women in sex appeal. For that reason, hosts sometimes find it prudent to send their Ganymede out of the dining room, temporarily replacing him with 'one of the fully grown, muscular fellows, a muleteer or stable-hand' to wait on lecherous guests. Martial indeed humorously protests that if guests are to be spared the temptation of making sexual passes at Ganymedes, these beautiful catamites must be replaced with masculine-looking, short-haired, and crinkly-haired slaves.[100]

This is the background against which Juvenal's contrast between the pretty boy and the aggressively masculine black groom must be seen. It is also important to note the muttered complaint of the hangers-on in this satirical picture: their grumbling about the black slave emphasizes his arrogance.

quando ad te pervenit ille?
quando rogatus adest calidae gelidaeque minister?
quippe indignatur veteri parere clienti
quodque aliquid posces et quod se stante recumbas.
maxima quaeque domus servis est plena superbis.

When will he get round to you? When will he come to serve the
hot or cold water you've asked for? He feels it's beneath his
dignity to take orders from you or attend to any request of yours.
It doesn't matter to him that you are a long-standing dependant
of his master. He even resents having to be on his feet while you
are reclining at table. All the great houses are full of arrogant
minions like him.[101]

The hangers-on are willing to accept that 'a Ganymede
purchased at the cost of so many thousands' is not allowed to serve
'bums' like themselves, and they can be content with the vicarious
pleasure they derive from ogling the pretty boy whose hand they
are not allowed to nudge. But they are shattered by the arrogance
of the stable-hand. A vision of this arrogance as 'uppity' (like
Wiesen's) is, however, most inappropriate. The black groom's
arrogance is encouraged by his master and is indeed a reflection of
his master's own contemptuous attitude towards the hangers-on.
The idea of the 'uppity black' (typical of racist contexts, where it
refers to behaviour on the part of a black, *qua* black, that
contravenes the canons of extreme deference prescribed by society
for his observance in the presence of a white, *qua* white) is very
obviously alien to the situation pictured by Juvenal, where the
black slave clearly feels free to treat his master's humble white
guests with scorn and arrogance in the presence of his master and
his favoured guests (all of them white), showing that he much
prefers his master's horses to these 'bums'.[102]

Several texts express a contrast between somatic blackness and
spiritual 'whiteness' in sentiments like 'black in body *but* white in
soul'. Comments in Christian literature, in particular, show a
'constant harping' on this theme:[103] for instance, the frequent
allegorical usage of the term *Aethiops* ('a black') to signify a person
of *any* colour or somatic type who is 'black' in spirit and 'without
divine light' by reason of the fact that he or she has not received a
Christian baptism.[104] Texts of this kind, which often give conscious
expression to the popular and negative symbolism of the colour

black as a mark of evil, ugliness, death, disaster, and the like, convey an evident derogation of nigritude, and even those scholars who have regarded the derogation as 'innocent' have felt a '*frisson* of unease' at the frequency with which it is repeated in the Christian literature of the Roman world.[105] One much discussed text of this kind is the third-century pagan epitaph of a black slave from Antinoe in Roman Egypt:

> Among the living I was very black, darkened by the rays of the sun. But beauty is less important than nobility of soul; and my soul, ever blooming with the whiteness of flowers, attracted the goodwill of my prudent master and embellished the blackness of my physical appearance.[106]

Another text to which much attention has appropriately been given is one of several relating to a test of spiritual 'whiteness' and Christian humility to which Abba Moses, an old *Aethiops* monk and fourth-century 'Desert Father' who had been a slave and armed robber in his youth, was reputedly subjected by his fellow clerics in an Egyptian monastery:

> It is said of Father Moses that, when he was invested with the long white priest's robe upon his ordination as a member of the clergy, the Archbishop said to him, 'See, Father Moses, you have become completely white.' The old man replied, 'Outwardly, Lord and Father. But am I also white inwardly?' Wishing to test him, the Archbishop said to the other priests, 'Whenever Father Moses comes into the sanctuary, drive him out and follow him in order to observe his reaction.' The old man came in and they abused him and drove him out, saying, 'Get out, Blackface!' As he was going out he said to himself, 'They have treated you properly, you sooty-skinned one, you black one! Since you are not human, why should you have entered the company of men?'[107]

It has been argued that these derogatory expressions carried the germs of 'disturbing developments' or 'dangerous ideas' with regard to black–white social relations in the Roman world.[108] Some have gone even further, maintaining that the negative symbolism of blackness and disparagement of blackness shown in these texts was integral to a social–psychological situation that encouraged 'a negative evaluation' of blacks.[109] Thus Étienne Bernand, noting the 'studied insistence' with which the notion 'black in body *but* white in soul' is developed in the above-cited epitaph of the black slave, concluded that 'people of colour' (not merely the colour of such people, but the people themselves) were held in low esteem *qua* people of colour. Devisse similarly pointed to certain socially 'dangerous' effects of the Christian vision of evil as black, with its implication that God is white and that black people are creatures of the Devil.[110] On the other hand, despite the clear evidence for irrational beliefs about blackness and black strangers, Snowden maintained that Roman society 'did not make color the focus of irrational sentiments',[111] and took the equally unacceptable view that the various instances of disparagement of nigritude have no bearing on the reality of black–white social relations, or even on that of the social–psychological dispositions of the most humble and indigent of blacks.[112]

In the above-cited piece of hagiography on Abba Moses, both the appellation *Aithiops* (which is flung at that black man in a derogatory tone, and which I have translated as 'Blackface') and the word *melane* ('you *black* one'), which he is made to apply in disparagement to himself, no doubt illustrate the Christian symbolic usage of these words in the sense of 'sinful' or 'Hell-black' (as in Ennodius' plea for sexual continence, which warns against the 'Hell-black face' of the temptress into sexual sin).[113] But the text on Abba Moses also relates to secular attitudes and behaviour. Attention has rightly been drawn to the notion of a black man as less than human contained in the soliloquy attributed to Abba Moses, and also to the actuality of the discriminatory treatment suffered by him and the 'open contempt' to which he is subjected.[114] Even though the situation was merely stage-managed in this particular case, the pattern of the testing of Moses in this and related accounts was obviously geared specifically to the psychology of *a black man of humble status*, and it cannot have occurred to the testers of Moses' spiritual 'whiteness' (or to the authors of these anecdotes, assuming that the anecdotes are wholly or partly fictitious) as a completely original idea. It must have been suggested by certain facts of contemporary secular life. Significantly, the fellow clerics of Abba Moses expected him to be 'upset' by the abuse to which they subjected him, even though the abuse was merely stage-managed; and, according to the report, he *was* 'upset', though he willed himself to overcome his wounded feelings in a spirit of true Christian humility.[115]

Some texts in this generally derogatory group pointedly dissociate ethnicity or colour of skin from personal worth; for example, the words of a queen of Aethiopia in a work of fiction of the third century AD to the effect that, *despite* their black colour, 'Aethiopians' are 'whiter and more resplendent in soul than the whitest of Greeks'; or again, the above-cited epitaph of the black slave whose whiteness of soul more than compensated for his physical blackness.[116] Statements of this kind do not, as Snowden held, (and indeed cannot) offer any proof of the absence of racism or colour prejudice.[117] As Wiesen, Cracco Ruggini, and others have rightly pointed out, any inference of that kind is a *non sequitur*.[118] Such sentiments may convey a great deal about the personal feelings and attitudes of individuals, such as the feelings of one Chimaerus and his wife, Aelia Carpime, towards their black servant, as indicated in the epitaph on the tomb set up by them at Halicarnassus in memory of the dead servant: the inscription declares that, while the tomb covers the servant's black body, his soul has been welcomed into the Island of the Blessed, and the deceased is addressed with the affectionate words

> Farewell, good Blackface. This your comfort be:
> We brought you home from Patara here to lie.[119]

But whatever the personal feelings and attitudes of the individuals voicing sentiments like 'black in body, white in soul', such expressions of sentiment can neither prove nor disprove the existence of structures of the racist kind. The only texts that can in themselves offer such proof with regard to blacks in Roman society are those which demonstrate the significance of the Roman concept *Aethiops*.[120] Snowden's arguments on this issue betray the unacceptable assumption that high-minded notions about the inner whiteness of blacks must actually have governed day-to-day social relations between blacks and whites. The sociological significance of such expressions of sentiment can, in fact, only be appreciated against a background of the ideology and structures of the society in which the sentiment is voiced, and only when the sentiment is realistically assessed as an indirect criticism of certain prevailing values and attitudes.[121] It is indeed very noteworthy that sentiments couched in language of the sort under discussion were voiced in the early Islamic world (where they have been interpreted by at least one scholar, rightly or wrongly, as evidence of an 'Alabama'-style social situation of 'color prejudice')[122] and even in some undeniably racist societies.

In the seventh-century Arab world (whose literature sometimes represents nigritude as a handicap of some kind) the black poet Suhaym declared

> Though I am a slave my soul is nobly free,
> Though I am black of color my character is white.

Similarly, the *dicta* of the prophet Mohammed are believed to have included the remark that, in Paradise, 'the whiteness of the Ethiopian will be seen over a stretch of a thousand years' and the injunction 'Obey whoever is put in authority over you, even if he be a cropped-nosed Ethiopian slave.' Again, an Arab writer of the eleventh century observed that 'God has decreed that the most devout is the noblest, even if he be a negress's bastard, and that the sinner and unbeliever is at the lowest level even if he be the son of prophets.'[123] Similarly, the anti-slavery literature of eighteenth-century America is replete with 'apologies' for the negro's blackness, like the observation of a clergyman that 'a dark complexion may cover a fair and beautiful mind.'[124] And William Blake (writing in a socio-cultural milieu that nurtured David Hume's conviction that blacks were naturally inferior to whites, and in which the racist pamphleteering of men like Edward Long and Samuel Estwick found numerous sympathizers in high places) could exalt whiteness of soul in blacks while also indirectly exalting somatic whiteness:

> My mother bore me in the southern wild,
> And I am black, but oh! my soul is white.
> White as an angel is the English child,
> But I am black, as if bereav'd of light.[125]

Even in the aggressively racist ambience of the nineteenth-century western European world (where blacks, *qua* blacks, however much 'equal in Christ', were definitely 'unequal in nature'), Victor Hugo could attempt to console a Haitian correspondent with '*Devant Dieu, toutes les âmes sont blanches*', while Kipling could exalt the white soul of his Gunga Din who 'for all 'is dirty 'ide', was 'white, clear white inside' and 'a better man than I am.'[126]

In the Roman texts conveying similar-sounding sentiments, the issue that really calls for consideration is one which scholars like Snowden have entirely neglected: namely, the very strong probability that the implicit disparagement of nigritude in such sentiments may have had an unwholesome effect on the psychological condition of some blacks in a society where preference for the somatic norm could find unabashed and public expression in the mocking of blacks by whites (as Juvenal and others show) and in the highly disparaging and contemptuous descriptions of blacks as 'frightful spooks' or as 'the shit of the Garamantes'.[127] Although Snowden rightly attempted to apply to the Roman situation Hoetink's notion of somatic norm image, he ignored the fact that Hoetink himself had illustrated the mental trauma that can take hold of people who, while personally very distant from the somatic norm image of their society, have been socialized into accepting it as their ideal.[128] Even in societies where worship of the somatic norm image is generally given more subtle expression than the kinds indicated for Roman society by several texts, that 'image worship' can have a disturbing effect on the somatically distant. C.C. Rogler found some forty years ago that, in Puerto Rico, the very white and fair-haired adolescent (especially if male) tended to feel self-consciousness and shame about his over-conspicuous 'paleface' appearance,[129] and Olaudah Equiano, one of the most prominent blacks in eighteenth-century England, confessed in his autobiography that, upon his first encounter with the European somatic type, his reaction was one of shock at 'the horrible looks, red faces and loose hair' of Europeans – yet a few years later, as a boy in England and a member of an English household, he had come to be 'mortified' at his own blackness and distance from the English somatic norm image.[130]

Even if Juvenal's *derideat Aethiopem albus* is a quotation or paraphrase of a proverb of the 'pot and kettle' sort (as Snowden maintained, and even Wiesen allowed as a probability),[131] it nevertheless contains the unavoidable message that (at the very least) there had once been a time when blacks, like cripples, were objects of mockery in Roman society. That message cannot be ignored or glossed over, as Snowden tried to do. The evidence makes it obvious that such mocking was in fact a constant feature of Roman behaviour in certain circles and circumstances, however humorous and good-natured the manner in which the mocking may have been conducted on occasion – for instance, by the light-ironic use of antiphrasis whereby a dwarf was named or addressed as 'Atlas' or 'Bigman' (*Magnus*), a black as 'Swan' or 'Silver' or 'Snow White', an ugly girl as 'Europa' (with the force of our 'Miss England' and the like), and a scabby mongrel as 'Tiger'.[132] Some references to blacks in the literary texts are in themselves instances of mocking, albeit by the written and publicly recited word as distinct from face-to-face mocking.[133] Moreover, Seneca actually attests to the reality of objectionable forms of open and unabashed face-to-face mocking of blacks by the very fact that he feels a need to deplore this behaviour: 'A person who disparages in an individual a defect that is in fact common to that individual's ethnic or national group (*commune vitium* or *vitium genti publicum*) is being unfair. The colour of the *Aethiops* is not remarkable among his own people; nor is blond and grease-knotted hair unbecoming for a male in Germany. One should not judge any characteristic remarkable or ugly in an individual if that feature is common to that individual's people.'[134] As for mockery of the decidedly unpleasant, insulting and abusive sort, it is enough to recall Juvenal's picture of the bullying, badgering, and status-symbolic thrashing of a *pauper* (a man also perceived as a probable 'Jewish beggar') by a complete stranger who happens to be socially superior to his victim and is the kind of man who cannot get to sleep at night until he has had a drunken brawl with some person socially safe to attack.[135] We also find allusions to the wretched life of indigents, entirely lacking in positive deference-entitling properties for whom death is the only release from indignities like mocking and thrashing at the hands of social superiors.[136] These examples, to be sure, relate to humble whites. But humble blacks were evidently also likely to suffer such indignities, and in their case the badgering will no doubt have included mocking references to their blackness, just as humble whites endured mockery of physical traits like snub noses.[137] Romans at all times showed a deep-seated tendency to indulge in open mockery of all sorts of odd or 'inappropriate' physical, cultural, behavioural, and social character-istics.[138] Given the fact that the population of the Roman world included a number of blacks, and given the strength of this urge towards caricature and the demonstration of acid wit and humour (*Italum acetum*)[139] in everyday life,[140] any notion of an absence of black victims of this behaviour would be beyond explanation.[141]

The mocking obviously took a variety of forms, ranging from gentle banter to cruel derision and insulting outbursts of disparagement.[142] So the really important questions posed by the allusions to the mocking of blacks are what kind of mocking these allusions represent, and whether or not blacks, irrespective of personal status, were apt to encounter mocking treatment by whites *qua* whites. The fellow clerics of Abba Moses were fully conscious of the fact that the treatment to which they subjected him, if applied to a humble black in the ordinary course of life, would greatly 'upset' that person, and Luxorius indicates that a black skin could be 'harmful' to its possessor in some way, though some blacks were (in some way, and for one reason or another) exempt from this 'harm'.[143] Evidently mocking of blacks was sometimes of the deliberately hurtful sort, the effect of which on the victim was an inner sense of 'hurt' and shame at his or her own physiognomy.[144] That feeling must sometimes have developed into the feeling of insecurity that Lucian calls *micropsychia* ('pettiness of mind' or, in effect, an inferiority complex), and even into self-hate, whether or not the victims developed defences like protective clowning and cunning, or the more constructive defence of a powerful striving for success.[145]

However, the 'Swan'/'Snow White' antiphrasis that was applied to blacks would seem to have been a usage belonging more to the category of banter – harmless and often affectionate in intent, whether or not it was always taken by the black recipient in that light. Wiesen supposed that this usage was usually a vehicle for 'cutting' mockery of 'the lowly blackness of the *Aethiops*.'[146] But that supposition is unwarranted. Admittedly, antiphrasis was used to convey insults of the most biting and hurtful sort, but that particular usage related only to criticism of moral and behavioural defects, as in 'calling a crook *Aristides* and a coward *Achilles*.'[147] So far as somatic 'defects' are concerned, criticism (as distinct from derision) does not arise, and the distinction between antiphrastic criticism and antiphrastic nomenclature relating to physique was noted by Romans.[148] If, as Lucian puts it, there were always plenty of ugly people who did not mind being flatteringly called names like 'Nireus' and 'Phaon',[149] it may be supposed that the same was true of blacks addressed by names like 'Silver', which represented banter and affection rather than insulting and abusive attitudes.[150] Martial's references to a dark-skinned girl euphemistically called

Chione ('Snow White') are pertinent: the joking at her expense verges on the 'cutting' only when it is extended to her supposed sexual frigidity by the satirical suggestion that only in that particular respect is she the fit and apt construction of her nickname '*Snow* White'.[151] Juvenal, to be sure, alludes to the usage in the general context of a cutting tirade against nobles who do not measure up to their distinguished family names, but his immediate context is in fact a warning to aristocrats not to allow their noble names to become the equivalent of mere antiphrastic jokes. John Ferguson aptly commented on Juvenal's allusion 'So we might call a six-footer "Tich", and *there was a day* when a black might be "Snowball"'.[152] That 'Snowball' antiphrasis went out of fashion in certain societies for the reason that it ceased to be seen as a humorous and affectionate usage by the blacks in those societies who have become increasingly programmed by certain social forces to see it as an insult, *despite* its essentially humorous and affectionate intent.

The Roman evidence, then, for the most part shows negativity. But the impression of a dominant negativity is a function of the upper-class 'bias' of this evidence and of the fact that some of the negative allusions to blackness and to blacks are popular clichés and indications of a convention in the use of language rather than indications of actual attitudes. Where the evidence does offer clear revelations of actual negative attitudes towards blacks, these all relate in some way to the fact that, in the experience of Romans, blacks were usually people of humble status. Sometimes the negative attitudes also relate to perceptions of *Aethiops* strangeness among people unfamiliar with the sight of black faces, but the second factor, to which most of these attitudes relate, is the prominence in the culture of the educated classes, of what I have called unashamed and open 'worship of the somatic norm image' and the consequently strong inclination of members of these classes to voice negative aesthetic evaluations of the black physiognomy on the basis of their own ethnocentric values and fashionable canons of beauty. It would be naive to suppose that this had no adverse psychological effects on those blacks who personally encountered such negative attitudes. But, despite earlier readings of the evidence, this material has to be interpreted not only in relation to the various expressions of positive attitudes (such as are shown in the allusions to black–white sexual relations and indications of other forms of intensive social relations between blacks and whites), but also in relation to the Roman ideology of status and deference. This second imperative arises particularly from the indications that some blacks were exempt from the handicap of blackness that is suggested by the negative evidence.

INTERPRETATIONS OF THE CONCEPT 'AETHIOPS'

Meaningful discussion of the subject of blacks in Roman antiquity evidently depends upon possession of a clear idea of the degree (or degrees) of somatic distance which, in the perceptual context of that society, separated blacks (*Aethiopes*) from the somatic norm. One scholar has asserted that study of this subject which limits its compass to 'the so-called pure Negro' and almost entirely ignores 'blacks of less pronounced Negroid characteristics' is of necessity 'as unrealistic and distorted as a study of the black population in the United States or Brazil would be if restricted to a consideration of 'pure' Negroes'.[153] That is not acceptable. The real imperative is a focus on the *Roman* concept of 'blacks' and avoidance of the false assumption that 'blacks' has been an unchanging concept throughout history. On the whole, the Roman evidence suggests that when Romans applied the term *Aethiops* to someone whom they saw in the flesh, the usage related to a particular combination of somatic traits describable as black or very dark complexion, 'tightly-curled' hair, 'swollen' lips, and broad or flat nose.[154] This concept needs clarification through discussion of the relevant evidence, but it is important to avoid the assumption that membership of the category *Aethiops* was, to all practical intents and purposes, determined by the mere fact of biological descent from an *Aethiops* parent, let alone grandparent or great-grandparent – an assumption that implies a social homogenization of people with black ascendants and a social definition of 'black person', and so also (however unconsciously) implies racism.[155] It will not do to say that '*the blacks* of the ancient artists' closely resemble persons today described as 'colored' or 'of mixed black and white descent', for such a statement presumes without warrant that artists of the Roman world shared a particular modern concept of 'the black person'.[156]

Beardsley and Snowden both operated on interpretations of the concept *Aethiops* that are clearly inappropriate. They both betrayed an assumption that the Roman concept signified a person with signs of 'negro blood' and that, in the Roman perceptual context, the category 'blacks' embraced a wide range of 'colored' types possessing somatic features 'not unlike those of the highly mixed American Negro' and even included 'Caucasoid-looking' people:[157] for example, a man whose portrait shows a so-called sign of negro blood 'in the lips'; or a person with features 'not strongly Ethiopian' but nonetheless presumed to be, in the ancient artist's intention, 'a member of this race'; or one with long wavy hair, a short nose and thick, protruding lips; or one with 'low forehead, nose short but not negroid, and thick, full lips' (a face quite reasonably seen by others as that of an Egyptian woman).[158] On this principle too, the Roman dramatist Terence, King Juba II of Mauretania, and the 'Moor' and Roman general Lusius Quietus can all be seen as 'black' or probably 'black' (as persons of 'unmistakable black–white extraction' or 'perhaps of Negroid descent'), and a catalogue of portraits of Roman blacks can contain items whose inclusion rests on the ground that some strain of 'negro blood' is discernible in their features. This mode of classification was rightly criticized by Raymond Mauny, who pointed out that these so-called signs of negro blood have been apparent in many Mediterranean whites.[159] Significantly, a portrait whose 'identity' as that of a black eludes the simple observer and is unlikely to have been apparent to persons whose visions were shaped in the Roman perceptual context, has been categorized by one scholar as that of a black (in so far as the 'curly but closely cropped hair, subnasal region and lips suggest Negroid admixture') and by another as a mixture of the 'aristocratic Negro' and Arabian types – a quaint description reflecting a now outmoded Anglo-Saxon tendency to equate with black nobility certain apparent combinations of 'Caucasian' and black African traits.[160] The taxonomic principle of so-called signs of negro blood has also fostered the unacceptable notion that a textual reference to any combination of two 'Negroid' traits must be a reference to an *Aethiops*, and it has likewise encouraged a tendency in some scholars to interpret as references to people of the *Aethiops* type far too many Roman descriptions of persons by the simple terms 'black' (*niger* or *melas*), 'dusky' (*fuscus*), 'curly-haired', and the like.[161] Thus, for Snowden, the Garamantes of the Fezzan (whom ancient texts usually distinguish from *Aethiops*) are 'black warriors';

and some sixth-century Moorish chiefs are 'black' simply because they are described in an epic poem by the word *niger*.[162] Without contextual support such descriptions cannot with certainty or high probability be held to have any more relevance to the theme of Roman attitudes towards blacks than the often derogatory references in the literature to swarthy and very sun-bronzed (*coloratus, ustus*) Mediterranean whites, such as Martial's description of the peasantry of Etruria as *colorati Etrusci* and the same poet's depiction of his 'Lycoris' as a woman of dark complexion (*fusca*) who is driven by the dictates of contemporary fashion to seek to acquire a lighter complexion, but turns 'black' (*nigra*) after one of her attempts at skin-bleaching.[163]

In the experience of Romans, people of the *Aethiops* type were not the only people with flat or snub noses or thick (or protruding) lips or 'tightly curled' hair; nor were they the only people whom Romans described as 'black' (*niger, ater, fuscus,* or *melas*).[164] There is therefore no justification for counting as 'Ethiopian' (in the Roman context) a Moorish captive described simply as 'black as a crow', or Glycon (an actor of the time of Nero) who is described as 'a tall, dark man with a pendulous lower lip', or a Christian convert represented as '*Aethiops* in colour'.[165] In this last example, indeed, the Latin description in itself obviously seeks to distinguish the man's appearance from that of an *Aethiops*, indicating a resemblance to the *Aethiops* type in colour only and so implying that the man was not actually perceived as *Aethiops*. This same type of description is actually applied by classical geographers and ethnographers to the Berber tribe known as the Asphodelodes, with the intention of conveying the same idea of a pronounced blackness of complexion combined with 'Caucasian' morphology, which was by implication perceived as different from the *Aethiops* type.[166] The appeal of scholars to a modern-style taxonomy in this matter avoids the crucial issue: namely, what would a Roman have meant if, on seeing a given person in the flesh, he described that person as *Aethiops*? For all their distinction and notability as historical figures, Juba, Terence, and Lusius Quietus are never described in ancient references as *Aethiops* or in language that might in any way suggest that Romans perceived them as men of the *Aethiops* type – as is suggested in the case of the celebrated fable writer Aesop by one unreliable source.[167] To be sure, portraits of Juba show him as a man with thick lips, but not one of the many ancient references to him connects him in any way with the *Aethiops* type of physiognomy. On the contrary, he is cited by Pliny, in a discussion on the very question of the *Aethiops* somatic type, in terms indicating a general assumption that he was not himself perceived by Romans as *Aethiops*.[168] And it is reasonable to suppose that literary references to famous people *would*, in any case, have sometimes alluded to their nigritude if they had been perceived as persons of that somatic type, for although Romans lacked the modern ideological urge to 'identify a man by his colour and shape',[169] comments on the physiognomy of famous people frequently appear in various types of literature.[170] Even Memnon, the protégé of Herodes Atticus, who earned literary notice solely because of his connexion with a distinguished family, is naturally described in that notice as *Aethiops*.[171] Juba, Terence, and Quietus may well have been 'coloured' men in the modern sense of the term, but that is entirely irrelevant if Roman perceptions did not associate them with the *Aethiops* category.[172]

Desanges interpreted the concept *Aethiops* as 'dark-skinned, not necessarily Negro' (in other words, as *homme de couleur* rather than *le Noir*), a definition which might include in the category very swarthy Moors, Melanogaetuli, and the like.[173] In defence of that position, he drew attention to Gsell's description of the 'negroids' found in modern times as indigenes of the oases of southern Tunisia: 'strong cheekbones; long, pear-shaped face; deeply notched nose; receding chin; skin very dark, a reddish brown; eyes deep black; hair only slightly kinky, and jet black'.[174] Gsell himself and a number of other scholars regarded this Saharan 'negroid' physiognomy as exemplifying *par excellence* the Roman concept *Aethiops*.[175] But these views have no sound basis: the physical appearance of modern Saharan negroids is quite irrelevant to the objective of grasping the *Roman* perceptual context, which can be attained only by close study of the few texts that actually offer the necessary information. Desanges, however, appropriately pointed out an anomaly in modern western perceptions, noting that people in the western world generally see 'white' as a category with firm and secure boundaries while relegating all notions of fluidity to the category 'non-white'.[176] Fluidity in the conceptualization of 'white' is, however, precisely what is to be expected in non-racist cultures such as ancient Rome must be presumed to have been – and will be conclusively shown to have been (particularly with regard to blacks) in the next chapter.[177]

Interpretations of the concept *Aethiops* naturally have a bearing on views about the proportion of 'blacks' in the population of the Roman world – a topic on which the evidence permits only vague speculations. Some have suggested that the number of blacks was quite large in the era of the emperors. It would seem that the number was generally larger in Egypt than elsewhere in the empire, while in most towns and villages outside Egypt, Italy, and parts of North Africa, the sight of black faces was more often than not a rare and almost unknown experience.[178] Finds of art objects depicting blacks offer no real evidence on this issue, since these often indicate nothing more than a taste for the exotic and an interest in legends like that of Memnon and Aurora in the localities in which they have been found.[179] Hardly more instructive are references to the enslavement of a thousand Nubian prisoners-of-war in 24 BC and to an all-black 'audience' in the theatre at Puteoli during the reign of Nero.[180] Since the all-black 'audience' is mentioned as an illustration of the 'brilliance and costliness' of the entertainment given by Nero to King Tiridates of Parthia, the reference to it is probably no more than a distorted report of a show with an all-black *cast* (which would certainly have rendered the show a rare, exotic, and expensive affair). As for the Nubian captives, the description of them as *Aethiopes* merely indicates 'nationals of the kingdom of Aethiopia' (the Meroitic kingdom); it cannot be assumed that the captives were, even for the most part, perceived by Romans as men of the *Aethiops* somatic type.[181] But even if they were all men of that type, their numbers would tell us little or nothing about their contribution to the size of the black population in Roman society in later generations, for that depends entirely on how Romans perceived the physical appearance of their offspring, born in slavery and of mating predominantly with non-black women (as will certainly have been the case, if they did mate and produce children at all).

In brief, lack of evidence precludes any meaningful estimate of the size of the black element even in a particular period, except in terms of its smallness – though the state of the evidence is itself testimony to the fact that Romans did not regard the black presence as a matter of particular importance.[182] Except in the case of recent history, the in-group references to a minority group that are most likely to offer evidence or clues as to the size of that minority tend to be of the sort associated with hostility and intolerance towards the minority, or disquiet about its presence: for example, the early seventeenth-century royal proclamation ordering the deportation of all blacks from the city of London on the grounds that they were too numerous and were exacerbating the hunger problem of the poor; or again, the estimates which in 1772 put the number of blacks in London at about 15,000 and which were motivated by antipathy towards the black presence.[183] It is extremely unlikely that any Roman city contained a black element nearly as large as that of Elizabethan London, let alone eighteenth-century London, for the black presence in London at those times was almost entirely the consequence of a large-scale and entirely black slave-trade, a phenomenon that Romans would have found incomprehensible. Beyond that postulate, it need only be said that those who interpret *Aethiops* in the same sense as the modern American concept 'black person', and those who see Roman descriptions of people by terms like *niger* and *melas* as practically always signifying the *Aethiops* somatic type, will arrive at estimates (*ceteris paribus*) considerably higher than those reached by scholars who see *Aethiops* as designating a combination of black pigmentation (ranging from light chestnut to jet black) and the characteristics platyrrhiny, tightly-curled hair, thick lips, and prognathism.[184]

THE DESIDERATA

The foregoing review reveals three interrelated matters which still very much require attention: first, clarification of the Roman concept *Aethiops* as a label for a distinct somatic type, and explanation of the significance of that concept with regard to Roman social ideology; second, examination of the appropriate texts for a definitive confirmation of the view (so far resting largely on circumstantial evidence and *argumenta ex silentio*) that colour prejudice (or racial prejudice) was unknown in Roman society;[185] third, explanation, in terms other than those of race, of the sociological significance of the various expressions of negative and positive attitudes to blacks already outlined in the foregoing comments on the negative symbolism of the colour black and the often related derogation of the black physiognomy, together with some discussion of the probable effects which this colour symbolism and derogation had on the psychology of blacks living in Roman social space. On this last matter the highly 'optimistic' position of Snowden clearly needs correction. Intelligent Romans, after all, have recorded that some Roman soldiers were induced by superstition (an aspect of the negative colour symbolism) to murder a black stranger because they saw their accidental encounter with him as a presage of disaster for themselves. This report at least indicates that Romans could *expect* that kind of reaction in such circumstances: that is, men driven by irrational fears (arising from the negative symbolism of blackness) into violent action against an innocent black stranger (thereby reacting like the bandits of Apuleius' novel, who instinctively seek to kill the ass that they believe has brought them bad luck), provided that the circumstances rendered it safe for them to indulge in such violence.[186] Blackness clearly *could* be a handicap in Roman society. But what kind of handicap, and how, and in what circumstances, did it arise and operate? Attention needs to be focused on the nature of the emotional responses of Roman whites to the sight of black faces in a context of local unfamiliarity with blacks, but also on the general question of black–white social relations and the psychological dispositions of blacks in a social situation in which physical 'defects' (including the 'ethnic' variety) were evidently often targets of acid wit and banter as well as badgering and bullying. Equally requiring study are the criteria that rendered individual blacks subject to, or exempt from, personal disparagement. These questions have hitherto failed to receive due attention owing to the bogus link with 'race' that has been imposed upon them, thereby obfuscating the issue of the Roman ideology of status and deference-worthiness which is evidently integral to the proper context in which disparagement or appreciation of blacks should be studied.[187] This approach stands to benefit from comparison of the Roman situation with those of certain more recent European societies of the non-racial kind, such as those of late medieval Italy and seventeenth-century England, in which blacks constituted a small numerical minority, though by no means a sociological minority (defined in terms of group degradation), and which had in common with Roman society two characteristics that have an important bearing on the issue of attitudes towards blacks: first, a definition of the rights of individuals in terms of *ordo* or estate, economic class, and degree of personal independence;[188] second, a habit of mentally associating blacks with low status (a habit arising in a natural manner from an objective situation in which blacks were mostly servants as well as being highly 'visible' people), and, indeed, of seeing them in the context of a pervading sense of rightlessness and powerlessness among the broad mass of poor commoners, irrespective of ethnic extraction.[189]

Chapter Two

THE *AETHIOPS* TYPE IN ROMAN PERCEPTIONS

THE TERM '*AETHIOPS*'

In the literature of the Graeco-Roman world the term *Aethiops* appears in four senses. In the oldest usage (the 'Homeric'), the plural form *Aethiopes* is a designation for the people of a utopian world of the remotest east who were imagined as possessing a sunburnt complexion-norm much darker than that of the world of Homer: the concept is evident in the very etymology of the word *Aethiops* ('sun-darkened face').[1] The second usage (again in the plural form *Aethiopes*) is a broad term conventionally applied to all peoples of the various ill-known or unknown parts of sub-Egyptian, Saharan, and sub-Saharan Africa which were all collectively called 'Aethiopia' ('the world of sun-darkened people'). The boundaries of this concept were defined by poetic convention in terms of exposure to the heat of the sun at its fiercest, and the usage, found, for example, in Strabo's reference to the Blemmyes, Trogodytes, Nubae and Megabari as 'those *Aethiopes* who live above Syene' (Aswan),[2] occurs mostly in literature of the non-empirical sort. In the third usage (and especially in Roman, as distinct from classical Greek, literature), *Aethiopes* and *Aethiopia* are national names for the population and the land of the Nilotic kingdom of Kush (Napata-Meroe).[3] In the fourth usage, *Aethiops* (the singular form) has a much more restricted import, designating a particular human somatic type that might today be described as 'black African'; in that sense the plural form *Aethiopes* refers to two or more persons of that anthropological type.[4] This concept had its genesis in Graeco-Roman acquaintance with Nilotic 'Aethiopia' and in actual experience of the black African somatic type, mainly in countries of the Graeco-Roman world itself. In the art of the Greek world (including that of southern Italy) from the sixth century BC onwards, and in Roman art from the third century BC, the realism with which this somatic type is portrayed clearly indicates direct experience of black Africans in Greek and Roman society, and points to a living concept of *Aethiops* as specifically connoting this anthropological type.[5] In literature this concept is apparent in descriptions of the type (or stereotype) as marked by a combination of black skin, crinkly hair, thick lips, and broad or flat nose,[6] and an early Roman experience of people of this type is reflected in an issue of coins in the third century BC depicting the head of a black African on the obverse and an elephant on the reverse.[7]

Most instances of the use of the plural form *Aethiopes* in Roman literature are not intended as references to people actually perceived by Romans as blacks, and do not offer any particular information about actual Roman perceptions of the *Aethiops* anthropological type.[8] Accordingly, it should hardly be surprising that some ancient African ethnic groups like the Blemmyes and Nubae, to whom the ethno-geographical label *Aethiopes* is sometimes applied in Roman writing, have been shown by modern archaeo-logical–anthropological investigations to have been only 'slightly influenced by negroid morphology'.[9] But notable in regard to actual Roman perceptions (as distinct from poetic and conventional usages of *Aethiopes* as a geographical term) is the comment of Philostratus on an artist's depiction of the mythical 'Aethiopian' king, Memnon: 'one would not describe Memnon as black [*melas*], for the pure blackness within him sends to the surface a rosy gleam.'[10] This comment not only shows that *Aethiops* conveyed the Roman concept 'black person'; it also betrays a common assumption that an *Aethiops* was a person of distinctly black complexion. It is on that general assumption that Philostratus attempts to rationalize the 'rosy' colour given by the artist to a man who, in the imagination of men of the Roman world, ought to have been black *qua* man of *Aethiopia*, and the rationalization resorts to the notion of an 'inner' and invisible blackness beneath the surface of the visible rosiness. This same conception of the *Aethiops* as characterized by a *remarkably* black colour is similarly implicit in Seneca's remark that 'the colour of the *Aethiops* is not remarkable among his own people.'[11] In a discussion of blacks in the Roman world (as distinct from the remote African habitats often assigned to so-called *Aethiopes* by geographers, ethnographers and mythographers), the relevant concept is clearly that of an anthropological type distinctly black in colour (according to Roman perceptions).

As Lesky has shown,[12] Greek legend originally conceived of *Aethiopes* as 'swarthy' people dwelling near the rising sun at the earth's eastern extremity. But when, in the course of the seventh and sixth centuries BC, Greeks became increasingly aware of a real land of 'blacks' in the region of the Upper Nile, the designation *Aethiopia* was given to that Nilotic and non-mythical land of 'sun-darkened peoples', and attempts were made to reconcile the old myths about *Aethiopes* with the newly-discovered ethno-geographical reality of the Upper Nile. In the mythic–utopian conception *Aethiopes* were men who differed from the Mediterranean somatic norm only in respect of their darker complexions, and so, in the processes by which 'science' sought to reconcile myth with the reality of Nilotic Aethiopia, mythical Aethiopians like Memnon were sometimes represented as 'black' Nilotics and sometimes as white or swarthy ancestors of the royal family of Nilotic Kush, this last solution resting either on the fact that, in the Mediterranean perceptual context, nationals of the Nilotic kingdom called 'Aethiopia' (Kush) were sometimes 'white' and sometimes 'swarthy' (as distinct from 'black'), or on the generally acknowledged 'genetic' principle that a black couple could produce legitimate 'white' children by biological regeneration or 'maternal impression'.[13] In this rationalization process the term 'Aethiopia' was also extended to the entire interior of Africa, and the designation *Aethiopes* was indiscriminately applied to all populations which could be located in this dimly conceived geographical entity of 'inner Africa'.[14] At the same time, however, empirical observation (for instance, Roman observation of blacks in Carthaginian armies) brought to the fore the concept *Aethiops* in the sense of the black African anthropological type.[15]

It is to that somatic type that Pliny refers when he asks, 'who ever believed in the existence of *Aethiopes* before actually seeing them?'[16] This question both alludes to ancient myths about *Aethiopes* and refers to a somatic type which Pliny and his contemporaries as well as earlier Romans had actually encountered – as a strange and unusual sight at first. Pliny obviously has that type (the black somatic type) in mind here when he speaks of

Aethiopes, and not the mere idea of 'Kushites' or of 'inhabitants of one of the lands called *Aethiopia*', for no one in Pliny's day would have needed to see an 'Aethiopian' in either of these two senses of the term in order to be convinced of their existence. The concept *Aethiops* as a distinct somatic type is similarly well indicated by the fact that, in imperial Rome, a stock theme in declamation exercises (*controversiae*) was *matrona Aethiopem peperit* ('A Roman married woman has given birth to an *Aethiops*'), the students' task being to argue before an imaginary jury an invented legal case hinging on the probability that a white woman with a white husband had given birth to a baby with the black African appearance (or a close approximation to it) without being guilty of adultery or premarital fornication with a black man. These imaginary defences and prosecutions of women on charges of adultery, which hinged on the popular notions of biological atavism and 'maternal impression', had some real-life counterparts in the courts of law.[17]

Some scholars have argued that this concept of *Aethiops* meant to Romans more or less what *Africain de couleur* (or even *homme de couleur*) means to a modern Frenchman.[18] But that is not supported by the evidence. For one thing, it is clear that the ethnic label *Leukaethiopes* or 'white people of black Africa' was coined by Greek geographers to meet a particular problem of terminology: certain African peoples (or at least one such ethnic group) located in the vaguely defined interior of Africa to which the term *Aethiopia* in its broad sense had come to be applied did not conform to the specific type that the term *Aethiops* connoted – indeed, they showed a very striking distance from the 'burnt face' image and so had to be sharply distinguished from *Aethiopes*.[19] Desanges saw the *Leukaethiopes* as a 'cross between *Aethiopes* and *Gaetuli*' and as 'a people of intermediate colour, like the Melanogaetuli' ('black Gaetuli') of the southern fringes of Roman Africa.[20] But just as the term *Melanogaetuli* definitely refers to the 'blackness' of skin which distinguished one people of *Gaetulia* from other Berber groups in that region of North Africa, so also *Leukaethiopes* evidently connotes 'whiteness' of complexion distinguishing one people of *Aethiopia* from other peoples in 'the land of dark-skinned and black peoples'. The prefix *Leuk-* must refer to whiteness, just as *Melano-* refers to blackness.[21] A terminological problem had arisen out of the conflict between the ethno-geographical concept *Aethiopia* and the more specific concept of a somatic type expressed by *Aethiops*: as a people of 'Aethiopia', the so-called *Leukaethiopes* were *Aethiopes*; but somatically they were white (in Greek and Roman perceptions), not *Aethiopes*. Hence the convenient term *Leukaethiopes*.

Ptolemy, in his survey of the peoples of Nilotic Aethiopia, shows the nature of the terminological conflict that lies behind the coinage of the term *Leukaethiopes*: he distinguishes between 'true *Aethiopes*' (in the more meaningful sense of 'black Africans') and others who are *Aethiopes* only in the sense of peoples of the geographical entity (or the national entity) 'Aethiopia'; he accordingly reports that neither the inhabitants of the northernmost sector of Nilotic 'Aethiopia' nor those located a little further to the south in the Triakontaschoinos were people of the black African somatic type (*Aethiopes*). Those of the Triakontaschoinos were dark-skinned, physically resembling the Garamantes of the Fezzan (who could be described as *melanes*), while those of the territory immediately bordering on Egypt were 'whites' of an even lighter complexion, and those of the region of Meroe were by and large the first 'real *Aethiopes*' to be encountered as indigenes in the traveller's southward progress.[22] Philostratus similarly contrasts with blacks (*Aethiopes*) the people of the area of Nilotic 'Aethiopia' around the first cataract of the river, and Pliny, citing Juba II of Mauretania, notes that the Nilotic peoples between Syene (Aswan) and Meroe were not blacks (*Aethiopes*), but 'Arabians' – that is, African peoples whose habitats were on the eastern side of the Nile, and who physically resembled the Trogodytes of the Red Sea coast of Africa and the Garamantes of the Fezzan.[23] These were evidently peoples of the types which, as Adams puts it, are describable as 'white' or 'black', depending on the operative perceptions and prejudices.[24] Ptolemy and Strabo also expressly distinguish the Garamantes from the *Aethiops* type, and they reveal a concept of 'inner Africa' as the habitat of the *Aethiops* type.[25] The very dark-skinned Berber group known as the Asphodelodes is likewise described as resembling *Aethiopes* only in colour but not in morphology.[26] The ethnic label *Melanogaetuli* ('black Gaetulians') is similarly a coinage reflecting the fact that this southern Berber people combined normal Mediterranean morphology with a very dark complexion.[27]

In Roman literature *Aethiopes* as a broad ethno-geographical term applied to non-blacks appears only in imaginative literature and in ethnographical writing that lacks a basis of empirical observation on the writers' part. Hence, in such literature the

Trogodytes of the Red Sea coast of Africa, the Garamantes of the Fezzan, and other 'swarthy' peoples of similar somatic appearance sometimes appear as *Aethiopes*, though they are usually contrasted with *Aethiopes*. Similarly, in the imagination of Claudian and Philostratus, the Berber Nasamones are a tribe of *Aethiopes*.[28] Naturally, however, it was mainly in the Roman world that Romans became directly acquainted with *Aethiopes*, and it was primarily this direct acquaintance that fostered and fortified the concept of *Aethiops* as a distinct somatic type that excluded not only people of the sort described as *Leukaethiopes* in the ethno-geographical literature, but also the Nilotic peoples contrasted by Ptolemy with 'real *Aethiopes*', meaning blacks – a type described by Roman writers as combining the somatic characteristics black skin, crinkly hair, thick lips and broad or flat nose.[29] This, to be sure, defines the somatic stereotype, for Juvenal's *decolor heres*, imagined as the fruit of a Roman woman's adultery with a black man, is still *Aethiops* in the satirist's imagination – an imagination which evidently reflects a real-life Roman perception of somatic distance from the Roman norm which placed some children of this kind of mixed parentage in the *Aethiops* category for the simple and natural reason that they combined a morphology of distinctly *Aethiops* appearance with the somewhat lighter-than-*Aethiops* complexion perceived by Achilles Tatius as common among children of mixed black and white parentage (*nothoi Aithiopes*).[30] The same perception is inherent in the declamation theme *matrona Aethiopem peperit*, which implies that some children, born of white mothers and presumed to have been the consequences either of sexual relations with black men, or of 'maternal impression', or of a biological atavism harking back to a black ascendant, were perceived as *Aethiopes* (as distinct from 'swarthy' or white).[31] The somatic type *Aethiops* can therefore only be properly defined by focusing on the themes of the Roman somatic norm and of Roman perceptions of distance from that norm.

'*AETHIOPS*' AND ROMAN PERCEPTIONS OF SOMATIC DISTANCE

A number of contrasts drawn by writers of the Roman world between the *Aethiops* and other somatic types have already been noted. The *Aethiops* type is contrasted with the physiognomy of

Indians, Moors, Egyptians and other 'swarthy' peoples of the sort that are today described as non-white but which are described in Roman literature by adjectives like *decolor* ('off-white'), *fuscus* ('swarthy', 'dusky'), *perustus* ('sun-bronzed'), and *coloratus* ('browned'). The peoples so described include swarthy Garamantes and northern Nilotic peoples, as well as the swarthiest known Berber peoples of the Maghreb, such as the very dark-skinned Melanogaetuli and the black-skinned Asphodelodes.[32] The *Aethiops* type is also contrasted with the blackest, most 'woolly-haired', and most flat-nosed of southern Indians, who are described in classical Indian literature itself as black, woolly-haired, and 'noseless'.[33] These contrasts indicate a Roman categorization of *Aethiopes* in somatic terms on the basis of a distinct perception which also registered a narrow somatic distance between certain southern Indians (Dravidians) and this *Aethiops* type.[34] Philostratus, for example, observes that Indians and *Aethiopes* are both black, and that their two countries are the only lands that 'produce black people'; some Romans even believed that 'the Aethiopians' were originally immigrants to Africa from India.[35] The contrast between the *Aethiops* type and the blackest of Indians or Berbers was probably therefore perceived only by people highly familiar with the *Aethiops* type,[36] but the perception is illustrated by Petronius' character Giton, whose viewpoint (in a passage to be quoted shortly) exemplifies a perceptual context in which a black skin alone did not qualify a person for membership of the category *Aethiops*.[37] In present-day white-dominated racist societies it is a relatively simple matter for a white person to pass as 'black'. Sometimes this can be done by a simple declaration of one's 'blackness'. In other cases success would require nothing more complex than a skilful application of ordinary cosmetics or a skin-dye.[38] Petronius' Giton, however, confidently dismisses the possibility of a white person in Roman society passing as *Aethiops*, because of what he sees as the impossibility of imitating the necessary *combination* of black African somatic traits (colour, hair, lips, and so on). Although some scholars have noted this,[39] they have not exploited the mine of sociological and cultural information offered by the text, especially with regard to the Roman concept *Aethiops* and Roman perceptions of somatic distance. The text presents an interesting little scene which confirms that, to experienced Roman observers, *Aethiops* connoted the black African somatic type, as distinct from other black-skinned or dark-skinned types.

Three characters, Encolpius, Giton and Eumolpus, are aboard ship at sea and the first two are desperately looking for a means of escaping recognition and punishment by the ship's captain and a female passenger. After a number of possibilities have been considered and rejected as futile, Encolpius suggests that he and Giton dye themselves black 'from hair right down to toenails' so as to be able to pass as black African slaves (*servi Aethiopes*) in the service of Eumolpus, who is not himself in any danger. But Giton sarcastically retorts:

> *quidni? etiam circumcide nos, ut Iudaei videamur, et pertunde*
> *aures ut imitemur Arabes, et increta facies ut suos Gallia*
> *cives putet; tanquam hic solus color figuram possit pervertere*
> *et non multa una oporteat consentiant ratione ut mendacium constet.*

Sure! And how about circumcising us to give us the Jewish look, or piercing our ears to make us look like Arabs, or plastering our faces with a chalk cosmetic so that Gaul may take us for her own people? As if black colour by itself can change our physiognomy! As if we wouldn't need a lot of matching details to make the deception work![40]

Giton then goes on to list the sort of 'matching details' which, along with blackness of skin, constituted the somatic stereotype of the black African slave: horribly 'swollen' lips (*labra tumore taeterrima*), a type of tightly curled hair that cannot be imitated by him and his companions even with the aid of a hot curling-iron, a 'scarred' forehead, bow legs with outer ankles almost touching the ground, and an alien kind of beard (evidently the sort described by Pliny as the 'curly' Aethiopian beard: *barba vibrata*).[41]

This text of Petronius' offers important information on the contemporary Roman perception of somatic distance in certain peoples. The 'Jewish look' (circumcision) is visible only in naked Jewish males. One recalls that, during the emperor Domitian's harsh exaction of the Jewish tax, males (by no means all of them Judaeans or devotees of Judaism) suspected of evading this special tax were sometimes stripped naked before the tribunal of the *fiscus Iudaicus* as an 'infallible' means of proving or disproving their 'Jewishness'.[42] Petronius implies that Judaeans and Arabs, if they adopted Roman styles of dress and deportment, would be indistinguishable from Romans in appearance: in other words, that people of these two groups conformed to the Roman somatic norm image, except for the artificial and culturally imposed marks borne by males of the groups. Israelites and Arabs themselves concurred with this perception. The former saw their own somatic norm as an intermediate colour and morphology between the extremes of 'nordic' whiteness and negro blackness, while Arabs contrasted their own somatic type both with the 'half-baked dough' of the northern European type and with the 'burnt crust' of the black African anthropological type.[43] If Romans had ever conceived the notion of turning Jews into a race (that is, subjecting them to *racial* discrimination), they would have found it necessary to impose a special uniform or 'identity card' on them – the inevitable refuge of the Third Reich and of the Spanish Inquisition.[44]

Petronius, however, shows that contemporary Romans perceived the peoples of 'Gallia' as somatically distant from themselves, since he represents whitening of the face with a chalk-based cosmetic as a crude attempt to achieve the 'Gallic' somatic appearance. Here 'Gallia' is shorthand for 'northern Europe' (indeed, 'central and northern Europe'), as Petronius himself shows in his reference to the cold winters of non-Mediterranean Europe by the phrase 'colder than a Gallic winter'.[45] The persistence of this shorthand and stereotype in later Roman times is shown in Christian literature which sets black Africans (*nigri Aethiopes*) at one end of the spectrum of somatic distance from the Mediterranean norm, and *candidi Galli* (the pale-white peoples of central and northern Europe) at the other extreme. Other late Latin writers also reflect this stereotype with contrasting references to black Africans and *candidi Germani* (German 'palefaces') or *candidi Saxones* (Saxon 'palefaces').[46] Romans evidently perceived these peoples of non-Mediterranean Europe as 'palefaces' in much the same way as Anglo-Saxons were perceived by the Indians of North America in modern times. In Petronius' context the details of the 'nordic' somatic stereotype are unnecessary (and would, indeed, have been otiose). They are therefore not listed. But they frequently occur in Latin literature: while the Mediterranean somatic norm is *albus* ('white', in the sense of pale-brown), the northern 'paleface' is *candidus* – marked by a very white, frosty complexion, blond or red hair, blue eyes, upturned 'snub noses', and an almost obscenely large frame and tall stature.[47] For a joke, a Roman male might play the 'paleface' by whitening his face with a chalk-based cosmetic and wearing one of the blond wigs which were part of the wardrobe of fashionable Roman women in and after the first century AD. In that way the humorous might achieve a crude imitation of the 'paleface' somatic characteristics described by Pliny as 'very white and glacial complexion' and 'long blond hair'.[49] But imitating the 'Gallic' look was evidently not a serious proposition. Petronius implies that this particular somatic stereotype (which included a 'vast and beastly size')[50] was as much beyond convincing imitation by a Mediterranean white man (*albus*) as was the black African combination of colour, hair, lips and nose; for all the various disguises suggested in the scene are represented as useless and ridiculous.

But if the suggested disguises are all ridiculous, they are not all equally so; Giton's sarcastic suggestions are in fact presented in descending order of impracticability as disguises. The Jewish 'disguise', a mere matter of circumcision, is the most idiotic since it relates to a part of the anatomy that would not even be on display. It merely serves to emphasize the lack of somatic distance between the Roman norm and the Judaean, as seen by Romans. So does the Arab 'disguise', which (amounting merely to ear-piercing for the insertion of earrings) is only slightly less ridiculous than the Jewish one. It is different, however, with the other two somatic images mentioned in the passage, where the notion of a disguise is not idiotic in itself: for, by contrast with Jews and Arabs, 'nordic' and *Aethiops* people are, in the Roman perceptual context, actually distant from Romans somatically. The disguise problem is that these two somatic stereotypes are too distant from the Roman norm to be convincingly imitated by a Roman. Just as the ease of assuming the appearance of a Judaean or an Arab highlights the conformity of those two groups to the Roman somatic norm, so the impossibility of achieving the 'nordic' or the *Aethiops* appearance emphasizes the distance which, in Roman perceptions, separated these two somatic types (or stereotypes) from the Roman somatic norm image.[51]

This text of Petronius further implies that, in the Roman perceptual context, the black African and the 'nordic' somatic stereotypes were at two extremes of distance from the Roman somatic norm,[52] although a much greater distance separated the

Aethiops appearance from that norm than was the case with the 'paleface' look. Although the various somatic types with which Romans were familiar included the type today called 'Mongoloid' (as Oost noted),[53] Romans tended to base their general allusions to somatic distance on the convenient and tripartite schema of blacks, Mediterraneans, and 'nordics' (*Aethiops-albus-candidus*).[54] This tripartite schema is evidently what Lucian has in mind when he asks whether an *Aethiops* whose knowledge, experience, and awareness of the world were limited entirely to the black African environment would assume that all human beings were black and that there were no *leukoi* or *xanthoi*.[55] Here *leukoi* is not, as the Loeb translator implies and Snowden suggests,[56] the equivalent of our 'the white man'; it is the equivalent of the Latin *albi*, meaning the Mediterranean somatic norm. As for *xanthoi*, both the Loeb translator and Snowden, to be sure, render it 'yellow men', obviously induced by certain modern assumptions to take this position, which suggests that Lucian is alluding to 'mongoloids' like the Japanese, the Chinese, or the Huns (who, according to a similar suggestion by S.I. Oost, were perceived by Romans as 'little *yellow* men').[57] But this particular concept of 'yellow men' is not only specifically modern European, it is of very recent origin, going back only as far as the nineteenth century.[58] Ancient Greeks and Romans did not use *xanthoi* (or *flavi*) in that sense, as a description of a natural complexion-type, for the simple reason that they, like the Japanese and Chinese themselves, perceived as white (*leukos, albus*) or as 'swarthy' men of the sort whom the prejudices of our own milieu induce us to call 'yellow'.[59] In Roman society *xanthos* or *flavus*, as descriptive of a human somatic type, focused attention mainly on *hair*-colour – blondness.[60] Like Latin *flavi* and *candidi*, the Greek term *xanthoi* conventionally conveyed the notion of 'nordics'.[61]

As in the Petronius passage, the anonymous *Moretum* similarly describes the black African complexion, hair, and lips, and Martial notes the detail of the flat or broad *Aethiops* nose (*sima nare*).[62] Our passage also illustrates two different depths of perception of somatic distance in the *Aethiops*. The standpoint of Giton is characteristic of the sort of Roman who was familiar with the black African somatic type – a familiarity which must usually have depended for the most part on residence in an area of the Roman world where blacks were a fairly common sight and were encountered in situations of close contact, even if only as servants. In the perception of experienced Romans (exemplified by Giton), for whom black skin was not in itself enough to warrant classification of a person as *Aethiops*, a black complexion combined with Mediterranean-type morphology must have suggested not an *Aethiops*, but an ethnic or national identity such as Indian, Egyptian, Asphodelodian, or Melanogaetulus. On the other hand, a more hazy type of perception is indicated by Encolpius' suggestion for a disguise, because it rests on the belief that application of an artificial but very pronounced blackness of colour can enable a Mediterranean white man to pass as *Aethiops*. This sort of perception, which is marked by a focus on colour to the virtual exclusion of the other somatic features of the black African type, may well have been characteristic of many (or most) of those inhabitants of the Roman world who had little or no personal contact or familiarity with black Africans. It is probable that at all times in the period from the first century BC to the end of the third century AD there were many Italians like Encolpius, who were entirely lacking in direct acquaintance with black Africans, as distinct from that acquired through the visual arts, literature and hearsay. But direct and close familiarity with black Africans can probably be postulated for a much larger proportion of Romano-Egyptians and inhabitants of the city of Rome, since these appear to have been the places where the black element in the population was most numerous.[63]

The proportion of blacks in the population of Roman Italy is, however, most unlikely to have been at any time as high as in eighteenth century Britain (where the number of blacks has been estimated at between 20,000 and 30,000), even when one allows for exaggeration in the British figures and also subtracts from those figures a considerable number of so-called blacks whom no Roman would have perceived as falling within the category *Aethiops*, but whose inclusion in the number of British blacks is demanded by modern prejudices and perceptions. Yet, despite the larger number of blacks in British society, by far the majority of indigenous Britons of the eighteenth century had no direct acquaintance with the black somatic type since the black element was concentrated in London and a few other ports.[64] Now, in comparing the Roman and British situations in this regard, it may be taken as almost certain that the black element in Roman Italy at the moment of its greatest numerical strength, though much smaller than that of eighteenth-century England, was less unevenly distributed, because slavery (the main source of the black presence in both cases) was fully institutionalized in Roman society but not in Britain; so the proportion of people in Roman Italy at that (uncertain and hypothetical) moment who had never actually seen an *Aethiops* is unlikely to have been as high as in eighteenth-century Britain. By the same token the proportion of Italians who, at the time when the black element was at its highest numerical strength, shared Giton's acute perception of somatic distance between *Aethiopes* and other dark-skinned persons is likely to have been much higher than the corresponding proportion of eighteenth-century Britons. Part of the explanation of this difference between the perceptual contexts of these two societies (perhaps even the main explanation as far as the cities of Rome and London are concerned) is the difference between the somatic norm images of the two societies. The somatic distance perceived by Romans between their own norm and the 'Egyptian look' (*Niliaco ore niger*) was slight enough to be bridged by a Roman who took a holiday in the sun[65] (and Iberians of the fifteenth and sixteenth centuries had a very similar perception),[66] so it was far easier for a Mediterranean white in Roman society (as it was also for an early modern Iberian) to distinguish between the swarthy Egyptian (or Indian) look – seen by many a Roman male as enviable – and that of the *Aethiops* than it was for the eighteenth-century white Londoner whose pale-white somatic norm was so distant even from the Egyptian or Indian appearance, and whose focus on colour-distance would incline him to lump together a variety of 'coloured people'. In Roman society, on the basis of Giton's type of acute perception, information about the distinctive features of the *Aethiops* anthropological type also circulated (through literature, the visual arts, and hearsay) beyond the various localities where *Aethiopes* actually resided at a given moment, and such information was also handed down to generations which themselves lacked first-hand experience of that somatic type (whether because a black presence established at a given time in a given locality did not persist for more than one or two generations, or because no blacks had ever appeared in a given locality at all), with the result that many people who had never actually seen an *Aethiops* would have been able to recognize one if the occasion arose, and to distinguish the type from other dark-skinned types, even if many of them were nonetheless likely to react in a negative manner (showing fear, disquiet, or a sensory aversion) upon their first encounter with an *Aethiops*.

If Petronius indicates a perceptual difference between experienced Roman observers (represented by Giton) and many other Romans (represented by Encolpius), he also suggests that, for both, *Aethiopes* were at a very great somatic distance from the Roman norm. In a society in which the somatic norm was the pale-brown Mediterranean shade of 'whiteness' (*inter nigrum et pallidum*, as Romans themselves put it), and in which numerous specimens of an even darker shade (often the result of regular exposure to the sun on the part of the labouring classes) were to be encountered,[67] a person with a physiognomy combining black skin with 'normal' morphological traits would have needed to be of a very black complexion in order to be perceived as *Aethiops*, even by an observer who had no personal contact and direct acquaintance with the black African somatic type. Even an Encolpius, unlike his eighteenth-century British counterpart, would not have confused *Aethiopes* with 'swarthy' (as distinct from very black) Egyptians, Moors, Indians, and the like. Several reports have shown that, even in the 1950s few Britons were able to distinguish between the various categories of 'non-white' immigrants to Britain, because most people found 'coloured' pigmentation so striking that they rarely noticed the ways in which some 'non-white' persons differed from others.[68] This suggests that a British Encolpius of the eighteenth century (as distinct from those of his compatriots who were familiar with black people) would have been unable to distinguish between various types of physiognomy perceived by him as 'non-white'; but the Roman Encolpius would have had this perceptual difficulty only in distinguishing between blacks (*Aethiopes*) and the very black-skinned Indian (whom even *cognoscenti* set at a minimal distance from the *Aethiops* somatic type) or the very black-skinned Moor who looked like a white man dyed jet black from hair to toenails. Indeed the Roman Encolpius must be contrasted in this respect even with his British counterpart of the first half of the present century, with whom he shared a heavy emphasis on colour in his visual registration of somatic distance from his societal norm. But here the difference between ancient Roman and modern British perceptions is largely to be explained by the racist dimension of the early twentieth-century British perceptual context, which complicated the optical registration with an ideological urge to assign a social definition to the appearance that met the eye.[69]

The difficulty which many Britons of the 1950s found in distinguishing between different categories of 'coloured people' is understandable in the conditions of the time, in which even the swarthy 'Pakistani look' was very distant from the norm. The same difficulty cannot have occurred in Roman society, where the degree of somatic distance separating the norm from the 'swarthy' appearance was relatively small and where even this slight distance could often be perceived in northern Mediterranean persons.[70] If the focus on colour displayed by Petronius' Encolpius reflects the fact that, in the popular Roman imagination, blackness of skin-colour was the most striking aspect of the *Aethiops* physiognomy, the blackness of the *Aethiops* very probably had this impact on most observers only as part of the total *figura*. That is the sense in which one must take the emphasis on colour found in certain texts, for instance, Seneca's statement that 'among his own people there is nothing remarkable about the black African's *colour*.'[71] It can hardly be supposed that a man like Seneca was unfamiliar with the morphology of the *Aethiops* somatic type which is so realistically described by contemporary and near-contemporary fellow residents in the city of Rome. Seneca must have been aware that his remark about the colour of the *Aethiops* applied equally to the entire combination of characteristics of that somatic type; but he singled out colour because of his awareness that it was the most striking feature of the black physiognomy, and that broad or flat noses (or 'snub noses'), thickness of lip, and hair-types meriting the descriptions 'woolly' or 'curly' or 'tightly-curled' were not peculiar to the *Aethiops*. Moors, Egyptians and others might have curly or tightly-curled hair; even Greeks (let alone 'nordics') might have snub noses; and non-blacks might have both dark skin and thick lips.[72] Evidently, in the Roman perceptual context, an African albino was white – which indeed corresponds with the general perception of many Africans today, even if in that perception the albino is 'white' but not 'a white', the latter being fundamentally a cultural concept in which physiognomy plays the role of symbol.

Although to Romans the designation *Aethiops* was almost certainly based on general impressions rather than on any rigid criteria of classification, and although their impressions must have varied according to the extent of the observer's familiarity with blacks, the confusions and errors of identification typical of Britons a generation ago can hardly have arisen in Roman society. Accordingly the focus on colour shown by an Encolpius should not be assigned the same significance as the apparently similar focus demonstrated by his modern British counterpart. Rather, it is to be compared with that of Britons in the sixteenth and seventeenth centuries, for whom the black African's colour was his defining trait, even though experienced observers were not unaware of the other details of the black African physiognomy. One such observer, in his record of a visit to West Africa, could thus use the simple term 'blacke' as an adequate description of the African physiognomy, without seeing any need to refer to any other physical characteristic. Similarly, another knowledgeable man, George Best, wrote in 1578, 'I my selfe have seene an Ethiopian as blacke as cole brought into England, who taking a faire English woman to wife, begat a sonne in all respects *as blacke as the father was*.'[73] The part of this last statement which I have emphasized is obviously something of an exaggeration, but it shows that the author is using the term 'blacke' as a kind of shorthand for 'black African in general appearance'. Observers in those early times similarly proclaimed the notion of human somatic diversity purely in terms of complexion: 'the tawney Moore, blacke Negro, duskie Libyan, ash-coloured [Asian] Indian, olive-coloured [American] Indian, the whiter European.'[74]

Even though, in the perception of Romans unfamiliar with the sight of blacks, extreme blackness of skin may have served in itself to connote *Aethiops*, other Romans obviously perceived *Aethiopes* (black Africans) as somatically distinct from other black-skinned and dark-skinned types. For such Romans, *Aethiops* designated a particular physiognomy constituted not only by skin-colour, but by a combination of traits which at least resembled the stereotype of black skin, crinkly hair, thick lips, and flat nose described by Petronius and other writers. The perception finds a more recent parallel in the European world of François Bernier, who in 1684 published the earliest comprehensive classification of human groups according to somatic type ('races') and counted North American Indians as whites, while placing black Africans (negroes) in a category of their own.[75] For Romans, the familiar somatic types included one broad category which was neither black-skinned, snub-nosed, and woolly-haired like the southern Indians, nor *Aethiops*, nor 'nordic' (*candidus, flavus*), nor representative of the Mediterranean somatic norm (*albus*). Individuals and groups in this broad category are frequently described in Roman literature as swarthy, dusky, or dark-skinned (*fuscus, subfuscus, decolor, coloratus,* and so on), or even loosely as 'black' (*niger, ater, melas,* and so on). Those placed in this general category include Egyptians, Moors, Indians, the emperor Constantius, the pretender Firmus (with regard to his *face*), Zenobia of Palmyra, and certain persons of mixed black and white parentage as well as some Italian groups and individuals.[76] The swarthy category clearly possessed a combination of predominantly 'normal' (that is, so-called 'Caucasian') morphology with darkness of complexion. It is also evident that only a slight distance separated persons of this 'swarthy' category from the somatic norm, the degree of proximity to the norm varying primarily in respect of the degree of swarthiness from person to person.

What was quite obviously *not* the yardstick by which the perception of membership of the category *Aethiops* operated was 'negro blood'. That is shown by an interesting and informative text of Pliny's.[77] Pliny's theme is the hereditary transmission of somatic resemblance, and he recalls the case of a famous boxer from Byzantium, Nicaeus, whose mother was the product of her own mother's adultery with a black African (*adulterio Aethiopis nata*). It is implied that the boxer's maternal grandmother was of the somatic type perceived by Romans as the norm (*albus*). But her daughter by the black African was 'in no way different from the rest in colour' (*nihil a ceteris colore differente*). Rackham's Loeb translation takes *a ceteris* as 'from other women', implying that this particular offspring of mixed black and white parentage had the normal Mediterranean colour, but he also suggests that the phrase might mean 'from the rest of her family', or even 'from other half-breeds'. The implication of the first of these two suggestions would not alter the substance of the passage, since it would still indicate that the daughter of a Mediterranean white woman by a black African lover had the same white colour as the typical Mediterranean woman, which was shared also by her mother, her mother's husband, and any genuine children of this marriage that may have existed. But 'other half-breeds' would imply that in the Roman perceptual context there was a 'half-breed' colour which characterized all persons of mixed black and white parentage, and which marked this particular 'half-breed'. Indeed, it would appear that most people of this kind of mixed parentage could be described as *decolor* (that is, having a complexion similar to that of swarthy peoples like the Indians, Moors and Egyptians): when Achilles Tatius describes some Nilotic pirates as 'dark-skinned' (*melanes tēn chroian*) while also contrasting their complexion with 'the pure darkness of the Indians' and likening it to the sort of colour that a person of mixed black and white parentage (*nothos Aithiops*) might have, he is evidently referring to a complexion which, in his own experience, could be seen as typical of persons of such mixed parentage.[78] But that cannot be Pliny's intention in this text, let alone the notion of a particular colour common to all black–white 'half-breeds', for Pliny's argument depends on the premise that persons of such mixed parentage varied greatly in colour (whatever the precise significance of the term *colore* in this context). 'Half-breed' is a single category, and it is moreover, determined by the mere fact of mixed parentage, embracing all persons of such parentage.[79] Pliny is not concerned with a single category of any kind, but with different categories of somatic appearance. His argument rests, moreover, on the principle that persons of exactly the same parentage may fall into different categories of somatic appearance, and his focus is on two of these categories: namely, the Mediterranean somatic norm, and the black African (*Aethiops*) type. It follows that, when he says that the daughter of parents representing both the Mediterranean norm and the *Aethiops* type had the same colour as 'the rest', he must mean by 'the rest' either other Mediterranean whites (or, at least, Mediterranean white females), or other black Africans, and the latter is ruled out by the fact that the daughter's colour contrasts both with that of her black father and with that of her son, who bore a close resemblance to the black African type (*avum regeneravit Aethiopem*). Pliny's intended message is obviously that the daughter of the adulteress had a colour no different from the normal Mediterranean type (*albus*).

The precise significance of the term *colore* in this context is another matter. The best route towards an understanding of Pliny's meaning lies in a consideration of his concluding remarks on this family's history in comparison with Juvenal's perception of a *decolor* infant as *Aethiops*.[80] In Pliny's account adultery with an *Aethiops* produces a child with the normal Mediterranean colour, while in Juvenal's picture a similar case of adultery produces an 'heir' who is both *decolor* (that is, not *albus*, but 'off-white') and *Aethiops*, since the cuckolded husband is *Aethiopis pater* ('father of a black African child'). In the perception illustrated by Juvenal's picture, the child is *Aethiops* evidently because of his general appearance (not his complexion, which is not typically *Aethiops*): his general appearance is a closer approximation to the *Aethiops* physiognomy than to any other type with which Romans were familiar, including the darker-than-normal Mediterranean type and the swarthy Indian and Moorish types for which the same term *decolor* and terms like *fuscus, perustus* and *coloratus* could serve as adequate descriptions. But the daughter in Pliny's account, who is white (*albus*) in complexion, and whose husband (as the account implies) is also white, produces a son who has 'regenerated his black African grandfather' (*avum regeneravit Aethiopem*). The 'regeneration' (biological atavism) cannot mean exact resemblance in all details, but it clearly means that this person was perceived as a closer somatic approximation to his black ascendant than to what Romans perceived as the 'swarthy type', let alone the Mediterranean norm (*albus*). Pliny's boxer, like Juvenal's 'heir of the wrong colour', though not possessing the precise complexion of the *Aethiops* somatic stereotype, is nevertheless *Aethiops*. The contrast between the boxer and his mother (in Pliny's intention) is therefore not merely one of skin colour. It is a contrast of general somatic appearance: in general appearance the boxer predominantly resembles his black ascendant, whereas his mother predominantly resembles her own white mother. Pliny's term *colore*, while emphasizing colour, also relates to general appearance.

We may compare the report of his personal experience given by the sixteenth-century Englishman, George Best, to the effect that the son of a black African by his 'faire' English wife was 'as blacke as the father was', in which the term 'blacke' signifies not only colour, but a general appearance perceived as a close approximation to the negro type and as very distant from the contemporary English somatic norm. Notable also are two reports by an eighteenth-century Fellow of the Royal Society on infants born in England to mixed black and white couples in 1766 and 1747 respectively. In the one case, the infant was perceived as 'entirely black, and in every particular of colour and features resembling the father' (a black African); in the other case, the infant daughter of a black Londoner and his white wife was 'as fair a child to look at as any born of white parents, and her features exactly like her mother's', although with 'the right buttock and thigh' as black as the father's.[81] This scientist took care to mention both colour and 'features' – unlike Pliny, who saw no necessity for so doing, and subsumed physiognomy in general terms under *color*. But, like the eighteenth-century scientist, Pliny intends to draw attention to a case of a person of mixed black and white parentage whose physiognomy is, in the contemporary perceptual context, in conformity with the somatic norm image. That intention corresponds with a belief (widespread in educated circles in Roman society) in the occurrence of this particular phenomenon as a natural biological fact, even if it was also believed that signs of such a white person's partly *Aethiops* ancestry might appear later in some of his or her descendants despite the fact of the latter having no additional black ascendants. This belief was supported by contemporary 'science', which held that the child resembles the parent whose seed has been 'more potent' in the act of procreation, and also that there is an 'ancestral seed' which runs in families from father to son and subsequent direct descendants, and which can therefore 'regenerate' in direct descendants the facial appearance, hair, limbs, and voice of father or mother, grandfather or grandmother, or a more remote ascendant.[82]

To be sure, Pliny's account is (in part, at least) open to question as a factual account of events in a particular family's history. Pliny himself sees the case of this white daughter of a black African as an unquestionable example (*indubitatum exemplum*) of a biological phenomenon that was well known to contemporary 'science', and there is every reason to believe that contemporary 'scientists' drew on empirical support of the kind presented by the eighteenth-century scientist cited above. But the facts surrounding the birth of Pliny's boxer may actually have been such as reasoned scepticism prompts one to postulate for the case in which, according to Plutarch, a Greek woman successfully rebutted an accusation of adultery with a black man by persuading all concerned that her 'black' (*melas*) child was to be explained simply by her own genetic status as the great-granddaughter of a black African.[83] This was no doubt a case of an adulteress with a black lover saved from the scandal and the legal consequences of adultery[84] by the profundity of the popular belief in what Pliny calls biological 'regeneration', and by the fact that no living person could contradict her claim to such a distant black ascendant. The white mother of Pliny's boxer may also have falsely claimed a black father as a means of explaining the blackness of a son who was actually the fruit of her own adultery with a black man. But that would not detract from the value of Pliny's report as evidence of Roman beliefs and of the nature of the Roman context in which somatic appearance was perceived: the account would still imply that the boxer's mother, though white, was (after the birth of her son) believed to be the daughter of a black man, just as the suspected adulteress of Plutarch's account retained her identity as a *Greek* (and white) woman after it came to be understood that she was the great-granddaughter of a black African. Thus, whether Pliny's account is taken at its face value (as Pliny himself wishes it to be), or merely as an illustration of popular beliefs and perceptions of somatic distance, it has an important sociological significance. The picture is, in both cases, one in which the society accepts as a natural phenomenon the fact of a black person, both of whose parents are white, and one of whose grandparents is black, with 'black' signifying the black African (*Aethiops*) type of physiognomy (including approximations to the somatic stereotype), and 'white' signifying the Mediterranean somatic norm as perceived by men of the Roman world.

The clear significance of this is that, in Roman society, the quality of Aethiopian-ness which distinguished the *Aethiops* from white men was merely a matter of outward physical appearance – *species*, as Christian writers would later express it. Categorization as *Aethiops*, or 'swarthy', or white (*albus*), or 'paleface' (*candidus* or *flavus*) was thus purely and simply a matter of the observer's optical registration of somatic distance or of the somatic norm, uninfluenced by the facts of the observed person's biological descent, and uncomplicated by any ideologically operative link with social role or social distance. Christian leaders were reflecting a long-standing Roman attitude when, in their discussions on the 'essential' and the 'accidental' qualities of man, they supported their doctrine by (*inter alia*) the argument that, although a black horse and an *Aethiops* both share the 'accidental' quality of blackness, the removal of this blackness leaves the horse still a horse, but entirely eliminates the quality of *Aethiops* from the *Aethiops*, who thereby becomes 'a white man like other men' (*erit eius species candida, sicut etiam aliorum hominum*).[85] These Christian arguments, to be sure, are lofty philosophical arguments aimed in part (like Seneca's argument on the theme of *communia vitia*) at allaying popular prejudices, and, like the proverb *Aithiopa smēchein* ('to wash an Aethiopian white'), they relate to the impossibility of actually removing the blackness of an *Aethiops*. But at the same time (again, like the proverb) they are clearly characteristic of a culture in which the defining quality of the *Aethiops* was simply physical appearance (*species*), irrespective of ancestry and parentage. In this perceptual context, most persons of mixed black and white parentage no doubt fell into the swarthy and black categories (by virtue of their *species*), but, as Pliny indicates, some were perceived as white. The Pliny text indicates that the black boxer's mother is white, even though she is separated from their common black ascendants by a narrower generation-distance than her own son who is black, and the distance separating the latter from his white relations is merely one of somatic appearance, not a social distance. Nor does the presence of a black relation in any way socially distance his white family members from their white peers outside the family circle. Any interpretation to the contrary is ruled out by the whole perceptual context, by the concept *Aethiops* emerging from the texts discussed above, and by the matter-of-fact presentation of this particular family history by Pliny (and of the 'scientific' theory by heredity of Lucretius and others).[86] It is very obvious that, in Roman society, somatic appearance was not an index of ascribed social roles, rights and status. None of the various 'non-normal' somatic categories known to Romans ('swarthy', *Aethiops*, 'nordic') was rigidly determined by biological descent from forebears of a given type. Petronius shows that a black skin alone did not make one an *Aethiops*; Plutarch's 'great-granddaughter of an *Aethiops*' is a *Greek* woman; and Pliny's 'daughter of a black father' is a white woman of Byzantium. Pliny's black son of a white woman is black not because he has a black ascendant, but because of his personal somatic appearance.

In such a context Martial and Juvenal naturally imagine that the black son and heir of an upper-class couple, who (uncharacteristically) has been allowed to survive infancy in the household, will enjoy a general social acceptance (despite the class prejudice of those of his neighbours who cannot be persuaded that he is anything but a *de facto* bastard of humble paternal extraction), and will inherit the eminent status and deference-position of his white parents.[87] The presumed black products of 'maternal impression' or biological atavism signalled by the declamation theme *matrona Aethiopem peperit* also have this same sociological implication of persons, irrespective of colour and shape, occupying the status and social roles to which the rank and economic standing of their legally and socially acknowledged white parents entitle them. To be sure, among the aristocracy, infanticide and infant exposure must in practice have always terminated the aristocratic careers of bastards of *Aethiops* appearance at a very early stage of their lives – as Heliodorus' romance presumes to be the first response of aristocratic mothers giving birth to infants who are somatically distant from both parents.[88] But the popularity of the beliefs in biological atavism and maternal impression clearly indicates the independence of social distance and somatic distance in Roman society. A parent would have got rid of an *Aethiops* infant (as an unwanted infant) not because blackness was in itself socially degrading (it was not), but first of all because children issuing from irregular sexual unions were for that very reason unwanted infants in the eyes of most parents; and second, because the retention and rearing of such an infant would be a clear and public confession of adultery, and of the husband's compliance with his wife's undeniable adultery– except in those cases where the child could be passed off as an adopted child or foster-child (*alumnus*), or in cases (no doubt largely restricted to the humbler segments of society) where a claim of biological atavism or 'maternal impression' could be persuasive. A third reason for getting rid of an infant of *Aethiops* appearance was the fact that the real father of such an infant would normally be, and would be assumed to be, a humble man; and that in turn, in the case of an upper-class adulteress, attached a social stigma to the adultery and its consequences, and rendered the infant a constant mark of this social disgrace. But if the bastard child resulting from an upper-class woman's adultery with an *Aethiops* happened to be of an appearance closely approximating to the somatic norm, however widespread the suspicions of adultery, those various considerations would not arise, and so it would be a simple matter to bring up the infant as a genuine child of the family and in enjoyment of its usurpation of upper-class status. Indeed, it is probable that the Pompeian graffito scribbled on a wall of that town's court-house (*basilica*) – '*non est ex albo iudex patre Aegyptio*' –[89] refers to a case of this sort.

Dölger (who noted that the term *Aegyptius* appears as a synonym of *Aethiops* in some Romano-African writings and as a synonym of 'black-evil' or 'black-ominous' in the Roman world at large) translated this graffito as 'The judge has no white Egyptian for a father', suggesting that *Aegyptius* here conveys the negative moral value judgement 'black-wicked', and *albus* the opposite.[90] There is evidently a play on both of the contrasting words *albus* (as white/pure/good/noble/proper/legitimate) and *Aegyptius* (as black/wicked/bad/improper/illegitimate). But the graffito scribbler's intention is not merely humorous. It is clearly also malicious. For that and other reasons his *albo* should be taken not as an adjective ('white'), but as an allusion to an *album*: the Pompeian *album decurionum* (roll of local city-councillors), or the *album iudicum* (the roll of judges), or better still the *album professionum liberorum natorum* (the register on which the births of legitimate children were recorded). The point or climax of the graffito is contained in the phrase *patre Aegyptio*, set at the very end and carrying an epigrammatic element of surprise: 'because his (true) father is an *Aegyptius* (i.e. a black man)'. Accordingly, if *ex albo* is taken as an allusion to the judges' roll or that of the local senators, the effect would be 'The judge comes not from the White (*album*), but from the Black, since he is the progeny of a black father.' By such a facetious 'not from the White' the scribbler may have intended the sort of adverse judgement on the moral character and behaviour of the judge that Dölger saw in the graffito, but even then the main intention will have been to impute to the man bastardy and an *Aethiops* father (as Martial does in the case of his imaginary 'thick-lipped and flat-nosed' brat of 'Marulla'), suggesting that he was for that reason not properly (*ex albo*) entitled to the position of judge, but ought to be a slave or commoner like his 'Egyptian' (black African) father. That is all the more reason why *ex albo* is best seen as a reference to the register of births, which pertained exclusively to legitimate children. For though the 'legitimacy' declared by this *album* was in effect merely a matter of children publicly acknowledged as legitimate,[91] the malicious might nonetheless use the phrase *ex albo* in the stricter sense of 'genuinely legitimate'. In that sense the intended message of this graffito would be: 'The judge, whatever the records may say, is an illegitimate son; his real father is a black man.'

Pliny's text confirms some of the conclusions already drawn from that of Petronius on the import of the concept *Aethiops* as a somatic type and on Roman perceptions of distance from their somatic norm while also offering further insights into the Roman perceptual context and the social and psychological dimensions of those perceptions. In sum, blackness of complexion did not, in itself, suffice to warrant classification as *Aethiops*. Classification of a person as belonging to the somatic category connoted by the term *Aethiops* (a usage quite different from the ethno-geographical and national concepts conveyed by the term *Aethiopes*) was determined by the personal perception of obsevers, but always with some reference to the kind of black African somatic stereotype and combination of traits (colour, hair, nose, and lips) described by acute observers like Petronius, Martial, and the anonymous author of *Moretum*. At the most discerning level of perception an *Aethiops* was a person whose visage presented a closer appproximation to that stereotype than to any other somatic type with which the observer was familiar. Hence the *decolor heres* of Juvenal's satirical picture, though lacking the full blackness of the *Aethiops* stereotype, is still *Aethiops*, and the same perception is illustrated by the concept *nothos Aithiops* found in Achilles Tatius in relation to the physiognomy of certain persons of mixed black and white parentage perceived as predominantly *Aethiops* in appearance.[92] But while some persons of such mixed parentage were perceived as *Aethiops* (and *nothos Aithiops* meant 'predominantly *Aethiops* in appearance', which is still in the category *Aethiops*), their complexions were shared by many who were not so perceived. The term *decolor* also described the complexions of persons contrasted with blacks, for example, Indians and Moors, and so it indicated a similarity of complexion between those 'swarthy' peoples on the one hand, and many persons of mixed black and white parentage on the other hand – both *nothoi Aithiopes* and others who were closer in appearance to the typical Indian, Moor, or Egyptian and so were perceived as 'swarthy' and not as *Aethiops* (or *nothos Aithiops*).[93] Less experienced observers, however, may have classified people as *Aethiops* by virtue of a pronounced blackness of skin which very appreciably distanced such persons from the 'swarthy' type of appearance represented by the typical Indian, Moor, or Egyptian, but also found among the labouring classes of the northern Mediterranean lands, and described in the literature as dark-skinned or sun-bronzed (*coloratus*, *perustus*, and the like). But, contrary to the opinions of scholars like Beardsley and Snowden, who set unwarranted store by the factor of 'negro blood', the less experienced Roman would classify as *Aethiops* a very black, flat-nosed and woolly-haired Indian whom he knew to be devoid of any connection with 'negro blood', while he would classify not as blacks, but as whites or as 'swarthy', people who were known to be possessors of 'negro blood' but who possessed a 'normal' or predominantly 'normal' morphology. The Roman perceptual context was therefore not of the kind designated in sociological theory as racial or racist, and this perceptual context is in itself the most important single indication of the non-racial character of Roman society – far more important than even the most meticulous balancing of favourable and negative ancient remarks about blacks or of artistic signals given by ancient portraits of blacks, and it constitutes a definitive indication of the error inherent in attempts to explain Roman social relations in terms of race.

In the parts of the modern world where such things matter, Pliny's boxer would be described by some ridiculous term like 'half-breed' or 'half-caste', and his mother would be perceived as 'coloured', certainly by those aware of (or believing in) her genuine or supposed identity as the daughter of a black African, and probably also by most observers to whom she was a mere stranger (assuming in this case that her claim to be the daughter of an *Aethiops* was genuine). That is because in such modern societies the observer's responses are not, like his or her Roman counterpart's, limited to the mere registration of somatic characteristics, but are complicated by an ideological urge to recognize some social-role significance in the somatic appearance that meets the eye. In such societies, somatic appearance, purity of descent from ancestors of the somatic type represented by the dominant group in the society, and descent (pure or not) from a representative of the somatic type that is correlated with inferior social roles and rights, all constitute indices of ascribed status and deference-position, positive or negative, in the society at large.[94] For that reason the eye can hardly ever be content, like the Roman eye, with registering general impressions of an observed somatic appearance. Hence the shock and trauma endured by two young white working-class women in Britain when their white husbands suddenly acquired 'Pakistani' faces as a result of the physiological condition known in medical circles as 'Nelson's syndrome', and when in consequence of this they faced ostracism (even by former friends) and a shattering of their erstwhile social lives.[95] That same kind of perception explains the invention of terms like 'mulatto', 'quadroon' and 'octoroon' to serve as precise labels of the degree of white or black 'blood' in the genetic composition of persons who, though somatically 'swarthy' or 'white' (as Romans would have perceived them), are *socially* defined as black or 'coloured' and ascribed appropriately inferior social roles and rights. Such labels accordingly have meaning or relevance only in societies in which somatic characteristics are *socially* significant and in which (for that reason) ideological motivation exerts enormous influence on perception – that is, only in the kind of society described by sociologists as racist.[96] Investigators of the perception of somatic distance in South Africa have, for instance, reported that Afrikaaners, when shown pictures of human faces, tended far more frequently than members of other segments in the same society to assign the faces to one or other of the two extremes of black and white somatic types, with correspondingly far fewer correct identifications of persons belonging to the intermediate segments of the population.[97] From such studies it has rightly been concluded that perception of somatic distance is greatly affected by the racist system of *socially* classifying people according to somatic appearance, since in that system the observed somatic appearances 'stand in a certain predictable relation' to the criteria of status and deference-position in the society concerned, and since the classification of people into sharply distinct social categories of this sort has a powerful emotional significance for the individual observer.[98]

By contrast with the ready ability to recognize signs of 'negro blood' that is engendered by the socio-cultural conditions of a race-relations situation (by the very fact that it gives people a heavy investment in the business of measuring somatic distance),[99] a social system like that of the ancient Romans institutionalizes, and internalizes in the individual, a simple perception and a fluid mode of classifying somatic types. Since Roman society did not link status in any predictable relationship with somatic appearance, one inevitably presents a distorted vision of that society by attributing to it concepts like 'mulatto', 'quadroon' and 'octoroon',[100] or by insisting (against all evidence) on seeing as 'black' the remote and white descendants of Roman blacks, or identifying as Roman portraits of blacks portraits which Romans would not have perceived as portraits of *Aethiopes*,[101] or writing of the Roman somatic category *Aethiops* in a manner which suggests that it was a socially defined category.[102] The tendency to project into Roman antiquity a modern concept of 'black person' (as a category defined in terms of possession of black ascendants) implicitly attributes racism to Roman society, however unwittingly, and this constitutes a serious internal contradiction in discussions whose intention is to argue against theses of a Roman race prejudice advanced by other scholars. This contradiction takes a particularly strange form in certain observations that have been made on the phenomenon which one may quite simply describe as constant absorption of black lineages into the mainstream of the white population in the genetic melting-pot of the Roman world. There can be little doubt that most blacks in Roman society took whites or 'swarthy' people as mates, if they mated at all. Since slavery was the main source of the black presence, it may be presumed that the ratio of male blacks (as distinct from progeny and descendants of blacks) to female blacks was, in any case, fairly high at all times. It is also clear that most of the progeny and descendants of blacks also took non-blacks as sexual mates. Hence there will have been a constant process of biological amalgamation of blacks into the mainstream of the white population, and we must accordingly reckon with the reality of a small black element whose presence was perpetuated by immigration rather than by procreation, with the result that a certain aura of strangeness continued to surround blacks in many localities of the Roman world.[103] But this process of biological amalgamation has sometimes been mentioned in very odd terms: with reference to a concept of *visible* blackness (blacks 'easily recognizable as Negroes'), as though there could have been some other category of blacks or one defined in terms other than physical blackness and so not easily recognizable as black;[104] or in the observation that the interbreeding process explains why 'outside art, it is not often easy to identify *negroes* in everyday life' and why 'documentary evidence' on blacks in Roman society 'is slighter than we should wish.'[105] In such observations the conceptualization is strangely out of joint, unconsciously categorizing as 'black' the remote and white descendants of blacks, and reflecting the notion of a non-physical definition of 'black' or 'negro' (characteristic of the racist perspective), instead of stressing that the familiar modern notion of 'black person', defined in *social* terms, was alien to Roman society, which knew no such thing as a black person (*Aethiops*) except in the obvious physical sense, and would have regarded as absurd the idea of a black person who was not physically (and visibly) black.

Pliny, Petronius, and Plutarch make it very clear that even a person with black ascendants, however recent, was black only if his or her personal somatic appearance merited that description.[106] And that should cause no surprise to those aware of the fact that, even in some modern societies whose histories have not been free of racism, a similar sort of perception, rather less rigidly conditioned than those of Anglo-Saxons and Frenchmen,[107] has been in operation and is reflected in records showing the proportion of whites to non-whites in those societies between the 1840s and the 1940s. Puerto Rican data reveal a gradual but steady rise in the proportion of that country's population represented by 'whites' from 50 per cent in 1846 to over 76 per cent in 1940; for Cuba, the corresponding rise is from 41.5 per cent in 1841 to almost 75 per cent in 1943; and in Argentina, which in 1852 had a non-white element constituting approximately 16 per cent of the total population (and in the capital 34 per cent), the non-white element entirely disappeared in subsequent generations.[108] The explanation of these demographic phenomena does not lie in differences in birth rates or mortality rates, or even in migration patterns, between the groups designated as 'white' and 'non-white'; it lies mainly in the simple fact of interbreeding and an almost Roman perceptual context (perception of so-called 'race'). The great majority of these 'whites' would have been accorded a rather different classification in certain other modern societies where shortness of nose or broadness of nose, or curly hair, or a suggestion of 'negro blood' in the lips, or the 'mulatto look' tend to be ideologically perceived as necessarily connoting 'non-white' or 'black'.

Chapter Three

THE EVIDENCE IN ITS IDEOLOGICAL CONTEXT

ROMAN GROUP-STEREOTYPING

Images (or mental pictures) of categories normally come from 'repeated experience with some class of objects', and an image is called a stereotype when it is 'an exaggerated belief' about a human category and serves the function of justifying other people's conduct towards that category of people and of impeding mental differentiation between individual members of that group. But the habit of categorical thinking and group-stereotyping, however deplorable in some situations, is integral to the human condition, since 'orderly living depends on thinking with the aid of categories' and since the mental process of typing and generalizing is 'a screening and selective device' that enables human beings to 'maintain simplicity in perception and thinking.'[1] Stereotypes of peoples may be highly exaggerated generalizations resting on the tiniest kernel of reality or even false images entirely lacking in any contemporary basis of fact. But, when negative, they often reflect a reality of group conflict or haunting memories of past tension and conflict, rationalizing and seeking to justify the positions of in-groups in those situations of conflict. Such images (which are kept alive by 'selective remembering and selective forgetting' and are socially supported by literature and other media of communication) often promote or sustain attitudes of hate, distrust, contempt, or fear towards members of out-groups in daily life, or at least function as an impediment to good personal relations between members of the different groups concerned.[2] Their influence on attitudes, behaviour, and social relations evidently depends on the prominence that they occupy in the thinking of the stereotypers about the stereotyped group. It has been shown that the attitudes and behaviour of Europeans towards blacks in the sixteenth and seventeenth centuries were influenced by a negative image of Africa as a continent 'divested of earthly goods, wild, and full of brutality', and by mental pictures of African 'savagery', backwardness, 'stupidity', heathenism and 'devilry', 'laziness', sensuality, and lustfulness.[3] But that was the image which at that time dominated the cognitive processes of Europeans with regard to Africa: no such importance can be attached to images of little or no prominence in the cognitive maps formed by members of one group about another, or to the sort of negative stereotype which has managed to outlive the particular social–psychological realities that it originally reflected and which is generally acknowledged as unrealistic. Such outmoded stereotypes serve, in radically altered climates, merely as material for humorous caricature or as convenient screens on which to project a personal dislike or personal conflict that has no genuine relationship to the stereotyping – as is evident when Catullus appeals to the outmoded image of the urine-bathing Spaniard for psychological support in his personal abuse of a rival in love.[4]

The literature of the Roman world reveals Roman visions of the place of the *populus Romanus* in the universal scheme of things as well as a variety of positive and negative images of non-Roman peoples, including *Aethiopes*.[5] Roman opinions about culturally distant peoples are usually heavily stamped with Romanocentrism. But the Romanocentric evaluations, while reflecting a bipolar conception of the world (the Roman *Kulturwelt* on the one hand, and the non-Roman or 'barbarian' world on the other), also reveal a mentality which habitually anchored evaluations of human groups on realistic scales of values and hierarchies of merits, even if not always on the true facts of particular barbarian cultural situations. If the ideological system was one in which the term *barbarus* conjured up a whole universe of negativity and inferior ways of life, the degree of barbarism of each 'known' barbarian people was qualitatively evaluated in terms of distance from Roman values and qualities (including material development). A given barbarian people could therefore be adjudged as barbarian in respect of some of its characteristics and un-barbarian in respect of others, and the total estimate varied from that of 'absolute barbarian' to that of *semibarbarus* or even exemplar of 'civilized life' (in Strabo's terms, *to hēmeron kai to politikon*),[6] each group above the level of 'absolute barbarian' being adjudged as possessing a particular mixture of cultural defects and good qualities. Elements of alien cultures might even be seen as worthy of appropriation and integration into the Roman system, but the bad was always seen as a scandal that must be rejected or even eliminated from the earth.[7] From this ideological perspective the various peoples of 'Aethiopia', as peoples outside the Roman world, were all 'barbarians' in some degree or other, but no more so than other barbarian peoples whose qualities, levels of material development, and modes of life (in so far as Romans had knowledge of these things or believed that they had) rendered them subject to the same Romanocentric evaluation.

The extent to which images of out-groups could be realistic inevitably depended on the relative availability of ethnological and historical data about them, and also on absence of the distorting influence of grave national conflict between them and the Roman people. Serious conflict (or haunting memories of such conflict) nurtured biased and negative stereotypes, while the absence of genuine ethnological–historical information about culturally distant peoples tended to induce images shaped by what Lonis calls '*l'approche mythique*' – the urge to view distant and remote barbarians through 'the deforming prism of myth', resulting in fantasy and stereotypes which might be favourable or unfavourable, but were in any case 'very distant from reality'.[8]

THE MYTHIC IMAGE OF '*AETHIOPES*'

The Roman image of geographically remote 'Aethiopians' which Snowden regarded as the one and only noteworthy Roman 'image of the black' belongs almost entirely to this mythic and unrealistic category. It arose from a literary tradition (part of the educated Roman's cultural heritage from the Greeks) which idealized 'the Aethiopians' and certain other spatially remote and ill-known peoples located (in the imagination, or at best in vague ethno-geographical reports) at the periphery of the 'inhabited world' (*oecumene*). This idealizing tradition, which goes back to Homer's idealization of 'the folk of sun-darkened face' (*Aithiopes*) as the most distant and most just of men, attributed to 'the Aethiopians' all the characteristics of a utopian people: innocence, love of freedom, peacefulness, moderation, longevity, handsomeness, a semi-divine tallness of stature, and a piety appropriately rewarded by divine favour. It was a utopian vision of remote 'Aethiopians' that was consistent with the situation of ethno-geographical ignorance in which it first emerged, relating as it did originally to a thoroughly nebulous world of the remotest east. But, even with the subsequent acquisition of ethno-geographical knowledge of Nubia (information which accumulated especially after the third century BC and established that Nilotic land in the consciousness of Greeks and Romans as 'Aethiopia' proper), the mythic image coexisted with the more realistic images arising from the ethnological data; it was actually reinforced, in the consciousness of members of the educated public, by historical and ethnological information about the Nilotic kingdom of 'Aethiopia' (Kush, or Napata-Meroe), and especially by data about the religious life of that ancient kingdom, whose monarchs had ruled Egypt as its twenty-fifth dynasty of pharaohs and had been accorded by history a grand reputation for virtue, generosity, piety, and justice.[9]

Many intellectuals evidently saw in some of this historical and ethnological information an obvious anthropological explanation of Homer's picture of 'the Aethiopians' as familiars of the gods, and in imperial Roman society the stereotype of 'Aethiopian' piety no doubt also drew strength from Roman appreciation of the contemporary reality of the cult of Isis: not only was this cult popular in the Roman world in the time of the pre-Christian emperors, but Romans envisaged the 'Aethiopian' capital, Meroe, as a place of pilgrimage to which devotees of the cult travelled from Rome to obtain holy Nile water for sprinkling in the temple of Isis in Rome. In later times Philae, the Nilotic 'Mecca' of the cult, was understood to be an 'Aethiopian' centre. Moreover, Romans associated black and swarthy people with expertise in the management of this cult.[10] Accordingly, writers and artists, following a tradition that was well established in the culture of the educated classes of the Roman world, continued for centuries to express the mythological and epic vision of 'the Aethiopians', recalling a legendary past in which *Aethiopes* had lived in close fellowship with the heroic figures of Graeco-Roman 'prehistory'. In that imaginary past Perseus, a son of the god Zeus or Jupiter, had married the 'Aethiopian' princess Andromeda, while Memnon, an 'Aethiopian' king who assisted the Trojans with his contingent of black troops, was the son of the Dawn goddess (Eos, or Aurora) –

by a black lover, in the imagination of some. Similarly Epaphus, son of Jupiter and Io, was the ancestor of the peoples of North Africa and of 'the Aethiopians', while Argos had fathered four *Aethiopes* on a daughter of Atlas, and seven of the daughters of Danaus had been born of an 'Aethiopian' mother.[11] In a similar spirit philosophy and astrology are represented as having come from 'the Aethiopians' to the Egyptians and thence to the Greeks and Romans through the intermediaries of the Chaldaeans, Scythians, and Thracians.[12] The romance of Pseudo-Callisthenes, written in the third century AD, presents an imaginary kingdom of 'Aethiopia' that is a wonderland of resplendent mountains, extraordinary fertility, fabulous fauna and flora, and fantastic royal luxury, with a people living in a sort of consanguinity with the gods, and a queen of semi-divine tallness, beauty and nobility of spirit whose wish is to ally her powerful country with Alexander the Great with the purpose of world conquest.[13] In the romance of Heliodorus, which belongs to the same era, the kingdom of Aethiopia is again a militarily powerful and extraordinarily fertile and rich wonderland, possessing an abundance of gold and a royal family descended from the gods as well as from the heroic figures Perseus, Andromeda, and Memnon. The king himself is 'the most just of men', a monarch who treats defeated enemies with extraordinary generosity, and his people are renowned for their religious piety, wisdom, and scientific eminence.[14]

Patristic interpretations of the biblical account of the Queen of Sheba's visit to Solomon also reflect the abiding influence of the epic image of remote *Aethiopes* in the cognitive maps formed by Christians and pagans alike in educated circles of Roman society in and after the third century: what is emphasized in this 'queen of the south' (envisaged as one of the great 'Aethiopians' of history) are her moral virtues and her pursuit of wisdom.[15] The epic poem of Quintus of Smyrna, probably written as late as the last quarter of the fourth century AD,[16] makes much of the legendary role of the 'Aethiopian' king Memnon and his black contingent at Troy. Much later still, Luxorius attests to the persisting vitality of the epic legacy and heroic image of 'the Aethiopians' when he directly (and in a spirit of admiration) assimilates the Memnon legend to the person of a successful and glamorous black jockey in sixth-century Carthage (*auriga qui semper vincebat*): 'Although Memnon was the son of Aurora, he fell at the hands of Achilles. Unless I am mistaken, Night is your mother and Aeolus your sire, and you, their son, were born to occupy Zephyr's cave. However, no Achilles will rise to conquer you. Although you are a Memnon in looks, you are not like him in your fate.'[17]

What is most significant in all this, as Warmington and Snowden rightly emphasized, is not the lack of a basis of black African (or even merely Nubian) contemporary reality for all or most aspects of this idealized image of remote *Aethiopes*, but the spirit and the mentality that sustained it (apparently to the end of Roman antiquity), and the message that it conveys with regard to attitudes towards blacks in Roman society.[18] The mythological lore which constituted the core of this image was evidently deeply rooted in the culture and consciousness of the educated classes of the Roman world, and, in so far as black Africans were generally subsumed (*inter alios*) under 'Aethiopians', the usage of that term both as a broad ethno-geographical label and as a national designation of the population of the Nilotic kingdom of Kush or Napata-Meroe, tempts one to interpret the idealized image as a reflection of the reality of a highly favourable public opinion of remote black African peoples, even though the image had little to do with evaluations of Nubian (let alone specifically black African) anthropological reality. In adopting that interpretation, some have not only seen this favourable mythic image as the dominant Roman view of 'the black', but have contrasted it with the negative early modern European image of 'the blacks' as primitive barbarians, and with the familiar and more recent mental linkage of black Africa with extremes of material poverty and backwardness, and with geopolitical and cultural insignificance. In making this contrast such scholars have rightly stressed that the idealized image attributed to 'the Aethiopians' a mastery of philosophy and science from very ancient times, a significant cultural stature, an important historical and prehistoric past, and a well-deserved reputation for love of peace and freedom, for religious piety, and for generosity.[19] But it would be a mistake to assume that this mythic and utopian image of 'Aethiopia' was shared by the unlettered masses of the Roman world.

Although the visual arts presented mythological themes relating to 'Aethiopians' of the heroic past,[20] the evidence on the whole suggests that the idealized image of 'the Aethiopians' was an aspect of a particular cultural experience that was practically restricted to the educated classes, who formed a small minority in a world in which the great mass of peasants, rural labourers, women and freeborn urban poor, as well as the majority of urban tradesmen and slaves (categories which themselves formed the bulk of the urban population) were illiterate.[21] To be sure, it is unduly pessimistic to suppose (as some have done) that 'there is almost no way of knowing what the mass of the population thought about those dark-skinned Africans who dwelt among them.'[22] Idealization of 'the Aethiopians' can hardly have been a matter of *public* opinion, except in a severely restricted sense of that term. It was in a large measure the consequence of a literary vogue – an urge 'more intellectual than emotional' to create an imaginary paradise, located on the periphery of the *oecumene*, and peopled by wise, just, innocent, and happy folk. The obverse of this urge was quite often a sense of disillusionment with certain realities of the writer's own society.[23] But the evidence leaves little room for doubt that, among the unlettered majority, the imagination with regard to *Aethiopes* was generally dominated by the negative symbolism of the colour black, which resulted in negative attitudes that were altered in individual cases only through increasing familiarization with blacks.[24] It is also clear that, in so far as the 'Aethiopian' wonderlands of Lucian, Pseudo-Callisthenes, and Heliodorus reflect elements of historical or contemporary African reality, they related specifically to Napatan-Meroitic civilization, which evidently evoked in educated Romans a measure of curiosity, kindly interest, respect, and admiration, not least because of the great contribution which (according to an opinion quite widespread in educated circles) that ancient civilization had made to the cultural progress of pharaonic Egypt.[25] Thus while the favourable and idealized image of *Aethiopes*, which was fortified by this intellectual wonderland-vogue, tells us nothing about attitudes among the uneducated masses, it can hardly have failed to obtain a sympathetic reception among a section (at least) of the reading public and, consequently, to occupy a place on the cognitive maps which that section of the public formed of distant *Aethiopes*.

R. Lonis, to be sure, takes a contrary view,[26] arguing that contemporary public opinion was perhaps not ready to share the sympathetic vision of *Aethiopes* presented by a Heliodorus or a Pseudo-Callisthenes. But he arrives at that position only on the false premise of a reading public motivated by anti-black race prejudice, which even induces him to suggest that Heliodorus makes his heroine the *white* daughter of a black royal couple as a sort of sop to his 'racially prejudiced' public's expected unreadiness to accept a fictional love between a *black* princess and a Greek noble. In all this there is a patent confusion of ethnocentrism with race prejudice. No doubt ethnocentric canons of beauty (and especially female beauty), as well as everyday experience, will have suggested to the generality of Heliodorus' readers a certain incompatibility between blackness and beauty in real life. But Pseudo-Callisthenes' extraordinarily beautiful 'black' Candace and the very beautiful 'black' mother of Heliodorus' own heroine show how small a problem this presented to the writer of romantic fiction, especially when (like these two romancers) he could follow the well established literary tradition on the love and marriage of Perseus and the (sometimes white, sometimes swarthy) 'Aethiopian' princess Andromeda and also draw on the notion of 'maternal impression' (as Heliodorus explicitly does).

The mythic image, then, often occupied the imagination of members of the educated classes, but it is absurd to see it as '*the* image of the black' in Roman antiquity. Other stereotypes of 'Aethiopia' and 'Aethiopians', more realistic and often also negative, were undoubtedly operative in the minds of educated Romans (let alone the uneducated) from time to time in the centuries from the late republican era onwards, though until the middle of the third century AD these mental visions of *Aethiopes* did not include the fixed image of contemporary 'Aethiopia' as a powerful country and military threat which Snowden imagines to have been a part of 'the image of the black' discussed above; nor was there in that period a dominant or prominent 'Roman view of blacks as warriors and enemies of Rome'.[27] In all the relevant ethno-geographical texts (especially Diodorus, Strabo, Pliny, and Ptolemy) from the late first century BC to the third century AD, 'Aethiopian' military power is a feature of a glorious Napatan-Meroitic *past*. The militarily powerful wonderlands of the romancers similarly have their dramatic settings in the distant past (the sixth and fourth centuries BC), and any hints that these romances contain of a perception of great 'Aethiopian' military power after these dramatic dates all relate to new developments in Nubia in the time of the writers themselves (the third century AD).[28]

IMAGES OF *'AETHIOPES'* ARISING FROM ETHNO-GEOGRAPHICAL LITERATURE

From the third century BC onwards, the ethnographical and geographical literature available to the educated public of the Roman world presented a considerable store of information on the alimentary habits, modes of life, religious beliefs and practices, levels of material development or degrees of backwardness, socio-political organization, dress, and physical appearance of various 'Aethiopian' peoples. From this literature the members of this restricted public could form their own judgements and find among *Aethiopes* (as they did also in the case of other out-groups) aspects of material and spiritual culture or of their general mode of life meriting admiration and approval or contempt and aversion. In this process there arose (on the one hand) a generally favourable opinion of the 'cultivated' population of the Meroitic kingdom, and (on the other hand) images of 'underdevelopment', primitive barbarism, savagery, and monstrosity among 'the majority of the Aethiopians.'[29] This tendency to separate the Meroitic *Aethiopes* from 'the majority' in Roman cognitive maps of 'Aethiopia' was no doubt reinforced by the mythic image itself, which, as has been noted above, related primarily (if not entirely) to an 'Aethiopia' imaginatively associated with Napatan-Meroitic antiquity. Diodorus, while reporting at considerable length information drawn from earlier Greek literature on backward black African and other 'Aethiopian' groups, lauds the *Aethiopes* of Meroe as civilizers of ancient Egypt; and in the same way Pliny's admiration for Meroe is as clear as his contempt and distaste for backward and savage 'Aethiopian' barbarians: offering a contemporary view of the Meroitic material condition, he sees the 'desertification' (*solitudo*) of the northern part of the kingdom as an unfortunate contemporary condition which calls for explanation precisely because it greatly contrasts with the once prosperous condition indicated by that country's glorious past, and he explains the contemporary situation as a consequence of exhaustion in ancient wars with Egypt in which the two belligerent nations had periodically exchanged with each other the positions of dominance and subjection.[30] Similarly Strabo, while noting the poor organization and equipment of the contemporary Meroitic army, categorizes the kingdom as an advanced or 'cultivated' society, by contrast with the wretched condition and primitive modes of life of other 'Aethiopian' (and indeed largely black African) societies which accounted for 'the majority of the Aethiopians'.[31]

This pattern of thinking about 'Aethiopia' in educated Roman circles was consistent with the fact that, in general, educated Romans had little interest in barbarian exemplars of extreme cultural distance (as distinct from 'cultivated' barbarians), unless political considerations were at work.[32] It was largely for this reason that the 'cultivated' society of the Meroitic kingdom long continued to attract much greater Roman interest than did those of other 'Aethiopians'; Roman contacts with 'Aethiopia' in and after the first century AD, though not inconsiderable,[33] hardly modified already existing attitudes. Indeed, references to *Aethiopes* in their African habitats were then for the most part inspired not by the contemporary realities of African life, but by existing literary traditions and by the imagination, which operated on a schema presupposing a correlation between a given people's geographical distance from the central areas of Roman civilization, on the one hand, and its cultural distance and degree of barbarism on the other hand.[34] In any case, the circulation of these 'realistic' negative and positive images of *Aethiopes*, no less than that of the utopian image, must have been practically confined to the educated classes. In the prevailing situation of widespread illiteracy the existing communications system was hardly capable of achieving a wide dissemination of the relevant anthropological information. Comparable in this regard is the fact that, although European experience of Africa between the sixteenth and eighteenth centuries was far greater than Roman experience of 'Aethiopia' (let alone black Africa) ever was, Africa remained during those centuries a practically meaningless concept to 'a French peasant, a German artisan, or an English farm labourer', whose societies were similarly characterized by very low rates of literacy.[35] In Roman society, to be sure, illiterate townsmen acquired some familiarity with certain stock stereotypes of foreign peoples which easily filtered down to the masses through the medium of public speeches, through the often caricatural representations of aliens on private and public monuments and on coins, and to some extent also through experience of triumphal ceremonies celebrating Roman victories over the more dangerous and belligerent barbarians.[36] But there is no good reason for supposing that 'anthropological' information about distant peoples, other than in situations of grave conflict with such peoples, enjoyed a wide circulation. Even in literate circles there was sometimes some confusion of *Aethiopes* with *Aegyptii*,[37] perhaps as a consequence of local experience of blacks largely in the context of 'Egyptian' (or broadly Nilotic) communities and cults, and of a stereotype of 'Egyptians' (as distinct from Alexandrians) as 'black' which went back to Herodotus' representation of Egyptians as 'black-skinned' (*melanchroes*).[38]

IMAGES ARISING FROM CONFLICTUAL RELATIONS

Some scholars have rightly noted the great influence of political considerations upon Roman perceptions of out-groups and on the directions assumed by Roman ethnography, leading to stereotypes that mirror Roman fears or ambitions with regard to particular foreign peoples, and sometimes even resulting in xenophobia.[39] Such were the circumstances in which arose the negative images of northern barbarians and Jews. The stereotypes of northern 'palefaces' (and especially Germanic barbarians) reflect not only Roman distaste for the habits and backwardness of northern barbarians, but also the Roman sense of the threat posed by them to the integrity of the Roman *Kulturwelt* and to the interests, institutions, and ambitions of the Roman people. Every educated Roman knew in outline the history of the northern menace from the Gallic sack of Rome in 390 BC to Arminius' destruction of the emperor Augustus' legions in Germany in AD 6 – an event which intensified latent Roman fears and haunted Roman memories for centuries thereafter, evoking visions of Germanic barbarians as subhuman embodiments of savagery, beastly cunning, and treachery.[40] Negative stereotypes of Jews similarly reflect Roman impatience with Jewish 'tribalism' or clannishness (*concordia*) and intransigent self-alienation, as well as suspicions of Jewish rebellion in the first and second centuries.[41] The absence of this pattern of stereotyping with regard to *Aethiopes* (and the persistence of an image of *Aethiopes* as a peace-loving folk) during the era of the high empire must be explained precisely by the fact that Romans were at no time before the middle of the third century AD motivated by fear of Nubia as a military threat of major proportions, or mentally preoccupied with *Aethiopes* as a serious danger to Roman interests.[42] Group stereotypes naturally undergo changes (sometimes even dramatic changes) under the impetus of changing political realities, adapting to 'the prevailing temper of prejudice or the needs of the situation' – as, for example, in the war-time and post-war American images of the Japanese and the Russians respectively,[43] and it is clear that a dominant Roman vision of *Aethiopes* as warriors and enemies of Rome was likely to arise only if there occurred political–military developments capable of leaving a deep, painful, and durable imprint on Roman minds.

Cracco Ruggini has suggested that such a development actually occurred in the latter part of the third century AD, with the serious menace which began to be directed at the southern provinces of the Roman empire at that time by barbarian peoples and bands of robbers located in the African 'interior' and including 'Aethiopians'. She allows that until this time 'the Aethiopians' had imposed no political and military preoccupations on the Roman mind, but she stresses that, after centuries of peaceful relations with the Meroitic kingdom, increasing instability set in on the Egyptian frontier as 'Aethiopians' (marauders and robbers, some of whom were undoubtedly black Africans) constantly menaced the countryside and emerald mines of Upper Egypt, and the caravan trade routes to the Red Sea. She notes also that the same era witnessed relentless pressure on the African provinces by 'Moors' and other *barbari* of the North African interior.[44] This situation of insecurity, in her view, bred an unfavourable image of 'black Africa' which for some time dominated the imagination of Romans with regard to *Aethiopes*, at least in the southern parts of the empire – an image which bore many of the negative traits of the contemporary stereotype of the dangerous, wild and belligerent northern barbarian, and inspired antipathetic attitudes towards black dwellers in Roman lands.[45]

The fact that only a minority (perhaps a very small minority) of these menacing warriors and marauders can actually have been blacks (as defined by Roman perceptions of somatic distance) does not in itself weaken this argument. To be sure, Roman experience of 'Aethiopia' was not an experience of a land of *blacks*; nor was the concept of sub-Egyptian Africans or Nubians (expressed in Latin by the term *Aethiopes* and in Greek by *Aithiopes*) synonymous with *blacks*; as has already been noted, Roman ethnographers point out that blacks (according to their perception of 'the black person') were not found as indigenous communities in the Nilotic region north of Meroe or in the adjacent deserts, and Romans in 'Aethiopia', like early modern Iberians in Africa, had no difficulty in distinguishing blacks from 'swarthy' and 'white' Africans.[46] But the cognitive maps formed by most educated Romans of the 'Aethiopians' in their distant African habitats grasped two categories of 'Aethiopians', distinguished in terms of cultural and developmental stature rather than in terms of somatic type.[47] Some modification of the idealistic perception of remote 'Aethiopians' is indeed suggested by the negative allusions to the mythical Memnon in post-Severan literature. While earlier literature presents a conventional picture of Memnon as a prominent figure in the utopian world of 'blacks' conjured up in the minds of educated Romans by the idealized image of remote *Aethiopes*, writers of the post-Severan era sometimes go out of their way to impress upon their readers' imagination the idea that this 'Aethiopian' king's arrival at Troy with his black troops (described now as *milia tetra*, or a 'hideous' or 'foul' contingent) was an ominous presage of disaster for his Trojan allies. In some texts of this period Memnon is even associated in the imagination with the highly detested 'Moorish traitor' Gildo and his black barbarian auxiliaries. These allusions bring to the fore the same negative symbolism that was conveyed by depictions of the dangerous sorceress Circe as a black woman. Another sign of this negative image of *Aethiopes* in this period appears in the fact that members of the educated elite could now unreservedly associate *Aethiopes* with backwardness and with scandalously barbaric practices like cannibalism. Christian leaders, for instance, often employ a wholly negative imagery of 'the Aethiopians' in propounding their faith and in explications of the scriptures. Origen, in conveying the message of the equality of all men before God, emphasizes the fact that this Christian message applies *even* to people like 'the Aethiopians who eat human flesh', the parricidal Scythians, and the Taurians, who perform human sacrifice using strangers as victims, and Jerome's exegesis of the psalmist's 'Ambassadors shall come out of Egypt; Aethiopia shall stretch out her hands to God' includes the comment that the *Aethiopes* got their name from their barbarous and savage habits.[48]

These negative presentations may have been influenced by the geopolitical considerations which (as Cracco Ruggini argues) came into play in the formation of xenophobic attitudes towards 'Aethiopian' barbarians in the third and fourth centuries, for 'men are rational enough to prefer plausible targets for their fears if they are available.'[49] The operation of '*l'approche politique*' is certainly clear in the work of the fourth-century court poet Claudian, who presents a picture of unrelieved 'Aethiopian' barbarism, unlike writers of the high empire, who commonly distinguish the Meroitic kingdom and its past from 'the majority of the Aethiopians'.[50] There are also hints in the literature of the post-Severan era that, in the imagination of Romans of the leisured classes, the utopian notion of remote, innocent, and wise *beati*, inventors of philosophy and astrology, was beginning to be associated in the main with nebulous peoples of the east rather than with 'the Aethiopians'.[51] Yet, as has already been observed, the favourable mythic image of *Aethiopes* continued to appear in Roman writing. Even as a mere literary *topos*, this epic theme can hardly have persisted (except in satire)[52] if its ideological premises were fundamentally unacceptable in the social–psychological climate of the post-Severan era.

It would seem, then, that for some time after the middle of the third century a negative image of distant *Aethiopes*, motivated by political considerations, often occupied the minds of upper-class Romans. This image was particularly marked and effective in the 'frontline' provinces of Egypt and North Africa, where it may also have seized the imagination of some people in the humbler ranks of society; we may reasonably suppose that in these 'frontline' provinces some people sometimes showed an inclination to 'identify' black strangers in their midst with the hated African barbarians beyond the imperial frontiers, thus displaying the human propensity for 'blaming our lot upon identifiable human agents (scapegoats).'[53] Post-Severan evidence of that predilection is offered by Synesius, for instance, who betrays an inclination towards scapegoating in his perception of Germanic slaves and public officials within the empire as brothers ('the same blond barbarians') of the menacing Germanic warriors then overrunning the imperial frontiers.[54] With regard to blacks, the same psychological disposition would seem to be reflected in the lines of Claudian already cited (in which the 'discoloured bastards' of this poet's imagination are placed in the same socio-cultural category as their black barbarian fathers rather than grouped with their Roman mothers), and also in the Romano-African epigram describing a black slave as 'a frightful spook' and linking him with external barbarians from the 'cesspits of the Garamantes'.[55]

But it is difficult (perhaps impossible) to say how widespread this scapegoating disposition was, even within the restricted circles of the upper classes, or how far-reaching its effects upon social relations were. The abusive testing of Abba Moses may reflect *inter alia* a contemporary secular habit of scapegoating internal blacks in Roman Egypt.[56] But the texts which suggest a scapegoating disposition represent only the responses of certain members of the upper classes, and we know that, throughout the Roman empire in the unsettled times after the middle of the third century AD, the response of the poor and the hungry to barbarian invasions was often that of seizing the opportunity to engage in looting, or that of fleeing their homes and turning to brigandage, 'driven by their afflictions into various criminal enterprises' (as one not unsympathetic, though upper-class, writer puts it), or filling the ranks of 'deserters, beggars, monks, and the merely desperate roaming loose from province to province.'[57] There is, in any case, no good reason for supposing that the conflicts in the southern provinces created a fixed image of black menace and militancy in the minds of the mass of the population in other parts of the empire where people's lives were not directly touched by this African barbarian menace. The populations of the other provinces were preoccupied with the more immediate and more dangerous menace of non-African barbarians like the Suebi, the Alamanni, and the Goths, who were even mentally associated with Gog, Magog, and the Apocalypse in the imagination of terrified Romans of the Christian faith.[58]

THE POPULAR DOCTRINE OF ETHNIC DIVERSITY

Among other Roman images of *Aethiopes* that are relevant to our discussion of Roman attitudes and behaviour towards blacks are some largely negative stereotypes arising from a climatic-astrological doctrine which went back, through the Greek philosopher Posidonius, to the Greek 'Hippocratic School'. The version of this doctrine that was most popular among educated Romans divided the known world into three main zones, on each of which a particular planet or combination of planets was believed to radiate its power: a cold northern zone, a temperate middle zone, and a hot southern zone. In the cold north, the lands of the 'nordic' barbarians, the human body supposedly absorbed the moisture from the atmosphere, and consequently these peoples of central and northern Europe were generally characterized by great size, deep voices, pale-white (*candidus*) and glacial complexions, blond or red hair, piercing blue eyes, and fullness of blood. In the hot south, where the humidity was absorbed by the fierce heat of the sun (which also accounted for the very dark or black complexions of southerners), the natives were by nature men of short stature, very swarthy or black skins, high-pitched voices, curly or woolly hair, black eyes, and deficiency of blood. The blood-constitution of the northern 'paleface' made him a brave warrior, but the climate of his zone made him dim-witted, so that his courage in battle was often mere foolhardiness. By contrast, the black or near-black southerner was endowed by the nature of his geographical environment with a sharp intelligence, while his blood-deficiency rendered him a coward and a poor warrior. The middle zone (sometimes equated in a chauvinistic spirit with Italy) was the Mediterranean area, which (according to this doctrine) blended the extremes of north and south into a harmonious moderation – a notion that served as an explanation of the dominance of Italy, whose peoples were 'the best proportioned' in both somatic form and mental acumen.[59]

A.J. Toynbee aptly contrasted this doctrine with modern racist explanations of ethnic differences, pointing out that, despite the intellectual vulnerability of the ancient explanation, it had the merit of seeking to explain perceived somatic and cultural differences 'as being the effects of diverse environments upon a uniform Human Nature, instead of seeing in them the outward manifestations of a diversity that was somehow intrinsic in Human Nature itself.'[60] But if this doctrine held that physical and temperamental differences among peoples were shaped by geographical environment, and if it represented blackness of skin or blond hair and blue eyes as a 'mere geographical accident',[61] it neither precluded nor discouraged sensory aversions to blackness, blue eyes and so on: it in no way established parity of esteem for all human complexions and somatic types. It was indeed (in Roman hands) thoroughly Romanocentric, and so Vitruvius, who presents the popular Roman version in great detail, can unreservedly describe the Italian somatic norm as 'the best proportioned' and as the ideal type of human physical appearance, implying that the 'paleface' and the black African were both unfortunate in the somatic endowments that nature (climate and geography) had given them.[62] And, of course, there is much evidence for sensory aversions (even strong aversions) to physiognomies distant from the Roman norm: for example, the already noted aversion of the Romano-African author of the epigrams on the 'frightful spook' at Hadrumetum, a black perceived as possessor of a terrible colour.[63]

In the images generated by the climatic-astrological doctrine, blacks and other southerners, despite their sharpness of wit, could never be a military match for Romans in view of their unwarlike temperament on the one hand, and Italian *gravitas*, superior courage, discipline and staying-power on the other hand. If beastly savagery (*feritas*) was the special mark of the 'paleface' barbarian, the most striking temperamental characteristics of the southern barbarian stereotype were self-delusion (*vanitas*), lack of purpose, and sensuality.[64] But it is noteworthy that the Roman stereotype of blacks arising from this doctrine shared neither the medieval Arab view of blacks (in their African habitats) as utterly lacking in 'the use of reason' and in 'dexteritie of wit and of all arts', nor the similar view of them as 'stupid' peoples 'blinded by folly' and 'without religion' expressed by some early modern European visitors to black Africa.[65] Admittedly, in this European view, black Africans were *innocent* victims of Satan; 'savagery' was still the criterion of the negative evaluation of peoples, and it was not until the eighteenth century that Africans ceased to be seen as 'innocent' and came to be regarded instead as people by nature stupid, bestial, immoral, and sinful.[66] It is indeed of some interest to trace the operation of the ancient doctrine of the influence of the physical environment in the ideological systems of its inheritors in the early Islamic world and in eighteenth-century Europe. For instance, in the work of the eleventh-century Moorish scholar, Sā'id al-Andalusî, the image of northern and central Europeans is more or less the same as that of the ancient Romans: in consequence of their geographical environment, these peoples are more like beasts than men; they have frigid temperaments and raw humours; they are gross-bellied palefaces with long, lank, blond hair; they lack keenness of understanding and clarity of intelligence, and are sunk in ignorance, dullness and stupidity. But the image of the southerner arising from the same environmental theory is no longer

102

the ancient Roman image, for in Sā'id's perspective the southern zone is coterminous with black Africa, and the whole of the Maghreb is chauvinistically set in the '*juste milieu*', whereas the classical intellectuals had set most of that territory in the hot southern zone.[67] Moreover, Sā'id's world is already one in which 'slave' can be mentally associated with 'black', and it is one in which information about black African societies has a solid basis in direct and extensive contacts with blacks in their African habitats – and, indeed, contacts occurring in contexts far from conducive to positive assessments of blacks. Hence it is no longer possible to abide by the classical notion of the sharp-witted southerner. The southern (*scilicet*, black African) characteristics now include (along with the lack of self-control, the fickleness, and the purposelessness attributed by the Romans) stupidity, ignorance, and lack of understanding.[68]

In the hands of the late eighteenth-century intellectuals of north-western Europe the ancient dogma underwent still further modification. Europe as a whole now falls within the '*juste milieu*', and Europeans are now a single cultural category. Dimness of wit is, accordingly, no longer a mark of the central and northern European. On the contrary, mental stature is now linked to an ascending scale of whiteness of complexion. The Roman ideological system set northern Mediterraneans (and especially Italians) at the top of the human hierarchy and denigrated the peoples of central and northern Europe as stupid and backward – without, however, condemning them or any other group to irredeemable inferiority. But, with the northward shift of the geopolitical centre of gravity in post-Roman times, the classical notions were adjusted to reflect the new realities of power and dominance, and the adaptations even included transferring the accolade of 'most perfectly constituted in somatic form' from the peoples of the Mediterranean to those of north-west Europe.[69]

It must further be stressed that Roman images of 'Aethiopia' and 'the Aethiopians' (in Christian as well as in pagan times), even when negative, were always free from the peculiar influences which helped to shape modern European images of Africa. Unknown in the Roman context were attitudes of self-righteous, puritanical antipathy arising from the frustrations and irritations experienced, by early modern Europeans in Africa in the face of black 'heathenism', 'beastly living', un-Christian 'venery' (seen as one of the most undesirable effects of the tropical climate), and what they thought to be extreme laziness, love of pleasure, and lack of 'laws'. Unknown also were the psychological influences which the existence or memory of an all-black slave-system and an all-white dominance have exerted on modern attitudes, creating an almost indelible mental association of blackness with the status of slave or subject and of whiteness with freedom and mastery, and establishing fixed assumptions about the biological and cultural superiority of 'whites'.[70] The overwhelming majority of slaves in Roman society was always white.[71] Indeed, the institution of slavery itself diverted the attention of Romans from ethnicity and from what is today popularly called 'race' towards the function of the slave as *worker and servant*. It was this worker role and servant role (and the conditions of those roles) that drew the social contempt of the freeborn (especially those of the leisured classes), not only for slaves irrespective of shape, colour, and ethnicity, but also for free men doing the same work as slaves. Among the leisured classes 'class attitudes and values overshadowed other kinds', and in the lower reaches of the social scale first polytheistic religious cults (many of them imported from foreign cultures), and later Christianity, aided the social integration of slaves, ex-slaves, and free commoners whose fellowship was very often institutionalized in religious–economic societies (*collegia*) organized by immigrant co-religionists to provide their members with social security, relief from loneliness, and a guarantee of a decent funeral.[72]

PHYSIOGNOMONIC LORE

In the Roman ideological system the climatic doctrine described earlier had much in common with notions arising from the pseudo-science of *physiognomonia*, whose adepts claimed to detect scientifically from physical characteristics (*qualitas corporis*) lineaments of personal character and temperament (*qualitas animi*). Their theories exercised a considerable influence both in educated circles and among the humbler ranks of society.[73] Common to *physiognomonia* and the climatic–astrological doctrine were the principles that the blood is the seat of the spirit (*anima*) and that, while abundance of blood strengthens the body and reduces the mental acumen, thinness and deficiency of blood weakens the body but sharpens the intellect, the mean between these two extremes achieving the perfect human combination of strength and wisdom. Both pseudo-sciences accordingly propagated much the same largely negative images of *Aethiopes*, Egyptians, Scythians, and other peoples located far outside the *'juste milieu'*. The *physiognomonici* fostered elaborate popular stereotypes of people of the 'hot and dry south' (associated with the 'hot' colours 'black' and 'swarthy') and people of the 'cold and wet north' (associated with the 'cold' colour 'white'), just as the peoples of the Mediterranean area were associated with the 'intermediate' colour pale-brown (*inter nigrum et pallidum*). Represented as 'southern' characteristics were black or swarthy skin, black and curly or woolly hair, black eyes, small bones, slim ankles, quickness of intelligence, sagacity, cowardice, rashness, untrustworthiness, craftiness, greed, mendacity, thievishness, love of pleasure, a powerful sexual urge, fickleness, and frivolousness. Inhabitants of the cold north, on the other hand, were broadly stereotyped as characterized by excessive tallness, lank blond or red hair worn long, light-blue eyes, upturned snub noses, large bones, obesity, huge bellies, simple-mindedness, dullness of wit and lack of intelligence, hastiness of temper, excitability, proneness to quick depression, lack of judgement, incapacity for reasoned and disciplined behaviour, courage, savagery, recklessness, drunkenness, laziness, and a tendency towards gambling and boasting. While admitting that biological intermixture among ethnic and national groups was a constant fact of life, the doctrine propagated this geographical distribution of somatic and temperamental traits as a general rule, noting also that the intensity of cold-northern or hot-southern characteristics decreased among peoples in proportion to their geographical distance from the far north or far south (or proximity to the *juste milieu*, whose peoples represented the ideal somatic, moral, and behavioral type).[74] The ideal somatic type (in respect of the male sex, at any rate) consisted of pale-brown complexion (described as *inter nigrum et pallidum* or the mean between the extremes of *Aethiops* blackness and 'nordic' whiteness), straight (but not large) nose, moist, bright eyes of a brown colour midway between jet blackness and pale-brown, brown hair (of a texture midway between the straight and the tightly-curled, and between excessive softness and extreme coarseness), lips neither thin nor thick, and moderate tallness.[75]

Beyond this broad ethnographic schema, *physiognomonia* also gave currency to numerous stereotypes applicable to individuals of all colours and shapes and linking particular somatic traits to particular mental and moral characteristics. Stiff woolly hair signified cowardice; very black hair signified both cowardice and greed; lank, straight hair (especially if blond) indicated stupidity and lack of culture; red hair signified beastliness, greed, and shamelessness; coarse hair signalled bravery. Similarly, extremely black or extremely white skin were traits which, in combination with certain other physical characteristics like paunchiness, shortness of neck, and roundness of face, indicated stupidity. A very black complexion in itself signalled cowardice and craftiness, while a dark olive skin indicated cowardice, gluttony, verbosity and irascibility. A pale white skin in a male indicated lack of manliness (this sort of complexion being associated with the female sex); red skin suggested the craftiness and deceit of the fox; blue eyes signalled savagery and lack of culture, 'black' eyes cultivation (though extremely 'black' eyes marked cowardice and craftiness), and dark-brown eyes meant strength and greatness of spirit. Again, a flat nose or snub nose was a sign of lechery, while thick lips proclaimed a crocodile-like gluttony.[76]

If the currency of some of these stereotypes was largely restricted to educated circles, many of the links between somatic and moral traits were no doubt part and parcel of Roman folklore, as tends to be the case with such notions in modern societies: the evidence indeed indicates that *physiognomonia* had adepts even in the humble strata of society. The vitality of some of the negative group stereotypes is also illustrated by the fact that Julius Caesar can treat as an established fact the image of northerners which rendered 'hastiness of temper and foolhardiness' an 'innate' characteristic of the Gallic Aedui.[77] Similarly, the image of northern barbarians as culturally alien blond giants retained its popularity and vigour despite empirical observation that not all northerners were blond or irrational; the discovery that the Silures of South Wales in Britain were dark of complexion and generally curly-haired readily induced the explanation that they were a tribe of Spanish origin.[78] Again, growing awareness of the fact that the Chatti of Germany did not quite fit the stereotype of the 'German mentality' merely rendered that people the exception that proved the rule – hence the observation of Tacitus: 'This people is distinguished by great physical hardiness, tautness of limb, savagery of expression, and *unusual* mental vigour; *for a German tribe*, they have a remarkable amount of judgement and degree of mental acumen.'[79] To Romans whose mental horizons embraced such peoples at all, terms like *Gallus*, *Germanus*, and *Aethiops* must often have served as what social psychologists call 'labels of primary potency',[80] disproportionately magnifying certain stereotyped 'attributes' of those peoples, and blinding the observer to the anthropological realities surrounding their lives, let alone the personal characteristics of individual *strangers* perceived as members of those stereotyped groups.

The stereotype associating blacks with hypersexuality (which recalls the similar image current among Europeans of the sixteenth and seventeenth centuries)[81] no doubt had considerable currency and vitality among Romans of all social classes.[82] It is implicit in several references and allusions, some of which indeed suggest that it gained some empirical validity in Roman eyes from events of daily life in the imperial capital and in other centres where blacks were a part of day-to-day experience. For instance, an assumption of a popular association of blacks with hypersexuality (and of Roman interest and curiosity about it) obviously underlies both the already discussed theme of declamation exercises *matrona Aethiopem peperit* ('a Roman married woman has given birth to a black baby'), and the apocryphal tale according to which Sextus Tarquinius, as early as the closing years of the sixth century BC, blackmailed the chaste Lucretia into submitting to his sexual desires by threatening to kill her and leave next to her on the bed the naked corpse of a black slave.[83] Satire similarly dwells on the xenophilic promiscuity of Roman women, whose favourite aliens supposedly included *Aethiopes*, and also attributes to women of the upper classes a powerful and uncontrollable urge for sexual intimacy with humble men – an urge which, if undoubtedly less rampant and widespread than is suggested by the exaggerated pictures of the satirists, has rightly been seen as a consequence of an affluent and luxury-swathed boredom felt by ladies of the leisured classes in a society that offered such women so few respectable outlets for their energies and talents that some were driven to seek outlets of licentiousness.[84] The fact that the macrophallic black is a traditional theme in Roman iconography also underscores the image of black sexuality which attributed to blacks (*qua* southerners) the possession of a sinister fascination for non-blacks of the opposite sex (and in some cases, even of the same sex), despite the negativity of the black somatic stereotype which included the feminine *vitia* of over-large breasts and perhaps also over-prominent buttocks.[85] Attestation of Roman sexual curiosity and interest with regard to *Aethiopes* is also given by the account of the emperor Heliogabalus' habit of frequenting black prostitutes, accompanied by 'unwilling' male friends, and perhaps also by the Pompeian graffito *quisquis amat nigra(m) nigris carbonibus ardet;/ nigra(m) cum video mora(m) libenter aedeo* ('Any man who loves a black girl is set on fire by hot charcoal flames; when I see a black girl I am ready and willing to eat that blackberry').[86]

Christianity did not eliminate this attitude; indeed the strong Christian linkage of blackness with sin favoured this association of *Aethiopes* with sexuality, inducing some people to see blacks as dark and mysterious sources of forbidden (and so heightened) sexual pleasure. Modern psychologists have noted that 'the elements of mystery and forbiddenness are present in sex appeal' and that 'differences in color and social status seem to be sexually exciting rather than repelling': such differences invite 'alternate ridicule and desire', the former arising from an urge to represent an 'inner temptation' as 'an outer threat'.[87] In early Christian society the ancient pagan notion of black hypersexuality became closely linked with that of the forbidden pleasures of sexual sinfulness, and this is apparent in several descriptions of black or 'Egyptian' tempters and temptresses, agents of the Devil often also represented as 'foul', 'ill-smelling', and 'ugly', that appear in Christian literature as well as in the contrasting imagery of *Aethiops* sexual continence that certain patristic texts seek to propagate with regard to evangelized and saintly blacks and their triumphs over the base demands of the flesh.[88] Blackness, linked with sin, was 'at once repulsive and alluring'.[89] Hence, on the one hand, the hagiographical tales and the Christian lessons directly reflecting the theme of a dangerous black sexuality, and, on the other hand, the writings which emphasize the chastity of the type of black who has attained true Christian 'whiteness'. To the first category belong accounts such as that of an ascetic tempted by a 'demon' in the form of an attractive black peasant girl, and warnings against the seductive charms of 'black girls' whose embraces 'befoul' one because of their 'Hell-black faces'.[90] Or again, the account of the temptation of Origen who, forced to choose between sodomy with an *Aethiops* and an act of implicit apostasy, chose the latter course as the lesser of the two evils; or that of the apparition (reported in the Egyptian Gnostic text *Pistis sophia*) of the demon Ariuth in the form of a completely black *Aethiops* woman; or the similar apparition of a 'foul-smelling and ugly' *Aethiops* woman; and again, that of 'the foulest of women, very much a black African, and not Egyptian, but completely black and filthy.'[91] To the second category belong the exegetical emphasis on the chastity of the Queen of Sheba (the 'queen of the south' and so of 'Aethiopia'), whose sole interest in visiting Solomon is represented as the quest for wisdom; and also the patristic interpretation of the baptism of the Candace's black eunuch as an example of 'the defeat of libido'; and again, the hagiographical tales of the transformation of the black slave Moses from lecher, armed robber, and murderer, to holy monk.[92]

On the whole, of course, the loves and lives of humble couples (of whatever colour or colours) held no interest for Roman writers. No Roman writer, for instance, shows the sort of interest demonstrated by the eighteenth-century English pamphleteer Edward Long, who in 1772 observed in strongly disapproving terms: 'The lower class of women in England are remarkably fond of the blacks, for reasons too brutal to mention.'[93] Interest in black sexual behaviour was restricted to situations in which the other partner was a member of the upper classes. But it was natural that blacks should have had intimate relations with non-blacks of their own social and economic peer groups, within and outside formal and semi-formal marital unions, as was the case with black domestics in England in the seventeenth and eighteenth centuries.[94] The near-total silence of the ancient texts on blacks and their sexual mates at humble social levels is itself an eloquent commentary on the spirit of the times. Pliny, as we have seen, refers in purely matter-of-fact terms to the adultery of a white woman with a black man, and the disapproving allusions to such relationships all centre on the *women's* adultery, not on the colour of the man. The tone of disapproval tends to recall Juvenal's reference to an innkeeper's wife pondering elopement with a cloak-seller, or Petronius' suggestion that *all* women are apt to be carried away by a mad passion for some stranger or other.[95]

COLOUR SYMBOLISM

In the Roman mind the concept 'black' in itself evoked negative images, and this was in every sense a popular conception. The negative symbolism of the colour black (associated with night, darkness, bad omens, death, evil, sin, disaster, sickness, unpleasantness, the malignant, the dirty, and the undesirable) in contrast with the colour white as a symbol of light, virtue, purity, good health, success, the pleasant, and the desirable, has been noted as an almost universal phenomenon, common among black as well as white peoples, and figuring 'prominently in the areas of human experience concerned with religion and the supernatural.'[96] In Roman antiquity this colour symbolism manifested itself even in usages of the words *niger* and *melas*('black') and their synonyms; like English 'blackmail', 'blackball', 'blacklist', 'black day', and so on, these Latin and Greek words were used metaphorically with the meanings 'spiteful', 'malignant', 'wicked', 'sinister', and the like.[97] In white or predominantly white societies it is perhaps natural (as some scholars hold)[98] that folklore and popular beliefs should relate this symbolism in some way to human strangers of a significantly darker complexion than the local norm, as well as to strange black animals and black inanimate objects; that was certainly the case with Roman superstitions, which were particularly vigorous in the lower ranks of society, though they also informed the outlook of many people of high education and status. Thus one poet disparagingly associates a black slave in an explicit manner with the ominous, the fearsome, and the world of the dead, and a similar sentiment is reflected in a depiction of Charon, the grim ferryman of the underworld, not only as black-skinned, but as an *Aethiops* (with snub nose and thick lips), and again in the use of black and Egyptian performers to play theatrical roles of inhabitants of the underworld.[99] Juvenal's satirical picture of a black Egyptian musician (*nigro tibicine*) also expresses this negative symbolism, for in that picture the black musician plays a leading role in a barbaric religious ceremony that ends in a scene of cannibalism, and in which the black is associated with the sinister, the evil, and the repulsive.[100] Similarly, in Claudian's picture of a violent imposition of black barbarian husbands upon aristocratic Roman women, this negative symbolism of blackness is evident in the poetic vision of 'discoloured bastards', where it is associated with anti-barbarism, xenophobia and paranoia about breaches of the rules of social hierarchy.[101].

To be sure, the 'black-hearted' and 'blackmail' type of usage ordinarily carries no conscious association with moral or social value judgements relating in a discriminatory manner to black or swarthy people; it acquires derogatory force with specific reference to such people only in the sort of social–psychological situation that makes it capable of serving as an unpleasant reminder to blacks (for instance) of their group degradation, and even in racist ambiences it does not always assume such a role.[102] But certain other aspects of this colour symbolism are likely to have influenced social relations in Roman antiquity, even if the relevant Roman evidence relates mostly to attitudes of members of the upper classes whose relations with blacks were, in any case, largely governed by considerations of status. As has already been observed, two Romano-African epigrams reveal a sensory aversion to the black physiognomy as well as personal antipathy towards one or more particular blacks, and a tendency towards scapegoating of blacks (*Anth.Lat.*, 182–183). Moreover, superstitious Romans of all social classes undoubtedly regarded as a bad omen not only an encounter with a strange black dog, but also a chance meeting with an *Aethiops* stranger; they might even seek to avert the 'evil omen' by pre-emptive violence against the 'ominous' black person if circumstances rendered it safe to inflict such violence, just as they instinctively thought of killing 'ill-omened' animals.[103]

In times before the beginning of Roman experience of black Africans, dark-skinned strangers of the 'Caucasian' type had evidently filled the role to which the evidence actually attests for *Aethiops*-type strangers in and after the first century BC. The Roman proverb conveying the notion of total ignorance (as in 'our 'not knowing from Adam'), which Catullus paraphrases in the words *nec scire utrum sis albus an ater homo* ('not knowing whether you are a white or a black'), probably goes back to the time when the very swarthy sort of Mediterranean white man was the only type describable as 'black' in actual Roman experience. That, in turn, would suggest a habit of applying the negative colour symbolism to very swarthy 'Caucasians' from early times. Clearly suggestive of such a habit in early Roman society are, first, the use of the term *Aegyptius dies* ('Egyptian day') as a synonym of *atra dies* ('black day'); second, the selection of Egyptians (along with blacks) to play stage roles of inhabitants of the underworld; and third, the fact that Christians of the Roman world, in an extension of this colour symbolism with specific reference to the Devil, associated Satan and his works not only with *Aethiopes* and black animals, but also with people of appreciably dark complexion in general.[102]

With the emergence of Christianity the negative symbolism of the colour black proliferated in images of the Devil, his demons and his works as black in colour.[105] From the late first century AD the Devil was labelled 'the Black One' (*ho melas*) and associated with night, while the son of God was associated with day, and this black demonology was particularly pronounced in Egypt, North Africa, Syria-Palestine, and Asia Minor from the third century AD onwards. The Egyptian Church leader Macarios recalls the Pauline doctrine that Christians are 'sons of Light' (*filii lucis*) and the ungraced *filii tenebrarum* ('sons of Darkness'), 'because the son of God is Day, while the Devil is symbolized by Night.' Similarly, Origen declares that the participant in the Christian sacrament is a son of God, while the ungraced is 'a spiritual *Aethiops*', and Peter of Alexandria attributes to the unrepentant sinner 'an unchangeable *Aethiops* skin.'[106] Church leaders, 'in their ever lively and fantastic representations of the Devil and his demons' missed no opportunity for emphasizing the nigritude of these beings. In their exegetical writings there is a common metaphorical usage of the term *Aethiops* ('black African') to designate 'dark-minded', 'black in soul', 'sunk in vice', and 'sin-stained'. As J. Devisse puts it, 'Christian exegesis and popular prejudice put together a stable image in which blackness was a sign of evil.'[107] In the exegetical terminology the expression 'black Africans' (*Aethiopes*) connoted all men, of whatever earthly colour and form, 'whose dark minds are not yet illumined by divine light' and whose souls can be purified only by penitence and by God's grace.[108] Likewise the term *Aethiopia* ('the dark land') symbolized the distant, as yet unevangelized, and spiritually unregenerated world of sin. To this metaphorical context belong observations like that of Gregory of Nyssa to the effect that Christ came to make 'blacks' white, and that in the City of God *Aethiopes* become white and prostitutes virgins.[109] Thus in the third and fourth centuries Egyptian ascetics who went into the desert 'to break the barrier of bodily will in order to attain the vision of God' commonly had visions of demoniac tempters and temptresses in the form of black men, women and boys, or black animals.[110] This image of the black demon and tempter or temptress pervaded lower class beliefs, especially in Egypt, North Africa, Syria-Palestine and Asia Minor; it was particularly prevalent among illiterates (the great majority of the population), who were deeply influenced by tales of the visions experienced by saints at moments when the personalities of the latter, if truth be told, had been 'disintegrated by self-inflicted hunger, thirst, exposure to desert heat and cold, and sleeplessness', as their lofty Christian ideals pitted them in an intense struggle against forbidden impulses.[111] Such apparitions multiplied in due course and were also reported in other parts of the Roman world: for instance, the dream attributed by the hagiography to Perpetua of Carthage in which, on the eve of her martyrdom, she was engaged in a struggle with the Devil in the form of a foul and ugly 'Egyptian' (*Aegyptius* here meaning, however, *Aethiops*); and, in Asia Minor, the dream-apparitions of an ugly, black, and filthy temptress, of a demon in the shape of a huge *Aethiops* 'black as soot', and of the Devil himself in the guise of the king of Aethiopia.[112] One of these texts from Asia Minor describes an apparition as *mulierem turpissimam, in aspectu Ethiopissimam neque Aegyptiam, sed totam nigram sordibus* ('the ugliest of women, in appearance very much a black African and not Egyptian, but completely black and filthy').[113] This shows that, although the deep blackness of the *Aethiops* was seen as the best symbol of demoniac power, such apparitions in human form ranged in colour and morphology from swarthy 'Caucasian' to negro African, and although references to Romano-African visions of demons use the term *Aegyptius* as a synonym of *Aethiops* (reflecting a usage commonly found in Romano-African writing),[114] it is clear that the degree of *nigritudo* characterizing these demoniac apparitions tended to vary according to the somatic norm of each particular area and its day-to-day experience of human beings 'blacker' than that norm. Thus in Egypt, where the bulk of the population was darker in complexion than the Roman norm, and where the black African element was larger than elsewhere, the apparitions were *Aethiopes* (darker than the local norm), while in certain other parts of the empire the swarthy Egyptian-type appearance was often adequate for this 'black' demoniac role. Indeed, in the iconographic expressions of the blackness–sin symbolism, the dark demons rarely bear a negroid facial morphology.[115]

IMAGES AND SOCIAL RELATIONS

Some of the images of *Aethiopes* outlined in the foregoing discussion obviously played a role (and in some cases probably a very vigorous role) in the formation of prejudgements of black strangers (as distinct from friends and acquaintances) in Roman society. Social relations were governed primarily by personal status: behaviour was regulated by recognition of certain acknowledged deference-entitling properties.[116] Most blacks in the Roman world (as distinct from progeny and descendants of blacks) were evidently people of humble status who had entered that world for the most part as slaves. There can be no doubt, therefore, that this humble status was what, above all, determined the treatment received by the majority of blacks (as individuals) at the hands of members of the leisured classes and commoners of superior personal status to their own. That was true of the humble generally, irrespective of ethnicity, colour, and shape. But it also seems clear that the behaviour of non-black individuals (including persons of the sort described in Roman literature as somatically 'swarthy') in encounters with black strangers was sometimes influenced by popular stereotypes of blacks: that of the sharp-witted and crafty southerner; or that of the lustful, darkly mysterious and sexually fascinating southerner; or that of the backward black barbarian addicted to horrid practices; or (in post-Severan Egypt and North Africa) the image of the militant 'black' warrior and marauder; or again, in educated circles throughout the empire, the mythic image of far-away 'blacks' as noble-natured and pious folk. It seems certain that, in the minds of the highly superstitious in all social strata and in all parts of the Roman world (particularly when previous experience of personal relations with blacks was lacking) the dominant emotion aroused by an encounter with a black stranger was quite often disquiet, suspicion of an ill omen, and even fear of the unfamiliar; in the early Christian world such prejudgements undoubtedly tended at times to associate the black stranger with 'a natural tendency to evil' as well as with bad luck of some kind. In encounters with black strangers the interaction must have depended greatly on Roman individuals' levels of education and degree of familiarity with blacks, as well as on their assessments of the blacks' social status and familiarity with Roman ways.

As early as the second century BC a Greek intellectual illustrated the effects of familiarization with blacks upon attitudes towards blacks in white communities. Agatharchides, while noting that black soldiers inspired fear in opponents unfamiliar with their somatic appearance, also stressed that in communities with current experience of blacks, this fear did not outlast childhood.[117] Modern psychologists have indeed shown that the young child has an instinctive fear of the strange and, for many, the strange obviously includes black faces. But, as Agatharchides saw, this fear, which is characteristic of infancy, has 'no necessary bearing upon the organization of permanent attitudes' towards blacks. Infants tend to adapt rapidly to novelties such as black faces.[118] An adult without previous relevant experience may be expected to show much the same anxiety as a child in confrontation with the unfamiliar, and that was the case, for example, with many people in eighteenth-century France, who reacted with fear at the sight of blacks, regarding them as grotesque. Similarly, the initial Portuguese reaction to the black African physiognomy was (like that of Olaudah Equiano in his first confrontation with the unfamiliar 'Caucasian' physiognomy) one of 'shock and horror' at a 'hideous and deformed' somatic appearance.[119] For Roman adults (*ceteris paribus*), the more mysterious and remote from normal experience blacks happened to be, the greater will have been the anxiety, fear, and antipathy aroused by the sight of a black face in a society in which folklore represented *Aethiopes* as harbingers of calamity and fostered mental association of black skin with dirtiness (*niger sordibus, Scybale, faex Garamantarum, carbo, cinis, foedus*, Memnon's *milia tetra*, are all expressions of this idea that occur in the references already discussed). And on the question of adaptation to, and familiarization with, blacks in Roman communities we must avoid the assumption that a black presence, when once established in a given locality, would necessarily continue through subsequent generations. The black presence in the Roman world was obviously not a matter of culturally cohesive black groups either eager or able to maintain their cultural and somatic identity in alien environments. There were, to be sure, bonds of a religious kind uniting some blacks living in the same social space, but even then not in exclusively black groups, but as communities with an Egyptian or Nilotic identity.[120]

As La Piana noted of the city of Rome, immigrants of the same nationality tended to cluster together for social and psychological security in particular districts and in self-imposed ethnic residential segregation, maintaining their language and culture for as long as they kept up their links with their native countries, and this attachment to their cultural traditions was supported by clubs or associations of a religious and economic kind (*collegia, hetairiai*), whose main attractions were the refuge that they offered from loneliness and the assurance of a decent funeral. But, except for the Jewish groups (and even these were not altogether immune to local cultural influences), members of these various national groups lived in ethnic seclusion only as a temporary expedient – until the individual newcomer had gathered the experience and the means to go out and join 'the current of a larger social life', and to assume his or her place in the particular stratum of the Roman social system for which he or she was qualified in terms of income and other status-criteria.[121] Not only were the 'ethnic' associations to which some blacks belonged (and it cannot be assumed that every black was a member of such an association) not black associations, black members were also very much in the minority in their various *collegia*. Moreover, our operative assumption must be that perpetuation of a black presence in a given Roman locality depended upon recurrent immigration of blacks, mostly through the slave trade, for in a society which encourages (or at any rate does not discourage) cultural assimilation and at the same time imposes no institutional barriers against 'miscegenation', a numerically small element of somatically distant immigrants (who, moreover, as individuals dispersed in various locations, lack the cohesion of an ethnic group with its own cultural identity) will quite rapidly become genetically and culturally fused with the dominant element in the population. This process was all the more inevitable in a situation like that of Roman antiquity, where the black immigrant was for the most part a slave who, despite his participation in an Isiac or similar *collegium*, was compelled to live in a Roman household amidst predominanty non-black fellow slaves of various national origins (where they were not locally born and bred *vernae*). Black slaves either did not mate at all, and died childless, or they must have mated mostly with white or 'swarthy' slaves, and one result of this interbreeding will have been the continuous process of somatic amalgamation to which reference has already been made.[122] That process, in turn, will have meant that a good number of Romans whose forebears had been familiar with the company of blacks did not themselves have that familiarity. Our assumption, then, is that the aura of strangeness surrounding blacks in Roman society (and especially in the less important centres) was on the whole more persistent than were individual black lineages.

That assumption renders it particularly important to take note of the work of modern psychologists on the subjects of social perception and the psychology of interpersonal relations. This literature[123] explains that individual adults, in encounters with other people, search with their senses for information about those persons that will enable them to act appropriately towards those people, and their feelings and behaviour will be more positive if the others are perceived as similar to themselves in personality, interests, attitudes, and values than if they are perceived as dissimilar or as unpredictable owing to their possession of an unfamiliar type of physiognomy. An encounter with a stranger of alien and unfamiliar physical appearance, about whom no other information is available, tends to trigger a psychological process leading to an unfavourable evaluation: the strange and unfamiliar is experienced as not fitting one's expectations, and it causes anxiety, insecurity, or fear owing to the fact that, in the absence of reassuring information, the unfamiliar appearance implies real differences in interests, values, and social characteristics, and renders questionable the observer's normal manner of relating to others. Resistance to the unfamiliar also has an aesthetic aspect, and the common reaction is the sort of aversion or uneasiness that often arises in meetings with physically handicapped strangers or mentally ill persons, where one can no longer assume that one's 'structured ways of behaving' are relevant. Where the other is perceived as a member of a negatively stereotyped group, the stereotype influences the psychological process, helping to reduce the observer's capacity to search for information about the somatically distant stranger as an individual person, and the other thus becomes a mere object, tagged with some 'label of primary potency' like 'black' instead of being seen as an individual with personal qualities.

Where, however, other information is available about the somatically distant stranger (indicating some personal similarity over and above the evident differences in physical appearance), and especially where there is awareness that the perceived somatic distance is the sole differentiating item, a positive interaction is to be expected, provided that the society is not of the sort which itself imposes social barriers on the basis of somatic appearance. Various studies have accordingly emphasized the importance of personal contact and familiarization with somatically distant people as an efficacious changer of attitudes towards such persons in social–psychological contexts in which a somatic appearance is disliked only because it is strange and disturbing and in which society imposes no fixed patterns on personal relations with representatives of the somatically distant group. It has been found that, even in racist contexts, the more one knows about a racized category (the category 'blacks', for instance), even if the knowledge arises from close contact with only one person of that category, the less likely one will be to see members of that category as mere objects; the greater the contact in terms of intensity (number of people involved, frequency, duration, and degree of intimacy), the greater is the change of the previously negative attitude towards members of that category. Two studies conducted in a context of racist structures (which the authors overlooked in the false belief that racial prejudice is simply a character-conditioned personal prejudice) are nonetheless relevant to the problem under discussion, since they show that in a non-racist context considerable attitudinal change would result from the process of 'getting used to' the initially strange and disturbing somatic appearance of blacks, and that behaviour towards the black stranger would then come to depend upon the degree to which that stranger is perceived as an asset or liability with regard to the realization of the white in-group's values.[124]

It is pertinent to note in this context some Roman indications of the importance of habituation and familiarization (*consuetudo*) in attitudinal change with respect to somatic traits widely regarded as 'inappropriate'. Lucretius observes that 'habituation arouses love', and he notes that, in the eyes of the familiarized man, a 'black' girl may be a 'honey-brown' (*melichrus*) or 'dusky' beauty, or a blue-eyed one 'Athena's image' (contrary to the conventional view of blue eyes as a somatic defect), or a thick-lipped one cherished as 'my living kiss'. Horace similarly notes that 'the lover is blind to his girlfriend's unsightly physical blemishes, or else he actually finds them charming, as Balbinus found Hagna's wen.' Ovid observes that 'the very passage of time removes defects from the body, and what was initially a flaw ceases to be so, owing to familiarization with a given appearance over time.'[125] In other words, while the familiar is perceived as 'good' and 'appropriate' and the strange as 'bad' and 'inappropriate', with time the strange becomes the familiar, and, as familiarity increases, the stranger moves from the category 'bad' to that of 'good' or 'acceptable'. This familiarization process, with regard to *Aethiopes*, was undoubtedly at work in Roman society, where most blacks lived as part of a *familia* of predominantly white fellow slaves, and in degrees of interpersonal closeness with the latter extending to the 'slave marriage' relationship in some cases. The anonymous author of *Moretum*, despite his own mockery of the physical appearance of the black slave-woman Scybale, stresses the intimacy which (according to his assumptions) would *naturally* exist between a peasant and his sole house-companion, who happens to be a black woman. Among free blacks (including ex-slaves) persons in occupational roles such as soldier, jockey, *venator*, gladiator, courtesan, and common prostitute also lived in constant contact with non-black colleagues, and occupational contact, when (as in Roman society) it is fully sanctioned by institutional supports, promotes interactions both extensive (close association in public) and intensive (eating and engaging in other social activities together, sexual relations, and marriage). The small number of Roman references to blacks as individual persons, named or anonymous, offers a good proportion of instances of this social integration: for example, Memnon in the household of Herodes Atticus, treated as a son by the latter; again, the black soldier and popular wag in the army in Britain; blacks as monks in monastic communities; popular jockeys in sixth-century Carthage, lauded by Luxorius; and the charismatic *venator* Olympius, popular and respected by his colleagues.[126]

An indication of this social integration in the city of Rome may also be seen in Pliny's story of the funeral of an amazing talking bird, believed to have been hatched in the precincts of the temple of Castor and Pollux and to have been given a home by a neighbouring shopkeeper who attached a religious significance to its place of birth. For several years the bird had kept up the habit of flying on to the *rostra* every morning, saying the name of the emperor, his son, and his nephew (Tiberius, Drusus and Germanicus), and then 'greeting' passers-by before flying back to the shop. But it was killed by the next-door tradesman 'either out of jealousy of his neighbour, or (as he wanted people to believe) because it had dirtied his shoes with its droppings.' According to Pliny, the killing aroused great public consternation, leading to the lynching of the 'murderer'; and the bird's funeral was celebrated 'with a very large cortège', the funeral-bed being borne on the shoulders of two *Aethiopes*, 'preceded by a flute-player and wreaths of all kinds.' Pliny observes that the last repects shown to this bird by 'the people of Rome' were particularly notable 'in a city in which the funeral remains of many leading citizens had gone unescorted', and he also contrasts the lynching of the bird's killer with the fact that 'no one had avenged the death of the great Scipio Aemilianus, conqueror of Carthage and Numantia.' The attitude to this bird obviously had to do with religious sentiment, and the role of the two blacks no doubt reflects their standing as devotees of the religious cult with which the bird was associated – ostensibly that of the Dioscuri; but the Dioscuri were often worshipped in association with the Nilotic deities Isis, Serapis, and Anubis and were, like these Egyptian deities, protectors of sailors. The event described by Pliny occurred in AD 35, and so belongs to a time of official hostility to the cult of Isis, whose temple on the Campus Martius had already been destroyed on the orders of the emperor Tiberius. That may well explain why the bird is associated only with the Dioscuri and not with an Egyptian cult, for this bird was probably an African (Aethiopian) parrot which for that very reason came to be called a *black* bird (*corvus*) in a subsequent distortion of the story – a distortion reproduced by Pliny.[127]

But in a socio-cultural ambience in which an active superstition about black strangers as ominous was part and parcel of the negative symbolism of the colour black, it would be naive to suppose that even the lofty ideals of the Church entirely eliminated negative and antipathetic attitudes towards black strangers, or that Christians were *all* able *at all times* to overcome the temptation to attribute to black and very dark-skinned strangers (as distinct from familiar black faces) the 'natural tendency to evil' which was attributed to the black monk Moses in his days as a 'lecherous' and murderous slave and armed robber.[128] That is not to suggest, however, that all (or even most) blacks necessarily took this superstition and symbolism seriously, or inevitably lived in fear of (or preoccupation with) possible ill-treatment or violence resulting from this symbolism at the hands of frightened and superstitious Romans. The account of the ominous encounter of the emperor Septimius Severus with a black soldier and army 'comedian' (an encounter listed by Aelius Spartianus among the portents of that emperor's death) suggests that the encounter (reputedly seen by the superstitious emperor himself as an alarming presage of his own death) was actually stage-managed as a practical joke by the black soldier, perhaps in collusion with some white soldiers of his unit.

> *post murum apud Luguvallum visum in Britannia cum ad proximam mansionem rediret non solum victor sed etiam in aeternum pace fundata volvens animo, quid ominis sibi occurreret, Aethiops quidam e numero militari, clarae inter scurras famae et celebratorum semper iocorum, cum corona e cupressu facta eidem occurrit. quem cum ille iratus removeri ab oculis praecepisset et coloris eius tactus omine et coronae, dixisse ille dicitur ioci causa: "totum fudisti, totum vicisti, iam deus esto victor."*

After inspecting the wall at Luguvallum (Carlisle) in Britain, he was returning to his nearby quarters as a conqueror who had firmly established peace for all time, wondering what omen might manifest itself before his eyes, when a black soldier from a *numerus*, a popular wag, well known for his constant practical jokes, ran up to him with a wreath of cypress branches. Severus, troubled by the man's ominous colour and by the equally ominous wreath, angrily ordered the man to be removed from his sight. But the black soldier is reported to have jokingly said, 'You have routed the world, you have conquered the world. Now, conqueror, become a god.'[129]

The *double entendre* 'become a god', of course, suggests 'meet your Maker' (as we might put it), and the whole anecdote attributes to this black man a disposition to make fun of the superstitious beliefs about black strangers. Like this black soldier, the black and Egyptian actors who were specially chosen for stage roles of people of the world of the dead similarly pandered to a popular stereotype of *Aethiopes* and were similarly disposed to play with the superstition about black strangers, for it cannot be assumed that they were all forced against their will to play these roles: some of them, at least, almost certainly had some independence of choice in the matter and were concerned only with earning a living and entertaining the public. Indeed, the particular instance of this sort of stage performance that our evidence associates with the ominous preludes to the assassination of the emperor Caligula was probably a drama inspired by Egyptian religious lore about the passion of the god Osiris.[130]

Yet there can hardly be any reasonable doubt that, in the minds of many illiterate and ill-educated folk, the Christian colour symbolism fortified the old pagan superstition which, as has already been noted, could lead to hostile behaviour towards black strangers. The Christian doctrine of the call to eternal salvation proclaimed the equality of all people before God, but it is of some significance that Christian leaders, almost in the manner of pagans like Seneca, offer 'apologies' for *Aethiops* blackness. The monk Meletius, in his work *De natura hominis*, attributes the diversity of human complexions to the Creator's loving care. Athanasius, like many a modern social psychologist, philosophically distinguishes 'the proper' in humankind (the essential defining attributes of rationality and mortal and immortal natures) from the 'subordinate' or 'non-essential' (colour, morphology, height, weight, and so on), which are due to 'accidents'. Boethius similarly proclaims the contrast between *rationale nigrum* (the black rational being) and *irrationale nigrum* (the black irrational creature), pointing out that it is only the non-essential or accidental quality *nigritudo* that creates the category *Aethiops*. Augustine in like manner proclaims that all people, of whatever colours and shapes, trace their origin to a single human form: 'Man was made one', and 'there are not several species of men as there are species of herbs, trees, fishes, birds, serpents, wild beasts, and grazing animals.'[131]

All this indicates the reality of a popular perception of *Aethiops* 'otherness' in many localities in the days of these writers. In such localities, as Courtès puts it, 'the symbolism of the black was so strong in influence that the theology of the divine image and likeness in man could do no better, all things considered, than to play down the nigritude − to pretend that it did not exist.'[132] Devisse similarly notes the 'contradictions', 'dreads and fears', 'enthusiasms and uncertainties' that were at work in many Christian minds with regard to the colour black and, by extension, in attitudes towards *Aethiopes*.[133] For undoubtedly the metaphorical usage of *Aethiops* linked images of the black to that of the Devil: hence, for instance, the pious warnings against 'Hell-black' temptresses into sexual sin.[134] Simple Christians in localities lacking familiarity with blacks must have found it very difficult to resist the notion that a person whose colour was the sign of sin and of the diabolical was himself a creature of the Devil. After all, even intellectuals of the early modern European world who were familiar with the appearance of blacks sometimes found it hard to resist that notion, and so the Frenchman Louis du May remarked of West Africa in 1681, 'the inhabitants are almost as black in soul as in body, and their bodies are as black as the paintings of demons that we see.'[135] One Roman account tells of the terror which the sight of the black Abba Moses brought upon the first monk he encountered in the desert during his flight from the law in quest of salvation (temporal and spiritual) and conversion to the Christian faith.[136]

J.M. Courtès concludes that, in the early Christian world, 'while the Ethiopians were in no sense relegated to spiritual ostracism, they suffered nonetheless by their metaphorical relationship with the demons' in the operation of colour symbolism.[137] Snowden expresses some dissatisfaction with that view, arguing that it is unlikely that blacks suffered 'in their day-to-day contacts with whites as a result of the metaphorical associations of this symbolism', and that Roman society in Christian as well as in pagan times 'was able to overcome whatever potential for serious anti-black sentiment there may be in color symbolism'. He rests his case on three points: the fact that the demonological texts are 'limited in scope', that Christian doctrine maintained 'the equality of the Ethiopians', and that a negative symbolism of blackness does not in itself mean antipathy to black people – all very true as generalizations, but hardly cogent grounds for dismissing colour symbolism as irrelevant to social relations in the specific case of Roman society.[138] This view shares with that of Courtès what is in fact the sole ground on which Courtès's conclusion is open to criticism at all: namely, the fact that it envisages 'the Ethiopians' and 'they' in blanket terms. In the light of the evidence it would be naive to suppose that the negative symbolism, however, lofty the intentions of the Christian exegesis, had no adverse effects at all on attitudes and behaviour towards humble black strangers, especially among the simple-minded and the illiterate in the several Roman communities where blacks happened at a given point in time to have been outside the normal local experience. But it is not legitimate to say more than that *some* blacks suffered ill consequences of the negative colour symbolism. For one thing, the role of personal status and deference-position cannot be overlooked. For another, the indications of black social integration discussed earlier are grounds for caution, even if the hagiographical anecdotes about Abba Moses clearly reflect attitudes of antipathy and apprehension of evil among simple-minded Christian folk in encounters with black strangers and the contemptuous behaviour that humble blacks sometimes met at the hands of whites of superior status. Sermons and conversations touching on black saints and monks like Abba Moses must have offered some reassurance to many a simple Christian mind, and familiarization with blacks (and, in consequence, intimate personal relations between individual blacks and whites) can hardly be presumed to have ceased to occur after the transition from paganism to Christianity.[139] The evidence so far considered suggests that the most significant factor in negative behaviour on the part of non-blacks towards blacks with whom they were personally unacquainted was the relative personal status of the individuals in the encounter. What distinguished an individual's attitude towards a black stranger from the same individual's attitude towards a white stranger was, *ceteris paribus*, personal unfamiliarity with *Aethiopes*, the cultural distance apparent in some blacks, and in some cases also superstitious beliefs arising from the deeply rooted symbolism of blackness.

THE IDEOLOGY OF ACCULTURATION

Ladislas Bugner noted that in Roman iconography the *Aethiops* is 'a figure that most distinctly expresses the differentiation of the foreigner.'[140] That perception of foreignness was at once somatic and cultural. In the absence of information to the contrary, Romans (like other human beings) will have tended to associate somatic strangeness with cultural alien-ness, and misperception of black strangers was obviously also aided by stereotypes and prior false beliefs. But, since the society was not racist, the problem will have been entirely constituted by the 'strangeness' of the black, and that establishes no more insuperable obstacle against social acceptance than does foreign birth.[141] Acceptance of a black into particular relationships clearly depended on the extent to which he had assimilated the ways of the host community. Correspondingly, the social distance observed with regard to a black stranger will have been the greater in proportion to the extent to which that stranger was perceived as unfamiliar with Roman norms or as a threat to Roman values.[142] It is noteworthy that Martial includes 'crinkly-haired blacks' in the category of foreigners in the city of Rome who are not so barbarian as to miss the opening of the Flavian amphitheatre, and who, though speaking languages of their own, are also Latin-speaking. Similarly, Lucian represents as 'the lowest of the low' in the slave population, not *Aethiopes*, but Lydians, Phrygians and Assyrians.[143] In social contexts where blackness is commonly associated with humble status *merely* because blacks are objectively people of humble status for the most part, the very system of status and deference ensures the social mobility of individual blacks who satisfy the operative criteria.[144] That was evidently the case in Roman society, where it was not at all inconsistent with the attested negativity of attitudes towards blacks – as Devisse seems to suggest for early Christian society when he observes (after attributing to blacks a *de facto* racial inequality), '*Yet* they were allowed to move upward in society, on two conditions: they had to get rich or demonstrate some ability entitling them to upward movement.'[145] The plain and simple truth is that this statement applies equally to humble folk of *all* colours and shapes in the Roman world. In the light of the foregoing discussion it may be assumed as a general principle that a Roman's perception of a black as 'different' was altered in a positive direction by assurances that that black was in fact Roman in culture and behaviour – unless it can be shown that the ideological system *discouraged* and distorted in Romans the natural human tendency to feel more comfortable in the company of people who exemplify the culturally familiar than in that of those exemplifying the unfamiliar. A brief discussion on Roman attitudes to cultural assimilation is thus appropriate.

Roman ideas of group temperaments and behavioural characteristics were much affected by the doctrine of the influence of the geographical milieu, but this doctrine was not a 'mechanistic' anthropogeography. The accepted notion of the remediability of ethnic, moral, and cultural defects was not linked in any mechanistic or essentialist manner to a change of geographical environment. In the sixteenth century, European intellectuals (who had inherited the basic beliefs of the classical anthropogeography) generally expected blacks to improve culturally if placed in a milieu (such as Europe) better than their tropical homelands, so Europeans of that era 'saw nothing extraordinary' in blacks in a European environment 'possessing talents equal to their own'.[146] Romans at all periods, accepted that 'barbarian' moral and behavioural defects could be socialized away, even in unfavourable habitats, by the civilizing influence of the Roman people, and their concept of an ethnic or national moral–behavioural trait as 'innate', like that of the early modern Europeans, meant 'deeply rooted', not 'ineradicable', so much more importance was attached to the role of the social and human environment in shaping culture than to that of geography and climate. The 'innate fraudulence' of the Carthaginians, for instance, was seen as a consequence not of nature (climate, geography, and biology), but of nurture, and all peoples were held to be equal in the capacity for learning and 'capable of attaining to excellence under the guidance of reason' in the appropriate social environment.[147] Nor did Romanocentrism result in blindness to 'the diversity of human cultures as a natural phenomenon arising from direct or indirect contacts between societies' (a criticism levied by Claude Lévi-Strauss against modern attitudes), even if it exemplifies what that same anthropologist in the same modern context describes as 'a false sociological evolutionism'.[148] For Roman intellectuals did postulate an almost unilinear process of 'development' within the *oecumene*: from savagery through barbarism to civilization; the degrees of cultural distance perceived in the various alien peoples were seen as stages on a ladder of 'development' which ended in the sort of material and moral culture that already marked the advanced peoples of the Mediterranean zone, the supreme example of which (in the apogee of imperial Rome) was Roman society itself. Just as a human group might have its passage along this developmental road accelerated by Roman assistance, so also 'development' was retarded or wholly prevented by isolation from such civilizing influences.[149]

This notion was the product of a mental and psychological process similar to that which Lévi-Strauss attributes to modern perceptions of cultural distance:

> Faced with the double temptation of condemning things that are offensive to him emotionally or of denying differences that are beyond his intellectual grasp, modern man has launched out on countless lines of philosophical and sociological speculation in a vain attempt to establish a compromise between these two

contradictory poles and to account for the diversity of cultures, while seeking at the same time to suppress what still shocks and offends him in that diversity.[150]

But, unlike many of their modern imperial counterparts, Romans accepted in an honest and realistic manner (despite their Romanocentrism) the human predicament here described by Lévi-Strauss. Just as medieval Christendom *wanted* the conversion of Jews and Muslims, so Romans wanted the elimination of systems of cultural otherness that offended them. This is a natural disposition, for 'if otherness is a scandal, the ideological system in which it is so perceived considers it eliminable'[151] – unless the context is that of an 'essentialist' ideology, such as those found in racist systems, where cultural otherness is simultaneously deprecated and perceived as irreversible, and 'the other' viewed with suspicion and distaste in proportion to his or her cultural proximity to the in-group. And a situation in which colour condemns the culturally assimilated to perpetual foreignness can hardly be seen as natural.[152]

Confidence in the superiority of their own system induced the Roman upper classes to show a consistent interest in the assimilation of Roman ways by other peoples, and especially by their ruling classes. To be sure, it has often been said that Romans did not impose their culture on other peoples.[153] But that is true only if one takes 'impose' in the crude sense of a hypothetical Roman official ordering Celtic barbarians (for example) to stop wearing trousers and don togas instead. It is more important to consider Roman attitudes towards Romanization and the fact that, in the geopolitical system dominated by Rome, inexorable social forces made Graeco-Roman culture a prerequisite for the individual's full realization of his or her talents and potential. Where necessary, the process was even overtly assisted by Roman officialdom.[154] Roman attitudes in this respect are clearly reflected in literature and art. In contrast with modern imperial powers, who have tended to prefer their 'natives' and other aliens in the 'unspoilt' state, the aliens whom Romans found preferable were the sort that most closely approximated to Roman ways; just as a preference for 'unspoilt natives' best suited the needs and interests of modern imperial powers in maintaining (as 'a rationalization of greed') the fantasy and false dogma of the irredeemability of the cultural and moral 'defects' of 'inferior' peoples, so the Roman preference for Romanized aliens harmonized with the Roman dogma representing alien cultural 'defects' as a scandal.[155] Thus, in officially commissioned art, barbarian enemies of the Roman order are intentionally depicted as wild savages, whereas Romanization is symbolically indicated by evenly-proportioned figures.[156] Similarly, the Roman attitude is clear in the younger Pliny's admiration of a perfectly Romanized Narbonese advocate, in Statius' enthusiastic commendation of an African who was as 'Italian' as one could possibly be, in Martial's laudation of a thoroughly Roman lady who was 'a descendant of woad-stained Britons', and in the elder Pliny's declaration that barbarians who remained unconquered by Rome (and so outside the Roman *Kulturwelt*) were unfortunate in the very fact of their political independence and cultural integrity – an ethnocentric affirmation of the Roman way of life (and a reflection on the Roman system of values) that evidently sums up the common attitude of the educated classes of the Roman world.[157]

That attitude, to be sure, called upon aliens in Roman society to make Romans 'the reference group in respect of language, manners and behaviour' (to use the words applied by Allport in a modern, but similar, context), and it exemplifies what in recent times has been negatively labelled 'the classical tradition of absolutist values' or pre-modern 'faiths in exclusive sets of values', in contrast with the 'faith in the pluralism of values' that has been much cherished by western intellectuals since the emergence of the science of anthropology in the nineteenth century, and is said to have given intellectuals 'both a new vision of the unity, and a new reverence for the diversity, of mankind.'[158] But it must not be forgotten that this 'pluralism' of values has not only never been given a mass acceptance in any modern society, but has often served as an excuse for bigoted opposition to the desire of others for social integration. Irritation at, or discouragement of, imitation of one's cutural norms by others can hardly be regarded as a *natural* human response, nor can an antipathy towards aliens that increases in proportion to the extent to which those aliens have assimilated themselves to one's culture. What Romans found odd and irritating in aliens exposed to Roman influences was failure and unwillingness to adapt and assimilate to Roman norms, and the obverse of this attitude was a prejudice which always led them to reward cultural conformism. Hence the annoyance of a Philostratus (*Vita Apoll.*, V

128

33), for instance, at the aloofness of Jews, their 'unsocial existence', and the fact that (as he saw it) 'they have nothing in common with other men, either food, or libations, or prayers, or sacrifices', and are therefore an unwelcome anomaly in the Roman world, 'more remote in those respects from us than Susa or Bactria, and more alien than the Indians' despite the greater geographical remoteness of the latter and the fact that they are outside the Roman empire. Philostratus evidently could not say this about any other body of aliens (*Aethiopes*, for instance) which, in his experience, resided within the Roman *Kulturwelt*. The Roman tradition of 'absolutist' values had at least the merit of basing differential treatment of individuals upon individual qualities judged in terms of cultural conformism, and so, however unequal the resulting treatment of individuals, that treatment was of the sort which (according to social psychologists) is not properly classed as 'discrimination'.[159]

IDEAL AND ESTEEMED SOMATIC TRAITS

A doctrine that seeks to explain the somatic diversity of peoples as a function of geographical milieu inevitably raises the question of whether somatic forms can be modified by migration and changes of climatic environment. In Europe in the fifteenth and sixteenth centuries the same anthropogeographical notions that had guided Roman intellectual thought actually inspired expectations that blacks transported to temperate climates would in due course shed their colour, and it was not until the late sixteenth century that these expectations began to be dismissed as baseless.[160] In the Roman world, some intellectuals (following a line of reasoning that went back to Posidonius) held that some modification of 'ethnic' physique was ultimately to be expected if a people migrated and settled in a different climate, but that belief is rarely expressed in the literature, and not at all in allusions to *Aethiopes*. A proverb of Greek origin in fact acknowledged the impossibility of 'washing an *Aethiops* white', and this clearly reflects the popular understanding of the matter in Roman society, at least after the third century BC.[161] Of course, European thinkers of the fifteenth and sixteenth centuries laboured under certain mental constraints imposed by the Christian doctrine of humankind's genesis which, allied to the old classical anthropogeographical notions, naturally led to the postulate that all people were originally white and that, where this primordial physique had been changed by climate, it could in due course be restored by the appropriate kind of climate. But the Roman intellectual tradition was established in an ambience free from such mental constraints, and it was much easier for Romans to reason (as they did) that, however much human physique was influenced by climate and geography, somatic traits were biologically transmitted, irrespective of habitat, by parents and inherited even from distant ascendants. The widespread Roman belief in 'regeneration' and in 'maternal impression' has frequently been noted, but even Christian doctrine maintained that, once the bodies of *Aethiopes* had become blackened by the rays of a sun hotter in Aethiopia than elsewhere, a *natural* blackness thereafter persisted in members of that '*gens*' as a result of 'biological inheritance of the defect.'[162]

This notion of blackness (*nigredo, nigritudo*) as a somatic defect (*vitium*) relates to the concept of 'somatic norm image' formulated by Hoetink, which is a valuable tool in the study of attitudes towards blacks in a context such as that of ancient Roman society, where the attitudes hinge on the 'strangeness' of the black anthropological type.[163] Hoetink maintains that every society (or societal segment, in the case of plural societies) has a distinct image of the appropriate or ideal or preferred form of human physical appearance, and that is as soundly based as is the view that each society at a given point in time has an image of 'ideal social types' (the images the average member of a society has as to the sort of person – soldier, entrepreneur, television personality, and so on – that he or she should ideally become).[164] Just as a society's ideal social type is subject to shifts and changes in consequence of changing socioeconomic realities, so too perceptions of 'appropriateness' of somatic appearance are modifiable (albeit with less dramatic rapidity) under the influence of social, economic, and political stimuli. Somatic norm images are governed by cultural habituation, and since the socialization that moulds people's attitudes in this respect is a continuous process, there is always the possibility of variations of preference between social classes in the same society.

A good illustration of this process and of its social–psychological consequences has been given by Hiroshi Wagatsuma in a study of Japanese perceptions from very early times. This study finds (*inter alia*) an idealization of feminine plumpness and roundness of face

130

yielding to idealization of slimness and facial slenderness in the female sex. Straight black hair was until the 1920s an imperative of both male and female beauty, and hair-straightening processes were adopted by persons whose natural hair did not conform to the ideal type. In the 1920s 'a subtle, not fully conscious trend toward idealization of Western features' gained momentum and became particularly pronounced after the Second World War, favouring curling and dyeing of naturally black and straight female hair, as well as plastic-surgical imitations of the 'Caucasian' appearance. But the constant in the Japanese somatic norm image over the centuries has been the Japanese type of whiteness of skin (often described in the west as 'yellow'): it has always been esteemed as beautiful, and remained an imperative of feminine beauty, lauded as 'snow-white' and artificially heightened by cosmetics, even when the bronzed complexion of the warrior had become the masculine ideal.[165]

Before the first century BC, the Mediterranean type of 'Caucasian' physiognomy with pale-brown (*albus*) skin and brown eyes represented the Roman somatic norm image, but a somewhat paler complexion symbolized feminine aristocratic privilege, and this *femineus pallor* was accordingly regarded in polite society as an essential mark of the feminine ideal of beauty, even if dark-complexioned women like the Carthaginian maid in Plautus' *Poenulus* could also be seen as beautiful.[166] The image of the preferred male appearance seems to have remained constant and without significant class variations throughout the era of the high empire; although fair-haired males like the Romanized German prince Italicus and Apuleius' fictional character Lucius, and swarthy men like the playwright Terence, are described as handsome, the literature dating from before the end of the third century AD generally presents as preferable a pale-brown 'Mediterranean' complexion (*inter nigrum et pallidum*, or 'slightly red and tawny whiteness', or 'neither white like a woman's nor over-bronzed like a slave's'), brown hair, straight (but not 'long') nose, and the moderate Mediterranean tallness.[167] But the importation of blond northern slave girls, together with the influence of Hellenistic fashions and tastes, introduced a change in the feminine ideal. Just as in the late nineteenth century the traditional Japanese idealization of feminine 'snow-whiteness' favoured a ready appreciation of the even paler complexion of 'Caucasian' females who 'did not need to have the help of powder and rouge',[168] so too Roman society's experience of 'nordic' feminine whiteness established the model of the blond, 'milk-white', and rosy-cheeked beauty in upper-class circles in the first century BC; thereafter smart Roman women whose natural complexions exemplified the feminine norm anyway emphasized their *femineus pallor* by the use of cosmetics, while the darker sort of woman (if she was fashionable) took pains to acquire a lighter complexion by creaming and bleaching.[169] Though the blond hair of barbarian males continued to be seen as comic, feminine blondness became highly fashionable in Roman society, and women habitually transformed themselves from natural brunettes into artificial blonds, using either dyes or wigs manufactured from natural blond hair clipped from barbarian heads.[170]

The bleached blond (but dark-eyed) look, though normally available to Mediterranean women only by artificial means, was lauded by writers (especially poets) as the ideal feminine type: they eulogized the golden blond hair, the dark eyes, the rosy (rouge-tinted) cheeks, and the 'ivory-white' or 'snow-white' or 'milk-white' faces, arms, necks, breasts and legs of this *candida* ideal, and mocked the deep ruddy tan of the peasant woman, whose colour betrayed regular exposure to the sun and ignorance of the refinements of the fashionable toilette.[171] In several epigrams Martial satirizes the artificiality of the contemporary feminine fashion, but he cannot conceal the attraction that the blond look holds for him, and his rationale is that 'rare things please one' (*rara iuvant*), though in his perception this blondness is appropriate only in women and in 'Ganymedes'. The puritanical Church leader Tertullian, with unequivocal hostility to the wig-wearing and hair-dyeing fashion, points to their health risks and ironically attributes the vogue for artificial blondness among the women of his Romano-African flock to an inferiority complex about their ethnic identity and a sense of regret that they were not born Germans or Gauls, but the ladies know that the true explanation is the current male preference for the blond look: 'We change our hair-colour to blond because gentlemen find us more attractive that way.'[172] This male attitude obviously explains Heliodorus' representation of his fictional 'Aethiopian' beauty Chariclea as golden blond.

But in a society in which the normal hair colour was brown, this blond ideal, with its heavy dependence on artificiality, was inevitably fragile. In a comparable cult of the blond and fair female look in fifteenth-century Spain and Portugal, upper-class women, under the influence of foreign fashions, came to see a swarthy complexion *in a woman* as ugly, so they took to the habit of painting their faces 'a white and red tint' and dyeing their hair blonde. But this was 'not a genuine expression of national taste' in either of these countries, where *most* men continued to prefer the swarthy Latin look in women, despite the attraction that feminine fairness held for males of the leisured classes.[173] The same would seem to have been true of Roman society. When Roman writers bow to the demands of conventional values or of high fashion only to the extent of offering 'apologies' for preferences and perceptions of female beauty that do not follow those dictates, they thereby show that, even among the leisured classes, the realities of daily life often bore little relation to the fashionable ideal. While the fashionable traits of female beauty lauded in the literature include the blond look (along with dark eyes, nose of modest size and length, height neither diminutive nor excessive, figure slim but not thin, breasts of modest size, and good gait), they also include hair of the colours dark brown, 'raven-black', honey-brown, and tawny. Men similarly found some dark-skinned women and short women beautiful, even if literary convention induced apologetic descriptions of them as 'black *but* beautiful' and the like, or apologetic similes likening their beauty to that of coals, which, when kindled, shine like rose-buds, or to dark violets and hyacinths.[174]

But some texts underscore the reality of unfashionable beauty when they handle the theme of men's 'blindness' to physical defects in their lady-loves. Roman adepts in the psychology of love noted that the besotted lover 'assigns to his beloved certain marks of excellence that she does not actually possess', seeing a dwarfish girl as 'a real cutie – from head to toe', a huge and ungainly Amazon as 'every inch a lady', a bundle of skin and bones as 'my slim gazelle', or a fat and big-breasted one as 'my Ceres'.[175] Even in upper-class circles, the blond *candida* ideal evidently often remained a mere ideal or cliché, as habituation effaced in individuals the narrowness of fashionable perceptions of beauty.[176] As for the broad masses, literary contrasts between the aesthetic values of Romans and those of other peoples indicate that most Romans remained untouched by upper-class fashion and maintained a general preference for the northern Mediterranean colour and features.[177] Most of the minority of ordinary Romans who happened to have been influenced by upper-class fashion no doubt kept the ideal of the blond and 'milk-white' beauty safely compartmentalized from everyday reality. Evidently, too, what is said about the blindness of the male lover will have been even more true of the female perspective, and particularly so at the lower levels of society.

The homage generally paid to the somatic norm image in upper-class circles is reflected in expressions of the sentiment 'black *but* beautiful', in references to black handsomeness as a kind of beauty that somehow transcends the purely somatic, and in descriptions of physique in documents from the Roman province of Egypt which repeatedly mention fairness of skin and straightness of nose.[178] Even when the references convey the notion 'black *and* beautiful', some accompanying note of 'apology' is sounded in deference to the dictates of the traditional and dominant values. Particularly instructive is Origen's exegesis of the *Song of Songs*, in which the biblical 'black bride', addressing the 'daughters of Jerusalem', declares: 'I am black and beautiful' (*melaina eimi kai kalē*, or, in the Latin version, *nigra sum et speciosa*). Origen recognizes that notion as one demanding explanation in a socio-cultural ambience dominated by a value system which holds whiteness of skin as a more or less essential constituent of beauty (especially female beauty). In that value system, this biblical text in its literal sense accordingly poses the questions, 'In what way is the spouse black?' and 'How can she be beautiful without whiteness?' Gregory of Elvira admits to being confused by the doctrine relating to this spouse as symbol of the Church among the gentiles, and so he asks, 'How can the Church say that she is black *and* beautiful, or beautiful if black?' Origen explains that the scriptural black spouse, allegorically representing the pagan converted to Christianity, continues after penitence to be black in soul from past sins; but this penitence nonetheless bestows in the interim a kind of beauty – 'something of what may be called an Aethiopian beauty' – pending the coming of the full white beauty that will be conferred by God's grace.[179] Throughout the discussions of these leaders of the Church, to be sure, the accent is on *spiritual* blackness and whiteness – on the symbolic equation of the bride with the Church of the gentiles and of blackness with sin, but the exegeses also reflect the values of the temporal and secular world in which whiteness of skin was generally regarded as an essential element of beauty, and which attached a high esteem to

conventional marks of beauty while generally finding '*Aethiops*
beauty' a difficult concept to comprehend and accorded little
favour to it, even as an acknowledged reality.[180] And for some
Romans black beauty evidently *was* a reality. For adaptation was a
two-way process, affecting the outlook of blacks in Roman
communities no less that that of members of the host community.

Several Roman comments on *Aethiopes* and on 'paleface'
barbarians attest to sensory aversions to what Romans called the
'shape' of such persons. A 'shape' (*aspectus, habitus, morphē, idea*) was
the totality of the visual impact made on one person by another: it
was not only a matter of natural somatic traits, for it included
dress, hairstyle, ornaments, facial make-up, and other visual effects
of cosmetic titivation, of hygienic or unhygienic habits, and of
affluence or indigence, and it could therefore be greatly modified
by human effort. The evidence suggests that Romans (and
especially those of the leisured classes) tended to focus on the
'artificial' aspects of 'shapes' as much as (and sometimes even
more than) they did on the natural somatic features. Crinkly
Aethiops hair, blond and greased German locks, and Celtic trousers
were among the ingredients of the alien 'shapes' that particularly
aroused sensory aversion and offended the aesthetic sensibilities of
Romans of the upper classes. An extremely alien 'shape' constituted
a *monstrum* (a disgusting freak), and it seems clear that among the
Roman upper classes reactions to such a shape differed little or not
at all from reactions to the sight of (for example) a dirty, blear-
eyed, snub-nosed Italian beggar with unkempt hair and shabby,
tattered clothing.[181] But even in the case of *Aethiopes*, cultural
assimilation included a Romanization of 'shape' – an index of a
process of socialization and adaptation which also modified
perceptions of somatic distance both on the part of blacks and on
that of the Roman whites with whom they associated. Winkes
(*ANRW* I.4, 909) pointed to examples of this Romanized black look
in Roman portraiture, indicating also that in the iconography it
usually occurs in portraits of well-to-do black men and women who
occupied positions of some esteem in Roman society. Black
courtesans, for example, achieved this Romanized black appearance
by their use of cosmetics, wigs, dress, and jewellery, and in their
general deportment.[182]

But the homage to the somatic norm image indicated by Origen
and others was often openly expressed in the form of mocking

comments on conspicuously distant deviations from that norm. The sort of mockery that poets directed at the complexions of Italian peasant women naturally also attended the very dark-skinned (and, *a fortiori*, the *Aethiops*) woman, whose complexion was even more distant from the norm, let alone from the fashionable *candida* ideal, and so some black women must quite often have felt the need of props for their self-esteem – as Ovid suggests when he makes a dark-complexioned lady take psychological support from the legend of Perseus' love for the beautiful and swarthy-hued 'Aethiopian' princess, Andromeda.[183] The biographer of the emperor Heliogabalus suggests a widespread upper-class conception of the least attractive woman as one who is both old and black, and in sixth-century Carthage, Luxorius, taking 'white' (indeed *candida*, as distinct from pale-brown) as typifying beautiful and 'black' as typifying ugly, satirized a contemporary lover of 'hideous and ugly black girls.'[184] But behind Luxorius' jibe is the assumption that some of his own peers, like the third-century emperor Heliogabalus, were attracted to black women. Notable, too, is the fact that the anonymous author of the already cited Pompeian graffito on the theme of prostitutes extols the sex appeal of black girls (or of a particular black girl in one of the city's brothels) without any allusion to the subject of beauty: his interest is entirely on what, for him, was evidently a more important consideration, namely, sexual attraction.[185] Similarly the peasant of *Moretum* is depicted as a man fully comfortable in, and satisfied with, the familiar company of a black slave woman as his sole house-companion, even if the author of the poem (like Luxorius) mocks the ugliness of this companion in the squalid life of her peasant master.[186]

Luxorius, whose jibes extend to dwarfs and dwarfish types, hunchbacks, old maids 'with elephant-like hides and faces', and ugly people in general, may strike the modern reader as 'most unkind to those afflicted with human failings and physical defects.'[187] But this 'cruelty' and mocking behaviour is no personal aberration. It accords with a deeply rooted Roman tendency to ridicule 'inappropriate' personal characteristics of all kinds, physical and non-physical. Romans even assumed that the physically handicapped god Hephaestus (or Vulcan) suffered daily mocking at the hands of his fellow deities on the grounds of his physical disability. Weird creatures of all kinds were objects of amused derision, though some provoked the even more negative reactions of fright and disgust.[188] Martial writes of a German mask, a Roman potter's caricature of a 'red haired Batavian' (evidently bearing a grotesque 'northern barbarian' appearance) which provoked derision in adults and the fear of a bogey in boys. Fright and disgust are stressed by Philostratus with regard to an 'Indian woman, black from head to breasts and white from breasts to toes'; but he also suggests that, even with a freak of this sort, familiarization eliminated the horror. Similar is Lucian's account of two *monstra*, one of which inspired fright and the other both fright and disgust among people unfamiliar with such 'novelties', but mere amusement and laughter among the more worldly-wise: a 'completely black' Bactrian camel, and 'a man of two colours, half jet-black (*akribōs melas*) and half extremely white (*es hyperbolēn leukos*), with the colours equally divided.' The negative reaction evidently related in part to the negative symbolism of the colour black in both cases, though Lucian attributes the absence of a popular reaction of admiration – in the case of the half-white man – to the strength of traditional aesthetic values which set great store by symmetry and 'beauty of form and line', and condemned to ridicule any incongruous and 'inappropriate' blend of whiteness and blackness, since 'even the combination of two fine things can be monstrous, the beauty of each being lost in the combination.'[189]

Caricature and mocking, then (in literature, art, and daily life), was far from being limited to alien somatic traits like those of the *Aethiops* and the northern 'paleface'; it was all-embracing, not even sparing gods, mythical heroes, and Romans of the highest social ranks. Most people lived at some risk of ridicule. The popular slogans included 'Better to make a joke than to *be* a joke' and 'Better to lose a friend than to lose the chance of a joke'.[190] Lack of a respectable income made one a target of open mockery and humiliation, and the great hope of every humble person of at least modest ambition was 'to live without being a joke to anyone, as a man among men, and to be able to walk with one's head held high.'[191] Walking in this manner was a privilege and a status symbol of the magnate and the comfortably-off: the symbols of humble status, no less than 'inappropriate' and odd alien dress or the sight of a lone raven amidst white swans, or a tiny black African on the back of an enormous elephant, attracted ridicule.[192] But mocking behaviour assumed several forms and dimensions: 'laughing down' (*deridere*) was more offensive both in intention and in effect than 'laughing at' (*ridere*).[193] The gentle dimensions (*ludimus innocui* is Martial's description) were jesting, banter or badinage, light irony, and practical joking, but mockery might also be cutting or brutally offensive disparagement and derision that 'drew blood'.[194] The victim of blood-drawing ridicule and disparagement was expected to feel anger, hurt, shame, or self-hate, whereas a similar reaction to mere teasing would be a sign of an inferiority complex – what Lucian calls 'pettiness of mind' (*micropsychia*).[195] But if, as Lucian implies, the *micropsychia* was often exhibited by men and women of the leisured classes in response to mockery, it was probably even more characteristic of the reactions of the humbler members of society, to whom the everyday realities of social and economic life offered far fewer grounds for self-esteem in the face of public disparagement, particularly when this treatment came from complete strangers. This *micropsychia* was no doubt particularly marked among people who were both humble in status and physically 'flawed', and it is evident that mocking of somatic 'defects' (including *communia vitia* like those of the *Aethiops* and the northern 'paleface') was sometimes highly upsetting and hurtful to the victim. The explicit references to this 'hurt', while indicating that the status and charisma of some blacks exempted them from hurtful treatment, suggest that those who did fall victim to it often reacted with feelings such as anger, tears, shame, self-hate, and of being less than 'a man among men' (as one of Petronius' fictional characters puts it).[196] For that reason we may suppose that they must also have been driven to develop ego defences of various kinds, for instance, avoidance of potential mockers where possible; seeking comfort, security, and self-respect in the bosom of an Isiac or other *collegium*; seeking revenge on mockers and potential mockers where possible (by cheating or harming them in some way when it seemed safe to do so); acting out (in protective clowning, for instance) the role or roles suggested by the disparagement; or the more positive defence mechanism of a powerful striving for success in a world whose popular slogans included 'A man's purse determines his worth' and 'Money makes the ugly handsome', and in which (as Seneca puts it) 'none are more ready to trample on others than those whom personal experience of insults has taught to be insulting.'[197] Luxorius suggests that the ego defence devised by one contemporary victim of public mockery, a hunchback, was the fantasy of noble lineage, and the unkind poet takes pleasure in puncturing this defence with the remark that the man's physical deformity is proof enough of his real ancestry.[198] We can never know for certain, but the career of many a black as popular practical joker (that of the black 'prankster' of the military *numerus* in Britain, for instance) may well have started as a defence mechanism of this sort.[199]

It has, however, been established that the notion of being treated as 'a man among men' (*homo inter homines*), or as less than human – a notion which loomed large in the minds of the humble in Roman society – can have nothing to do with race prejudice, as some have believed in respect of applications of this pattern of thought to humble blacks.[200] In societies organized, like that of the ancient Romans, on the premise of inequality of 'estates' or 'orders' (*ordines*), there is often a tendency among the upper ranks to see the lower orders as 'non-men' or 'less than human'.[201] The attitude is reflected in the soliloquy attributed by the hagiography to Abba Moses, which makes him see himself as disparagingly as his social betters see him – as subhuman (*mē anthrōpos*). For even though in this particular case the mocking epithets 'Blackface' (*Aithiops*) and 'Black one' (*melane*) are almost certainly Christian metaphorical expressions of the notion 'Creature of the Devil' and are applied in a religious context, they none the less also reflect a secular pattern of disparagement of a humble 'sooty-skinned' folk as less than men among men (*homines inter homines*). This pattern, which is also evident in the epigrammatic derision of humble black as *faex* ('riff-raff', or 'shit'), human only in speech, seems comparable with that of the Arab world of the seventh and eighth centuries in which a 'white' fellow poet could ridicule the black poet Nusayb in the verses

> I saw Nusayb astray *among men*;
> > his color was that of *cattle*.
> You can tell him by his shining blackness;
> > even if he be oppressed, he has the *dark face of an oppressor*.

Nusayb retorted, 'all he has done is call me black, and he speaks the truth;' but his ego defence, no less than that attributed to Abba Moses (a will to succeed as a holy monk), highlights the handicap borne by humble blacks: 'Blackness does not *diminish me* . . ./the verses of my poems are *my lineage*!/ How much better a keen-minded, clear spoken/black than a mute white!'[202]

In Roman society the contrast between human and subhuman was a distinction between socioeconomic categories (which in the province of Egypt amounted also to a distinction between *cultural* categories). It is the same distinction (demarcating rustic clodhopper from polished and urbane gentleman, or Hellenic and Hellenized from 'imperfectly civilized Egyptian peasant') as rendered the word 'Egyptian' itself a derogatory epithet in the language of the propertied and leisured classes of society in Egypt. The distinction is voiced in precisely that manner by a member of the privileged classes who writes to some of his friends in mock-apologetic tones, 'Perhaps, my brothers, you think I am some barbarian or *subhuman* Egyptian' (*Aigyptios anathrōpos*).[203] The same derogatory concept is expressed in Latin by *agrestis ac inhumanus* ('uncivilized peasant' or 'subhuman peasant')[204], and it is interesting to note that an imperial *epistula* of AD 215 reflects this ideology of status, ordering the expulsion of all 'Egyptians' from the city of Alexandria, particularly 'the countryfolk who have fled from other parts' and who, 'by the numbers of *their kind* and their *uselessness*, are disturbing the city' to which they have fled from their own districts 'to escape rustic toil'. The document goes on to exempt from this ban those who have come as tourists 'to view the glorious city of Alexandria' or to enjoy 'a more civilized life (*politikōtera zōē*) or for incidental business.' And it also confidently declares that 'the *true Egyptian* (*alēthinoi Aigyptioi*) can easily be recognized by his speech, which proves him to have assumed the appearance and dress of another class; moreover in his mode of life his far from civilized manners (*enantia ēthē apo anastrophēs poleitikēs*) show that he belongs to the category 'Egyptian peasant' (*agroikoi Aigyptioi*).'[205] In Roman Egypt 'Greeks' (a category that included Hellenized Egyptians) and Jews alike 'scorned or disliked the peasants of the soil' (the *agroikoi Aigyptioi*), 'and wished to hold themselves aloof.'[206]

Even in the absence of personal experience of overt and public disparagement, some people with distinct somatic 'defects' (such as *Aethiopes*) no doubt felt about their conspicuous distance from the Roman somatic norm image a self-consciousness or a 'mortification' similar to that noted by Rogler among 'palefaces' in Puerto Rico or that which the African Equiano admitted in himself in eighteenth-century England.[207] But blacks in Roman society did not constitute a single socio-cultural category; nor were there any such categories consisting exclusively of blacks. And whatever the sense of abuse or of oppression felt by members of socio-cultural categories like the 'subhuman Egyptian', these were nonetheless in principle open-ended categories, not closed to all escape by any deterministic ideology – hence the not undistinguished careers of black entertainers, or that of an Abba Moses (who entered the Church after a long life as slave and desperado); or the similar careers of the several other humble blacks who became monks and earned respect; or that of the celebrated 'Jew-baiter' Apion, who, though of indigenous Egyptian stock, was not an *Aigyptios ananthrōpos*, but a prominent member of the 'Hellenic' ruling class of Roman Alexandria. The fundamental element in the distinction of social categories was property and income: the 'Hellenes' of partly or wholly indigenous Egyptian ancestry were all people of considerable wealth, largely concentrated in Alexandria and the Delta, for, in general, only the wealthy and important families among the indigenous population possessed the means of acquiring a thorough education and Hellenization.[208]

Since the rights and obligations of the individual person are an aspect of the structure of society, the 'problem' surrounding blacks in the Roman world, as in late medieval Tuscany and in seventeenth-century England, can be related entirely to the issues of personal status and black 'strangeness' – somatic as well as cultural in the case of relative newcomers (especially 'heathen' newcomers in Christian times). The attitudes underlying disparaging comments on the physiognomy of blacks were no different in kind from those shown by (for instance) Viking references to North American Indians as 'those swarthy and ugly men' who 'arrange their hair in an unpleasant fashion', or disparaging comments by early modern Europeans on the somatic features of Malays and Eskimos, or on the 'horrid Curles' and 'disfigured' lips and noses of black Africans, or on the 'large Breastes' of negro women.[209] In those more recent societies, as in the Roman world, this perception of ugliness was linked with a tendency to associate negro blackness with 'the soiled and dirty' and with the sun-darkened complexions of the local labouring classes; the fact that, in people's experience, blacks in these societies were mostly humble folk, also gave rise to a tendency to associate blacks with humble status. But people adapted to the initially strange sight of black faces – as is only to be expected in situations where the more powerful segments in the society do not have any vested interest in popular antipathy towards blacks; and humble blacks, like humble people in general, could move up the social scale depending on their possession of the appropriate attributes universally acknowledged in the society as deference-entitling (which, in the Christian societies, included Christian baptism), though the poor and indigent black, *qua* poor and indigent person, naturally suffered the extreme privations, the grim struggle for survival, the squalor, the rightlessness and the lack of social justice that went in all these societies with what Juvenal sarcastically called the 'liberty of the poor man' in relation to his own society: poverty and lack of personal independence in a pre-industrial society.[210] In Elizabethan England, for example, blacks underwent a process of cultural assimilation, and some were 'securely lodged at various social levels' of that society, some as 'humble but prosperous Englishmen', some as 'firm favourites' in wealthy households, protected by the wealth and rank of their masters.[211] For this reason it is important to consider the question of personal behaviour and attitudes towards blacks in Roman society in relation to personal status.

THE IDEOLOGY OF STATUS

Status was evidently the major factor in the regulation of Roman social relations. Social behaviour is always based on some degree of either appreciation or derogation of the relative worth of the other, assessed on the basis of individual perceptions of deference-entitling properties in their various weights and measures, even if 'in most actions the appreciative and derogatory elements are mingled with others like commanding, coercing, cooperating, purchasing, loving' and so on.[212] But not all qualities admired and esteemed by a society are deference-relevant or significant of the location of people in that society's stratification system. For instance, deference is distinct from the esteem attached to personal qualities (as Lucian clearly indicates in the case of Roman society in his contrast between appreciation of beauty and strength on the one hand, and 'respect' for an occupational role on the other hand).[213] In relation to modern western societies, social scientists distinguish from deference-relevant factors such qualities as kindness, manliness, tallness, obesity and their opposites, while they include among deference-entitling properties occupational role, accomplishment in an occupational role, wealth, type of wealth, income, mode of acquisition of income, lifestyle, level of educational attainment, political or corporate power, connections (by kinship or otherwise) with persons of high status, 'performance on behalf of the community or society in relation to external communities or societies', 'possession of objective acknowledgements of deference like titles or ranks', and ethnicity.[214]

In Roman society the esteemed or disparaged qualities which lacked deference-relevance included (along with moral qualities and behavioural traits like kindness or alcoholism) physical 'virtues' and 'defects' like beauty, ugliness, thinness, obesity, whiteness and blackness of skin, and the facial and general somatic morphology of the various anthropological types; ethnicity was deference-relevant only in so far as it could function as symbol of the prestige (or lack of it) of an individual's area of origin (*origo*) or of a particular degree of proximity to (or distance from) Roman urbanity and Roman cultural norms in the case of strangers about whom no other information was available. In Roman comments of the sort contained in the epitaph declaring that a black slave's non-physical qualities compensated for the defects of his physical blackness, the inherent notions of esteem and disparagement are of the kind that bear no relation to deference and status.[215] The deference-entitling properties all related in some way to one or more of the three dimensions of the stratification-system: rank or 'estate' (*ordo*), economic class (level of wealth and income), and power (in the widest sense of the term). Each person's status was an amalgam of acknowledged positions on each of these dimensions: their deference-positions summed up their ratings in terms of the various deference-entitling properties and the relative weights attached to each. It was on these deference-entitlements that attitudes and behaviour towards blacks (as towards all members of the population) evidently hinged: rank, property and income-level, mode of acquisition of income, power and authority, degree of personal independence, connections (relative proximity to persons in powerful social roles, including the primordial connection with dead and living persons of high or humble status which we call 'birth'), occupational role and performance in that role, style of life, educational attainment, and contribution to one's community's or to the whole society's charisma.[216] While the superior deference-worthiness of certain occupational roles was beyond question (the 'liberal' role of advocate compared with the 'vulgar' role of barber or auctioneer, for instance), cases of status-inconsistency occurred frequently, arising from individual combinations of high ratings in respect of some of the deference-entitling properties and low ratings in respect of others: for instance, a millionaire ex-slave whose low rank and level of education were inconsistent with his great wealth and economic power; or a slave in the emperor's household who possessed slaves of his own and lived in luxury and affluence, but was at the same time legally the chattel of another person; or an ex-slave in the imperial service who, by virtue of his powerful connections, amassed great wealth, exercised great influence, and commanded deference 'from all but the highest aristocracy', but had a low rating in terms of rank. The black 'Hercules' and the black jockey lauded by Luxorius and lionized by their townsmen and townswomen also provide examples of this status-inconsistency – men with low status-ratings in terms of birth, rank and occupation (the 'vulgar' occupation of public entertainer as *venator* or *auriga*), but possessing very high ratings in terms of performance in their occupational roles, considerably high ratings in terms of income, and (overall) an enormous popular esteem.[217]

Behaviour was governed in large measure by this sense of hierarchy, and dishonour accrued from 'marrying down' socially (*impares nuptiae*), as is emphasized in Claudian's emotive picture of barbarian blacks wedding noble Roman ladies, and equally in Apuleius' romance. The negative properties from which the negative deference positions of Claudian's black barbarians derive include ethnicity, but only because in their cases ethnicity functions as a symbol of barbarism.[218] An inscription offering advice to 'all who desire to live a good and free life' emphasizes deference by enjoining its readers, in the first place, to 'show respect where it is due', and secondly, to 'desire your master's good.'[219] Such behaviour was ideologically demanded not only of slaves, but of social inferiors in general. Every Roman citizen was born into a clearly defined rank (*ordo*): either one of the the three ranks of 'respectable people' (*honestiores*) – senatorial (*clarissimus*), equestrian (*egregius*), and curial – or the broad plebeian rank of so-called 'commoners' (*humiliores*). In addition, the population embraced the *ordo* of ex-slaves and the categories of free non-citizens and of slaves. The link between rank, income, and power found expression *inter alia* in the legally recognized minimum property-ratings (*census*) required for membership of the higher

144

ranks, and in the fact that people of those higher orders (the *honestiores*) formed the ruling class whose members, even when miscreants, must be treated with respect and not like common plebeian criminals.[220] Humble men received more severe and more degrading sentences in the courts than *honestiores* found guilty on the same charge, and people of low status had little or no prospect of success as plaintiffs in civil actions against people of high status. The dual-penalty system reserved for people of humble status capital sentences like crucifixion and *damnatio ad bestias* (a mauling to death by wild animals in the arena), and the harsher non-capital penalties like hard labour in the mines, flogging, and chained imprisonment. Nor were *humiliores* allowed to bring against their 'betters' civil actions like those of fraud, theft, and grievous bodily harm, for such charges, by their very nature, would involve derogation of the respectability (*honestas*) of people of rank and high status and a denial of the deference (*reverentia*) that was their due.[221]

While the 'respectable' were separated from 'commoners' by a great gulf of status and privilege, the ranks of the 'respectable' were themselves distinguished from each other by important degrees of status. But the orders were not closed castes: despite the great emphasis on maintenance of the boundaries of rank, there was always some degree of social mobility, as individuals with the requisite education, wealth, drive, luck, and connections rose in the hierarchy of ranks and economic grades, or some unfortunates became declassed. Army veterans and their children, for instance, automatically ranked as 'respectable', enjoying a prestige that was due at once to their station as honourably discharged soldiers and to ownership of the property that their occupation permitted them to acquire. This applied specifically to ex-soldiers who were Roman citizens, but the prestige of the military also attended those like the black soldier of the Britain-based *numerus* who probably never became Roman citizens.[222] None of the available evidence otherwise suggests that any black person held a Roman rank (inherited or earned) above that of commoner. Despite the satirists, we may be sure that any black bastards fathered on upper-class women by black men will have been rapidly disposed of as unwanted infants: any *de facto* bastards arising from such adulterous unions and yet brought up as upper-class children will have been of a somatic appearance perceived, not as *Aethiops* (which would have rendered avoidance of the scandal and the penalties of adultery practically impossible), but as white or swarthy.

The slogans 'Money is king' and 'Your purse determines your worth' did not accurately reflect the attitude of all commoners, and still less so that of 'respectable' people. Wealth, after all, was not exactly synonymous with power (*potentia*), which Cicero aptly described as 'the possession of resources sufficient for preserving one's own interests and weakening those of others.'[223] Wealth was not the only constituent of what Cicero calls 'resources', but it was the basic ingredient. A large income was a prerequisite for the good life, for leisure, for a variety of status symbols, and, for the freeborn, it was also the essential basis of personal independence.[224] Accordingly, wealth that was not paraded for admiration as a symbol of status and power was seen as 'useless to its possessor' and as practically non-existent.[225] Roman literature is replete with such observations, which must be taken as expressions (however exaggerated) of social values and attitudes: a rich man whose riches cannot be seen is 'no better than a tramp'; money makes people 'handsome, wise and strong, lending them honour and esteem' and bringing them admiration, renown, and 'homage from all', including the favours of women, since it precludes its possessor from being 'wholly ugly'. Not only was handsomeness not deference-relevant; a wealthy person could in the most literal sense improve his or her looks by fine dress and by a command of the services of the most expert beauticians and the best beauty aids.[226]

That the economic system operated distinctly to the benefit of those already in possession of considerable wealth is particularly evident in the grossly disproportionate scales of salaries, gratuities, and even famine relief, which reflected the inequalities of the social scale, but were deemed appropriate on the principle of giving more to those who already had much.[227] The abjectly indigent, the simply poor, and those of modest means often cringed before the rich, bowing and scraping to the power of wealth, and so an ex-slave 'loaded with the stuff', having risen to riches through huge legacies from his former master and through his own entrepreneurial flair, was apt to be treated in some ways like an aristocrat by freeborn people of modest means, even if he had 'a foreign accent' and lacked certain other deference-entitling properties.[228] Satirical literature, with characteristic exaggeration, tells of the sudden enrichment of 'plenty of men who yesterday hadn't a penny to buy a piece of rope with.' Instances of such enrichment undoubtedly occurred from time to time as a result of legacies obtained from rich 'connections' by relatives, toadies, or 'lewd slaves held in high esteem in a household since the days of their wanton youth' when, like Petronius' fictional character Trimalchio, they had served their masters *inter alia* as homosexual pets, or their masters' wives as gigolos, or both (or, in the case of female slaves, had been favourite bedmates of their masters). Several Roman comments indicate that these 'lewd slaves' included blacks (*Aethiopes*), like the youth pictured by Martial as his master's 'sombre-faced' pet, and the black wrestler and father of one of the children of Marulla in another of that same poet's satirical pictures.[229] But the most common instances of advancement up the economic scale were evidently cases of people 'who started with some minor skill or minor sum of money' and rose to a 'relative affluence' that gave them relative power and a command of relative deference in a social situation in which indigence was widespread.[230]

This is the general context in which the evidence on the positive deference-entitling properties of individual blacks must be viewed. It has been convincingly shown that blacks occupied a variety of social and economic positions, and in some cases positions of considerable esteem. Some blacks may well have been indigent and destitute, but at any given time in the period from the first century BC to the third century AD most were domestic slaves,[231] assured of food, clothing, and shelter, and also more likely to receive an education than the average poor Roman of free birth and free status.[232] Others were labourers of various sorts, while a few served as priests and minor officials of the Isiac cult and as soldiers, and a good number as actors, jockeys (racing charioteers), and public entertainers in other branches of 'show business' (*ludicrae artes*).[233] Marble portraits of black individuals who occupied relatively esteemed social positions reflect the status of such blacks, like Memnon, the protégé of an aristocratic family: in these portraits the artists, without underplaying the nigritude of the subject, but giving clear expression to his or her 'Romanized shape', took pains to give the face the proportion usual in Roman portraiture, thus indicating that such blacks were perceived not as barbarians, but as persons integrated into Roman society and fully accepted in the strata appropriate to their positive deference-entitling properties.[234] Free blacks in 'show business' had opportunities for upward social mobility, even if advancement was often aided by their playing the gigolo or courtesan (routes to success that were open even to slaves).[235] The satirical literature frequently contrasts the genteel poverty (*paupertas*) of men in 'liberal' professions (poets, advocates, professors, and schoolmasters) with the affluence that often accrued to soldiers, gigolos, and people in the 'vulgar' occupations of actor, gladiator, jockey (*auriga*), animal-fighter in the arena (*venator*), auctioneer, and barber. The earnings of the *auriga* and the *venator* were indeed substantial, and the most successful of them made fortunes in prize money. Many of them began their careers as slaves (as will almost certainly have been the case with the blacks attested to in these occupations) and earned their freedom as a reward for success, often in consequence of a popular demand by the adoring spectators.[236] From the first century AD onwards success in the 'vulgar' occupation of jockey had more charisma than modest performance in the 'honourable' or 'liberal' professions, and outstanding jockeys like the blacks commemorated in the iconography and literature were even honoured with statues and other monuments by their communities.[237] A similar charisma or glamour attended success in all the main fields of popular entertainment; and not only do blacks appear to have been well represented in such occupations, but some are known to have had outstanding success, even if in brief and dangerous careers. And, for the successful, blackness was no handicap (as Luxorius puts it) in the ordinary course of life, even if upper-class values represented these glamorous occupations as 'vulgar'.[238]

One aspect of the distinction between 'honourable' or 'liberal' professions on the one hand and 'vulgar' or 'dishonourable' (*inhonestae*) occupations on the other was the status-relevance of education, and especially that of a higher education.[239] The glamour of 'show business' occupations illustrated the status-inconsistency of men of low rank who were at the same time affluent and popular heroes in their communities.[240] For if the mass of the population (including most aristocrats) lionized the successful 'show business' star, the conventional upper-class attitude saw 'vulgar' wage-earning occupations as placing the worker in the position of a servant under the orders of a master – hence the notion that 'the very wages of the labourer are badges of slavery.' For that reason, even if a man with some pretensions to respectability fell on hard times away from his home town and condescended to temporary manual work *faute de mieux*, there was a widespread tendency to see such work as labour of the thoroughly degrading kind which set a man in the role of 'some Indian or Scythian slave'. The dominant values took account of the gradations of status attaching to the various means of acquiring an income, maintaining the division between 'liberal' professions (inseparable from a higher education) and vulgar trades and occupations, and deterring snobbish men of 'genteel poverty' from entering even highly remunerative professions like medicine and architecture, which were deemed honourable only for 'the kind of people to whose status they are appropriate'[241] – commoners who might thereby achieve affluence and a consequent command of considerable deference.

The deference-relevance of education was naturally enhanced by the prevailing state of widespread illiteracy (comparable with the typical situation in 'the less Protestant parts of pre-industrial Europe'[242]). A higher education was all the more deference-relevant as it was obtained only by a small proportion of the minority in possession of the basic ability to read and write – an ability that was proportionately less rare among slaves in grand households than it was among the freeborn poor.[243] This is of some significance for the theme of blacks in so far as the evidence suggests that, at any given point in the history of the high empire, a good proportion of the blacks in Roman society consisted of slaves in wealthy households and ex-slaves connected with such households. Moreover, there is some evidence for blacks with a higher education: Philostratus refers in admiring tones to the learning of Memnon, the protégé of Herodes Atticus, and some statues of black youths have with some plausibility been interpreted as relating to blacks undergoing the tertiary education[244] that was a prerequisite for 'liberal' occupations and careers. Such an education was also a deference-entitling property the importance of which is emphasized in allusions to it as a property in which parents with adequate means were prepared to invest considerable sums, in references to upward social mobility from an occupational role like that of porter to that of advocate, in pictures of the deference granted to the advanced education of a man of genteel poverty by prosperous but ill-educated businessmen, and in disparaging allusions to the status-inconsistency of the unlettered rich.[245] The powerful black eunuch and 'minister in charge of all the treasures' of the Meroitic Candace (queen or queen mother) mentioned in the *Acts of the Apostles* (8.27f.) was, admittedly, a visitor of some distinction from a foreign land and not a resident in Roman social space, but he displayed some of the symbols acknowledged in Roman society as symbols of high status: literacy (probably in Greek), possession of a carriage and horses, and attendance by personal servants. It is significant that in this event, which occurred in the early first century AD, this black man's possession of these status symbols is not represented as having occasioned any surprise in the observant apostle Philip. The situation pictured in this account is one in which a black's possession of such status symbols simply and naturally proclaimed him as a man of considerably high status, and in this particular case information about the black's ocupational role in his own country ensured recognition of him as 'a man of authority' (*dynastēs*).

But the realities of power could be particularly abhorrent to people who possessed the high education, tastes and social-role expectations of 'respectable people' without the corresponding level of property and income. Such people often found it necessary to court the powerful and arrogant slaves of powerful men and to face insults from *parvenus* whose memories of insults endured in their own former days of powerlessness rendered them particularly apt to insult inferiors in status once they had attained positions of power through recently acquired wealth or rank, or even merely through their connections with powerful people.[246] One of the attractions of the life of the hanger-on in the household of a magnate (or of an *alumnus* like the learned black Memnon in the home of Herodes Atticus) was, in fact, the consequent deference-entitling property of connections with a grand house. Lucian even emphasizes the social esteem obtainable merely from being *seen* in the company of well-born and richly dressed men.[247] Attitudes and behaviour towards inferiors and superiors were responses to perceptions of status symbols, positive or negative (a 'slave name', torn and shabby dress reminiscent of 'common beggars at the crossroads', or absence of slave-attendants were all symbols of low status). No one, and least of all ignorant and uneducated people lacking in self-esteem, wanted to be seen near a shabbily dressed person.[248] A person bearing the negative status symbols of a slave (even as a pose) could expect to be treated as a slave, and equally, one who dressed and acted the part of a magnate with some conviction was treated like a magnate by strangers for as long as he could maintain the pretence – but exposure was a humiliating experience.[249]

In this value system the social interaction of status-equals was (*ceteris paribus*) far less complex than the behaviour of superiors towards inferiors and vice versa. For instance, in the fictional work of Apuleius, the mocking and taunting of one humble man by another not surprisingly results in an angry and violent exchange of insults.[250] But in that same work an encounter between a junior army officer (*procerus miles*) and a peasant illustrates the greater complexity of relations between unequals in status. The soldier, with brusque arrogance, requisitions the peasant's ass, but the peasant, not understanding Latin, fails to make an appropriate response, and so the soldier, interpreting this as unacceptable 'insolence', pushes the peasant off his donkey and begins to give him a thrashing. The peasant grovels and begs, but to no avail. Then, in sheer desperation, he draws upon his superior physical strength to give his social superior a savage beating, after which he rides off on his way, leaving the officer prostrate in the road. But he instantly and instinctively realizes that he must now go into hiding if he is to escape a terrible retribution from the forces of law and order.[251] This scene, though fictional, mirrors social reality. People of low status were acutely conscious of their lack of rights in such an encounter; and here it is pertinent to recall that most blacks in the Roman world were of such status. In the era of the high empire, when even privates in the legions had the privileged position of *honestiores* in the eyes of the law and lawsuits involving soldiers came before a military court, the humble civilian plaintiff (let alone the humble civilian defendant) had little or no prospect of success in a civil action. Such a person would indeed ordinarily lack the effrontery to strike a soldier or bring a legal action against one who had maltreated him. Several instances of soldiers harshly requisitioning the animals and other property of civilians by force are actually documented.[252] In response to this kind of institution-alized oppression even commoners of considerable means could plaintively ask, 'what use are laws when money calls all the tunes and people without a gentleman's income have no real rights at all?'[253]

When unknown in a given community, even prosperous people might be 'of little account' until they could establish some connection with the name of some local magnate, and assessment of a person as 'of no account', when realistically based upon absence of positive status symbols, usually prompted contemptuous treatment (which might include a status-symbolic thrashing) at the hands of social superiors.[254] Lucian offers a picture of a frequent recipient of such treatment: a snub-nosed cobbler who has 'no stake in life' (no farm, no tenement-block to bring in an income from rents, no cash or movable property, no reputation, no status, no statues), and for whom death is the only release from the harsh attentions of creditors, from iniquitous taxation, from hunger and cold, and from thrashings at the hands of social superiors.[255] Juvenal, with his usual exaggeration, similarly illustrates the contemptuous treatment of men of low status in his picture of an upper-class youth selecting from among nocturnal passers-by a much older man who looks safe to thrash both from the social and from the physical point of view. But the satirical lines leading up to this thrashing scene are no less significant: there the satirist explains that, for all his drunkenness and hot-headedness, the young aristocrat, who has nothing but contempt for the obviously humble, 'makes sure he keeps his distance from the passer-by whose scarlet cloak and retinue of slaves proclaim his lordly status.'[256]

The exemption of blacks like the charismatic arena-performer, Olympius, from the 'handicap' of blackness (liability to mockery and to other unwelcome behaviour prompted by the negative symbolism of blackness) was evidently a consequence of the deference commanded by individual blacks on the score of their deference-entitling properties (in the case of Luxorius' black stars in the world of popular entertainment, the attributes described earlier as 'accomplishment in an occupational role' and 'level of income').[257] The sole limitations on the Roman propensity towards open and unabashed mockery of alien or 'inappropriate' character-istics were, in fact, those imposed by the ideology of deference: respect for (or fear of offending) people of superior status, whether these socially superior persons were themselves marked by the mockable characteristics or were powerful protectors of the individuals so marked. Significantly, in Petronius' novel, some status-inferiors of a multimillionaire ex-slave instinctively repress the urge to laugh openly at the comic sight of this man's shaved head: only the thoughtless among them (*imprudentes*) 'allow a laugh to escape', and they instantly seek to cover up their *faux pas*.[258] Similarly, although a combination of baldness, flat nose, and wrinkles might ordinarily be a target of ridicule, it was not so in a person of superior status, or even in a relatively humble man with powerful connections. Wealth, even in itself, could often command deference, and, as Lucian puts it, money and power transformed physical ugliness into beauty and handsomeness. The ugly, pale-complexioned and pot-bellied multimillionaire, despite these somatic 'defects' was (like the black aristocratic youths of Martial's imagination, mocked by that poet's *persona*) mockable by inferiors in status only from a safe and secret distance, and negative perceptions of the physiognomy of a deference-worthy black were appropriately modified by perceptions of his positive deference-entitling properties.[259] This psychology evidently related to the whole gamut of interpersonal relations between inferiors and superiors in status.

If, in Apuleius' novel, the behaviour of an old female innkeeper (who feels free to speak disparagingly of a local man of superior status in his absence) appears not to fit this prescription of mocking from a safe distance, inasmuch as she speaks in the presence of an upper-class youth, it is nevertheless clear that the old plebeian woman's free speech is rendered safe by another of the principles of the Roman ideology of status and deference: the social superior mocked in his absence by this plebeian woman actually lives 'like a tramp', commanding no deference on the score of his lifestyle and his hidden wealth. Perceptions of men of this sort were influenced by the idea that 'no one is well off unless people know about it', and that a rich man who habitually dined alone and failed to surround himself with a throng of slave attendants and a retinue of free dependents was 'no better than a tramp'. Moreover, Apuleius' noble youth, in whose presence the plebeian woman disparages a social superior, is a complete stranger in that particular community; having just set foot in the town, he can for the moment be seen as a person 'of little account' in the affairs of that particular town.[260]

In grand Roman households, slaves (like the black groom of Juvenal's picture) could be openly contemptuous of their masters' guests or of other socially superior visitors and callers only when that attitude was an extension of that of their masters, and so rested on the positive deference-entitling property of 'connections'.[261] As Reekmans has shown, the particular extent of the role of 'connections' that is illustrated by such behaviour on the part of social inferiors was an aspect of a modification of traditional opinions of social hierarchy and a reflection of an increasing incidence of nonconformity to traditional social roles and social positions which distinguished Roman society in and after the first century BC from the pattern of earlier times. The prominence of money-worship and the greater power and privilege that were attached to material wealth in this later period were consequences of a process of socio-structural change which diminished the degree of social distance that had earlier separated some social categories, while increasing the distance between other categories, particularly in the imperial metropolis itself.[262] Aliens were the greatest beneficiaries of this process of social change, among the aspects of which were behavioural phenomena like the xenophilic promiscuity of some women of high rank and their taste for intimate relations with slaves and other humble men, including blacks. The process introduced and institutionalized a high revaluation of the status and material rewards of certain inferior and 'vulgar' occupational roles like those of jockey, gladiator, and other purveyors of public entertainment, and narrowed the social distance between aristocrats and their domestic slaves, and between well-to-do Romans and foreign purveyors of foreign cults and fashions (including blacks as devotees of the cults of Isis and othe1 Egyptian deities), to the point where members of these previously distant social categories regularly enjoyed extensive and intensive interactions with one another.[263]

None the less, the humble generally gazed in awe or envy at the powerful and made due obeisance to them, while the latter generally viewed the poor and unprivileged with contempt and often subjected educated but poor dependants to degrading treatment, sometimes requiring them to bow their heads and grovel before them.[264] We cannot rightly think of blacks in Roman society without imagining some of them, *qua* humble people, in invidious situations of this sort – in a system in which 'the powerful' (*potentes* or *hoi dynatoi*) and 'the arrogant rich' exerted cruel pressures against the weak and the poor, and enjoyed extra-legal power and influence.[265] Resentment at the inequalities and iniquities of the system on the part of men of the 'shabby genteel' category is quite widely aired in the satirical literature, and hints of similar resentment among the humbler classes may be contained in expressions like the complaint of a fictional character to the effect that 'the little man suffers, while the big man's jaws celebrate the Saturnalia every day', or in the astrological prediction of the third century AD, promising 'tumult and war' which 'will go badly for the rich', whose arrogance will be cast down, and whose goods will be 'confiscated and delivered over to others' in a reversal of the existing social order in which 'the poor will be exalted and the rich humbled'.[266] But although some magnates lived in fear of slave plots, resentment among the have-nots rarely surfaced in individual action (let alone collective action), except in so far as it was reflected in the ubiquitous activity of gangs of armed robbers, and in the sympathy often shown to these bandits by the poor.[267] Some friction, occasioned by the gross inequality of wealth, sometimes came to the surface in times of grave food-shortages, and after the middle of the third century AD the ranks of bandits were regularly filled by hungry and desperate men of the oppressed classes, including blacks like the brigand (later monk) Moses. But the deference-system found general acceptance among all social classes. The clearest indication of this acceptance is the perennially pervasive institution of clientship (*clientela*), with its vertical ties binding together in mutual sympathies and obligations individuals and groups among the *humiliores* on the one hand, and patrons among the *honestiores* on the other hand.[268] The common attitude of acceptance is also frequently reflected in Roman literature, for instance, in the episode in Apuleius' novel in which the civic leaders of a town feel obliged to offer profuse apologies to a young visitor of high rank for a practical joke (*lusus*) at his expense which has been shared by the local *plebs* and has caused the young aristocrat tears and shame.[269] As social psychologists have often pointed out, envy and resentment at social and economic differentiation 'seems to appear only when the distance between ourselves and those more fortunate than ourselves is small enough so that we can reasonably compare ourselves with them'.[270] It hardly appears in conditions resting on the premise of the inequality of social estates.

Such were the conditions of Roman society. Black members of that society had to adapt to the rules of the system. On the very reasonable assumption that blacks entered the Roman world for the most part as slaves, and that in the minority of instances where this was not the case the black newcomer was usually a person of quite modest means, it follows as a general rule that the fortunes of the black individual depended upon the rapidity and thoroughness of that adaptation. As a first step, the black barbarian had tö debarbarize himself or herself. Thereafter, his or her prospects of escape from the harsher indignities and deprivations that attended the lives of the humble, and from what has been described earlier as the 'handicap' of blackness, though dependent to a considerable extent on luck and connections, will have rested anyhow on his or her acquisition of positive deference-entitling properties.

CONCLUSION

In the foregoing discussion an attempt has been made to interpret various references and allusions to blacks and blackness in Roman writings, and portrayals of blacks in Roman iconography, in their proper social–psychological and ideological context. Parts of the exercise may have the appearance of a laborious enterprise with disproportionately small results: *parturient montes, nascetur ridiculus mus.*[1] But one major objective of the study has been to demonstrate decisively the fact (hitherto the subject of considerable and sometimes polemical argument) that Roman attitudes towards *Aethiopes*, even at their most negative, have nothing to do with the familiar modern phenomenon of *race* and are of a kind very different from those commonly described by social scientists by the terms 'racist', 'racial prejudice', 'colour prejudice', and 'racism'. An inextricably related objective has been to underscore the extent to which a proper historical understanding of these Roman attitudes depends upon our own self-understanding and our awareness of how we have come to be subject to certain prejudices and to hold certain assumptions which, though highly questionable, generally pass unquestioned. These two aims, however imperfectly achieved in this *opusculum*, largely constitute whatever importance the results of the work may have.

The 'problem' surrounding the presence of blacks in Roman society (in so far as it may be seen as a problem) was entirely one of Roman perceptions of the strangeness (sometimes not only somatic, but also cultural) of *Aethiopes*. The Roman concept *Aethiops* meant the black African somatic type, and it embraced all somatic appearances perceived by Romans as matching or very closely approximating to the image of the black African type as a

157

combination of black skin, crinkly hair, thick lips, and flat nose which Romans carried about in their heads, but it was perceived as distinct from 'swarthy' and 'very swarthy' types (what we would describe as 'swarthy Caucasian' and 'Caucasian-type' morphology combined with very dark skin), and even from types combining black skin with predominantly 'normal' (in our terms, 'Caucasian') morphology. In modern western societies children of mixed black and white parentage are invariably regarded as 'non-white', and there is often also a tendency to accept as incontrovertible Madison Grant's dogmatic principle that 'the cross between a white man and a negro is a negro; the cross between a white man and a Hindu is a Hindu; the cross between any of the three European races and a Jew is a Jew.'[2] But in the Roman perceptual context the progeny, let alone more distant descendants, of an *Aethiops* did not necessarily fall into the category of *Aethiops*: some were perceived as 'swarthy' (in our terms, 'swarthy Caucasian' and types of physiognomy combining black skin with 'Caucasian' morphology), some as 'white', and some as *Aethiops*, the classification in all cases depending entirely on the individual's physical appearance; there was no assumption inherent in the structures of the society that neither the black newcomer nor his descendants could 'ever become full members of the society because of the presence of the visible factor of colour' or shape.[3] Nor was there any predictable link between physical appearance and status, even if the fact that most people in the *Aethiops* category were objectively humble people did foster a habit of mentally associating *Aethiopes* with humble status. The treatment received by an *Aethiops* at the hands of a non-black person depended above all on the personal status and deference-position of each of the parties in the encounter, and there was considerable variety in the statuses and (positive and negative) deference-positions of blacks, even if few blacks or none at all were to be found in social stations above the rank of plebeian. A black like Memnon, an *alumnus* in an aristocratic household, lived a life of upper-class affluence and dignity, enjoying the deference due to a man closely connected with the aristocracy, even if his own legal status was in fact that of a plebeian of slave origin and a black in possession of symbols of high status received appropriate deference from those of lower (genuine or apparent) status, irrespective of colour and ethnic identity or origins, even if he happened to be passing through a district whose population lacked current familiarity with the sight of black faces. Thus the black eunuch of Candace, a man of great authority (*dynastēs*), as he rode through Judaea and Palestine in his carriage (in itself a symbol of high status) appropriately attended by servants, was perceived by on-lookers like the apostle Philip as a man of obviously high status and accorded appropriately high respect.[4]

But since the majority of blacks in Roman society were humble folk, the question of Roman attitudes relates mostly to humble blacks. Attitudes towards humble blacks on the whole varied from community to community, depending on whether a given community's population currently included blacks or had included blacks in very recent generations and therefore on whether the community had some direct or almost direct experience of, and familiarity with, blacks. For familiarization naturally reduced (and tended to eliminate) the antipathy towards blacks which the initially strange sight of blacks tended to arouse – unlike the process observed in several modern societies, where increasing familiarity with the sight of black faces and growing acculturation of blacks have been concomitant with increasing hostility and discrimination against blacks.[5] But diverse attitudes might be shown in one and the same Roman community at one and the same moment in time. This diversity related in the first place to a diversity of perceptions based on the differences of rank and class between the upper and the lower orders of society. It is chiefly on the writings of men of the leisured upper classes that we depend for information, and the various written comments and allusions to blacks largely (but not always exclusively) illustrate upper class feelings and attitudes, for instance, the sensory aversion to *nigritudo* that is evident in descriptions of the *Aethiops* physiognomy by writers like Martial, Petronius, the Romano-African author of the epigrams on the black slave at Hadrumetum, the poet who envisages a black military contingent as *milia tetra* or 'a horrid host', and the several Christian writers who refer to 'ugly' and 'foul' demons in the shape of *Aethiopes*; similarly, the very hostile reception given by Claudian to the idea of a black man (presumed to be for that reason a humble man) marrying a noble Roman lady; and again, the evident displeasure of a Martial or a Juvenal at the adultery of upper-class women with black slaves and other humble *Aethiopes*, and castigation of this adultery as a threat to the maintenance of the boundaries of rank.[6] But the comment of the anonymous author of the poem *Moretum*, while reflecting that writer's own negative attitude to the somatic appearance of a humble black slave woman and to the squalid peasant life that she shares with her peasant master, at the same time reveals his assumptions with regard to the sort of relations that were naturally expected to occur between a humble peasant and his black female slave who was also his sole house-companion: intimate social relations are assumed to be the natural concomitant of such a situation.[7] Similarly, the numerous allusions to the negative symbolism of the colour black and to the related superstitions about blacks reflect attitudes current at all levels of society. Upper-class attitudes and behaviour towards blacks reflect the fact that members of the upper classes were in general socially remote from blacks, and usually in the master–servant relationship if there was any direct relationship (or even familiarity with blacks) at all, and although barriers of rank and class did not always preclude intimate personal relations with humble blacks, on the whole those barriers made for attitudes of indifference, or antipathy, or paternalistic kindliness and affection towards particular black individuals, or curiosity, or appreciation (from a standpoint of social superiority) of the success and achievements of certain charismatic black performers in 'show business' (the *ludicrae artes*).

A certain air of indifference is suggested by the very nature of much of the written evidence, in which blacks receive only coincidental notice and are not treated as social objects attracting the writer's interest or concern *qua* blacks.[8] To the indifferent, an *Aethiops* was just a humble slave, a musician, an *auriga*, and so on, meriting no more attention than was ordinarily deserved by persons of such a social station – that is to say, little or none. This indifference did not, to be sure, extend to learned blacks like Memnon or to foreign black dignitaries like the Kushite royal treasurer mentioned in the *Acts of the Apostles*. But blacks of such social stature were evidently encountered only very rarely. Antipathy, on the other hand (at any rate, antipathy towards a particular black person as well as distaste for the black physiognomy), is evidenced by rare texts like the epigrams on the black slave at Hadrumetum, which have a decidedly hostile tone.[9] Some degree of antipathy is also attested to by texts and iconographic items which merely illustrate a sensory aversion to the physiognomy of blacks, but attitudes and feelings of kindliness and affection of a paternalistic kind emerge clearly from texts like the epitaph of the black slave at Antinoe (a monument set up by the slave's master, in which the latter expresses his kindliness through the mouth of the dead slave, observing that the slave's blackness, though far from being an esteemed characteristic, covered a variety of excellent ('white') non-corporeal qualities). A less self-conscious affection is displayed by a similar epitaph of another black servant, set up at Halicarnassus by one Chimaerus and his wife in honour of their departed 'Blackface', whose remains they insisted on bringing home from Patara where the slave had died.[10] But Chimaerus and his wife, Aelia Carpime, may well have been merely well-to-do plebeians (as distinct from upper-class persons) whose relations with their black servant were accordingly more intimate and intensive than would normally have been the case among the upper classes, and should perhaps therefore be compared with the peasant of *Moretum* rather than with the owner of the Antinoe slave.

Upper-class curiosity about *Aethiopes* appears in three forms: first, an interest and curiosity relating to the Napatan-Meroitic kingdom and its glorious historical past; second, a sort of scientific curiosity about the *Aethiops* physiognomy and biology (in the latter case, especially with regard to the reproductive processes and results of the mating of blacks with whites), which we see in the works of men like Pliny and Lucretius;[11] and third, a sexual curiosity and interest that often took the form of an urge to have sexual relations with blacks and resulted in the satisfaction of that urge either in adulterous relationships of upper-class women with humble blacks, or in sexual liaisons between upper-class men and their own black slaves (male and female), black prostitutes (who were often slaves), or black courtesans (who were perhaps often ex-slaves).[12] Fulsome expressions of appreciation of the success of particular blacks in the 'vulgar' world of popular entertainment are particularly evident in the epigrams of Luxorius.[13] This poet, to be sure, belongs to the world of Vandal, as distinct from Roman, Africa, but his cultural traditions are Roman and his writings reflect attitudes that had for centuries characterized aristocratic society in Roman Africa and in the Roman world in general.[14] Indeed, a Roman marble relief honouring a black jockey (*auriga*), and literary references to similar honours, point in exactly the same direction as the encomiums addressed by Luxorius to black 'stars' in the arena or race-course in sixth-century Vandal Carthage.[15]

Just as paternalistic kindliness was demonstrated in different degrees, so too were negative attitudes among the leisured classes. The intensity of negative attitudes varied according to circumstances: hostile scapegoating of a black at Hadrumetum (arising no doubt from an atmosphere of conflictual relations with Saharan tribes); superstitions about black strangers as ominous or as creatures of the Devil; or sensory aversions to *nigritudo*, given public expression in mockery of blacks. And in all of these various expressions of negativity there will have been a tendency on the part of the Romans concerned to conceive of the term *Aethiops* as a 'label of primary potency' and thereby to see black strangers through the deforming prism of stereotypes rather than as individual persons. But, even among the upper classes, much depended on the degree of contact and familiarity which the observer actually had with blacks; and, by contrast with the tendency of people less familiar with blacks to see *Aethiops* as a label of primary potency, which blinded the perceiver to the qualities of a given *Aethiops* stranger as an individual person, it may be noted that even Martial's black wrestler, Pannychus, is conceived as an individual whose facial features (not to speak of his non-somatic qualities) are his own and do not exactly match those of any other person.[16] Again the only social 'pressures' against people forming their own individualistic judgements of *Aethiopes* were in the nature of the stereotypes and false popular beliefs about *Aethiopes*. The structures of society carried no inherent prejudice against blacks *qua* blacks, and so the processes of cultural assimilation and adaptation of blacks to Roman ways and habits (including the acquisition of 'Romanized black shapes' by well-to-do blacks, which rendered them sexually attractive to many Romans) were in themselves no less important as factors in the elimination of the initially antipathetic attitudes towards blacks than was the process of adaptation by whites to the initial strangeness of blacks. This adaptation process naturally occurred in all the various Roman communities whose populations included blacks. But because of the constant process of interbreeding which regularly placed progeny and descendants of *Aethiopes* in the somatic categories 'swarthy' and 'white', a continuous presence of blacks in a given community depended on regular immigration of black newcomers, and negative attitudes were most pronounced in situations where blacks were rarely or never encountered, and where mental pictures of 'the *Aethiops*' rested largely or entirely on ideas derived from the information media, including hearsay. In any case, blacks who were humble folk suffered, *qua* humble folk, the various privations of humble folk in a society structured on the premise of inequality of rank and class: like their non-black peers, some humble blacks endured poverty as well as oppression at the hands of *potentes*; and those in particularly indigent circumstances were condemned to a life of squalor in their grim struggle for survival, while many more suffered upper-class contempt. Equally, well-to-do blacks lived lives characteristic of the well-to-do generally.

The psychological condition of blacks in contact with members of the leisured classes depended on their personal self-esteem,and that, in turn, largely depended on their personal status and deference-position in society. The individual victim of upper-class mockery was no doubt driven by his or her hurt feelings into a variety of ego-defences: in some cases, avoidance of potential mockers and addicts of status-symbolic thrashing where avoidance was possible; in others, seeking security and props for their self-esteem in the haven of a *collegium*; in others, cheating and attempting to harm disparagers; in others, a resort to protective clowning; and in others, a relentless striving for success. But even possession of a 'Romanized black look' did not necessarily preclude in such blacks the sort of self-consciousness and mortification about their blackness which Olaudah Equiano felt in eighteenth-century London. And, as Juvenal (II 23, III 278f.) implies, even after familiarization had eliminated the particular forms of antipathy typical of people unfamiliar with blacks, a person of superior social status, bent on inflicting a status-symbolic thrashing on a humble black, *qua* humble person, might still refer abusively to the blackness of his humble victim; and even a white peer might cast in the teeth of a personally disliked black the more negative stereotypes of blacks, in the manner of Catullus' abuse of Egnatius as a urine-bathing Spaniard.

With regard to lower class attitudes and behaviour, we must bear in mind that the negative messages contained in the iconography – mockery and caricature of blacks – are in many cases the work of craftsmen and artists who belonged to plebeian social strata, even if they must be located in the most prosperous of those strata. But (as Rolf Winkes showed) the iconography often also distinguishes between well-to-do and culturally assimilated blacks on the one hand, and humbler or 'barbarian' blacks on the other.[17] The plebeian artist who created the surviving portrait of Memnon, a protégé of a wealthy and aristocratic household, quite obviously viewed that particular black man with a deference due to his superior position in society, so he naturally produced a portrait showing 'a black, noble of visage, calm, marvellously expressive.'[18] A similar attitude of respect and deference may be inferred from other portraits of blacks to which Winkes drew attention.[19] At the humble levels of society appreciation of the achievements of a black 'star' in the world of popular entertainment was in every sense a genuine hero-worship (*populi amor*, as Luxorius describes it), and blacks were granted the deference due to their status when they were persons of superior status.[20] If the negative colour symbolism and the superstition about black strangers as ominous were at their strongest among the lower orders, sensory aversions to the physiognomy of *Aethiopes* were less powerful and durable among humble Romans than they were among members of the leisured and educated upper classes, since the ideals of beauty and of 'the appropriate' in facial and bodily shape were generally much more remote from everyday reality among the humble and toiling masses than they were among the refined and leisured rich. This is shown by (*inter alia*) the fact that the physical appearance of white peasants and members of the white 'sordid *plebs*' like Lucian's snub-nosed cobbler were targets of upper-class mockery just as much as was the *Aethiops* physiognomy. Moreover, *ceteris paribus*, adaptation to the initial strangeness of blacks was evidently a more rapid process at the lower levels of society than it was among the leisured classes, owing to the absence of barriers of rank and to the higher frequency and greater intimacy of contact with blacks that marked social relations at the humble levels of society. Naturally, it was also at the humbler levels of society, and especially among the slave population, that occurred for the most part the constant process of integration and genetic absorption of blacks into the white population which has been indicated.

NOTES

INTRODUCTION

1 Especially F.M. Snowden, *Blacks in Antiquity: Ethiopians in the Greco-Roman Experience* (Cambridge, Mass. 1970) – cited hereafter as *Blacks*; id., *Before Color Prejudice: The Ancient View of Blacks* (Cambridge, Mass. 1983); L. Cracco Ruggini, 'Leggenda e realtà degli Etiopi nella cultura tardoimperiale', *Atti del IV° congresso internazionale di studi etiopici*, I (Rome 1974) 141–93 – cited hereafter as Cracco Ruggini 1974; ead., 'Il negro buono e il negro malvagio nel mondo antico', in Marta Sordi (ed.), *Conoscenze etniche e rapporti di convivenza nell' antichità* (Milan 1979) 108–33 – cited hereafter as Cracco Ruggini 1979; J. Vercoutter, F.M. Snowden *et al.*, *The Image of the Black in Western Art*, I (New York 1976), II.1 (Cambridge, Mass. 1979) – cited hereafter as *Image*.

2 I note the general satisfaction with the state of the question of 'race relations' in the Roman world that has been expressed by scholars like R. MacMullen (*Roman Social Relations*, New Haven/London 1974, vii) and D.B. Saddington (*ANRW* II.3, 1975, 119–20).

3 See C.R. Whittaker, *Phoenix* 25 (1971) 188.

4 Cf. L.A. Thompson, 'Observations on the perception of "race" in imperial Rome', *PACA* 17 (1983) 1–21.

5 On the sociological concepts 'race' and 'racism', see J. Rex, *Race Relations in Sociological Theory* (London 1970) 159–60; id., 'The concept of race in sociological theory', in S. Zubaida (ed.), *Race and Racialism* (London 1970) 48–54; id., *Race, Colonialism and the City* (London 1973) 190–1, 202–3; Colette Guillaumin, *L'idéologie raciste: genèse et langage actuel* (Paris 1972); P.L. van den Berghe, *Race and Racism: A Comparative Perspective* (New York/London 1967) 11–12. For some appropriate diagnoses of Roman attitudes towards out-groups in general, see Cornelia Cogrossi, 'Preoccupazioni etniche nelle leggi di Augosto sulla *manumissio servorum?*', in Marta Sordi (ed.), *Conoscenze etniche e rapporti di convivenza nell' antichità*, 158–77; L.A. Thompson, 'The concept of purity of blood in Suetonius' *Life of Augustus*', *Museum Africum* 7 (1981) 35–46; K.R. Bradley, *Slaves and Masters in the Roman*

Empire: A Study in Social Control (Coll. Latomus 185, Brussels 1984) 83f., 148–9; Saddington, *ANRW* II.3, 134; F.W. Walbank, 'Nationality as a factor in Roman history', *HSCP* 76 (1972) 156; Y.A. Dauge, *Le barbare: recherches sur la conception romaine de la barbarie et de la civilisation* (Coll. Latomus 176, Brussels 1981) 281f., 318f., 471, 477f.; J. Vogt, *Kulturwelt und Barbaren: zum Menscheitsbild der spätantiken Gesellschaft* (Wiesbaden 1967); K. Christ, 'Römer und Barbaren in der hohen Kaiserzeit', *Saeculum* 10 (1959) 273–88; E. Demougeot, 'L'idealisation de Rome face aux barbares à travers trois ouvrages récents', *REA* 70 (1968) 408; L. Cracco Ruggini, 'Pregiudizi razziali, ostilità politica e culturale, intoleranza religiosa nell'impero romano', *Athenaeum* 46 (1968) 139–52. Useful also, despite its highly inappropriate and misleading title, is A.N. Sherwin-White, *Racial Prejudice in Imperial Rome* (Cambridge 1967) 73f., 83 (rightly criticized on the ground of misconception of 'racial prejudice' by M.D. Biddis, *Race* 9, 1968, 402–3 and Cracco Ruggini, op. cit. 139–52). S.I. Oost (*Galla Placidia Augusta: A Biographic Essay*, London/Chicago 1968, 15) also appropriately comments on the 'emphatic cultural prejudice' of the Romans, noting that 'although Negroids and Mongoloids were known to them', representatives of such somatically distant peoples excited 'only curiosity or at most perhaps derision' in Roman observers.

6 A. Montagu, *Man's Most Dangerous Myth: The Fallacy of Race* (5th edn.) (London 1974) 4; cf. M. Banton, 'What do we mean by racism?', *New Society* no. 341, April 1969, 351.

7 N.H. Baynes, 'The decline of Roman power in western Europe', *JRS* 33 (1943) 33; cf. M. Banton, *The Idea of Race* (London 1977) 2; Colette Guillaumin, 'Les ambiguités de la catégorie taxonomique "race"', in L. Poliakov (ed.), *Hommes et bêtes: entretiens sur le racisme* (Paris 1975) 203–8; ead., *L'idéologie raciste* 55–62.

8 The exceptions are Cracco Ruggini 1974 and 1979; cf. ead., *Athenaeum* 46 (1968) 140. On the issue of Roman 'antisemitism' an appropriate conceptualization of 'race' is also demonstrated in J. Mélèze-Modrzejewski, 'Sur l'antisémitisme paien', in M. Olender (ed.), *Pour Léon Poliakov: le racisme. Mythes et sciences* (Paris 1981) 414–15.

9 A failing particularly evident in Grace H. Beardsley, *The Negro in Greek and Roman Civilization: A Study of the Ethiopian Type* (Baltimore 1929), and in the contributions of Snowden (*Blacks; Before Color Prejudice*; and 'Iconographical evidence on the black populations in Graeco-Roman antiquity', in *Image* I, 133–245, 298–307).

10 Snowden, *Blacks* 176, 183; id., *Before Color Prejudice* 67–8. 107–8.

11 J. Devisse, 'From the demoniac threat to the incarnation of sainthood', in *Image* II.1, 50–1.

12 A. Bourgeois, *La Grèce devant la négritude* (Paris 1971) 26–9, 119–20; R. Lonis, 'Les trois approches de l'Ethiopien par l'opinion gréco-romaine', *Ktema* 6 (1981) 74, 81–7 (my italics); cf. J.P.V.D. Balsdon, *Romans and Aliens* (London 1979) 2; W.J. Watts, 'Race prejudice in the satires of Juvenal', *Acta Cl.* 19 (1976) 83–104. But see J. Rex, *Race Relations in Sociological Theory*.

13 On these matters, cf. J. Gagé, *Les classes sociales dans l'empire romain* (2nd edn.) (Paris 1964); M.I. Finley, *The Ancient Economy* (London 1973); J.A. Crook, *Law and Life of Rome* (London 1967); R. MacMullen, *Roman Social Relations*; P. Garnsey, *Social Status and Legal Privilege in the Roman Empire* (Oxford 1970); Dauge, *Le barbare*; K.E. Müller, *Geschichte der antiken Ethnographie und ethnologischen Theoriebildung von den Anfängen bis auf die byzantinischen Historiographen*, II (Wiesbaden 1980); W. Speyer and I. Opelt, 'Barbar', *JbAC* 10 (1967) 251–90; M. Benabou, 'Monstres hybrides chez Lucrèce et Pline l'Ancien', in L. Poliakov (ed.), *Hommes et bêtes* 143–52; Erna Lesky, *Die Zeugungs- und Vererbungslehren der Antike und ihr Nachwirken* (Akad. der Wiss. und der Lit., Mainz 1950) 108; P.A. Brunt, *Italian Manpower: 225 BC – AD 14* (Oxford 1971) 113f.; A.N. Sherwin-White, *The Roman Citizenship* (2nd edn.) (Oxford 1973) 221f.; Saddington, *ANRW* II.3, 134; H. Solin, 'Juden und Syrer im westlichen Teil der römischen Welt', *ANRW* II.29.2 (1983) 654–779. Balsdon's (op. cit., 2) 'master race' is a carefree and misleading translation of Pliny's (*Pan.* 51.3) *populus victor gentium*, which means nothing more sinister than 'world-conquering people'; as is very well known, that 'people' was extremely mixed, in terms of what Romans called *genus* and what moderns popularly call 'race', during the era of the emperors.

14 P.A. Brunt, 'Reflections on British and Roman imperialism', *Comparative Studies in Society and History* 7 (1965) 287; cf. L.A. Thompson and J. Ferguson (eds), *Africa in Classical Antiquity* (Ibadan 1969) 26.

15 On those aspects of what MacMullen (*Roman Social Relations*, vii) calls 'race relations' which have to do with the presence of blacks (*Aethiopes*) in Roman society in the long period (50 BC to AD 284) covered by his own discussion of social relations, his satisfaction with the state of the question was evidently a tribute to Snowden's painstaking work, *Blacks in Antiquity*. For a similar tribute to that work, see Saddington, 'Race relations in the early Roman empire', *ANRW* II.3, 119–20; cf. Cracco Ruggini 1979, 118 (acknowledgement of the same work as a comprehensive survey of the iconographic, literary, hagiographical, papyrological, epigraphic, numismatic, and archaeological material relating to blacks); J.M. Cook, *CR* 22 (1972) 253–5; P. MacKendrick, *AJP* 94 (1973) 212–14.

16 On this last subject the only books and monographs known to me are those of Beardsley (op.cit.), Snowden (*Blacks*, and *Before Colour Prejudice*) and the collaborative work *The Image of the Black in Western Art* (volumes I and II). A. Bourgeois' book *La Grèce devant la négritude* devotes only a few pages to Rome. Notable works on barbarians are: J. Jüthner, *Hellenen und Barbaren* (Leipzig 1923); T.J. Haarhoff, *The Stranger at the Gate* (London 1948); G. Walser, *Rom, das Reich und die fremden Völker in der Geschichtschreibung der frühen Kaiserzeit* (Basel 1951); K. Christ, *Saeculum* 10 (1959) 273–88; J. Vogt, *Kulturwelt und Barbaren*; W. Speyer and I. Opelt, *JbAC* 10 (1967) 252–90; Dauge, *Le barbare*. With regard to the theme of Jews and antisemitism, the extensive

bibliography listed by J.N. Sevenster in his *The Roots of Pagan Antisemitism in the Ancient World* (Leiden 1975) well indicates the vigour of that particular interest, which has undoubtedly been prompted largely by the remarkable continuity of the Israelite people, and of Judaism as a religion and way of life, from ancient to modern times: as Michael Grant (*The Jews in the Roman World*, London 1973, xi) puts it, while the ancient Assyrians, Babylonians, Persians and Romans are gone forever, 'the Jews are still with us.' Cf. H. Solin, *ANRW* II.29.2, 787.

17 Cf. J. Dowd, *The Negro in American Life* (New York 1926) 456; M. Banton, *The Idea of Race*, 49; H. Hoetink, *The Two Variants in Caribbean Race Relations* (London 1967) 78f.; P.D. Curtin, *The Image of Africa: British Ideas and Action, 1780–1850* (London 1965) 28f.; E. Shils, 'Color, the universal intellectual community, and the Afro-Asian intellectual', in J.H. Franklin (ed.), *Color and Race* (Boston 1968) 4–5; Han Suyin, 'Race relations and the third world', *Race* 13 (1971) 1–20; Beardsley, *op. cit.*, ix.

18 Cf. T. Reekmans, 'Juvenal's views on social change', *Anc.Soc.* 2 (1971) 144.

19 Cf. W.D. Jordan, *White over Black: American Attitudes towards the Negro, 1550–1812* (Chapel Hill 1968) 586; W.B. Cohen, *Français et Africains: les noirs dans le regard des blancs, 1530–1880* (Paris 1981, trans. C. Garnier), 15; Banton, *The Idea of Race*, 106. There has, to be sure, been some criticism of Snowden's indiscriminate use (*Blacks*) of 'mythological material, history and romantic narrative', and of his citing at face value 'anything from Homer to Heliodorus' (Morton Smith, *AHR* 76 [1971] 139–140). But it cannot seriously be argued that any given ancient literary genre is inherently superior to others as evidence on *attitudes*, and the real force of the criticism in question lies in the fact that attention to context is the primary guarantee against misrepresentation of a text. Some scholars have rightly stressed the importance of works of fiction as evidence on attitudes: cf. F. Millar, 'The world of *The Golden Ass*', *JRS* 71 (1981) 63–75; J.E. Ifie and L.A. Thompson, 'Rank, social status and esteem in Apuleius', *Museum Africum* 6 (1977–1978), 21–36; P. Veyne, 'Vie de Trimalcion', *Annales* 16 (1961) 213f.; G.K. Hunter, 'Elizabethans and foreigners', in A. Nicoll (ed.), *Shakespeare in his Own Age* (Shakespeare Survey 17, Cambridge 1964) 37–52; id., 'Shakespeare and colour prejudice', *Proc.Brit.Ac.* 53 (1967) 139–63.

20 On the Roman ideological system, see Dauge, *Le Barbare*; D.C. Earl, *The Moral and Political Tradition of Rome* (London 1967); P. de Francisci, *Spirito della civiltà romana* (Rome 1952); H. Bardon, *La génie latine* (Brussels 1963); M. Mazza, *Storia e ideologia in Tito Livio* (Catania 1966); U. Knoche, *Vom Selbstverständnis der Römer* (Heidelberg 1962); O. Seel, *Romertum und Latinität* (Stuttgart 1964); K.E. Müller, *Geschichte der antiken Ethnographie*; J. Gaudemet, 'L'étranger dans le monde romain', *Studii Clasice* 7 (1965) 37–47; id., 'L'étranger au Bas-Empire', *Rec.Bodin* 9 (1958) 209–35; F. de Visscher, 'La condition des pérégrins

à Rome jusqu' à la constitution antonine de l'an 212', *Rec.Bodin* 9 (1958) 195–208.

21 Both R. Winkes, on the limited scale of his study of Roman portraiture ('Physiognomonia: Probleme der Characterinterpretation römischer Porträts', *ANRW* I.4 [1973] 899–944), and R. Lonis, in his article on Graeco-Roman attitudes towards 'the Ethiopians' (*Ktema* 6, 1981, 69–87) attempted something of this kind.

22 J.M. Courtès, 'The theme of "Ethiopia" and "Ethiopians" in patristic literature', in *Image* II.1, 9–32 (discussion of the sources at 9–10).

23 *Mon.Germ.Hist.*, VII, 246 (Ennodius, *Ep.* VII 21): *sic tua non maculent nigrantis membra puellae, / nec iaceas propter Tartaream faciem* ('So don't let the body of a black girl blacken and dirty yours. Because of her Hell-black face, you shouldn't go to bed with her'); cf. Courtès, op. cit., 22.

24 P.L. Shinnie, *AHR* 89 (1984) 103.

25 Lucian, *Somnium* 8; cf. Plut., *Pericles* 2.1; Cic., *Brut.* 257; Alison Burford, *Craftsmen in Greek and Roman Society* (London 1972), 11–14, 23– 7, 41; J.P.V.D. Balsdon, *Life and Leisure in Ancient Rome* (London 1969) 134–5; Susan Treggiari, 'Urban labour in Rome: *mercenarii* and *tabernarii*', in P. Garnsey (ed.), *Non-slave Labour in the Greco-Roman World* (Cambridge Philological Society, suppl. vol. 6, Cambridge 1980), 48f.

26 Cf. L. Bugner, 'Introduction', in *Image* I, 22; J. Desanges, 'The iconography of the black in ancient north Africa', ibid. 258f.; J. Leclant, 'Egypt, land of Africa, in the Graeco-Roman world', ibid 273f.

27 Snowden, *Blacks* 144–82, 194; id., *Before Color Prejudice* 50–9, 67–87; Winkes, *ANRW* I.4, 908f.; Cracco Ruggini 1974, 147f.; ead., 1979, 113f; Lonis, *Ktema* 6 (1981) 69–87; cf. B.H. Warmington, *Afr.Hist.St.* 4 (1971) 384–5.

28 Cf. M. Banton, *White and Coloured: The Behaviour of British People towards Coloured Immigrants* (London 1959) 39; E.J.B. Rose, *Colour and Citizenship: A Report on British Race Relations* (Oxford 1969) 15f.; Guillaumin, *L'idéologie raciste*, 66.

29 Cf. G.W.Allport, *The Nature of Prejudice* (Boston, Mass. 1954) 165f.; R. Bastide, 'Color, racism and Christianity', in J.H. Franklin (ed.), *Color and Race*, 34; E. Shils, ibid., 1-3. K.J. Gergen ('The significance of skin color in human relations', ibid., 113) suggests that extreme distance from a given population's somatic norm in terms of colour is more 'visible' (and so charged with greater significance for the observer) than extreme distance in height or weight. But colour distance acquires its significance in every case from the observer's mental selection and interpretation of his own impressions, in the light of his *prior experience*, so Gergen's point is little more than a restatement of Seneca's distinction (*De ira*, III 26.3) between the 'absolute somatic defect' (exemplified by the likes of giants, dwarfs and hunchbacks in *all* societies, and a not uncommon sight everywhere in pre-industrial times), and, on the other hand, the *commune vitium* or 'ethnic defect' (exemplified by blacks in a white society or by 'palefaces' in a non-

white society, and so likely to be a less familiar sight than dwarfs and the like in pre-industrial societies). If as François Raveau suggests ('An outline of the role of color in adaptation phenomena', in Franklin, ed., *Color and Race*, 99), a different-coloured person 'stands out' more conspicuously than a cripple of 'normal' colour, that can only be because non-conformity to this colour norm (in the given society) is more rarely experienced in that society than the cripple's type of deviation from the somatic norm – unless the society is of the (racist) sort in which colour is a deference-entitling property and, as such, is very closely monitored as a symbol of high or low status (because people in such a situation have, as it were, a high investment in such a monitoring process).

30 The point is emphasized by M.I. Finley, *The Use and Abuse of History* (London 1975) 68f.; cf. S. Piggot, in P.J. Ucko, Ruth Tringham and G.W. Dimbleby (eds.), *Man, Settlement and Urbanism* (London 1972), 949.

31 L. Febvre, *Combats pour l'histoire* (2nd edn.) (Paris 1965) 215.

32 Cf. Snowden, *Blacks*, 178; W.L. Westermann, *The Slave Systems of Greek and Roman Antiquity* (Philadelphia 1955), 104; K.E. Müller, *Geschichte der antiken Ethnographie*, II, 16 ('sehr bemerkenswerterweise'). In a recent work Snowden actually proposed to 'discover the reasons for the *absence* of bitter antagonism toward blacks in the ancient world' (*Before Color Prejudice*, vii – my italics).

33 Guillaumin, *L'idéologie raciste*, 65–7, 13; cf. Thompson, *PACA* 17 (1983) 1; J. Pitt-Rivers, in *Race* 9 (1968) 400–1; G.K. Hunter, *Proc.Brit.Ac.* 53 (1967) 158f.

34 Cf. Guillaumin, op. cit., 9–16, 33f.; Jordan, *White over Black*, 3f., 94f., 216f., 153f.; Cohen, *Français et Africains* 84f., 99f., 114f.; P. Mason, *Patterns of Dominance* (London 1970), 31–2; Banton, *The Idea of Race*, 27f.; G.K. Hunter, in A. Nicoll (ed.), *Shakespeare in his Own Age*, 38; J. Rex, *Race, Colonialism and the City*, 186; Dauge, *Le barbare*, 381f.; Müller, *Geschichte der antiken Ethnographie* II, 14–15, 118–21.

35 Jordan, op.cit., 164; P. Bairoch, 'Écarts internationaux des niveaux de vie avant le revolution industrielle', *Annales* 34 (1979) 145f.; id., *La révolution industrielle et sous-devéloppement* (Paris 1967); F. Chabod, *Storia dell'idea d'Europa* (Bari 1962), 60–109; D. Hay, *Europe: The Emergence of an idea* (2nd edn) (Edinburgh 1968), 56, 96f., 117–32; Y. Lacoste, *Géographie du sous-développement* (Paris 1967); I. Sachs, *The Discovery of the Third World* (Cambridge, Mass. 1976) 146f.

36 Cf. Jordan, op. cit. 71f., 257; O.C. Cox, *Caste, Class and Race: A Study in Social Dynamics* (2nd edn.) (New York 1959) 330f.; P. Mason, *Patterns of Dominance*, 31–2; Banton, *The Idea of Race*, 27f.; id., *Race Relations* (London 1967), 117; id., *White and Coloured*, 57–9, 68f.; Cohen, op. cit., 99f.; Rex, *Race, Colonialism and the City*; H.R. Isaacs, 'Group identity and political change: the role of color and physical characteristics', in J.H. Franklin (ed.), *Color and Race*, 75–6; Thompson, *PACA* 17 (1983) 2–3; J.A. Rogers, *Sex and Race: Negro-Caucasian Mixing in All Ages and All Lands*, I (9th edn.) (New York

1967), 207 – citing the London magazine *Titbits* of 21 July, 1917, where one reader wrote drawing attention to the threat to 'the eternal supremacy of the white over black' posed by intimate relations between English women and black soldiers and stage-performers. See also E.J.B. Rose, *Colour and Citizenship*, 591.

37 E. Shils, in J.H. Franklin (ed.), *Color and Race*, 2; cf. Hay, op. cit. (n. 35), 117–23; Chabod, op. cit. (n. 35), 60–109; Thompson, *PACA* 17 (1983) 3; Jordan, op. cit. (n. 34), 164.

38 Cf. Pliny, *HN* IV 88, VI 53, VII 9–12; Strabo IV 5.4; L.A. Thompson, 'Strabo on civilization', *Platon* 31 (1979) 219–21; id., *PACA* 17 (1983) 2–3; Chabod, op. cit. (n. 34); J.B. Duroselle, *L'idée d'Europe dans l'histoire* (Paris 1965); Hay, op. cit. (n. 34); Müller, op. cit. (n. 34), II, 78f., 97–105, 114–21, 194f., 230f.

39 Cf. Vitruv. VI 1.3–11; Pliny, *HN* II 189–90; Anon., *De physiog.* (ed. André) 79, 90–2; Suet., *Iul.* 76.3; Seneca, *Polyb.* 18.9. In this literature Mediterranean 'whiteness' is consistently perceived as an intermediate colour between 'black' and pale 'nordic' whiteness (cf. Anon., *De physiog.*, ed. André, 88: *inter nigrum et pallidum*). Cf. André, *Étude sur les termes de couleur dans la langue latine* (Paris 1949 – cited hereafter as André, *Étude*), 123–30, 327; Balsdon, *Romans and Aliens*, 59f., 214f.; Benabou, in Poliakov (ed.), *Hommes et bêtes*, 143–152; Thompson, *Platon* 31 (1979) 213–30; id., 'On development and underdevelopment in the early Roman empire', *Klio* 64 (1982) 383–401; id. *PACA* 17 (1983) 2–3; Duroselle, op. cit., 29f., 38f.; Hay, op. cit. (n.34), 4–16.

40 Cf. Jordan, op. cit. (n. 34), 216–17; Cohen, op. cit. (n. 34), 98–9, 122–42; Shils, op. cit. (n. 37), 2.

41 Cf. Vitruv. VI 1.3–7, 10–11; Pliny, *HN* II 189–90; Müller, op. cit. (n. 34), II, 107f.; Thompson, *Platon* 31 (1979) 213–30; id., *Klio* 64 (1982) 383–401; Duroselle, op. cit. (n. 38), 38f., 298f.; Hay, op. cit. (n. 34), 4–16; Saddington, *ANRW* II.3, 117.

42 Blake, 'The little black boy', in *Songs of Innocence* (1789); E. Bernand, *Inscriptions métriques de l'Égypte gréco-romaine* (Paris 1969), no. 26; Victor Hugo, cited by Cohen, op. cit. (n. 34), 308 (*'Devant Dieu, toutes les âmes sont blanches'*); B. Lewis, *Race and Color in Islam* (New York 1970), 12. Similar is the hagiographical description of a black 'Desert Father' of the monastery at Scete in fourth-century Roman Egypt (Abba Moses) as a man who, *despite* his somatic blackness (symbolically associated with spiritual 'blackness'), 'had a soul more radiantly white than the splendour of the sun' (*Vita S. Moysis Aethiopis*, 1, in V. Latyshev [ed.], *Menologii anonymi Byzantini saeculi X quae supersunt*, St Petersburg 1912, fasc. 2, 330).

43 A.H. Richmond, *Readings in Race and Ethnic Relations* (Oxford 1972), 1; cf. M. Leiris, 'Race and culture', in Leo Kuper (ed.), *Race, Science and Society* (Paris/London 1975), 168; Jordan, *White over Black*, 608.

44 P.D. Curtin, *The Image of Africa*, 28–29; cf. M. Banton, *Race Relations*, 12; H. Hoetink, *The Two Variants in Caribbean Race Relations*, 78f.

45 J. Rex, *Race, Colonialism and the City*, 195; J. Stone, 'James Brice and

the comparative sociology of race relations', *Race* 13 (1972) 325; E.C. Hughes, 'Race relations and the sociological imagination', *Race* 5 (1964) 3f.

46 A. Montagu, *Man's Most Dangerous Myth: The Fallacy of Race* (5th edn.) 4, 54; N.H. Baynes, *JRS* 33 (1943) 33; cf. Banton, *The Idea of Race*, 2; Guillaumin, in Poliakov (ed.), *Hommes et bêtes*, 203–8; ead., *L'idéologie raciste*, 55–62.

47 Guillaumin, *L'idéologie raciste*, 1–5, 64; Rex, op. cit. (n. 45), 203.

48 A.J. Toynbee, *A Study of History* (London 1935), I, 208; cf. Curtin, op.cit. (n.44), 375–377; Banton, *Race Relations*, 26–30; Cohen, *Français et Africains*, 297f.; Guillaumin, op. cit. (n. 47), 45–73.

49 B.G. Trigger, 'Nubian, negro, black, Nilotic?', in Sylvia Hochfield and Elizabeth Riefstahl (eds.), *Africa in Antiquity: The Arts of Ancient Nubia and the Sudan* (New York 1978), I, 28; cf. W.Y. Adams, 'Continuity and change in Nubian cultural history', *Sudan Notes and Records* 48 (1967) 15–16.

50 Cf. Guillaumin, op. cit. (n. 47), 32f., 44, 93; Banton, *The Idea of Race*, 4.

51 Especially after the publication (in 1684) of François Bernier's pioneering distribution of humanity according to 'races'. Cf. E. Pittard, *Les races et l'histoire* (Paris 1924), 3–4; M. Radin, *The Jews among the Greeks and Romans* (Philadelphia 1915) 48f.; Banton, *Race Relations* 16–18; id., *The Idea of Race*, 16f.; Guillaumin, op. cit. (n. 47), 55f., 69f.; Cohen, op. cit. (n. 48), 31–2.

52 P. Mason, 'An approach to race relations', *Race* 1 (1959) 44. Since the seventeenth century, 'races' (defined in the two popular senses of 'people' and 'somatic type') have also often been associated with particular temperamental and behavioural characteristics, explained by geographical or historical circumstances, just as was the case with *genera* or *gentes* in Roman usage; cf. Thompson, *PACA* 17 (1983) 4.

53 The same conceptual overlap is also apparent in the recent ruling of the House of Lords that British Sikhs are a 'race' under the law since they constitute a distinct ethnic group (though in the somatic sense they are a part of the so-called 'race' popularly described by the term 'Asians')

54 As Erna Lesky has pointed out (*Die Zeugungs- und Vererbungslehren der Antike und ihr Nachwirken*, 108), 'race' as a genetic concept was unknown in classical antiquity.

55 Mart. VI 61.3: *PG* LXVI.1092–1097 (Synesius); cf. Claudian, *Bell. Gild.*,419 (*flavi Sygambri*), *In Ruf.* II 108–10 (*flavi Galli*), *Cons. Stil.* II 240–241 (*flava Gallia*), *In Eutrop.* I 390 (*flavi Suebi*).

56 *Moretum* 31–5.

57 Gell. XI 18.6; Livy XXI 22.3, XXX 12.18; Suet., *Aug.* 4.2; Cic., *Phil.* IV 13. Livy's notion of a 'mixed Libyan-Phoenician *genus*' (XXI 22.3) is paralleled by Sir Walter Scott's description of the Normans as a 'mixed *race*' (Banton, *The Idea of Race*, 18 – my italics).

58 Cf. Bourgeois, *La Grèce devant la négritude*; Lonis, *Ktema* 6 (1981) 69-87; Sherwin-White, *Racial Prejudice in Imperial Rome*; W.J. Watts, *Acta Cl.* 19

(1976) 83-104; Saddington, *ANRW* II.3, 112-37; Walbank, *HSCP* 76 (1972) 158; S. Davis, *Race Relations in Ancient Egypt* (London 1951); Cohen, *Français et Africains*; Mason, *Race* 1 (1959) 41-52; id., *Race Relations* (Oxford 1970); Curtin, *The Image of Africa*. Not surprisingly, the same notion is commonly reflected in the comments of scholars whose subjects are matters other than 'race relations'; hence E. Courtney (*A Commentary on the Satires of Juvenal*, London 1980, 27), whose vision of *Hispani, Galli, Afri* and *Graeculi* as 'races' easily leads him into the error of equating xenophobia with 'racial prejudice' and, consequently, of speaking of Juvenal's resentment at 'foreign upstarts' as an attitude that combined class prejudice and *'racial* prejudice' (my italics).

59 M.I. Finley, 'Race prejudice in the ancient world', *The Listener* 79 (1968) 146.

60 G.W. Allport, *The Nature of Prejudice*, 6-9.

61 J. Rex, *Race, Colonialism and the City*, 202-3, 217f.; Guillaumin, *L'idéologie raciste*, 27-43.

62 E. Shils, 'Deference', in J.A. Jackson (ed.), *Social Stratification* (Cambridge 1968) 104-106.

63 Cf. Rex, op. cit. (n. 61), 203, 217f.; id., *Race Relations in Sociological Theory*, 114f., 160; Shils, op. cit. (n. 62), 129-30; Guillaumin, op. cit. (n. 61), 27-43.

64 W.G. Sumner, *Folkways: A Study of the Sociological Importance of Usages, Manners, Customs, Mores and Morals* (Boston, Mass. 1906), 13; O.C. Cox, *Caste, Class and Race* (2nd edn.) 321, 478-9; I. Sachs, *The Discovery of the Third World*, 2f.

65 The tendency is also evident in discussions of social relations in more recent history, for example, P. Mason, *Race*, 1 (1959) 41-52; id., *Race Relations*, 30-1; Cohen, *Français et Africains*, 404. But see Cracco Ruggini 1979, 113; ead., *Athenaeum* 46 (1968) 140; J. Mélèze-Modrzejewski, in M. Olender (ed.), *Pour Léon Poliakov: le racisme. Mythes et sciences*, 414-15; and especially the three works of John Rex cited previously; also A.H. Richmond, 'Theoretical orientations in studies of ethnic group relations in Britain', *Man* 57 (1957) art. no. 145, 120–1; Guillaumin, *L'idéologie raciste*.

66 Cf. Snowden, *Blacks* 183; id., *Before Color Prejudice*, 67, 107-8; Winkes, *ANRW* I.4 908f.; Saddington, *ANRW* II.3, 119-20; P. Mayerson, 'Anti-black sentiment in the *Vitae patrum*', *HTR* 71 (1978) 304-11; J. Ferguson, (ed.), *Juvenal: The Satires* (New York 1979) 128, 212; D.S. Wiesen, 'Juvenal and the blacks', *Cl.et Med.* 31 (1970) 132-50; R. Lonis, *Ktema* 6 (1981) 69-87; J. Devisse, in *Image* II.1, 50-1.

67 Cf. K.L. Little, *Negroes in Britain: A Study of Racial Relations in English Society* (London 1948), 95 (my italics); P. Mason, *Prospero's Magic: Some Thoughts on Class and Race* (London 1962) 54-60; id., *Patterns of Dominance*, 30-1; G. Boquet, 'L'image des Africains dans le théâtre élisabéthain', *Annales* 24 (1969) 894.

68 Allport, *The Nature of Prejudice*, 90.

69 *PACA* 17 (1983) 5.

70 A good example of this particular failing is Philip Mason's conviction
    (*Race*, 1959, 46-8) that Nazi and 'Teddy Boy' violence, and the
    incipient riot provoked by the local silversmiths at Ephesus in the
    name of Diana of the Ephesians (*Acts of the Apostles* 19), all represent
    manifestations of one and the same kind of prejudice and group
    antipathy. W.B. Cohen (op. cit., [in n. 65], 72-81, 142-6, 395-404)
    similarly sees nineteenth-century French anti-black racism as merely
    a more intense development of a negative attitude displayed by
    French people towards blacks since the sixteenth century.
71 J. Rex, in S. Zubaida (ed.), *Race and Racialism*, 48; id., *Race, Colonialism
    and the City*, 203, 217f.
72 Cf. A.H. Richmond, *Readings in Race and Ethnic Relations*, 1; M. Banton,
    The Idea of Race, 148; Guillaumin, *L'idéologie raciste*, 5. Some social
    scientists have spoken of 'invisible races' referring to racized groups
    which are indistinguishable from the dominant group in the same
    society in terms of somatic appearance and yet are marked out by
    ascriptive criteria, for instance, the Burakumin of Japan, or the
    Iberian *Conversos* of the era of the Inquisition. Cf. G.D. Berreman,
    'Race, caste and other invidious distinctions in social stratification',
    Race 13 (1972) 393; W.G. Runciman, 'Race and social stratification',
    Race 13 (1972) 499; P.L. van den Berghe, *Race and Racism*, 12. But the
    term 'invisible race' pays unnecessary homage to the popular concept
    of 'race' as somatic type. The sociological concept constitutes the
    reason why (for instance) the idea of a French racism inferiorizing
    Portuguese immigrants as a group cannot be dismissed, as Cohen
    (*Français et Africains*, 400) believed, *solely* on the ground that the
    Portuguese belong to the same 'race' as the French (that is, the same
    somatic type). Since the late eighteenth century, rationalization of
    racism has usually appealed to data from the biological sciences, but
    it has taken other forms at other times, not at all depending on the
    'organized scientific knowledge' that tends to be seen (wrongly) as a
    sine qua non of racism (for this error, cf. Cohen, op. cit., 144; Cox,
    Caste, Class and Race (2nd edn.) 322, even suggests that pre-capitalist
    society is by definition immune to the virus of racism); for examples of
    pre-capitalist society (and 'pre-scientific') racism, cf. Runciman, op.
    cit.; Berreman, op. cit.; L. Poliakov, *The History of Antisemitism*
    (London 1974) II, 224f. Equally perverse is the notion that whites
    (expecially 'nordics') have always had some sort of innate urge to
    racize darker peoples (suggested by Han Suyin, *Race* 13, 1971, 1-20;
    cf. Hoetink, *The Two Variants in Caribbean Race Relations*, 86f.). See S.
    Zubaida, in Zubaida (ed.), *Race and Racialism*, 4; Rex, *Race Relations in
    Sociological Theory*, 159-60; Toynbee, *A Study of History*, I, 207f; Banton,
    The Idea of Race, 4-5; Guillaumin, *L'idéologie raciste*, 9-13, 29-40.
73 Rex, *Race Relations in Sociological Theory*, 159; cf. Guillaumin, op. cit., 36.
74 Allport, *The Nature of Prejudice*, 136.
75 L.P. Gartner, *The Jewish Immigrant in England: 1870-1914* (London
    1973), 278; cf. Runciman, *Race* 13 (1972), 500.
76 S.I. Oost, *Galla Placidia Augusta*, 39 (but despite Oost, 'yellow men' –

flavi or *xanthoi* – meant to Romans, not 'mongoloid peoples', but blond-haired 'nordics'); cf. Sherwin-White, *Racial Prejudice in Imperial Rome*, 51-60 (Roman derogation of northern barbarian somatic traits); cf. Thompson, *Museum Africum* 7 (1981) 35-46; Cogrossi, in Marti Sordi (ed), *Conoscenze etniche e rapporti di convivenza nell'antichità*, 158-77.

77 The true nature of the 'antisemitism' of the Roman world has been rightly diagnosed as a cultural and power-political group-antagonism: the *Iudaeus* was always free to cease being a Jew and become Roman in culture and habits if he or she so desired; so too the barbarian was free to debarbarize himself or herself and to encourage the Romanization of his or her progeny as a guarantee of escape from adverse ethnocentric Roman attitudes. Cf. I. Heinemann, 'Antisemitismus', *RE* Suppl. 5 (1931) 3-43; J.N. Sevenster, *The Roots of Pagan Antisemitism in the Ancient World*; C. Levy, 'L'antijudaisme paien: essai de synthèse', in V. Nikiprowetski (ed.), *De l'antijudaisme antique à l'antisémitisme contemporaine* (Lille 1979), 51-86; L. Mélèze-Modrzejewski, in M. Olender (ed.), *Pour Léon Poliakov: le racisme*, 411-439; Cracco Ruggini, *Athenaeum* 46 (1968) 139-147; Dauge, *Le barbare*, 294f., 325f., 396f., 463f., 476f.; Vogt, *Kulturwelt und Barbaren*; E. Demougeot, *REA* 70 (1968) 392-408; Saddington, *ANRW* II.3, 118-119, 120-132; G. Walser, *Rom, das Reich und die fremden Völker*, 70f.; Christ, *Saeculum* 10 (1959) 273-288; Speyer and Opelt, *JbAC* 10 (1967) 231-290.

78 Cf. Snowden, *Blacks*, 178, 188, 218; id., *Before Color Prejudice*, 88f., 66; Winkes, *ANRW* I.4, 908f.; Devisse, in *Image* II.1, 50f.; Courtès, ibid. 19-20 ('a certain racism', supposedly evidenced by disdainful Christian references to foul, malodorous and ugly demons in the shape of blacks); Wiesen, *Cl. et Med.* 31 (1970) 132-50; Beardsley, op. cit., 20f., 37f., 62f., 65, 82f., 111f., 116, 120f.; Lonis, *Ktema* 6 (1981) 82-7; Morton Smith, *AHR* 76 (1971) 139-40. Snowden, of course, allows only the possibility of a mild 'color prejudice' in Roman society (similarly Saddington, *ANRW* II.3, 119-20, and J. Ferguson [ed.], *Juvenal: The Satires*, 128, 212), and even the admission is of the involuntary sort (*Blacks*, 176, 183; *Before Color Prejudice*, 67-8,107); but his conceptualization is not essentially different from that of the 'race prejudice school': he even shows an inclination to see an explanation of racism in a white population's unfamiliarity with blacks living in their midst (*Before Color Prejudice*, 130 n. 2), a notion which is very easily discouraged by a recollection of the fact that the two factors of 'blacks living amidst whites' and cultural homogeneity of the black and white populations have endured for numerous generations in societies that are nonetheless racist (cf. Allport, *The Nature of Prejudice*, 517). In all these works 'racism' is mistakenly seen as a personality-conditioned prejudice, a misconception that also explains why other scholars have interpreted the Roman material as evidence of an anti-black prejudice distinguishable from modern race prejudice only in degree of intensity and in scale (cf. P. Mayerson, *HTR* 71, 1978, 304-11; J. Desanges, 'L'Afrique noire et le monde méditerranéen dans

l'antiquité: Éthiopiens et Gréco-Romains', *RFHOM* 62, 1975, 410-11; id., 'L'antiquité gréco-romaine et l'homme noir', *REL* 48, 1970, 87-95; Saddington, op. cit.; M. Rosenblum, *Luxorius: a Latin Poet among the Vandals*, New York/London 1961, 209; F. Paschoud, *Roma aeterna: études sur le patriotisme romain dans l'occident latin à l'époque des grandes invasions*, Rome 1967, 140; J. Ferguson, op. cit.; W. Den Boer, *Mnem.* 24, 1971, 439). Even Lellia Cracco Ruggini (1974, 1979; cf. *Athenaeum* 46 [1968] 139-52), who distinguished the Roman 'prejudice' from modern racism, saw some of its manifestations as very close to modern racist behaviour. There is, however, an interesting difference between Beardsley's outlook and the more recent points of view on this matter: whereas the latter rest on the assumption that public and unabashed derogation of nigritude, if fairly widespread, must indicate racism (that is, ascription of an inferior group status to blacks), Beardsley assumed that even the existence of such a group status does not constitute racism if the disparagement of blacks is suitably counterbalanced by expressions of a paternalistic white 'goodwill' towards black individuals. In either case the assumption is drawn from the social–psychological milieu of the author, and in either case it is indefensible.

79 Cf. Vell., II 117.3, 118.1; Tac., *Ann.* II 14.2, XI 16-19, 23-4, XIII 55-6; *P.Oxy.* 1681.5f.; Themistius, *Or.* I (11b-12c Dindorff); Cic., *Phil.*VIII 9; Galen, *De tuenda sanitate* I 10.17; Apul., *Met.*IV 4 (violent contempt for the *volgus ignobile* and its *inculta pauperies*, which is a condition of a very different order from genteel *paupertas*); cf. Cracco Ruggini, *Athenaeum* 46 (1968) 139-47; Dauge, *Le barbare*, 463f., 476f.; Sherwin-White, *Racial Prejudice in Imperial Rome*, 44f.; Walbank, *HSCP* 76 (1972) 145f.; Saddington, *ANRW* II.3, 120-22; Vogt, *Kulturwelt und Barbaren*, 11-12, 17f., 34f.; Balsdon, *Romans and Aliens*, 18f.; MacMullen, *Roman Social Relations*, 88f.; L.P. Gartner, *The Jewish Immigrant in England*, 278; Runciman, *Race* 13 (1972) 499f.; Rex, *Race, Colonialism and the City*, 186-7; id., in Zubaida (ed.), *Race and Racialism*, 49; O.C. Cox, *Caste, Class and Race* (2nd. edn.), 331.

80 Among the phenomena of later times with which these contemptuous Roman stereotypes are comparable are the attitudes shown towards Irish people by medieval Anglo-Norman nobles, who loaded the appellation *Hibernicus* ('Irish') with contempt; cf. H.S. Deighton, 'History and the study of race relations', *Man* 57 (1957), art. no. 147, 123; cf. Sherwin-White, op. cit., 44f.; Dauge, op. cit., 463f.; Thompson, *Klio* 64 (1982) 389f.; id., *Platon* 31 (1979) 214f.

81 H.R. Isaacs, 'Blackness and whiteness', *Encounter* 21.2 (1963) 15; Colette Guillaumin, in Poliakov (ed.), *Hommes et bêtes*, 20.

82 The concept 'somatic norm image', formulated by the Dutch sociologist Hermann Hoetink, is defined as 'the complex of somatic characteristics accepted by a group as its norm and ideal.' (H. Hoetink, *The Two Variants in Caribbean Race Relations*, 120f.).

83 Cf. C.C. Rogler, 'The role of semantics in the study of race distance in Puerto Rico', *Social Forces* 22 (1944) 451; J. Walvin, *The Black Presence:*

A Documentary History of the Negro in England, 1555-1860 (London 1971) 74f., 86-92. It is interesting to note in this connection that a Japanese scholar found in operation among some post-war Japanese an absolutist standard of beauty (a consequence of western 'Caucasian' influence) and a feeling of mortification at their own personal distance from that 'international' somatic norm image (Hiroshi Wagatsuma, 'The social perception of skin color in Japan', in J.H. Franklin (ed.), *Color and Race*, 146-8 – essay reprinted in Melvin M. Tumin (ed.), *Comparative Perspectives on Race Relations*, Boston, Mass. 1969, 124-39).

1 REVIEW OF THE MODERN LITERATURE

1 Cf. S. Reinach, *Répertoire de la statuaire grecque et romaine* (Paris 1897) III, 158; E. von Stern, 'Bronzegefass in Bustenform', *JOAI* 7 (1904) 197–203; A.J.B. Wace, 'Grotesques and the evil eye', *ABSA* 10 (1903–1904) 107; F. Poulsen, 'Tête de prêtre d'Isis trouvée à Athènes', *Mélanges Holleaux* (Paris 1913) 221; C.T. Seltman, 'Two heads of negresses', *AJA* 24 (1920) 14.

2 Cf. Beardsley, *The Negro in Greek and Roman Civilization*, xi; Snowden, *Blacks*, 187f.

3 W.G.Waddell, *Selections from Menander* (Oxford 1927) 152. The same assumption also appears in some literature of more recent date, cf. A.J. Arkell, *A History of the Sudan to 1821* (2nd edn., London 1961) 113; P. Green, *Juvenal: The Sixteen Satires* (Harmondsworth 1967) 75; P. Mayerson, *HTR* 71 (1978) 307.

4 Cf. Snowden, *Blacks*, 169.

5 J. Dowd, *The Negro in American Life*, 456; cf. M. Banton, *The Idea of Race*, 49.

6 Beardsley, op. cit.

7 But Cracco Ruggini 1979, 1974 differ considerably from the general pattern.

8 To be sure, this misguided question was explicitly posed only by Beardsley (op. cit., ix, 116), but it is implicit in the works of several other scholars, for example, Snowden, *Blacks* 184–6; id., *Before Color Prejudice* 17 ('*the position*' of '*the Ethiopian*' – my italics); Wiesen, *Cl. et Med.* 31 (1970) 148f. ('estimate of *the Negro*', position of blacks as a race – my italics); Bourgeois, *La Grèce devant la négritude*, 120 ('unequal *race*' – my italics). The same implication is inherent in the *assumption* (evident in several discussions and comments) that blacks in Roman society were necessarily treated as a *racial* group, and so, that it is invariably appropriate to speak of the black element in the population as a collectivity *vis-à-vis* whites, in terms of 'they' and 'them'; cf. Courtès, in *Image* II.1, 20–1; Devisse, ibid., 50–1; Wiesen, op. cit., 138f., 133–7; Den Boer, *Mnem.* 24 (1971) 439; Lonis, *Ktema* 6 (1981) 82–7; E. Bernand, *Inscriptions métriques de l'Égypte gréco-romaine*, 143–7; G.R. Dunstan and R.F. Hobson, 'A note on an early ingredient of racial prejudice', *Race* 6 (1965) 334–9. The implication is again

inherent in discussions like that of Winkes (*ANRW* I.4, 908f.), which see in the Roman situation a parallel with a modern race relations situation.

9 A.H. Richmond, *Man* 57 (1957) 120–1; M. Banton, *White and Coloured*, 39, 84; J. Rex, *Race, Colonialism and the City* (passim); E.J.B. Rose, *Colour and Citizenship*, 14, 590.

10 Beardsley, op. cit., ix-xii, 115–20, 125f.; cf. 20f., 37f., 62f., 79, 82f., 111f. Beardsley envisaged this racism (or 'racial feeling') as the inevitable consequence of increasing black numbers in the first century AD, which breached the Roman threshold of intolerance (op. cit., 115–20). But it may be noted as a general principle that, according to social psychologists, the sort of 'growing density' of blacks postulated by Beardsley 'is not in itself a sufficient principle to explain prejudice', though it may cause the 'aggravation of whatever prejudice already exists' (Allport, *The Nature of Prejudice*, 229).

11 Wiesen, op. cit. 132f.; Morton Smith, *AHR* 76 (1971) 139–40; Bourgeois, op. cit. 119f.; Lonis, op. cit. 69f.

12 Desanges, *REL* 48 (1970) 92f.; id., *RFHOM* 62 (1975) 408f. Desanges' position has not been subtle enough to avoid being taken as basically supportive of the racial prejudice position (cf. Cohen, *Français et Africains*, 21; Sachs, *The Discovery of the Third World*, 42); cf. W. Den Boer, op. cit. 439 (restricting the Roman 'race prejudice' to the early Christian world); P. Mayerson, *HTR* 71 (1978) 304f. (again, restricting the prejudice to the Christian world).

13 M. Rosenblum, *Luxorius*, 209.

14 F. Paschoud, *Roma aeterna*, 140, Courtès, op. cit., 19–21; Devisse, op. cit. 50–1.

15 Winkes, *ANRW* I.4, 908f.

16 Bernand, op. cit. (n. 8), 143–7; Wiesen, op. cit., 133f., 137–9, 141–3, 147–8.

17 Bourgeois, op. cit. (n. 8), 119f.; Devisse, op. cit. (n. 8), 37–8, 50–1, 61–2.

18 J. Ferguson (ed.), *Juvenal: The Satires*, 128, 212.

19 Snowden, *Blacks*, 176, 182f.; id., *Before Color Prejudice*, 67–8, 107–8; Saddington, *ANRW* II.3, 120; cf. Winkes, op. cit. 908–11.

20 Snowden, *Blacks*, 217–8; id., *Before Color Prejudice*, 63–108; Saddington, op. cit. 119–20; cf. B.H. Warmington, *Afr.Hist.St.*4 (1971) 383–6; J.M. Cook, *CR* 22 (1972) 253–5; Desanges, *REL* 48 (1970) 87–95; id., *RFHOM* 62 (1975) 391–414; C.R. Whittaker, *Phoenix* 25 (1971) 186–8. The position of Cracco Ruggini (1974, 1979) is more subtle and nuanced than that of any other contributor to the debate, but her view that in some parts (at least) of the Roman world in late antiquity there was a widespread colour prejudice against people of black pigmentation is, nevertheless, likely to be seen quite widely as supportive of the racial prejudice position.

21 Wiesen, op. cit., 135–6; Snowden, *Blacks* 28, 180–8; id., *Before Color Prejudice*, 80–2, 134–6 n. 57.

22 Cf. Beardsley, op. cit., ix-xii, 20–21, 37f., 62f., 65f., 78–9, 82f., 111–16,

125f.; Wiesen, op. cit., 137–9, 141–3, 147–8.

23 Cf. Snowden, *Blacks*, 134–6 n. 57 (a tendency criticized by Wiesen, op. cit. 134f., 136–7; Desanges, *REL* 48 [1970] 92–3; id., *RFHOM* 62 [1975] 410–11; Sachs, op. cit. [n. 12], 42; H. Deschamps, *Africa: J. Int.Afr.Inst.*41 [1971] 68; Devisse, op. cit. [n. 8], 50–1; H.J. Diesner, *Gnomon* 56 [1984] 373–4).

24 Wiesen, op. cit., 139f., 149–50.

25 Snowden, *Blacks*, 176, 183; id., *Before Color Prejudice*, 67–8, 107–8; cf. Saddington, op. cit., 119–20.

26 Cracco Ruggini 1979, 108f., 112f., 117; ead., 1974, 147.

27 Mayerson, op. cit., 304, cf. Devisse, op. cit. 37–8, 50–1, 61–2; Courtès, op. cit. 19–20; Desanges, *RFHOM* 62 (1975) 410f.; Morton Smith, *AHR* 76 (1971) 139–40; Lonis, *Ktema* 6 (1981) 82f.

28 See Chapter 3, 'The ideology of status'.

29 Cf. Snowden, *Blacks*, 180–1.

30 Snowden, in *Image* I, 229–32; Desanges, ibid., 251–8; Leclant, ibid., 273.

31 Bugner, ibid., 12–13; Snowden, ibid., 229–32; Desanges, ibid., 258.

32 Snowden, *Blacks*, 176, 181f., 186–92 and figs 70, 72–4; id., *Before Color Prejudice*, 63–4, 80f.; id., in *Image*, I, 238 and figs 251–2, 333, 336–7. Against those who would see the iconography as a mere expression of an *Aethiops* somatic stereotype (cf. Morton Smith, AHR 76, 1971, 140), both Snowden and Winkes drew attention to several highly individualized portraits of blacks that are evidently portraits of real people (Snowden, *Blacks*, 28, 187–8 and figs 70, 73, 75, 115–16; id., *Before Color Prejudice*, 15–16, 80–2; Winkes, *ANRW* I.4, 909–10; cf. G. Becatti, *The Art of Ancient Greece and Rome*, New York 1967, 274). L. Bugner (in *Image*, I, 12) similarly notes the individuality of the marble head that is generally accepted as that of Memnon, the black protégé of Herodes Atticus, 'a black, noble of visage, calm, marvellously expressive'. This bust (now in the East Berlin Museum) was discovered at Thyreatis among a number of others with bases intact and with the names of the models – names also mentioned by Philostratus (*Vita Apoll.* III 11, *Vitae sophist.* II 588) along with that of Memnon as names of members of the household of Herodes Atticus. See Snowden, in *Image*, I, figs 336–7 (=*Blacks*, fig 68). The iconography suggests a considerably high concentration of blacks in domestic slave roles like those of groom, cook, and bath-attendant, but blacks are also depicted as jockeys (racing-chariot drivers), circus performers, and musicians (Bugner, op. cit., 18; Snowden, in *Image*, I, 184, 220, 224, 232; Desanges, ibid., 257–65). For depictions of blacks as priests, musicians and dancers in relation to the Isiac cult, see Leclant, ibid., 278–85; Desanges, ibid., 258.

33 Bugner, ibid., 16. Bugner notes that even a turned-up snub nose could be used by artists to serve this negative and caricatural function. Cf. Leclant, ibid., 273–8 and figs 374–6, 378; J.P. Cèbe, *La caricature et la parodie dans le monde romain des origines à Juvénal* (Paris 1966) 345f., 354; Winkes, *ANRW* I.4, 910; P. Perdrizet, *Bronzes grecques d'Égypte de la*

collection Fouquet (Paris 1911) 55, no. 88 and figure 23; H.A. Grüeber, *Coins of the Roman Republic in the British Museum* (London 1910) I, no. 3468; Beardsley, op. cit., 81; Seltman, *AJA* 24 (1920) 14; G. Becatti, 'Negro', *EAA* V (Rome 1963) 353–400.

34 Winkes, op. cit., 909–10; cf. Cèbe, op. cit., 345f.

35 Cf. Morton Smith, *AHR* 76 (1971) 139–40; Wiesen, *Cl. et Med.* 31 (1970) 132f.; Desanges, *REL* 48 (1970) 87–95; id., *RFHOM* 62 (1975) 391–414; Lonis, *Ktema* 6 (1981), 74, 83f.; J. Devisse, in *Image*, II.1 37–8, 50–1, 61–2.

36 Mart., VI 39.1–9. The sequel relates to the other five 'brats', whose natural fathers are imagined as white men.

37 Wiesen, op. cit., 141–3.

38 Juv. VI 600; Claudian, *Bell. Gild.*, 193.

39 Cf. J. Rex, *Race Relations in Sociological Theory* (passim),

40 Snowden, *Blacks*, 322–3 n. 82; cf. Cracco Ruggini 1979, 118; E. Courtney, *A Commentary on the Satires of Juvenal*, 30; Juv. VI 599f.; Mart. VI 39; Petronius, *Sat.* 126.5–7.

41 Mart. VI 39.6–9; cf. *Spect.* 3.10; *Moretum* 31–35; Pet., *Sat.* 102; Snowden *AJP* 68 (1947) 288f.; id., *Blacks*, 178f. But Snowden also failed to note the positive significance of Martial's use of the verb *incedere* ('strut about') in the Marulla epigram (VI 39).

42 Juv. VI 600; Claud., *Bell.Gild.*, 193. These and many other instances of mocking are somehow overlooked by Snowden.

43 Cf. Cracco Ruggini 1979, 118. The class prejudice that marks Martial's *persona* is well expressed by Ovid's remark (*Her.* IV 34) that when a lady of rank commits adultery with a humble man the breach of the boundaries of rank offends more than the adultery itself (*peius adulterio turpis adulter obest*). Cf. J.P. Sullivan, 'Martial's sexual attitudes', *Philologus* 123 (1979) 287; T. Reekmans, *Anc.Soc.* 2 (1971) 128f.

44 Cf. Juv., XII 126; Hor., *Epodes* 15.18; Claud., *Bell.Gild.*, 194; Lucian, *Catap.* 16 (*semnōs probainein*); MacMullen, *Roman Social Relations*, 195 n. 68. This point is somehow overlooked by those, like Beardsley, who see this epigram as proof of so-called racial prejudice.

45 Juv. VI 597–601. On the word *decolor*, cf. André, *Étude*, 126. E. Eyben ('Family planning in antiquity', *Anc.Soc.* 11–12 [1980–1981] 15) notes that the practice of killing or abandoning malformed infants at birth 'was routine'. A *decolor infans* might be seen as 'malformed' by some parents, and many who did not see it in that light would still find it 'unwanted', especially as, among the poor, inducements towards bringing up such an infant arising from beliefs in biological 'regeneration' and 'maternal impression' had to compete with the inducement towards killing or abandoning it arising from poverty. As explanations of a baby of 'the wrong colour', in any case, these popular 'genetic' ideas must have met with considerable scepticism among upper-class husbands. Noteworthy is the discussion by J.A. Rogers (*Sex and Race* I (9th edn), 158, 175) on the vitality of these ancient beliefs in Europe as late as the 1930s. Rogers cites instances

where attempts by middle-class women to attribute their babies 'of the wrong colour' to biological atavism were thwarted by sceptical acquaintances who were able to obtain evidence of the women's intimacy with black men. Heliodorus (IV 8) suggests that upper-class women giving birth to such a baby would immediately seek to get rid of it.

46 Claud., *Bell.Gild.*, 188–95.

47 Cf. J. Vogt, *Kulturwelt und Barbaren*, 12, 15, 18–28, 35–48, 65f.; Dauge, *Le barbare*, 281–329; Paschoud. *Roma aeterna*, 42f., 135f.; G.G. Belloni, 'Aeternitas e annientamento dei barbari sulle monete', in Marta Sordi (ed.), *I canali della propaganda nel mondo antico* (Milan 1976), 220–8; K. Christ, *Saeculum* 10 (1959) 279; J. Gaudemet, *Rec.Bodin* 9 (1958) 222–235; Cracco Ruggini, *Athenaeum* 46 (1968) 148f.

48 Cf. M. Gluckman, 'How foreign are you?', *Race* 4 (1962) 20. The bitterness of Claudian's vision is exacerbated by a deep sense of Roman impotence; cf. *Bell.Gild.* 73, 166–8, *Cons. Stil.*I 264–9; A. Cameron, *Claudian: Poetry and Propaganda at the Court of Honorius* (Oxford 1970) 192–8, 370; Paschoud, *Roma aeterna*, 135–54; Walbank, *HSCP* 76 (1972) 158; Dauge, *Le barbare* 294–5, 311f. On the general upper-class xenophobia towards Gildo's menace, see Augustine, *Contra litt. Pet.* II 23.53; Amm., XXIX 5.37; H.J. Diesner, *Der Untergang der römischen Herrschaft in Nordafrika* (Weimar 1964) 13f., 97f., P. Romanelli, *Storia delle province romane dell'Africa* (Rome 1959), 606. On the belief that the Nasamones were a tribe of *Aethiopes*, see Philostratus, *Vita Apoll.* VI 25; Desanges, *Catalogue*, 154–5, 195; cf. Dauge, op. cit. 361f.; Claud., *Cons. Stil.* I 248–61, 275–6, 351, 354–6.

49 These lines of Claudian recall the contrasting image of Virgil's *despectus Iarbas* and the rejection of his barbarian marriage-proposal by *Sidonia Dido* (Virgil, *Aen.* IV 36–8). In Claudian's picture and general usage, *Maurus* is a genetic term for 'North African barbarian' in contrast with 'Roman-African' (cf. *Bell.Gild.*70–4); but, in respect of 'barbarism', he makes no distinction between Gildo's 'Moors' and his 'Aethiopians'. On children's fear of the dark and of the unaccustomed sight of black faces, see *GGM* I 118 (Agatharchides); A. Dihle, 'Zur hellenistischen Ethnographie', in *Grecs et barbares* (Entretiens sur l'Antiquité Classique 8, Fondation Hardt, Geneva 1962), 214f.; Den Boer, *Mnem.* 24 (1971) 439; P. Mason, *Race Relations*, 64; W.B. Cohen, *Français et Africains*, 38f. On contemporary physiognomonic lore, see Johanna Schmidt, 'Physiognomik', *RE* 20.1 (1941) 1064–74; Elizabeth C. Evans, *Physiognomonics in the Ancient World* (passim). The moral content of Claudian's allusion to the blackness of the 'bastards' fathered by Gildo's 'blacks' is also present in his disparagement of the Huns (*In Ruf.* I 123f.) for their 'ugly facial appearance and repulsive-looking bodies' (*turpes habitus obscenaque visu/corpora*), which again also reflects the aesthetics of the somatic norm image.

50 The word *Aethiopem* is both emphatic and negative. For another indication of a habit of mentally associating blacks with low status, cf. Origen, *Hom. in cant. canticorum* II 377, 373-374; cf. (for Menander's

Hellenistic world) Men., frg. 612 (ed. Koerte): 'nobly-born, *even if* he be a black.'

51 Cf. Beardsley, op. cit., 115-20; Rosenblum, *Luxorius*, 195.

52 Wiesen, op. cit., 133f., 138f.

53 *Moretum*. 31-5.

54 Desanges, *RFHOM* 62 (1975) 409-11.

55 Ibid., 410; cf. Diesner, *Gnomon* 56 (1984) 373-4.

56 Pet., *Sat.*, 102.

57 Snowden, *Before Color Prejudice*, 76-9, 134-6 n. 57; cf. Seneca, *De ira* III 26.3; Juv., XIII 162f.

58 Hoetink, *The Two Variants in Caribbean Race Relations*, 120f.

59 Luxorius, to be sure, lived and wrote in Vandal Carthage, but his cultural traditions are Roman, and his work reflects attitudes that had been characteristic of Roman society for centuries.

60 Luxorius 67.6–14 (=*Anth.Lat.* 353.6–14). The opening lines extol the countless victories and the popular acclaim of this *venator*, 'a Hercules in neck, shoulders, back and limbs' who bears a name (Olympius) that rightly links him with divinity; cf. Luxorius 68 (=*Anth.Lat.*354), the epitaph of the same champion composed by the admiring poet and posthumously recalling his glory with the words, 'your glory will live forever, and Carthage will always be saying your name.'

61 Cf. Virg., *Ecl.* 10.37–9, 2.16–18; *Anth.Gr.* V 121, 210. Snowden saw the above-cited text of Luxorius and a number of others as passages extolling 'the beauty of blackness'. But none of the texts so cited can rightly be seen in that light (and, indeed, except for the two cited from Luxorius, both in praise of Olympius, they cannot rightly be taken as references to an actual perception of the *Aethiops* somatic type). Herodotus' reference to the 'Macrobian Aethiopians' as 'the handsomest of men' relates to the utopian world of sunburnt men (*Aethiopes*) mirrored in Homer's epics (Herodotus III 20; cf. Hom., *Iliad* I 423–5, XXIII 205–7; *Od.* I 22–4, IV 84, V 282; cf. A Lesky, 'Aithiopika', *Hermes* 87, 1959, 27–38; Desanges, *Catalogue*, 191); the courtesans mentioned by poets as 'black', 'curly-haired', 'honey-brown' and the like (or people described as *colore fusco*) cannot be presumed to have been perceived as belonging to the *Aethiops* category; cf. *Anth.Gr.* V 121, 210; Theocr. 10.26–9; Mart. I 115, 72, IV 62, VII 13; André, *Étude*, 123f.; Morton Smith, *AHR* 76 (1971) 139–40; Saddington, *PACA* 12 (1971) 58; Whittaker, *Phoenix* 25 (1971) 187.

62 R.W. Garson, 'Observations on the epigrams of Luxorius', *Museum Africum* 6 (1977–1978) 10; cf. Origen, *Hom in cant. canticorum*, I 4.6, the secular dimension of which is evidently a contemporary notion of 'something that may be called an *Aethiops* beauty', which lacks the esteem accorded to conventional beauty, even when it can be recognized as beauty; cf. *CCL* LXIX.176 (Gregory of Elvira).

63 Luxorius 43, 71, 78 (*Anth.Lat.* 329, 357, 364); cf. Gregory of Elvira, *In cant. canticorum* (*CCL* LXIX.176) for an indication of a secular puzzlement at the notion 'black *and* beautiful' (a combination of

concepts conventionally seen by members of the educated classes as mutually exclusive, especially with regard to the female sex): this Christian leader says of the Church of the Gentiles (symbolized by a black woman) 'How can she say she is black *and* beautiful, or beautiful if black?' Luxorius' contrast between *Pontica*-beautiful and *Garamas*-ugly is an adaptation of the conventional Roman contrast between 'nordic' Scythian and black *Aethiops*, but, as Desanges (in *Image* I, 268) suggests, the adaptation perhaps idealizes 'nordic' feminine beauty, reflecting perhaps a certain Germanization of outlook among descendants of the old Romano-African upper class at Carthage under the Germanic regime of the Vandals.

64 B. Lewis, *Race and Color in Islam*, 11–13 (citing verses of these poets).
65 *Ktema* 6 (1981) 83. Lonis acknowledges that, in Heliodorus' romance, a white Chariclea permits the author a greater complexity and excitement of plot than would otherwise have been possible. But that does not in itself explain the writer's attitude in making his heroine golden blond.
66 Cf. E. Feuillâtre, *Étude sur les Éthiopiques d'Héliodore* (Paris 1966) 11–41.
67 That position rests on the all too common misconception of 'racism' and abuse of the term 'racist' already noted in the foregoing. It is noteworthy that Philip Mason, a well known writer of modern race relations, interpreted Roman attitudes in much the same way as Lonis, stressing (like Devisse, Den Boer, and others) the powerful and negative influence of the symbolism of blackness upon attitudes and behaviour towards people of black skin, and concluding that Roman attitudes (no less than those of Europeans of more recent times) amounted to a 'colour prejudice' or 'race prejudice' or 'racialism' of a sort not expressed in the form of institutions (P. Mason, *Patterns of Dominance*, 30; id., *Race Relations*, 63–4; id., *Prospero's Magic*, 59–74; cf. Devisse, in *Image*, II.1, 80, 62; Courtès, ibid. 32).
68 Juv. II 21–8.
69 P. Green, *Juvenal: The Sixteen Satires*, 75; cf. Beardsley, op. cit., 119.
70 Snowden, *Blacks*, 322 n. 82.
71 Wiesen, *Cl. et Med.* 31 (1970) 138f., 133–137 (my italics); cf. Beardsley, op. cit., 37, 20–1, 78 (speaking, like Wiesen, of iconographic and literary association of the negro not only with the hunchback, but also with the cretin); Bernand, *Inscriptions métriques de l'Égypte gréco-romaine*, 143–7 (speaking of a 'low esteem accorded to people of colour'). With regard to Juvenal's text, it should be noted that the object of the satire is not male homosexuality *tout court*, but grown men in the *passive* role in sodomy (cf. J.P. Sullivan, *Philologus* 123, 1979, 294–5).
72 Wiesen, op. cit., 138–9.
73 Cf. Juv. XIII 162–6; Sen., *De ira* III 26.3.
74 Sen., *De ira* III 26.3.
75 Ibid.; cf. Juv. XIII 162–6; Luxorius 10, 24, 29 (=*Anth.Lat.* 296, 310, 315); Courtney, *A Commentary on the Satires of Juvenal*, 127. For mocking in the medium of literature, cf. Mart VI 39.6–9, VII 89.2; *Anth. Lat.* 182–3.

76 Agnar Mykle, *The Song of the Red Ruby* (Panther edn., London 1963), 54.

77 Cf. Adamantius, II 36 (R. Foerster, ed., *Scriptores physiognomonici Graeci et Latini*, I, Leipzig 1893); Lucian, *Anach*.25, *Dionys*. 2, *Menipp*.11, *Merc.cond*. 42, *Dial. meretr*. 2. 282, 3. 285; Mart. XIV 176; Lucretius, IV 1149–1207; Ovid, *Rem. am*. 315–44, *Ars am*.II 653f., *Am*. III 3.2–9, 7.7–8.

78 Cf. Juv. XIII 162–166; Sen., *De ira* III 26.3; Pet., *Sat*. 102; *Moretum* 34; *PG* LXVI.1092f. (Synesius); Mart., I 62.5, 115.2, II 34.2, IV 62.1; Hor., *Epodes* 2. 41; Lucian, *Dial. meretr*. 1. 282; Watts, *Acta Cl*. 19 (1976) 86.

79 Wiesen, op. cit., 138f. Snowden (*Before Color Prejudice*, 76) rightly observed that there were whites who did not conform to the Roman somatic norm image.

80 Wiesen, op. cit., 137; Juv. XIII 162–6; Sen., *De ira*, III 26.3. Wiesen (op. cit., 143–5) disagreed with Sherwin-White's interpretation (*Racial Prejudice in Imperial Rome*, 57–85) of certain texts as signs of a negative Roman perception of 'the vast and beastly size' of northern European barbarians, preferring to see such texts (without convincing argument) as indicative of Roman admiration of 'nordic' size (cf. Caes., *BG* I 39.1, II 30.4, IV 1.9; Livy VII 9.8–10.12; Tac., *Germ*, 20.1, *Ann*. I 64, II 14, 21, *Agric*.11.2). But on 'nordic' and *Aethiops* 'defects' see André, *Étude*, 70, 82, 140, 176–80; G.J. de Vries, *Mnem*.ser. 3, 12 (1945) 160.

81 *Anth.Lat*., 183. This epigram perhaps relates to an atmosphere of violent conflict with Saharan barbarians; a similar relationship has been attributed to the marble statue of a black boy, erected at Hadrumetum, the town to which the epigram relates; cf. Snowden, *Blacks*, fig. 58; L. Foucher, *Hadrumetum* (Paris 1964) 170–1 and plate 12d.; but Desanges (in *Image*, I, 265) questions the relevance of the statue to Saharan campaigns, while noting the psychological interest of the epigram and translating the word *faex* as 'shit' (ibid. 257).

82 *Anth.Lat*., 182.

83 Cf. Cracco Ruggini 1979, 108f.; Desanges, *REL* 48 (1970) 92f.; id., *RFHOM* 62 (1975) 408f.; Lonis, *Ktema* 6 (1981) 74f.

84 Desanges, in *Image*, I, 257f.

85 Ibid., 257.

86 Cf. Foucher, op. cit., 170f.

87 Cf. Lonis, op. cit., 87f.

88 Desanges, *RFHOM* 62 (1975) 409–11; cf. id., in *Image* I, 257.

89 Lewis, *Race and Color in Islam*, 12, 33–6; cf. Allport, *The Nature of Prejudice*, 300–4.

90 Juv. V 52f. 'Saharan groom' is Green's (*Juvenal: The Sixteen Satires*, 118) very apt rendering.

91 Juvenal's language does not declare the groom to be an *Aethiops*, particularly as slaves of North African origin ('swarthy' rather than black) were fashionable as stable staff. But Wiesen convincingly argued that the satirist's intention is to represent the two slaves in this

picture as complete opposites: Ganymede of untanned whiteness and *Aethiops* in a conventional contrast between extremes of somatic appearance (Wiesen, op. cit., 140; cf. R. Marache, ed., *Juvénal: saturae III, IV, V*, Paris 1965, 24; Jennifer Hall, 'A black note in Juvenal: satire V. 52–5', *PACA* 17, 1983, 108). For a similar description (and generalization) of fashionable stable staff as *niger*, cf. Mart., XII 24.6 (*rector Libyci niger caballi*, which recalls Juvenal's *nigri manus Mauri* and the vogue for having slaves of North African origin as grooms; cf. Sen., *Ep.*123.7; Lucian, *Philops.* 20; Mart., X13). The vogue is also indicated by a mosaic of Capsa (Gafsa) in Roman Tunisia depicting a very swarthy groom (Desanges, in *Image* I, fig. 349). Desanges (op. cit., 265) also notes the 'conventional theme' of dark-skinned grooms in Roman iconography, a motif which may well reflect the fact that black (*Aethiops*) grooms were a common feature in the stables of wealthy households; cf. Bugner, in *Image*, I, 18. In any case, Juvenal's imagination pictures the two slaves as examples of the conventional contrast between *candidus* and *Aethiops*; cf. Vitruv. VI 1.3–4 (*candidus* and *fuscus*); Pliny, *HN* II 189–190 (*candidus* and *Aethiops*); Firmicus Maternus, *Math.* I 2.1 (*candidus* and *Aethiops*); Ptolemy, *Tetrab.* II 2.5 ('palefaces' and blacks).

92 Cf. Mart., VIII 51, II 43, IV 42, 66, IX 73.6, XIII 42, X 66, 98, III 58, XIV 205, VI 39.13; Juv. IX 46–7, XIII 42; Sen., *Ep.* 95.24; Lucian, *Symp.* 15, *Sat.* 38, 26, *Nigrin.* 22, *Dial. mort.* 19.362, *Gallus* 11, *Merc. cond.* 16; Ps.-Lucian, *Amores* 14; cf. Pliny, *Pan.* 48 (*femineus pallor*).

93 Beardsley, op. cit., 119; Wiesen, op. cit., 139.

94 Wiesen, loc. cit. (my italics).

95 Ibid., 141 (my italics).

96 Sen., *Ep.* 95.24, *De brev. vitae* 12.5; cf. Mart. III 58, IV 42, VI 39.13, IX 73.6, X 66, 98, XI 8, 26, XIV 205; Juv. IX 46–7; J. Gérard, *Juvénal et la réalité contemporaine* (Paris 1976) 124–5.

97 Juv. V 54 (*et cui per mediam nolis occurrere noctem/ clivosae veheris dumper monumenta Latinae*). This comment on the black slave also contains an allusion to the superstition according to which a chance meeting with a black stranger was a bad omen; cf. Sen., *Apocol.* 13: 'a black dog that you certainly wouldn't want to run into in the dark' (*canem nigrum. . .sane non quem velis tibi in tenebris occurrere*); cf. Courtney, *A Commentary on the Satires of Juvenal*, 238; J. Ferguson (ed.), *Juvenal: The Satires*, 177; Jennifer Hall, *PACA* 17 (1983), 109.

98 Ferguson (op. cit., 177) rightly notes the heavily homosexual atmosphere of the picture; cf. Courtney, op. cit., 231, 238–9; Marache, op. cit. (n. 91), 24.

99 Cf. Mart., I 20, II 43, III 60, 82, IV 42, VI 11, IX 2, X 98; Lucian, *Sat.* 38, 22, *Symp.* 15, *Merc. cond.* 26. Pliny (*Ep.* II 6), who denounces the habit, shows that some Romans actually gave dinner parties of this type, shamelessly discriminating between major and minor guests. Cf. Pliny, *HN* XIV 91; Courtney, op. cit., 231. The Ganymede's career as favoured waiter and homosexual bed-mate was,

however (like that of the female sex-object), rather short in duration, ending at the onset of obvious adulthood (Ps.-Lucian, *Amores* 10, 26).

100 Mart., X 98, IV 42; Lucian, *Symp.* 15, *Sat.* 38, *Merc. cond.* 26.

101 Juv. V 62–6; cf. Lucian, *Sat.* 38.

102 Cf. Jennifer Hall, op. cit., 108; Gérard, op. cit. (n. 96), 126. The term 'bums' is borrowed from Green's (op. cit., 118) translation.

103 B.H. Warmington, *Afr.Hist.St.* 4 (1971) 385.

104 Cf. *PG* LXIX.1188 (Cyril of Alexandria); Snowden, *Blacks*, 200.

105 Warmington, op. cit.; cf. Desanges, *REL* 48 (1970) 92f.; id., *RFHOM* 62 (1975) 408f.; Cracco Ruggini 1979, 108f.; ead., 1974, 147f.; Lonis, *Ktema* 6 (1981) 74f.; Courtès, in *Image*, II.1, 9–32; Devisse, ibid., 37f.; Den Boer, *Mnem.* 24 (1971) 439.

106 E. Bernand, *Inscriptions métriques de l'Égypte gréco-romaine*, no. 26.5–10.

107 *PG* LXV.284. This is one of a series of closely related anecdotes on the 'testing' of Abba Moses (cf. *PG* LXVII.1377b–d; *PL* LXXIII.959, XLIX. 563–4).

108 Desanges, *RFHOM* 62 (1975) 408f.; Devisse, in *Image*, II.1, 37–8, 50–1, 61–2; cf. Cracco Ruggini 1979, 112f.

109 Cracco Ruggini 1979, 112f.; Den Boer, *Mnem.* 24 (1971) 439; cf. G.R. Dunstan and R.F. Hobson, *Race* 6 (1965) 334–9; Paschoud, *Roma aeterna*, 140; Courtès, op. cit., 20; Devisse, op. cit. 50–1.

110 Devisse, op. cit., 37–80; Morton Smith, *AHR* 76 (1971) 140; cf. *PG* XLIV.792.

111 Snowden, *Blacks*, 176, 181f.; id., *Before Color Prejudice*, 63–4, 80f. Arguments of this sort have earned Snowden's work epithets like 'highly optimistic' and 'irenic'; (cf. Devisse, op. cit. 37f., 50f.; Lonis, op. cit. 74f.; Courtès, op. cit., 9–32; Deschamps, *Africa: J.Int.Afr.Inst.* 41 (1971) 68; Sachs, *The Discovery of the Third World*, 42; Desanges, *REL* 48 (1970) 92f.; id., *RFHOM* 62 (1975) 408f.

112 Snowden, *Blacks*, 196–7.

113 *Mon.Germ.Hist.*, VII, 246.

114 Cf. Mayerson, *HTR* 71 (1978) 304–7; Cracco Ruggini 1979, 108–18; ead., 1974, 147–8; Devisse, op. cit., 37–8, 50–1. 61–2.

115 *PG* LXV. 284; cf. Juv. II. 23; Cracco Ruggini 1979, 108–18.

116 Ps.-Callisthenes III 18.6 (*Hist. Alex. Magni*, ed. Kroll); cf. *GGM* I, 118; Bernand, op. cit. (n. 106), no. 26; *Vita S. Moysis Aethiopis* (Latyshev, *Menologii anon. Byz. saec. X quae supersunt*, fasc. 2, 334); Cracco Ruggini 1979, 108f.

117 Snowden, *Blacks*, 176; cf. W.L. Westermann, *The Slave Systems of Greek and Roman Antiquity*, 104; J.M. Cook, *CR* 22 (1972) 254; Den Boer, *Mnem.* 24 (1971) 437–8.

118 Wiesen, *Cl. et Med.* 31 (1970) 136; Cracco Ruggini 1974, 147–8; ead., 1979, 108f.; cf. Lonis, *Ktema* 6 (1981) 83–4.

119 *SEG* IV 192 (trans. Cook, op. cit. 254).

120 See below, Chapter 2.

121 Cf. H.C. Baldry, *The Unity of Mankind in Greek Thought* (Cambridge 1965), 138, rightly stressing that the philosophical standpoint of Menander's character (frg. 612, Koerte: 'if a man's natural character

is good, then he is nobly-born, *even if* he be an *Aethiops*) merely proclaims merit as 'the criterion by which men *should be* judged' (my italics). The idea, which has many parallels in Roman literature, was in fact a literary cliché; cf. Sen., *De ben.* III 28.1, *Ep.* 44.5, 47; Lucian, *Toxaris* 5, *Anach.* 17; Juv. VIII; Courtney, *A Commentary on the Satires of Juvenal*, 381.

122 B. Lewis, *Race and Color in Islam*. My cautious 'rightly or wrongly' is an acknowledgement of my ignorance of Arabic and of the society which is the subject of Lewis' study. But if his English translations of Arabic texts and occasional allusions to social structures are correct, then he is wrong in suggesting that the Islamic situation falls within the typology of social situations classified in sociological theory as 'race relations situations' or 'racism'. Far less doubt is aroused by the conclusion of L.C. Brown ('Color in northern Africa', in J.H. Franklin, ed., *Color and Race*, 186–204, and especially 190–2) that 'the spectrum of black–white relationships' in Islamic northern Africa has always been explainable in terms of personal status and not in terms of 'race'.

123 All quotations from Lewis, op. cit., 11, 20–2. Of similar import is the old Moroccan maxim (cited by Brown, op. cit., 192) 'A fertile negress is better than a sterile white woman', which (as Brown notes) shows a prejudice of the sort amounting merely to aesthetic preference (what I have called 'worship of a somatic norm image'), or at most one arising from the fact that, in that society, the imagination could easily associate blacks with humble status.

124 Cited by W.D. Jordan, *White over Black*, 258.

125 Blake, 'The little black boy' (*Songs of Innocence*, 1789).

126 Cf. P.D. Curtin, *The Image of Africa*, 42f.; R. West, *Back to Africa* (London 1970) 13–14; Victor Hugo, cited by W.B. Cohen, *Français et Africains*, 308; M. Banton, *The Idea of Race*, 67; Kipling, *Barrack Room Ballads* (1892).

127 *Anth.Lat.* 183, cf. Juv. II 23.

128 H. Hoetink, *The Two Variants in Caribbean Race Relations*, 134; cf. F. Raveau, in J.H. Franklin (ed.), *Color and Race*, 99.

129 C.C. Rogler, *Social Forces* 22 (1944) 451.

130 J. Walvin, *The Black Presence*, 74f., 86–92; cf. Hiroshi Wagatsuma, in J.H. Franklin (ed.), *Color and Race*, 146–8.

131 Snowden, *Blacks*, 322 n. 82; id., *Before Color Prejudice*, 76–7, 134–6 n. 87; Wiesen, op. cit., 138 n. 23; cf. Courtney, op. cit. (n. 121), 127.

132 Cf. Juv. VIII 30–8; Mart. III 34; Jerome, *Ep.* 40.2; Isidore, *Etym.* I 37.24; Hor., *Sat.* I 343–54; J. Ferguson (ed.), *Juvenal: The Satires*, 255; Courtney, op. cit. (n. 121), 390–1.

133 For instance, *Anth.Lat.* 182–3, 329; Mart. VI 39.6–9, VII 89.2; Pet., *Sat.* 102; *Moretum* 31–5.

134 Sen., *De ira* III 26.3; cf. Juv. XIII 162–6.

135 Juv.III 278–99; cf. Apul., *Met.*IX 39–40; Courtney, op. cit. (n. 121), 191–2; Cèbe, *La caricature et la parodie*, 345–56; Reekmans, *Anc.Soc.* 2 (1971) 152–3 (rightly seeing the practice of mocking, badgering and

thrashing as a socially valid way of expressing one's superiority of status).

136 Lucian, *Catap.* 15, *Gallus* 14.

137 Cf. Lucian, *Catap.* 15. Despite his irenic tendency, even Snowden was unable completely to deny what is in fact an undeniable element of caricature of blacks in the iconography (*Before Color Prejudice*, 80; *Blacks*, 182; cf. Cèbe, op. cit., 345f.; Winkes, *ANRW* I.4, 910; Desanges, *REL* 48 [1970] 93; G. Becatti, 'Caricatura', in *EAA* II [Rome 1959] 342–8).

138 Cf. Lucian, *Prom. Litt.* 4–5, *Zeus trag.* 6, 27, *Anach.* 16; Mart. I 104.10, VI 77.8, XIV 176; *Anth.Lat.* 296, 301, 310, 315, 361 (= Luxorius, 10, 24, 29, 75); Pet., *Sat.* 46.1–2, 61.4; Quintilian, VI 3.28; Cèbe, op. cit. 345f.; U.E. Paoli, *Rome: Its People, Life and Customs* (London 1963) 267f.

139 Horace's (*Sat.* I 7.32) description of the sharpness characteristic of Roman wit.

140 Cèbe, op. cit., 345f.; Paoli, op. cit., 267f.

141 Snowden gave far too little acknowledgement to the social–psychological reality of public and unabashed mockery, apparently allowing his examination of the evidence to be compromised by an instinctive feeling (not essentially different from that shown by Wiesen and others of the race prejudice school) that open and shameless mockery of nigritude by whites is fundamentally inseparable from 'racism' and must accordingly be glossed over by any available means in order to avoid conflict with the thesis of a non-racist Roman world; cf. *Blacks*, 182; *Before Color Prejudice*, 75–82.

142 Cf. Cèbe, op. cit., 140, 224f.; Pet., *Sat.* 61; Mart. VII 12; Lucian, *Prom.* 8–9.

143 *PG* LXV. 284; LXXIII. 970–1; Luxorius 67.6 (= *Anth.Lat.* 353.6).

144 Cf. Sen., *De ira* III 26.3 (*dedecet*); Luxorius 67.6 (*nocet*); *PG* LXV.284 (*etarachthēn*); *PL* LXXIII.970–971; Juv. XIII 162–6.

145 Cf. Allport, *The Nature of Prejudice*, 142–61; Lucian, *Prom.* 8–9.

146 Wiesen, *Cl. et Med.* 31 (1970) 143–144. Others see the usage as undifferentiated from the mocking indicated by Juvenal's (II 23) *derideat Aethiopem albus*: 'a white man may mock a black'; cf. Reekmans, *Anc.Soc.* 2 (1971) 153 n. 23; Courtney, *A Commentary on the Satires of Juvenal*, 390.

147 Plut., *Quaest. symp.*, II 1.6 (632a, d).

148 Isidore, *Etym.* I 37. 24; cf. Jerome, *Ep.* 40. 2.

149 Lucian, *Pro imag.* 2.

150 It may be noted that the examples of the usage mentioned by Juvenal include one that is very much like the 'flattering' euphemisms mentioned by Lucian ('Nireus' and 'Phaon'), namely the antiphrastic appellation of the 'Miss England' type applied to an ugly girl.

151 Mart. III 34, XI 60, VI 77.7; cf. Pliny, *HN* VII 75; Prop., IV 8.41; Quintilian II 5.1; Pliny, *Ep.* IX 7; Jerome, *Ep.* 40.2; Ovid, *Rem. am.* 327–40, *Ars am.* II 657–62; Hor., *Sat.* I 3.22–54; Lucretius, IV 1160–9; P. Howell, *A Commentary on Book One of the Epigrams of Martial* (London

1980) 345 (on Mart. I 115). Notable is Horace's (*Sat.* I 3.45–8)
reference to the affectionate habit whereby the Roman father fondly
spoke of a squint-eyed son as having 'a slight cast', or called a
miserably undersized son 'Chick' or a boy with knock knees 'Big
Ankles'. A similar (though in no way euphemistic) usage is indicated
by the statement of Ausonius (*Parentalia* 5.4–5) that his grandmother
was called 'Maura' ('Darkie') by her childhood friends because of her
swarthy complexion. Significantly, the attested cases of euphemistic
naming are mainly household pets like the dwarfs in grand
households who were amusingly and affectionately called Magnus,
Andromeda, and the like.

152 J. Ferguson (ed.), *Juvenal: The Satires*, 235 (my italics).
153 Snowden, *Before Color Prejudice*, 65–6.
154 Cf. Pet., *Sat.* 102; *Moretum* 31–5; Mart., VI 39.8–9; Lonis, *Ktema* 6
     (1981) 69–70.
155 This assumption is particularly obvious in Beardsley's book (op. cit.
     82–108, 125–133), but it is also implicit in many of Snowden's
     comments (*Blacks*, vii, ix, 2, 181, 184–185, 329 nn. 159–161; *Before
     Color Prejudice*, 1–17, 63–66, 90–92; *Image* I, 134–135, 174). Similarly,
     in response to the comment of W.Y. Adams (*Nubia: Corridor to Africa*,
     London 1977, 8; cf. B.G. Trigger, in Hochfield and Riefstahl [eds.],
     Africa in Antiquity, I, 27) that ancient Nubians are 'black' or 'white'
     depending on one's prejudices, Snowden made the unacceptable
     comment that Romans 'were far from unclear' in this matter, thus
     implying that Romans, like those who share his perception, had no
     doubts about the blackness of Nubians (Snowden, *Before Color
     Prejudice*, 16). That view is plainly contradicted by the evidence (cf.
     Strabo XVII 1.53, XVI. 4.4; Pliny, *HN* VI 177; *Oxford Latin
     Dictionary*, 'Aethiops'). On the sociological implications of a definition
     of the Roman concept *Aethiops* in terms of mere descent from an
     Aethiops in recent generations, cf. J. Rex, *Race Relations in Sociological
     Theory*, 114–20; id., in Zubaida (ed.), *Race and Racialism*, 46–54; W.D.
     Jordan, *White over Black*, 167–169; A.H. Richmond, (ed.), *Readings in
     Race and Ethnic Relations*, 1–3.
156 Snowden, *Before Color Prejudice*, 17 (my italics); ibid., fig. 25; id.,
     Blacks, fig. 67; id. in *Image* I, figs. 231–3, 265, 286, 290–2, 300, 303,
     334 (portraits suggesting 'miscegenation').
157 Snowden, *Before Color Prejudice*, 17; the view that an ancient
     description of physical appearance which mentions any two 'negroid'
     traits must be a reference to an *Aethiops* (id., *Blacks* 14, 6) is as
     unacceptable as Beardsley's idea (op. cit. 63f.) that, in red-figured
     vases, any two of the traits short nose, thick lips, and prominent jaw,
     prove an artist's intention to depict an *Aethiops*. In discussing the
     iconography, Snowden also speaks of 'a wide range' of black types
     showing 'varying degrees of Caucasoid admixture' (*Image*, I, 242, cf.
     174) and of depictions of 'blacks' resembling in general appearance
     'many a descendant of black–white mixture in various parts of the
     world today'; he finds examples of 'crossbred features of the black'

(ibid., 174, 183–4, 216, 238, figs. 228–9, 329) in portraits in which others easily fail to see any nigritude. For instance, the face of an ancient statue perceived by Snowden and others of similar vision as that of a black boy (Snowden, *Before Color Prejudice*, 63–6; id., *Blacks*, 88 and fig. 63; cf. D.K. Hill, *Catalogue of Classical Bronze Sculpture in the Walters Art Gallery*, Baltimore 1949, xvi-xvii) has been seen by a European scholar as that of a Greek boy of the lower classes (W. Zschietzschmann, *Hellas and Rome*, London 1959, 150). Similarly, a portrait seen by F. Poulsen (*Catalogue of Ancient Sculpture in the Ny Carlsberg Glyptotek*, Copenhagen 1951, 166, no. 229b) as that of a white 'lad of distinctly plebeian type', is perceived by Snowden (*Image* I, 184) as 'a young mulatto'. Again, a first-century BC limestone head of a bald man, seen by N. Bonacasa as an Egyptian or Libyan (*Ritratti greci e romani della Sicilia*, Palermo 1964, 25–6, no. 27, pl. 12, 1–2; cf. E.S.G. Robinson, *Catalogue of the Greek Coins of Cyrenaica*, Bologna 1965, xxxiii), is, for Snowden, a well-to-do 'black' (*Image* I, 238 and fig. 329); and F. Cumont's negroid 'goddess Libya' (*Mon.Piot* 32, 1932, 41–50 and fig. 4) is perceived by Snowden (*Image* I, 217 and fig. 285) as 'a mulatto or quadroon', where the 'negritude' is probably non-apparent to most observers. Similar interpretations of the concept *Aethiops* abound in Beardsley's book (cf. ix–xii, 1–4, 75–108, 125f.). But it is perhaps significant that a marble bust of the first century AD described by Snowden in one place as 'a Negro' whose 'woolly hair and lips leave no doubt as to the Negroid characteristics' (*Blacks*, 187 and fig. 115; cf. *Image* I, 214) is elsewhere seen by him as offering no warrant for classification as 'Negroid' apart from 'a slight thickness in the lips' (*Image*, I 305 n. 233 and fig. 280), and a marble statue of a woman (from Lower Egypt, and dating from the first century AD), interpreted as a personification of 'Africa', is at once a 'mulatto woman' with 'flat nose, thick lips (neither very pronounced) and long, flowing hair' (ibid., 217 and fig. 286) *and* 'a charming Negro woman' (id., *Blacks*, 91 and fig. 67).

158 Beardsley, op. cit., 75, 82, 86–7, 95, 108, 125, fig. 13; for a similar vision, cf. A.J.B. Wace, *ABSA* 10 (1904) 107. There is little doubt that most people would, like Becatti (*EAA* V, 399), see simply a 'Caucasian' with somewhat full lips in the piece of sculpture (*Image*, I, fig. 230) whose 'rather full lips' have been enough to suggest 'mixed ancestry' to Snowden and others (*Blacks*, 329 n. 159; *Image*, I, 183–4 and fig. 230); cf. D.E.L. Haynes, *Fifty Masterpieces of Classical Art in the British Museum* (London 1970), no. 87; A.W. Lawrence, *Later Greek Sculpture and its Influence on East and West* (New York 1969), 18, whose perspective stands in strong contrast with the preoccupation with the taxonomic principle of 'negro blood' that led Beardsley to quarrel with German archaeologists whose discussions of the iconography made no distinction between 'negro' (*Neger*) and 'Moor' (*Mohr*), and with French scholars who used the term *nègre* 'to cover all variations of dark skin regardless of the features of hair' (Beardsley, op. cit., xi): here we see in operation the assumptions or that scholar's own milieu,

which excluded 'Moors' from the category 'blacks' on the principle that a Moor with negro blood was not a Moor, but a negro, and hence that a Paul Robeson was unfit for the role of Shakespeare's Othello since 'Othello was a Moor', while 'Robeson is an Ethiopian' (J.A. Rogers, *Sex and Race* I (9th edn.), 208; cf. W.B. Cohen, *Français et Africains*, 340).

159 Snowden, *Before Color Prejudice*, 65f., 88, 93f., figs. 25, 49, 53; id., *Blacks*, 143, 270, figs. 63, 67–8; id., *Image*, I, 174, 183f. 213–17, 229–38, figs 228–9, 233, 282–3, 285–6, 329–32, 334. But see R. Mauny, *J.Afr.H.* 12 (1971) 157–8; id., *Gnomon* 43 (1971) 830; Shinnie, *AHR* 89 (1984) 103; Desanges, in *Image*, I, 260, 265, 312 n. 145; J. Leclant, ibid., 282–5 (for perceptions different from Snowden's).

160 Snowden, *Blacks*, fig. 68; id., *Before Color Prejudice*, 88 and fig. 49; cf. C.C. Vermeule, *AJA* 68 (1964) 336. But, for a different kind of perception, see Shinnie, op. cit. 103; Mauny, op. cit.; Bonacasa, op. cit. (n. 157), 25–6; Haynes, op. cit. (n. 158), no. 87. On the tendency to see 'aristocracy' in blacks with 'regular' features, cf. Cohen, op. cit. (n. 158), 308–13.

161 So, Snowden (*Blacks*, 15–21) lists 54 names of so-called blacks, the vast majority of which cannot be shown to be names of persons actually perceived by Romans (or Greeks) as belonging to the category *Aethiops*, but are mentioned in the sources simply as Axumites, Trogodytes, Nubians or Moors, or are described as 'curly-haired' or by adjectives which need mean no more than 'swarthy' (*fuscus, niger, melanchroos, melas, melaneusa*); cf. André, *Étude*, 53f.

162 Snowden, *Blacks*, 4, 12, 182; id., *Before Color Prejudice*, 32–3; Corippus, *Ioh.* VIII 415–6 (*nigro de corpore*), 482 (*nigrique secat fera colla Mamonis*). Even the description of Moorish captives as 'black as crows' (ibid. VI 92–4) has no clear significance for Roman perceptions of the *Aethiops* somatic type: whatever it tells us about Corippus' poetic imagination, it is not a description of people actually perceived by him as belonging to the category *Aethiops*. Like Claudian (*Bell.Gild.* 192–3) and Philostratus (*Vita Apoll.* VI 25), Corippus imagines the Berber Nasamones to be a tribe of *Aethiopes*; cf. Desanges, *Catalogue*, 154–155. On the imprecision of Roman usages of the word *niger*, cf. André, *Étude* 125–7. For ancient distinctions between Garamantes and *Aethiopes*, cf. Strabo II 5.53, 33; XVII 3.19; Dionys. Perieg., 217–18 (=*GGM* III, 114); Ptolemy, *Geog.* I 9.7–10, I 8.5–7, IV 6.5; Gilbert and Colette Picard, *Daily Life in Carthage* (London 1961) 215; Desanges, *Catalogue*, 95 n. 4.

163 Mart., X 68.3, cf. VII 13; Cat., 39.12; André, *Étude*, 124f., 324.

164 Cf. Tac., *Agric.* 11 (curly-haired and dark-skinned Silures of Wales); HA *Firmus* 4 (curly-haired and dark-faced, but 'white', Firmus); Lucian, *Philops.* 34, *Navig.* 2, 45; Arrian, *Ind.* 6.9; Claud., *In Ruf.* II 108–10; Pliny, *HN* VI 70 (Indians); Ach. Tat. III 9.2 (Egyptians). Lucian's 'learned and extraordinarily able man' from Memphis has a flat nose and protruding lips (*simos, procheilos*) but is Egyptian, not *Aethiops* (Lucian, *Philops.* 34; cf. *Navig.* 2, 45; André, *Étude*, 55f. 123f.;

Mauny, *J.Afr.H.* 12 [1971] 157–8). Similarly, ethnic and national labels like *Afer* ('African'), *Maurus* ('Moor') and *Indus* ('Indian', referring to the Indian Ocean and Red Sea coasts of north-east Africa) offer no particular information about somatic appearance. Cf. J. André, 'Virgile et les Indiens', *REL* 27 (1949), 157–63; A. Lesky, *Hermes* 87 (1959) 27f.; J.Y.N. Nadeau, 'Ethiopians', *CQ* 20 (1970) 338–49; id., 'Ethiopians again and again', *Mnem.* 30 (1977) 75–78; Whittaker, *Phoenix* 25 (1971) 187; Desanges, 'Une mention altérée d'Axoum dans l'*Expositio totius mundi et gentium*', *Annales d'Ethiopie* 7 (1967) 148; D.B. Saddington, *ANRW* II.3, 119; R. Mauny, *J.Afr.H.* 12 (1971) 157–8; id., *Gnomon* 43 (1971) 830f. Among the texts in which *Indus* appears as a clear allusion to sub-Egyptian Africa and the Red Sea–Indian Ocean littoral of north-east Africa are Virgil, *Georg.* IV 293 (allusion to the Nile as sweeping down from the 'sun-bronzed *Indians*'), Ovid, *Ars am.* I 53 (reference to 'Aethiopian' Andromeda brought by Perseus 'from the Indians'), Mart. VII 30.4 ('the black Indian from the Erythraean Sea'); cf. Philostorgius, *Hist. eccles.* II 6 (*PG* LXV.469); Pet., *Sat.* 57; Lucian, *Gallus* 14, *Pro imag.* 5, *Navig.* 6; Ps.-Lucian, *Amores* 26, 40. The 'red' *Aethiopes* of Statius (*Theb.* V 427–8) is evidently an allusion to the Red *Sea* area, and not (as Snowden believes) a reference to 'Negroes of a red, copper-coloured complexion' (Snowden, *Blacks*, 4).

165 Snowden chooses to see these people as blacks (*Blacks*, 163; *Before Color Prejudice*, 8). For the textual references, Corippus, *Ioh.* VI 93–4 (Moorish captive); *Schol. in Pers.*, ed. Kurz, 5.9 (the actor Glycon): *staturae longae, corporis fusci, labio inferiore demisso*; *PL* LXV.378 (Fulgentius): description of the Christian convert, a native of some hot country distant from Roman Byzacena in Tunisia. Persius comments only on Glycon's 'silliness' (Persius, 5.9). The Christian convert should be seen as a very dark-skinned man of the 'Caucasian' type; cf. Diod., XX 57.5. It is also significant that the Christian missionary Theophilus is designated 'Indian' (that is, 'Nubian' or 'sub-Egyptian African') or 'Blemys' or 'Libyan'; but never '*Aethiops*' (Philostorgius, *Hist. eccles.* II 6 = *PG* LXV.469; ibid., III 4–6 = *PG* LXV. 481–8; Greg. Nyss., *Contra Eunomium*, 1 = *PG* XLV.264; cf. Desanges, *Annales d'Éthiopie* 7, 1967, 146–8. This missionary was evidently not perceived (as Snowden supposes) as *Aethiops*.

166 Diod., XX 57.5; cf. Ach. Tat. III 9.2; Adamantius II 31 (in R. Foerster (ed.) *Scriptores physiognomonici Graeci et Latini*, I). The term *nothos Aithiops* used by Achilles Tatius (III 9.2), however, describes a person who, though his complexion can be described as *decolor* (as distinct from black), has a facial morphology perceived as *Aethiops*. This *nothos* sub-category of *Aethiopes* may well have included the sort of appearance illustrated by the face of the groom depicted in a Hellenistic marble relief described by Snowden (*Image*, I, 184, fig. 232) as 'the pronounced Negro type'.

167 *Prooem. vitae Aesopi* (in B.E. Perry, ed., *Aesopica*, I, 215): Aesop is here attributed black skin, flat nose and protruding lips, with the additional

comment 'hence his name; for *Aesopus* is the same as *Aethiops*'. The sources speak of Lusius Quietus simply as a 'Moor' (*Mauros* or *Maurus*) or 'man from Mauretania' or from some semi-barbarian group in North Africa beyond the imperial frontiers (Cassius Dio LXVIII 32.4; HA *Hadrian* 5.8; Themistius 250; Dindorff). Den Boer's view that Quietus was a 'full-blooded Ethiopian' has no evidence in its favour, and rests on interpretation of *Mauros* as 'black' and on a comment by the *physiognomonicus* Polemo on aspects of the appearance of an important (but unidentifiable) person, thought to be Quietus, which was intended as an indication of the link between those physical traits and the person's negative moral traits. Even if it were absolutely certain that Polemo's 'the man from Qwrnyn' is an allusion to Quietus (and caution certainly forbids such an assumption), Polemo's allusion offers no suggestion at all that the person in question was an *Aethiops* (cf. Evans, *Physiognomics in the Ancient World*, 12). Snowden (*Blacks*, 143, *Before Color Prejudice*, 33) does not question the view of Quietus as *Aethiops*; but Den Boer's unconvincing case has rightly been dismissed by A.G. Roos (*Mnem.* 3, 1950, 158–65, 336–8) and L. Petersen ('Der mauretanische Reitergeneral Lusius Quietus', *Das Altertum* 14, 1968, 211–17). To be sure, J. Desanges (*Image*, I, 312 n. 148) sees Quietus as 'an Ethipianfrom Cerne', a place which he woudl identify with Mogodor; but his 'Ethiopian' is the equivalent of 'homme de couleur', not of 'negro' or 'le Noir' or the Roman concept *Aethiops* (ibid. 247, 308 n. 20; id., *RFHOM* 62, 1975, 409), and that is more or less the position first taken by Den Boer, who argued that Quietus was a 'coloured man', by which he meant 'not wholly of white descent' (*Mnem.* 1, 1948, 327–337).

168 Pliny, *HN* VI 177. For portraits of Juba, cf. J. Mazard and M. Leglay, *Les portraits antiques du Musée Stéphane Gsell* (Alger 1958), figs 6–8; E. Boucher-Colozier, 'Quelques marbres de Cherchel au Musée du Louvre', *Libyca*: Arch.-Epigr. 1 (1953), 23–8 and fig. 1 (noting the thick lips as well as the curly hair); cf. *MEFRA* 58 (1941–1946), 340. J. Desanges (*Image*, I, 265) considers it 'permissible' to detect negroid features in some portraits of Juba (ibid., figs 363–4), but that tells us nothing about Roman perceptions.

169 Whittaker, *Phoenix* 25 (1971) 188.

170 Cf. Evans, op. cit. 13f. (on the influence of *physiognomonia* on several authors of the Roman world, especially biographers and the historian Ammianus Marcellinus).

171 Philostratus, *Vita Apoll.*, III 11, *Vitae sophist.*, II 588.

172 For the false assumption that modern taxonomic principles are relevant, cf. Beardsley, op. cit. 75–108, 125f.; Snowden, *Blacks*, 163, 186f., 270 n. 3; id., *Before Color Prejudice*, 11, 17, 56–66, 88–9, 92–3, 114 n. 33; id., in *Image*, I, 216–17, 238, 242. Despite some support for Snowden's vision of nigritude from scholars like Beardsley (op. cit., 75 and fig. 13), C.T. Seltman (*Greek Coins*, (2nd edn.) London 1955, 183 and pl. xlii.6), F. Cumont (*Mon.Piot* 32, 1932, 41–50 and pl. 4), and F. Poulsen (*Mélanges Holleaux* 217–23 and pl. 6), several of his

identifications of 'blacks' in the iconography have rightly been
questioned: cf. R. Mauny, *Gnomon* 43 (1971) 830; id. *J.Afr.H.* 12
(1971) 157–8; P.L. Shinnie, *AHR* 89 (1984) 103; J. Desanges, in *Image*
I, 260, 265, 312 n. 145; J. Leclant, ibid., 284–5; Thompson, *PACA* 17
(1983) 14. Among earlier commentators who were apparently unable
to perceive the nigritude subsequently seen by Snowden in some items
of the iconography (*Image*, I figs 228–30, 233, 282–3, 285, 286
[=*Blacks*, fig. 67], 303, 331) are R. Brilliant, *The Arch of Septimius
Severus in the Roman Forum* (Rome 1967=*Mem.Am.Ac.* 29), 247 and pls
78 cd, 80a, 81; E.S.G. Robinson, *Catalogue of the Greek Coins of Cyrenaica*
(Bologna 1965) xxxiii; G. Becatti, *EAA* V, 399; Haynes, op. cit. (n.
158), no. 37; Bonacasa, op. cit. (n. 157) no. 27; Poulsen, op. cit. (n.
157), no. 229b; and F.W. von Bissing, *AM* 34 (1909) 29–32.

173 Desanges, *RFHOM* 62 (1975) 409; id., in *Image*, I, 247, 308 n. 20. As
Desanges himself notes, *homme de couleur* is not as ambiguous as it may
appear to be, since (in French usage) it is never applied to the so-
called 'yellow' peoples of the Far East.

174 S. Gsell, *Histoire ancienne de l'Afrique du Nord*, I (Paris 1920) 294; cf. R.
Collignon, 'Étude sur l'ethnographie générale de la Tunisie', *Bulletin
de Géographie Historique et Descriptive*, 1 (1886) 309–15; H. von
Fleischhacker, 'Zur Rassen- und Bevölkerungsgeschichte Nordafrikas
unter besonderer Berücksichtigung der Aethiopiden, der Libyen und
der Garamanten', *Paideuma* 15 (1969) 12–53; G. Camps, 'Recherches
sur les origines des cultivateurs noirs du Sahara', *Revue de l'Occident
Musulman et Méditerranéen*, 7 (1970) 35–45; J. Desanges, in *Image*, I, 308
n. 20, 247–8, 309 n. 47; id., *RFHOM* 62 (1975) 408f.; id, *Catalogue*,
15–16.

175 Gsell, op. cit.; Camps, op. cit., 35f.

176 Desanges, *RFHOM* 62 (1975), 408; cf. M. Banton, *White and Coloured*,
63–4, 84.

177 As W.Y Adams has observed (*Nubia: Corridor to Africa*, 8), Nubians
are describable as white, non-white, or black, depending on the
prejudices of the observer's environment and temperament; cf.
Trigger, in Hochfield and Riefstahl (eds.), *Africa in Antiquity*, I, 28.
For fluidity in the conceptualization of 'white' in some modern
societies, cf. H. Hoetink, *The Two Variants in Caribbean Race Relations*,
185f.; id. *Slavery and Race Relations in the Americas: Comparative Notes on
their Nature and Nexus* (London 1973), 187–8.

178 Snowden, *Blacks*, 110–11, 183f., 284–5 n. 41; id., *Before Color Prejudice*,
65–7, 131 n. 2; cf. Cracco Ruggini 1979, 119–22; ead., 1974, 147; R.
Mauny, *J.Afr.H.* 12 (1971) 159; id., *Gnomon* 43 (1971) 831; id., in
Cambridge History of Africa, II (Cambridge 1978) 272f.; Warmington,
Afr.Hist.St. 4 (1971) 383–5; Desanges, *REL* 48 (1970) 94; id., in *Image*,
I 257–68; Leclant, ibid., 270; Morton Smith, *AHR* 76 (1971) 140;
Whittaker, *Phoenix* 25 (1971) 187; M. Bang, 'Die Herkunft der
römischen Sklaven', *RM* 25 (1910) 248. It has been noted that the
Egyptian element in the population of the city of Rome was fairly
parts of the Roman empire, see Desanges, op. cit. 258 and fig. 346 (a

large and that it included Nilotic blacks; cf. M. Malaise, *Les conditions de pénétration et de diffusion des cultes Égyptiens en Italie* (Leiden 1972) 71–5, 159f., 321–30; Leclant, in *Image*, I, 282; J. Baumgart, *Die römischen Sklavennamen* (Breslau 1936) 64; Bang, op. cit. 248; Desanges, *Image* I, 257. For iconographic allusions to blacks in Egyptian cults in various parts of the Roman empire, see Desanges, op. cit. 258 and fig. 346 (a second-century mosaic panel from Lepcis Magna conveying an image of the life-giving Nile, with two black musicians in front of a nilometer; cf. J.M.C. Toynbee, *The Art of the Romans*, London 1965, fig. 78); Leclant, op. cit. 278–85 and figs 375, 383–4 (a second-century marble relief from Aricia depicting an Isiac ceremony with black and swarthy musicians and dancers; cf. Snowden, *Blacks*, fig. 5); Leclant, op. cit., 315 n. 80; Snowden, op. cit., figs 118–19; id., *Before Color Prejudice*, figs 60–1; id., in *Image*, I, figs 288–9 (mural paintings of the first century AD from Herculaneum, showing respectively a black Isiac dancer with a swarthy sistrum-shaking priest, and a swarthy musician with a black sistrum-shaking priest). Juvenal's satirical picture of a black musician (*nigro tibicine*) in a barbaric religious festival at Ombi in Egypt (Juv. XV 49), perhaps a fertility ritual (J. Lindsay, *Daily Life in Roman Egypt*, London 1963, 115ff; cf. Courtney, *A Commentary on the Satires of Juvenal*, 592), may very well have been prompted by experience of the role of Nilotic blacks as musicians, dancers, and singers amidst lighter-hued Egyptians and Nubians in Isiac ceremonies in Rome and other Italian cities.

179 Desanges, in *Image*, I, 258f.; cf. Leclant, ibid., 273f.
180 Strabo XVII 1.54; Cassius Dio LXIII 3.1–2.
181 Cf. W.Y. Adams, 'Post-pharaonic Nubia in the light of archaeology', *JEA* 51 (1965), 161f.; Whittaker, *Phoenix* 25 (1971) 187. Strabo's usage of the term *Aethiopes* in this context (as a designation of a *nation*) contrasts with, for instance, Pliny's reference to a circus performance by a hundred *Aethiopes* in Rome in 61 BC, which refers precisely to the black African anthropological type (actually seen by Romans in the circus as *venatores*); cf. Pliny, *HN* VIII 131.
182 Cf. Snowden, *Before Color Prejudice*, 63; Courtès, in *Image*, II.1, 10, 26.
183 J. Walvin, *The Black Presence*, 12–16; id., *Black and White: The Negro in English Society* (London 1973), 8–10, 46f.
184 Lonis, *Ktema* 6 (1981), 69–70.
185 Even when earlier discussions have rightly placed the issue of blacks in Roman society in the context of the well known antithesis between Roman and barbarian (a context which rules out the idea that somatic type was a determinant of social roles and rights, and instead makes debarbarization the primary prerequisite for the social integration of blacks, while also presupposing an ideology of social classification on the basis of deference-entitling properties like wealth and education – cf. Winkes, *ANRW* I.4, 909f.; Dauge, *Le barbare*, 390f., 511f.), those same discussions have arrived at inconsistent conclusions implying a Roman context of racism (for instance, by suggesting that the situation was actually rather like that of the United States some

decades ago, and hence that black social positions in the Roman world were effectively positions in a system of stratification applicable only to a black 'community' or 'race' (cf. Winkes, op. cit., 909f.; Lonis, op. cit., 82–7). Nor has this contradiction been resolved by the work of Snowden, since those contributions have continued to reflect a false (and essentially racist) vision of the Roman concept 'black man'(cf. Snowden, *Blacks*, 143, 163, 186f., 270 n.3; id., *Before Color Prejudice*, 17, 56, 88, 92; id., in *Image*, I, 174–84, 216, 238; cf. Cook, *CR* 22 (1972), 253–5).

186 Plut., *Brut.*, 48, Appian, *BC* IV 17.134; Florus II 17.7–8; Obsequens, 70; cf. Apul., *Met.*, VI 26; Ps-Lucian, *Lucius* 22. Similarly, some characters in Petronius' novel (*Sat.* 74) immediately decide to kill a cock whose crowing is interpreted as a bad omen.

187 Cf. Juv. III 278–301; Pet., *Sat.*, 32, 43, 57, 117, 124–5; Mart., VI 39.6– 7; Lucian, *Prom.*, 57–8, 82, *Menipp.* 11, *Navig.* 45, *Charon* 1, *Timon* 23, 27, *Catap.* 16, *Gallus* 12, *Zeus trag.* 14; Ps.-Lucian, *Nero* 7; Claudian, *Bell. Gild.*, 194; *Anth.Lat.* 353; Reekmans, *Anc. Soc.* 2 (1971) 153.

188 Cf. MacMullen, *Roman Social Relations*; Garnsey, *Social Status and Legal Privilege in the Roman Empire*; M. Bloch, *Feudal Society* (trans. L.A. Manyon, London 1961), 241–79; G.A.J. Hodgett, *A Social and Economic History of Medieval Europe* (London 1972), 88f., 173–5; Betty Behrens, in *Cambridge Economic History of Europe* (2nd edn.) (Cambridge 1967), V, 549–620; Colette Guillaumin, *L'idéologie raciste*, 28f.; K.L. Little, *Negroes in Britain*, 171f.; Devisse, in *Image*, II.1, 57.

189 Cf. I. Sachs, 'Le noir dans l'art européen', *Annales* 24 (1968) 887–8; Little, op. cit., 198–202; Walvin, *The Black Presence*, 13f., 61f. That a mental association of blacks with low status was operative in Roman society is obvious from certain pieces of evidence, including satirical comments on adultery between Roman ladies and black men, where the writers' disapproval rests entirely on the *assumption* that realism demands representing the black paramour of an upper-class woman as a slave (or, at best, a free man of low rank); cf. Mart., VI 39.6–9; Juv. VI 599–601; Claudian, *Bell. Gild.*, 192–3. The assumption is also apparent in Christian texts offering allegorical interpretations of the scriptures relating to the 'black and beautiful' *Aethiops* bride of the *Song of Songs*, or the black spouse of the patriarch Moses, seen in either case as an allegory of the Church among the Gentiles and 'black *by* her low origin' (cf. Origen, *Hom. in cant. canticorum*, II 377; also ibid. 373–4, where the *Aethiops* Abdimelech, saviour of Jeremiah in the biblical account, is a black stranger *presumed* to be of 'ignoble stock', and also seen as symbolic of the Church among the Gentiles). See also Jerome, *Ep.* 22.1; Augustine, *Enarr. in psalmos* 73.16; Cracco Ruggini 1979, 124–5, 112; Ifie and Thompson, *Museum Africum*, 6 (1977–1978), 26; cf. Pet., *Sat.*, 14, 37–8, 77; Apul., *Met.*, I 5, 23, II 18; Lucian, *Merc. cond.*, 9, *Scytha* 8–9; Ps.-Lucian, *Lucius*, 4.

2 THE *AETHIOPS* TYPE
IN ROMAN PERCEPTIONS

1 Cf. A. Lesky, *Hermes* 87 (1959) 27f.; L.A. Thompson and J. Ferguson (eds), *Africa in Classical Antiquity*, 26.

2 Strabo XVII 1.53 (misinterpreted by Snowden on the erroneous assumption that Nilotic peoples labelled *Aethiopes* were always blacks in the perception of Romans: *Blacks*, 118, vii-viii, 4f., 8f; *Before Color Prejudice*, 17; but see Strabo XVI 4.4. and Pliny *HN* VI 177; cf. *Oxford Latin Dictionary*, s.v. 'Aethiops'; Desanges, *RFHOM* 62 (1975) 392f.; id., *Catalogue*, 15–16; id., *REL* 48 (1970) 88; id., in *Image*, I, 246–8, 308 n. 20; Cracco Ruggini 1979, 109; Whittaker, *Phoenix* 25 (1971) 187–8.

3 Cf. Strabo XVII 1.53–4; *Mon. Ancyranum* 5. 26.18–22; *ILS* 8995; Diod., III 2.3–7, 4–8; Pliny, *HN* VI 181–2.

4 *Oxford Latin Dictionary*, s.v. 'Aethiops' 2.

5 On this realism, cf. Snowden, *Blacks*, 22f.; Beardsley, op. cit., 36.

6 Cf. Pet., *Sat.* 102; Mart., VI 39.6–9; *Moretum* 31–5; Diod., III 8.2, 28.1; Pliny, *HN* II 189–90; Sextus Emp., *Adv.math.* XI 43; Ptol., *Geog.* I 9.7–10, *Tetrab.* II 2.56; Arrian, *Ind.* 6.9; Curtius Rufus IV 7.19.

7 Snowden, *Blacks*, 130–1 and figs 41a–c; id., *Before Color Prejudice*, 31–2 and figs 31ab.

8 Cf. Whittaker, op. cit., 187–8.

9 Ibid.; cf. W.Y. Adams, *JEA* 51 (1965) 161; id., *Sudan Notes and Records* 46 (1967) 12.

10 Philostratus, *Imag.* II 7; cf. id., *Vita Apoll.* VI 2 ('Indians and *Aethiopes* are both black').

11 Seneca, *De ira*, III 26.3.

12 Lesky, *Hermes* 87 (1959) 27f.

13 On mythological themes in art relating to 'Aethiopians', see Snowden, *Blacks*, figs. 18,26,76,90; id., *Before Color Prejudice*, figs. 17,21; Desanges, in *Image*, I, 258–60 and figs. 356–7. Cf. Gellius XIX 7.6; Cat., 66.52; Manilius, *Astron.*I 767; Ovid, *Am.* I 8.3–4, *Pont.* III 3.96, *Her.* 15.36; Virg., *Aen.* I 489; Sen., *Agam.*, 212.

14 Cf. Desanges, *REL* 48 (1970) 89; id., *Catalogue* 15–16.

15 Cf. Snowden, *Before Color Prejudice* 26–34; Desanges, *Recherches sur l'activité des méditerranéens aux confins de l'Afrique: VIe siècle avant J.-C. – IVe siècle après J.-C.* (Paris 1978 – cited hereafter as *Recherches*) 217f.

16 Pliny *HN* VII 6 (*quis enim Aethiopas antequam cerneret credidit?*)

17 Cf. Calp. Flacc., *Decl.* 2 (Lehnert); Quintil. frg. 8 (Lehnert); *CCL* LXXI. 38 (Jerome); Snowden, *Blacks* 194; cf. Plut., *De sera num. vind.* 21. 563a.

18 Cf. Desanges, *RFHOM* 62 (1975) 400; id., *Catalogue* 15–16; id., in *Image* I, 248; S. Gsell, *Histoire ancienne de l'Afrique du Nord* I (Paris 1920) 294; G. Camps, *Revue de l'Occident Musulman et Méditerranéen* 7 (1970) 35f.; H. von Fleischhacker, *Paeduma* 15 (1969) 12f.

19 Cf. Pliny *HN* VI 187, VII 6, V 43; Mela I 23; Ptol., *Geog.* IV 6.5–6.

20 Desanges, *Recherches* 140 n. 128; id., in *Image* I, 248.

21 Gsell (op. cit., in n. 18, 289; cf. ibid. V, 1927, 9 n. 7) saw this; but he

came to the odd conclusion that the whiteness was an artificial colouring applied to 'black' bodies. O. Bates (*The Eastern Libyans*, London 1914, 44 nn. 1–2) rightly related the label 'Leukaethiopes' to a Graeco-Roman contrast between whites and blacks in northern Africa, and (again, rightly) saw 'Melanogaetuli' as a description of a Berber people who generally resembled blacks in colour.

22 Ptol., *Geog.* I 9.7–10; cf. IV 6,5, I 8.5.

23 Philostr., *Vita Apoll.* VI 2; Pliny *HN* VI 177 (*non Aethiopum populos, sed Arabum*); cf. Strabo XVII 3.19, 22, II 5.3; XVI 4.4.; Ptol., *Geog.* IV 6.5, I 8.5.

24 W.Y. Adams, *Nubia: Corridor to Africa*, 8; cf. B.G. Trigger, in Sylvia Hochfield and Elizabeth Riefstahl (eds), *Africa in Antiquity*, I, 26–35.

25 Strabo XVII 3.19, 23, II 5.33, 53; cf. Ptol., *Geog.* IV 6.5, I 8.7; Dionys. Perieg., V 217–8 = *GGM* III 114.

26 Diod., XX 57.5.

27 Ptol., *Geog.* IV 6.5–6; cf. Desanges, *Catalogue* 219–20; id., in *Image* I, 248.

28 Cf. Strabo XVII 1.53; Lucan IV 679; Arnobius 6.5; Ptol., *Geog.* I 8.5; Solinus 30.2; Isidore, *Etym.* IX 2.128; *Schol. in Theocr.* 7.114a (Blemmyes as *ethnos Aithiopikon melanochroun*); Philostr., *Vita Apoll.*, VI 25; Claud., *Bell. Gild.*, 192. But see Strabo II 5.33, XVII 3.19; Dionys. Perieg. 217–8 = *GGM* III 114; G. and C. Picard, *Daily Life in Carthage*, 215; Desanges, *RFHOM* 62 (1975) 391f.; id., *Catalogue* 15–16, 93–5, 155, 185f., 195; id., in *Image* I, 248–58; J.Y.N. Nadeau, *CQ* 20 (1970) 338f.; id., *Mnem.* 30 (1977) 75–8; Saddington, *ANRW* II.3, 119.

29 Cf. Pet., *Sat.* 102; *Moretum* 31–5; Mart. VI 39.6–9.

30 Juv. VI 600 (the infant is imaginatively perceived as *Aethiops* in so far as the cuckolded husband, socially and legally recognized in this picture as its father, is '*Aethiopis pater*'). Achilles Tatius (III 9.2) conveys the same idea of this combination of somatic traits not by the bald term *Aethiops*, as Juvenal does, but by the term *nothos Aithiops*. The face of the groom depicted on an Athenian marble relief of the third century BC (National Museum, Athens, no. 4464) which Snowden describes as 'the pronounced Negro type' (*Image* I, 184, and figs. 231–232) may in fact have corresponded to the sort of mental picture held by Juvenal of his *decolor heres* and by Achilles Tatius of his *nothos Aithiops*.

31 Cf. Calp. Flacc. 2 (Lehnert); Quintil., frg. 8 (Lehnert).

32 Diod., XX 57.5; Sextus Emp., *Adv. math.* XI 43; Strabo XVII 3.19; Ptol., *Geog.* IV 6.5; Pliny *HN* VI 70; cf. Pet., *Sat.* 102; Manilius, *Astron.* IV 722–30; Arrian, *Anab.* V 4.4., *Ind.*, 6.9; Philostr., *Vita Apoll.* VI 2.

33 Pliny *HN* VI 70; Arrian, *Ind.* 6.9; cf. Christine Bolt, *Victorian Attitudes to Race* (London/Toronto 1971) 187–8.

34 The contrasts occur in texts from a variety of literary genres, ranging from epic and elegiac poetry to historiography, biography, essays and encyclopaedic compilations. See above, nn. 32–3.

35 Cf. Philostr., *Vita Apoll.* VI 2, 11, 16, III 20.

36 Pliny *HN* VI 70; Diod., XX 57.5; Arrian, *Ind.* 6.9.

37 Pet., *Sat.* 102.

38 Cf. J.A. Rogers, *Sex and Race: Negro-Caucasian Mixing in All Ages and All Lands*, II (New York 1942) 379; J.H. Griffin, *Black Like Me* (2nd edn.) (New York 1977).

39 Snowden (*Blacks* 6, and *Before Color Prejudice* 10) gives passing notice to this text, but the main line of his argument is unaffected by it.

40 Pet., *Sat.* 102.

41 Ibid.; Pliny *HN* II 189.

42 Suet., *Dom.* 12.2; cf. L.A. Thompson, 'Domitian and the Jewish tax', *Historia* 31 (1982) 339.

43 Cf. S.W. Baron, *A Social and Religious History of the Jews* (2nd edn.) (New York 1952) II, 238; B. Lewis, *Race and Color in Islam*, 33–4; Snowden, *Before Color Prejudice*, 134 n. 156.

44 Cf. Thompson, *PACA* 17 (1983) 8.

45 Pet., *Sat.* 19.3 (*frigidior hieme Gallica*).

46 *PL* LXII. 695; cf. Pliny *HN* II 189; Vitruv. VI 1.3–4; Ptol., *Tetrab.* II 2.56; Firmicus Maternus, *Math.* I 2.1; Snowden, *Blacks* 262 n. 32.

47 Cf. Caes., *BG* I 39.1, II 30.4; Hor., *Epodes* 16.7; Vitruv. VI 1.3; Ovid, *Met.* VI 715; Strabo IV 4.2; Lucan II 54; Sen., *De ira* III 26.3; Pliny *HN* II 189–90; Lucian, *Dial. meretr.* 2. 282; Amm., XV 12.1; Tert., *De cultu fem.* II 6.1; Claud., *Carm. min.* 17.41, 196–197, *In Ruf.* II 108–110, *In Eutrop.* I 380; Polemo 32, 41 (Foerster); Adamantius II 31 (Foerster); Sherwin-White, *Racial Prejudice in Imperial Rome* 57–8; Balsdon, *Romans and Aliens* 60f., 216.

48 Cf. Pet., *Sat.* 110; Mart. V 68, IV 37.2; Lucian, *Dial. meretr.* 5. 290, 11. 309, 12. 314; Tert., *De cultu fem.* II 7.1, 6.1–3.

49 Pliny *HN* II 189 (*candida atque glaciali cute. . .flavis promissis crinibus*).

50 Sherwin-White, *Racial Prejudice in Imperial Rome*, 57; cf. André, *Étude* 176f.

51 Significantly, the two characters settle for a disguise that proves to be quite effective (until their identity is betrayed by the *voice* of one of them): complete shaving of heads and eyebrows, together with a skilfully painted imitation of branding on the forehead with the mark of the recaptured runaway slave, *FVG(itivus)*: Pet., *Sat.* 103–5.

52 The several conventional contrasts of this kind cited by Snowden (*Blacks* 171f.) point to the same perception on the part of the Romans.

53 S.I. Oost, *Galla Placidia Augusta*, 39.

54 This too is the import of the frequent conventional contrasts noted by Snowden (*Blacks*, 171f)

55 Lucian, *Hermotimus* 31.

56 Snowden, *Before Color Prejudice* 37.

57 Ibid.; cf. Oost, op. cit. 39 (my italics).

58 Cf. Colette Guillaumin, *L'idéologie raciste* 65.

59 Cf. Hiroshi Wagatsuma, in J.H. Franklin (ed.), *Color and Race* 129f.; H.R. Isaacs, ibid. 91–2.

60 Although these terms might occasionally describe a tawny complexion, that usage does not appear in conventional contrasts

between somatic types, and it is evident that Lucian here rests his choice of examples upon a conventional and convenient contrast of somatic types: *Aethiops–albus* (or *leukos*)–*candidus* (or *xanthos*, or *flavus*).

61 Cf. Ps.-Arist.67; Adamantius II 31; Polemo 36 (all in R. Foerster, ed., *Scriptores physiognomonici Graeci et Latini*); Snowden, *Blacks* 171f., 262 n. 32; Claud., *Bell. Gild.* 419, *In Eutrop.* I 380, *In Ruf.* II 108–10, *Cons. Stil.* II 240–1.

62 *Moretum* 31–5; Mart. VI 39.6–9; cf. Diod., III 8.2, 28.1; Ptol., *Tetrab.* II 2.56; Pliny *HN* II 189–90; Sextus Emp., *Adv. math.* XI 43; Arrian, *Ind.* 6.9. No other classical writer mentions the trait described by Petronius as 'scarred forehead' (*cicatrices*), but the fact that it is occasionally portrayed by artists on faces of blacks suggests that some Romans did see it as a mark of blacks, or at least black slaves; cf. Snowden, *Before Color Prejudice*, 15.

63 Cf. Cracco Ruggini 1979, 121–2; ead., 1974, 147; Mauny, *J.Afr.H.* 12 (1971) 159; Desanges, *REL* 48 (1970) 94; id., in *Image* I, 257–68; J. Leclant, ibid., 270; Snowden, *Blacks*, 183f.; id., *Before Color Prejudice*, 65–7; Warmington, *Afr.Hist.St.* 4 (1971) 385.

64 R. West, *Back to Africa*, 15. K.L. Little (*Negroes in Britain*, 218) observes that, even in 1948, 95 per cent of white Britons had no first-hand personal knowledge of 'coloured people'. Cf. Christine Bolt, *Victorian Attitudes to Race*, 5.

65 Mart. X 12.

66 Cf. Cohen, *Français et Africains*, 62, 158.

67 André, *Étude* 124f.

68 Banton, *Race Relations* 374.

69 Ibid.

70 Cf. Cat., 39. 12; Mart. X 68.3; André, *Étude* 47, 55, 123f. In regard to British perceptions some thirty years ago, my own personal experience suggests that, when attempts were actually made to distinguish blacks from 'Pakistanis', the distinction was often erroneous. I recall witnessing an English observer approach a group of students consisting of two Caribbean blacks (both undoubtedly *Aethiops* in the Roman perceptual context) and one white South African, and 'identify' the lighter-coloured of the two blacks as 'Pakistani'. That observer owed his acquaintance with the 'Pakistani appearance' almost entirely to the presence of a Pakistani cricket team in England at the time (summer 1954).

71 Sen., *De ira* III 26.3; cf. *Actus Petri cum Simone* (in *Acta apostolorum apocrypha*, ed. R.A. Lipsius and M. Bonnet) 22, where a demoniac apparition is described as *in aspectu Ethiopissimam, neque Aegyptiam, sed totam nigram* ('in appearance very much a black African; not Egyptian, but completely black'), a description in which 'completely black' in itself sums up the totality of the black African appearance. Cf. Diod. III 29.1 (*melanes kath' hyperbolēn*); Ptol., *Geog.* I 9.7 (*katakorōs melanes*); Heliod. II 30 (*akribōs melas*); *GGM* I 148: Agatharchides (*melanes exaisiōs*); Lucan X 221–2; Pliny *HN* XXII 2; Isidore, *Etym.*, I 37.24; Jerome, *Ep.* 40.2.

72 Cf. Mart. VI 39.6; Lucian, *Navig.* 2, 6, 45, *Gallus* 13, *Philops.* 34; Adamantius II 31 (in R. Foerster, ed., *Scriptores physiognomonici Graeci et Latini*, I).

73 Remarks all cited by W.D. Jordan, *White over Black*, 5, 15 (my italics); cf. Cohen, *Français et Africains* 26f.; D.B. Davis, *The Problem of Slavery in Western Culture* (New York 1966) 447.

74 Cited by Jordan, op. cit. 12. See also above, n. 71, for similar usages of terms meaning 'extremely black' in Graeco-Roman writing.

75 Cf. Cohen, op. cit. 31–2.

76 HA *Firmus* 4 (*capillo crispo. . .vultu nigriore*), *Tyr. trig.* 30.15; Amm., XXII 16.9, 16.33; Cat., 39.12; Mart., X 68.3; Ach. Tat. III 9.2; cf. André, *Étude* 47, 55, 123f.; Snowden, *Blacks* 258 n. 10, 161 n. 28.

77 Pliny *HN* VII 51.

78 Ach. Tat. III 9.2.

79 Cf. *Bell. Afr.* 19: *hybrida*, referring however to persons whose parentage is 'mixed' not in the sense of mixed somatic types (in popular modern terms, mixed 'races'), but in terms of legal status. Cf. Val. Max., VIII 6.4; Suet., *Aug.* 19. For earlier Roman awareness of the great diversity of somatic appearance that was possible in persons of mixed black and white parentage, cf. Lucretius IV 1218–26; Arist., *Hist. an.* VII 6. 586a, *Gen. an.* I 18. 722a. See also Antigonus, *Mir.* 112; Plut., *De sera num. vind.* 21. 563a; Erna Lesky, *Die Zeugungs- und Vererbungslehren der Antike*, 88f.

80 Juv. VI 600.

81 For George Best's report, cf. W.D. Jordan, *White over Black*, 15; for that of the Fellow of the Royal Society, cf. F.O. Shyllon, *Black People in Britain: 1555–1833* (London 1977) 104.

82 Cf. Lucretius IV 1210–32; Arist., *Gen.an.*, IV 3. 769a, *Hist.an.*, VII 6. 586a; Lactantius, *De opif. dei*, 12; Antigonus, *Mir.* 112; Plut., *De sera num. vind..*, 21. 563a; Pliny, *Ep.* I 12.4; Cyril Bailey (ed.), *T. Lucreti Cari, De rerum natura libri sex* (Oxford 1947), III, 1313–16; Erna Lesky, op. cit. (n. 79), 88–94; G.E.R. Lloyd, *Science, Folklore and Ideology: Studies in the Life Sciences in Ancient Greece* (Cambridge 1983) 58–111.

83 Plut., *De sera num. vind.*, 21. 563a.

84 Cf. H.M. Last, 'The social policy of Augustus', in *Cambridge Ancient History* X (Cambridge 1952), 443–7; M.N. Andreev, 'La lex Julia de adulteriis', *Studii Clasice* 5 (1963) 165–80; J.F. Gardner, *Women in Roman Law and Society* (London 1986), 117–31; A.N. Sherwin-White, *The Letters of Pliny: a Historical and Social Commentary* (Oxford 1966), 393–4 (on Pliny, *Ep.* VI 31.4–6).

85 *PL* LXIV.30,56,79,132–3,145–6 (Boethius); cf. *PG* LXIV.1279–82 (Meletius); *CSEL* XXVIII 1.78 (Augustine): Aug., *De civ. dei* XVI 8; Courtès, in *Image*, II.1, 11–14.

86 See above, n. 82.

87 Juv. VI 599–601: Mart., VI 39.6–9.

88 Heliod., IV 8; cf. E. Feuillâtre, *Étude sur les Éthiopiques d'Héliodore*, 11, 19; Snowden, *Blacks*, 96–7. For one thing, it was obviously less easy for a socially prominent white adulteress than for a humble one to

make a convincing claim to a black ascendant as the explanation of a black or *decolor* infant produced by her, since the facts of her ancestry would be far less open to misrepresentation. Moreover, upper class husbands were evidently more inclined than their humble counterparts to be sceptical about the popular 'genetic' explanations when the issue concerned infants produced by their own wives, so they would usually see a 'black heir' as proof of adultery with a humble black man. Cf. Rogers, *Sex and Race*, I (9th edn.), 158, 175. On the general theme of unwanted infants, cf. J.P.V.D. Balsdon, *Life and Leisure in Ancient Rome* (London 1969) 82f.; id., *Roman Women: Their History and Habits* (London 1962) 193–9.

89 *CIL* IV 1943; *CLE* I, 40.

90 F.J. Dölger, *Die Sonne der Gerechtigkeit und der Schwarze: eine religionsgeschichtliche Studie zum Taufgelöbnis* (Liturgiegeschichtliche Forschungen 2, Münster 1918), 52–3. For metaphorical usages of *Aegyptius* and *Aegyptiacus* in the sense of *Aethiops* (or *niger* and *ater*), cf. *TLL* I, 963.

91 Cf. F. Schulz, 'Roman registers of birth and birth certificates', *JRS* 32 (1942) 78–91, *JRS* 33 (1943) 55–64.

92 Juv. VI 599–601 ('*Aethiopis* pater'); Ach. Tat., III 9.2 (*nothos Aithiops*), with the emphasis on *Aithiops*, and suggesting a person whose colour is 'brown' rather than 'black' (cf. ibid. IV 5.2: the blackness of the *Aithiopis chroia*), but whose morphology marks him out as *Aethiops* in general appearance, in contrast with the Nilotic pirates of this scene, who have a similar 'brown' colour but a 'caucasian' morphology.

93 For *decolor*, cf. Ovid, *Ars am.* III 130, *Met.* IV 21, *Trist.* V 3.24; Prop., IV 3.10; Juv., VI 600.

94 Cf. J. Rex, *Race Relations in Sociological Theory*; M. Banton, *White and Coloured*, 39; H. Tajfel, 'Social and cultural factors in perception', in G. Lindzey and E. Aronson (eds.), *The Handbook of Social Psychology*, III (2nd edn) (Reading, Mass. 1969), 323f.

95 The earlier of these two cases (documented on British television) occurred sometime in the 1970s. The second was documented on TV-am, London, on 20 May 1986, and in the London *Star* of 20 and 21 May 1986. Of much significance is the powerful urge displayed by the women to divorce their 'black' husbands; and in the more recent case the wife actually obtained the desired divorce, leaving her 'black' husband in order to marry a 'white' man.

96 Cf. Rex, op. cit.

97 T.F. Pettigrew, G.W. Allport, and E.O. Barnett, 'Binocular resolution and perception of race in South Africa', *Brit.J.Psych.* 49 (1958) 265–78.

98 Cf. Tajfel, op. cit. (n. 94), 329.

99 Ibid., 329; Allport, *The Nature of Prejudice*, 133.

100 Cf. Snowden, *Blacks*, 182f., 270 n. 3; id., *Before Color Prejudice*, 15–17, 95, figs. 20–1, 25ab; id., in *Image* I, 184, 216–17; Leclant, ibid. 315 n. 80.

101 One must indeed largely agree with R. Mauny (*J.Afr.H.* 12, 1971, 158; *Gnomon* 43, 1971, 830) and others (Shinnie, *AHR* 89, 1984, 103;

Desanges, in *Image* I, 260; Leclant, ibid. 282) in questioning a number of such identifications of 'blacks' in the cultural context of the ancient iconography (for example, Snowden, *Blacks*, figs 63,67,68,75,86,101; id., *Before Color Prejudice*, figs. 25,49,53,58; id. in *Image* I, figs.275,285,286,300,321,331–2,334). In the Roman perceptual context such faces will have been seen as 'swarthy' for the most part, and in some cases as 'white', rather than as representative of the *Aethiops* type.

102 This is noticeable in the works of Beardsley, Snowden, Wiesen, and Devisse discussed earlier.

103 A similar process of biological absorption was at work in Britain between the sixteenth century and the eighteenth, and indeed even in the nineteenth century (J. Walvin, *Black and White: The Negro in English Society*, 46–100, 197–9; cf. M. Banton, *The Idea of Race*, 54; K.L. Little, *Negroes in Britain*, 190–1). But perhaps a closer similarity with the Roman situation should be seen in that of Argentina, whose 'non-white' population, amounting to 16 per cent of the total in 1852, had entirely disappeared into the 'white' mainstream by the early twentieth century (H. Hoetink, *Slavery and Race Relations in the Americas*, 187–8). A very similar process was also operative in Puerto Rico and Cuba (see below, n. 108). On the question of the supply of Roman slaves, cf. W.V. Harris, 'Towards a study of the Roman slave trade', *Mem.Am.Ac.* 36 (1980) 117–40; K.R. Bradley, 'On the Roman slave supply and slavebreeding', in M.I. Finley (ed), *Classical Slavery* (London 1987), 42–64.

104 Snowden, *Blacks*, 184–5.

105 J.M. Cook, *CR* 22 (1972) 254 (my italics).

106 Pliny, *HN* VII 51; Pet., *Sat.* 102; Plut., *De sera num. vind.*, 21. 563a.

107 H. Hoetink, *The Two Variants in Caribbean Race Relations*, 180f.; W.D. Jordan, *White over Black*, 169; W.B. Cohen, *Français et Africains*, 157–9.

108 Hoetink, *The Two Variants in Caribbean Race Relations*, 185f.; id., *Slavery and Race Relations in the Americas*, 187–8.

3 THE EVIDENCE IN ITS IDEOLOGICAL CONTEXT

1 G.W. Allport, *The Nature of Prejudice*, 20f., 189f.

2 Cf. A.H. Richmond, *Man* 57 (1957) art. no. 145, 120–1; M. Gluckman, *Race* 4 (1962) 18–19; Allport, op. cit., 191f.

3 W.D. Jordan, *White over Black*, 11–43; W.B. Cohen, *Français et Africains* 9–14, 21–7. 52f.; J. Walvin, *The Black Presence*, 12–13; I. Sachs, *The Discovery of the Third World*, 26–7.

4 Cat., 39, 37; cf. Allport, op. cit. 191f.

5 Cf. Y.A. Dauge, *Le barbare*, 396f., 463f.

6 Cf. Strabo II 5.6, 5.8, 5.32, IV 5.4, III 2.15, XVII 1.3; Suet., *Iul.* 76.3 (*semibarbari*); Sen., *Polyb.* 18.9 (*barbari humaniores*); cf. L.A. Thompson, *Platon* 31 (1979) 213–29; J. Vogt, *Kulturwelt und Barbaren*, 35–48.

7 Cf. Dauge, *Le barbare*, 381f., 413f., 485f., 511f.; J. Gaudemet, *Studii Clasice* 7 (1965) 37f.

8 R. Lonis, *Ktema* 6 (1981) 74, cf. 82f.; K.E. Müller, *Geschichte der antiken Ethnographie* II, 1–19.

9 Cf. Diod., III 2.2–3.1; Sen., *De ira* III 20.2; Lucian, *Zeus trag.* 37, *Prom.* 17, *De sacrif.* 2; Ps.-Lucian, *Philopatris* 4; Paus., I 33.4; Philostr., *Vita Apoll.* VI 4, 21; *Imag.* I 7, II 7; Dionys. Perieg. 559–61 = *GGM* III 139; Heliod., IX 20–1, 24, 26, X 39; A. Lesky, *Hermes* 87 (1959) 27–34; Cracco Ruggini 1974, 142f.; ead. 1979, 109f., 119f.; J. Desanges, *REL* 48 (1970) 91; Lonis, op. cit. 74f.; E. Lévy, 'Les origines du mirage scythe', *Ktema* 6 (1981) 57f.; R. Drews, 'Aethiopian Memnon: African or Asiatic?', *Rh.M.* 112 (1969) 191–2; K. Trüdinger, *Studien zur Geschichte der griechisch-römischen Ethnographie* (Basel 1918) 133–46.

10 Juvenal (VI 527–529), the last hostile witness to the popularity of this cult, complains (of upper-class Roman women): *ibit ad Aegypti finem calidaque petitas/ a Meroe portabit aquas ut spargeret in aede/ Isidis antiquo quae proxima surgit ovili.* Cf. M. Malaise, *Les conditions de pénétration et de diffusion des cultes Égptiens en Italie* (Leiden 1972) 68–75, 102f., 111, 127–41, 317–330; J. Leclant, in *Image* I, 278–85; Snowden, *Blacks* 191–2.

11 Cf. Ovid, *Ars am.* I 53, *Am.* I 8.3–4, 13.33–4, III 5.43–4, *Pont.* III 3.96–7; Virg., *Aen.* I 489; Sen., *Agam.* 212; Cat., 66.52; Gell., XIX 7.6; Manil., *Astron.* I 767; Corippus, *Ioh.* I 186; Cracco Ruggini 1979, 119–20; Snowden, *Blacks* 144–55 and figs. 18, 26, 90; id., *Before Color Prejudice*, 71–3 and figs 17, 19–21, 42–3; id., in *Image* I, figs. 155–7, 167–73; Desanges, ibid., 258–60 and figs 356–7. Cf. Lonis, op. cit. 75f.

12 Lucian, *Fugitivi* 8, *De astrol.* 3–5; cf. Philostr., *Vita Apoll.* VI 6–17, 22–23; Steph. Byz., *Ethnika* (ed. A. Meineke, Berlin 1849, repr. Graz 1958) 47 'Aethiops': *Aethiopes* were the first 'to have honoured the gods and to have used laws.'

13 Ps.-Callisthenes III 21–3 (Kroll); cf. Lonis, op. cit. (n. 8) 82.

14 Heliod., IV 8.3, 12.1, VI 1–2, IX 1.5, 4.4, 26.2, X 4.1, 5.2, 16.5–10, 23.4, 25.1; Lonis, op. cit. (n. 8), 81–2; E. Feuillâtre, *Étude sur les Éthiopiques d'Héliodore* (Paris 1966) 11–41.

15 Origen, *Comm. in cant. canticorum* II 367–9; Greg. Naz., *Oratio* 40 = *PG* XXXVI. 397; cf. J.M. Courtès, in *Image* II.1, 22; Snowden, *Before Color Prejudice*, 102.

16 This seems generally accepted, although somewhat earlier dates have been assigned to the poem by some scholars; e.g., F. Vian in his Budé edition of the work (Paris 1963), xix-xxii. The persisting vitality of the epic and utopian theme of *Aethiopes* is also indicated by Lactantius Placidus (*Comm. in Theb.*, ed A. Jahnke, Leipzig 1907, 5.427), Stobaeus (IV 2.25: a 'golden age' innocence attributed to 'the Aethiopians'), and Stephen of Byzantium (*Ethnika*, ed. Meineke, 47: religion and law 'invented' by 'the Aethiopians').

17 Luxorius 7 (trans. Rosenblum). According to the legend, Zephyrus (the West Wind) was Memnon's brother; cf. C.J. Fordyce (ed.),

Catullus (Oxford 1961) *ad* Cat. 66. 52–8. But the poetic linkage of the black *auriga* to Aeolus and Zephyrus emphasizes his great speed as a racing charioteer.

18 Warmington, *Afr.Hist.St.* 4 (1971) 385; Snowden, *Before Color Prejudice*, 69.

19 Cracco Ruggini 1979, 109f., 119f.; ead. 1974, 142f.; Warmington, op. cit. 385; Snowden, *Before Color Prejudice*, 69, 71–3, 127–8 n. 87; cf. Lucian, *De astrol.* 31, *Fugitivi* 8; Philostr., *Vita Apoll.* VI 6–17, 22–23; Diod., III 2.2–3.1.

20 Cf. Snowden, *Blacks* 144f., 181–2, figs. 18, 26, 90; Desanges, in *Image* I, 258–60 and figs. 356–7.

21 Cf. W.V. Harris, *ZPE* 52 (1983) 87–111; H.C. Youtie, *ZPE* 17 (1975) 202; id., *HSCP* 75 (1971) 161–76; A.H.M. Jones, *The Later Roman Empire*, II, 997.

22 P.L. Shinnie, *AHR* 89 (1984) 103.

23 Lonis, *Ktema* 6 (1981) 82–83; cf. Cracco Ruggini 1979, 119f.; E. Lévy, *Ktema* 6 (1981) 57f.; K.E. Müller, *Geschichte der antiken Ethnographie*, II, 135–48.

24 Graeco-Roman literature indicates some awareness of the psychological process of adaptation to strange or 'inappropriate' somatic characteristics – a process which has been studied in modern contexts by several social scientists; cf. F. Heider, *The Psychology of Interpersonal Relations* (New York 1958) 188f.; G.W. Allport, *The Nature of Prejudice*, 129f., 261–81, 300f.; H.E.O. James and Cora Tenen, 'How adolescents think of peoples', *Brit.J.Psych.* 41 (1951) 145–72; eid., *The Teacher was Black* (London 1953); cf. Hiroshi Wagatsuma, in J.H. Franklin (ed.), *Color and Race*, 150–3. For ancient comments on this phenomenon, cf. *GGM* I, 118 (Agatharchides); Lucretius IV 1283 (habituation renders one blind to physical *vitia*); Ovid, *Am.* II 653–4 (physical defects cease to exist in the eyes of those who become habituated to them over time).

25 Cf. Lucian, *Fugitivi* 8, *De astrol.* 3; Philostr., *Vita Apoll.*VI 6–17, 22–23; Diod., III 2.2–3.1; Snowden, *Before Color Prejudice*, 51, 69, 71f.

26 Lonis, op. cit., 83–4.

27 Snowden, *Before Color Prejudice*, 58. That argument, indeed, hardly harmonizes with Snowden's own outline of the importance of the mythic image as an indication of Roman attitudes. As we shall see, even the Graeco-Roman doctrine of ethnic diversity as a function of climate and geography stereotyped *Aethiopes* (along with all other southern peoples) as unwarlike, in contrast with northern barbarians, and a stereotype of blacks as 'cowardly' was also part of Roman physiognomonic lore; cf. Strabo XVII 1.54; Vitruv., VI 1.5–11; R. Foerster (ed.), *Scriptores physiognomonici Graeci et Latini*: Adamantius II 33, 37, Polemo 36, 54, Ps.-Arist. 9; Thompson, *Platon* 31 (1979) 228–9.

28 Cf. Diod., III 2–7; Strabo XVII 1.54; Pliny, *HN* VI 182; Ptol., *Tetrab.* II 2.56; Heliod., II 31.3–4, 32.1–3, VI 1–2, IX 4.4; Ps.-Call., III 23. 8–12; E. Feuillâtre, op. cit. (n. 14), 13, 21, 37–8, 41; Cracco Ruggini 1974, 160f., 171–8; ead. 1979, 120f.; A.M. Demicheli, *Rapporti di pace e*

di guerra dell' Egitto romano con le populazioni dei deserti africani, 127–58.

29 Cf, Strabo XVIII 1.3 (the majority of the *Aethiopes* are backward, owing to the natural deficiencies of their habitats), XVII 1.54; Ptol., *Tetrab.* II 2.56 (most *Aethiopes*, like most Scythians, are savages owing to their unfavourable climate and geographical milieu); Paus., I 33.4 (the 'most just' *Aethiopes* live in Meroe and 'the Aethiopian plain'); Diod., III 2–3.7, 8.3–5, 9.2, 12–27, 34.7–8; Pliny, *HN* IV 35, V 46, VI 35, 188, 194–195; Philostr., *Vita Apoll.* VI 2; Solinus 30.7; Origen, *De princip.* II 9.5; Thompson, *Platon* 31 (1979) 228–9; id., *Klio* 64 (1982) 383f.

30 Diod., III 2–3.7, 4–8; Pliny, *HN* VI 182: *nec tamen arma Romana ibi solitudinem fecerunt: Aegyptiorum bellis attrita est Aethiopia vicissim imperitando serviendoque.* Cf. Thompson, *Platon* 31 (1979) 228–9.

31 Strabo XVII 1.54; cf. Ptol., *Tetrab.* II 2.56; Thompson, op. cit. (n. 30) 228f.

32 Cf. Müller, *Geschichte der antiken Ethnographie, II*, 16f.; M. Benabou, in L. Poliakov (ed.), *Hommes et bêtes*, 149–51; Germaine Aujac, *Strabon et la science de son temps* (Paris 1966) 307–9; Lonis, *Ktema* 6 (1981) 87.

33 Cf. Desanges, *Recherches*, 3f.; A.M. Demicheli, op. cit. (n. 28) 18f.

34 Cf. Müller, op. cit. (n. 32), II, 1–19, 77, 97, 107f.; Demicheli, op. cit. (n. 28), 12–13; Desanges, *Recherches*, 3f.

35 R. Hallet, *The Penetration of Africa* (London 1965) 38; cf. I. Sachs, *The Discovery of the Third World*, 17–18; C. Cipolla, *Literacy and Development in the West* (Harmondsworth 1969); R.S. Schofield, 'Dimensions of illiteracy: 1750–1850', *Explorations in Economic History* 10 (1972–1973) 445f.; F. Furet and J. Ozouf, *Lire et écrire: l'alphabétisation des Français de Calvin à Jules Ferry* (Paris 1977); L. Stone, 'Literacy and education in England: 1640–1900', *Past and Present* 42 (1969) 69–139; Harris, *ZPE* 52 (1983) 87–111; Youtie, *ZPE* 17 (1975) 202; id., *HSCP* 75 (1971) 161–76; Jones, *The Later Roman Empire*, II, 997; Desanges, *Recherches*, 3f.

36 Cf. F.W. Walbank, *HSCP* 76 (1972) 157; Saddington, *ANRW* II.3, 115; P. Bienkowski, *De simulacris barbarorum gentium apud Romanos* (Cracow 1900); Annalina Calo Levi, *Barbarians on Roman Imperial Coins and Sculpture* (New York 1952); Winkes, *ANRW* I.4, 899f.; Müller, *Geschichte der antiken Ethnographie*, II, 11–12; Lonis, *Ktema* 6 (1981) 85–6. Public speakers often found it convenient to trot out caricatures and negative stereotypes of foreign peoples, and this was all the more to be expected in situations of genuine conflict between Rome and foreign peoples (cf. Cic., *Flacc.* 9–12, 66–9, *Prov. cons.* 10, *Scaur.* 42–4; Quintil., XI 1.89; Livy, XXXVI 17.5; Balsdon, *Romans and Aliens*, 30f.; Cèbe, *La caricature et la parodie*, 138f).

37 A confusion particularly noticeable in parts of Roman Africa: cf. *Anth.Lat.* 182–3, 293, 353–4; *Passio Perpetuae* 10 (in J.A. Robinson, *Texts and Studies: Contributions to Biblical and Patristic Literature*, I.2, Cambridge 1891, 76); F.J. Dölger, *Die Sonne der Gerechtigkeit und der Schwarze*, 52–3.

38 Herodotus II 104; cf. Mart., IV 42.5, X 12.12; *TLL* I, 963 (*Aegyptius*

and *Aegyptiacus* as synonyms of *niger* and *ater*). Alexandria, after all, was not *in* Egypt, but *near* Egypt (*ad Aegyptum*).

39 Cf. Lonis, op. cit. (n. 36). 86, 81; Müller, op. cit. (n. 36), II, 1–19; J. Glissen, 'Le statut des étrangers à la lumière de l'histoire', *Rec.Bodin* 9 (1958) 27f.

40 Cf. Vell., II 117–18; Sen., *De ira* I 11.3–4; Tac., *Ann*, II 14.2f.; Claud., *Bell. Get.* 423–34; Themistius 11b–c (Dindorff); Prudentius, *Contra Symm.*, I 449f., II 807f.; Dauge, *Le barbare* 213f.; Vogt, *Kulturwelt und Barbaren*, 10, 17f., 34f., Cracco Ruggini, *Athenaeum* 46 (1968) 146f.; Walbank, *HSCP* 76 (1972) 158; Saddington, *ANRW* II.3, 120–122; Thompson, *Klio* 64 (1982) 383–401; id., Platon 31 (1979) 213–30.

41 Cracco Ruggini, *Athenaeum* 46 (1968) 141f.; ead. 1979, 109–21; ead. 1974, 151f., 171f.; Dauge, *Le barbare* 136–7, 211–304, 472–8; Sherwin-White, *Racial Prejudice in Imperial Rome*, 86f.

42 Lonis' argument to the contrary (op. cit. 86), suggesting a Roman military concern about Aethiopia since the last quarter of the first century BC, is not acceptable; cf. Cracco Ruggini 1974, 161f.; ead. 1979, 120; Desanges, *Recherches* 321–66; Demicheli, op. cit. (n. 28), 127–58.

43 Cf. Allport, *The Nature of Prejudice*, 191–204, 367f.

44 Cracco Ruggini 1974, 160f., 173–8; ead. 1979, 120f.; cf. Demicheli, op. cit. (n. 28), 127–58; Desanges, *Catalogue*, 154–5, 195; id., *Recherches* 321–66; P, Romanelli, *Storia delle province romane dell'Africa*, 606f.; H.J. Diesner, *Der Untergang der römischen Herrschaft in Nordafrika*, 13f. For the notion of 'Aethiopian' involvement in these conflicts, cf. Claud., *Bell. Gild.*, 188f.; Corippus, *Ioh.* IV 197–8.

45 Cracco Ruggini 1974. 151f., 161f.; ead. 1979, 119f.

46 Cf. Pliny, *HN* VI 177; Ptol., *Geog.* I 9.7–10, IV 6.5, I 8.5; W.B. Cohen, *Français et Africains*, 158, 31–2, 62.

47 Although the ethnographers distinguished between certain peoples of 'Aethiopia' in terms of physical appearance, even indicating that some of these so-called 'Aethiopians' were not people of the *Aethiops* somatic type, the salient distinction made by the reading public in general was undoubtedly the one indicated by the ethnographical contrasts between a 'cultivated' minority and an 'uncivilized' (*agrios*, in the Greek texts) 'majority of the Aethiopians'; the educated public will have made the distinction as a habit of mind established by what Allport (*The Nature of Prejudice*, 20f., 189f.) calls the 'screening and selective' mental process that serves the human urge 'to maintain simplicity in perception.' Cf. Diod., III 2–7, 8.3–5, 9.2, 12.27, 34.7–8; Strabo XVII 1.3, 1.54, 3.19, II 5.3, XVI 4.4.; Pliny, *HN* V 46, VI 188, 194–195, 182, 177; Ptol., *Tetrab.*, II 2.56, *Geog.*, I 9.7–10, IV 6.5; Paus., I 33.4; Philostratus, *Vita Apoll.* VI 2. This pattern of thinking, emphasizing cultural rather than somatic 'Aethiopian' categories (cf. Philostratus, *Imag.* II 7, *Vita Apoll.* VI 2), was obviously also encouraged by the fact that in everyday life and experience in the Roman world *Aethiops* had the specific meaning of 'black African', designating a somatic type.

48 *PL* XXV. 1091–2 (Jerome); cf. *Psalms* 67 (68).32; Origen, *De princip.*
II 9.5; Claud., *Bell. Gild.*, 188–92, *Cons. Stil.* I 264–9; A. Cameron,
Claudian, 192–8; J. Devisse, in *Image*, II.1, 61. For a depiction of Circe
as black, cf. Snowden, *Before Color Prejudice*, fig. 43 (terracotta skyphos
in the British Museum).
49 Allport, *The Nature of Prejudice*, 368.
50 Claud., *Carm. min.* 23 (74).1–2, 25 (30, 31).61–3, 28 (47).16–23, *Cons.
Stil.* I 351, *De tert. cons. Hon.* 20–1; cf. Cracco Ruggini 1979, 120f.;
Lonis, *Ktema* 6 (1981) 86.
51 Cracco Ruggini 1974, 161f.; ead. 1979, 120; cf. Philostr., *Vita Apoll.*,
VI 6–17, 22–3.
52 Cf. Lucian, *Bis acc.* 2; Ps.-Lucian, *Philopatris* 4 (satirical tones in
allusions to the Homeric theme of *Aethiopes*).
53 Cf. Allport, *The Nature of Prejudice*, 170.
54 *PG* LXVI. 1092–7.
55 *Anth.Lat.* 183; Claud., *Bell. Gild.*, 188–95.
56 *PG* LXV. 284, LXVII. 1377b–d; *PL* LXXIII. 959, XLIX. 563–4.
57 Anon., *De rebus bell.*, 2.3; R. MacMullen, *Enemies of the Roman Order:
Treason, Unrest and Alienation in the Empire* (Cambridge, Mass. 1967),
192f., cf. 164–85, 249–54 (riots arising mostly from hunger in times of
acute food-shortages which 'badly strained the social fabric' and often
led to destructive violence of humble against humble). Cf. A.H.M.
Jones, *The Later Roman Empire*, III, 1059f. (general apathy of the
humble).
58 Cf. Dauge, *Le barbare*, 211–19; Vogt, *Kulturwelt und Barbaren*, 34f.;
Cracco Ruggini, *Athenaeum* 46 (1968) 147–51; ead. 1979, 133; Müller,
Geschichte der antiken Ethnographie, II, 194–258.
59 Vitruv., VI 1.3–11; Diod., III 34.7–9; Hippoc., *Aer.* 12, 17–24, *Diait.*,
2.37; Cic., *De div.*II 84, 89, *De fato* 7; Lucretius VI 722, 1109; Ovid,
Met. II 235–6; Lucian X 221–2; Sen., *QN* 4a.2.18; Mela I 68, II 16f.,
76, III 33; Pliny, *HN* II 189–90; Strabo II 3.7, III 1.1, VI 4.1, XV
1.22, XVII 1.3; Ptol., *Tetrab.* II 2–4; Manilius, *Astron.* IV 711–59;
Tert., *De anima* 20, 25; Paus., IX 21.6; Firmicus Maternus, *Math.*, I 1;
Claud., *In Eutrop.* I 380, *In Rufin.*, II 108–10, *Cons. Stil.*, II 240–1, *Bell.
Gild.*, 419, *Carm. min.*, 23 (74).1–2; Macrob., II 5. 10–12; E. Bernand,
Inscriptions métriques de l'Égypte, no. 26.5–6; Erna Lesky, *Die Zeugungs-
und Vererbungslehren der Antike*, 95f., 107–9; Germaine Aujac, *Strabon et la
science de son temps*, (Paris, 1966) 270–3; Trüdinger, *Studien zur Geschichte
der griechisch-römischen Ethnographie*, 37f., 120f.; Müller, op. cit. (n. 58),
I, 137f, 310f., II, 14f., 107–15, 141f., 172–80, 195, 230–58; Dauge, *Le
barbare*, 476f.
60 Toynbee, *A Study of History*, I, 253.
61 Snowden, *Blacks*, 176; id., *Before Color Prejudice*, 85–8.
62 Vitruv., VI 1.10–11; cf. Ptol., *Tetrab.* II 2.56; Müller, op. cit., II, 172.
63 Desanges, in *Image* I, 257; *Anth.Lat.* 183,, cf. 182, 189. Some
iconographic caricatures which grotesquely exaggerate *Aethiops*
somatic 'defects' also indicate a sensory aversion to the negroid
physiognomy on the part of their creators (cf. Bugner, in *Image*, I, 16;

Leclant, ibid., 273–8; Cèbe, *La caricature et la parodie*, 345–54).

64 Vitruv., VI 1.10; cf. Dauge, op. cit., 470f., 361f.

65 W.D. Jordan, *White over Black*, 33–4, 171f., 216f., 227; W.B. Cohen, *Français et Africains*, 23 (citing Arab sources, including the Europeanized Arab, Leo Africanus); ibid., 9–14, 21–4, 38–45, 52f., 62. This early European stereotype also branded blacks as pleasure-loving, excessively lazy, fond of dancing, and 'without laws' (ibid., 52f.), as Tacitus (*Hist.* I 11) says of Egypt at the time of its annexation by Rome (*insciam legum*).

66 Cf. Cohen, op. cit., 42–5, 85–9; Jordan, op. cit., 78f.

67 For the location of the North African littoral in the *juste milieu* and the hinterland in the southern zone, cf. Ptol., *Tetrab.*, II 2–3; Mela I 40; Strabo XVII 3.7, 3.15; Claud., *Cons. Stil.*, I 337–8, II 257.

68 Cf. B. Lewis, *Race and Color in Islam*, 35–8; D.B. Davis, *The Problem of Slavery in Western Culture*, 50.

69 Cf. J.B. Duroselle, *L'Idée d'Europe dans l'Histoire*, 49–57, 105f. D. Hay, *Europe: The Emergence of an Idea* (2nd edn) 104f.; Jordan, *White over Black*, 254–9; P.D. Curtin, *The Image of Africa*, 51, 65f., 377f.; Cohen, *Français et Africains*, 308.

70 Cf. Jordan, *White over Black*, 3–43, 78f., 94f.; Cohen, *Français et Africains*, 9–14, 21f., 38–46, 52f., 60f., 85f., 308; J. Walvin, *Black and White: the Negro in English Society, 1555–1945* (London 1973), 16f.; E.J.B. Rose, *Colour and Citizenship*, 14, 591; M. Banton, *White and Coloured*, 57–9, 68f.

71 A point rightly stressed by B.H. Warmington, *Afr.Hist.St.* 4 (1971) 384–5, and Snowden, *Before Color Prejudice*, 70–1.

72 Cf. M.I. Finley, *The Listener*, 79 (1968) 147–8; C.R. Whittaker, *Phoenix* 15 (1971) 188.; R. MacMullen, *Enemies of the Roman Order*, 173f.; J.P. Waltzing, '*Étude historique sur les corporations professionnelles chez les Romains depuis les origines jusqu'à la chute de l'empire d'Occident*, I (Louvain 1885) 415f.

73 Anon., *De physiogn.* (ed. J. André) 2; cf. Johanna Schmidt, 'Physiognomik', *RE* 20.1 (1941) 1064–74; Elizabeth C. Evans, *Physiognomics in the Ancient World*. The influence of this 'science' among the humbler classes of society in the Roman world is suggested by Pliny's (*HN* XI 274) reference to its doctrines as *vulgo narrata* and by the fact that Petronius attributes expertise in it to an *ancilla* in his fictional work (*Sat.*, 126.3).

74 Cf. *Scriptores physiognomonici Graeci et Latini* (ed. R. Foerster), I: Adamantius II 31; Polemo 32–3, 36, 40–1; Ps.-Arist., 9, 67, 69; Anon., *De physiogn.* (ed. André), 9, 12, 14, 81, 88; Sherwin-White, *Racial Prejudice in Imperial Rome*, 9f.

75 Anon., *De physiogn.* (ed. André), 14f., 23f., 48, 51, 79, 92–3; *Scriptores physiogn.* (Foerster), I: Polemo 25–6, 32–3, 35–6, 39–44, 56; Ps.-Artist., 9, 13, 61, 67–9; Adamantius II 31–3, 35–7, 46–7.

76 See above, nn. 74–5.

77 Caes., *BG* VII 42.2.

78 Tac., *Agric.* 11 (*colorati vultus, tortique plerumque crines, et posita contra*

Hispaniam Hiberos veteres traiecisse easque sedes occupare fidem faciunt). This explanation may not have been altogether unfounded, but its ready acceptance no doubt owed much to the stereotype association of these physical traits with the south, and of blondness and pale whiteness with the north.

79 Tac., *Germ.* 30. In a recent discussion on a similar theme, B.D. Shaw ('Eaters of flesh, drinkers of milk: the ancient Mediterranean ideology of the pastoral nomad', *Anc.Soc.* 13/14, 1982–1983, 5–31) likewise notes the vitality of the pastoralist stereotype, which is a constant theme in classical literature and 'seems to have overridden any empirical investigation of barbarian peoples' (ibid., 24). Cf. Müller, *Geschichte der antiken Ethnographie*, II, 13–14; Vogt, *Kulturwelt und Barbaren*, 14.

80 Cf. Allport, *The Nature of Prejudice*, 165–180.

81 Cf. J.M. Courtès, in *Image* II.1, 22; Jordan, *White over Black*, 33f.; J. Walvin, *Black and White*, 11f.; Cohen, *Français et Africains*, 46f.

82 Cf. Courtès, op. cit.

83 Servius, *ad* Virg., *Aen.* VIII 646; Calp. Flacc. frg. 2 (Lehnert); cf. Balsdon, *Romans and Aliens*, 218.

84 Cf. Mart., VI 39, IV 42.3–4, VII 30; Juv. VI 83–4, 592–601; Pliny, *HN* VII 51; Plut., *De sera num. vind.* 21. 563a; Pet., *Sat.* 110, 126.5–7; Ovid, *Her.* IV 34; Lucian, *Sat.* 29, *Gallus* 32; M.I. Finley, *Aspects of Antiquity* (Harmondsworth 1972) 127f.; J. Carcopino, *Daily Life in Ancient Rome* (Harmondsworth 1962) 107f.; J.P.V.D. Balsdon, *Roman Women: Their History and Habits* (London 1962) 79, 197–9, 209f.; id., *Life and Leisure in Ancient Rome* (London 1969) 283, 297.

85 On the black female stereotype, cf. *Moretum* 31–5; Juv. XIII 163; Lucretius IV 1168; Gell., III 12; Snowden, *Blacks* 182 and fig. 5; ibid. 272–73 n. 4. Just as early modern Europeans commented unfavourably on the 'large Breastes' of West African women (Jordan, *White over Black*, 8–10), Romans regarded excessive mammary endowment as a defect (*vitium*) in a woman, or even as a divine curse (cf. G.J. de Vries, 'Maiorem infante mamillam', *Mnem.*ser. 3, 12, 1945, 160). On black macrophallism as an iconographic theme, cf. Cèbe, *La caricature et la parodie*, 351, 354; Snowden, *Blacks* 180; id., in *Image* I, 220 and fig. 284; Desanges, ibid. 257, 260, fig. 347. J. Leclant (ibid. 273, 278) observes that statuettes of macrophallic blacks 'were often symbols of fertility and fecundity in the Graeco-Roman world'; and A.J.B. Wace (*ABSA* 10, 1903–1904, 110) saw them as potent charms. Martial (I 87) satirizes a contemporary who kept a sombre-faced *Aethiops* boy as a homosexual pet; cf. Epiphanius, *Adv. haeret.* 64.2 (alleged temptation of Origen into sodomy with an *Aethiops*).

86 *CIL* IV 6892 (The author may have been a slave; *nigra* in the context of a group of prostitutes in a brothel, as in this particular case, can hardly refer to any but an exotic or rare type of physical appearance: the scribbler's sentiments presuppose such a rare type as distinct from a merely dark-skinned girl or a brunette, and so the graffito should be taken as alluding either to black prostitutes in general or to a

particular black prostitute. But, in any case, it clearly exudes sexual curiosity and emphasizes the exoticism of one or more black prostitutes (probably slave-girls) as sex objects offering a *rare* experience in Pompeian brothels. Cf. *CIL* IV 1520. The customers of these slave-girl prostitutes were mostly slaves, but they also included men of the upper classes, especially youths (cf. Balsdon, *Roman Women*, 25–26). On the escapades of Heliogabalus with black prostitutes, cf. HA, *Heliog.* 32.5.

87 Allport, *The Nature of Prejudice*, 374.

88 Cf. Courtès, in *Image* II.1, 19–22.

89 J. Devisse, in *Image* II.1, 62.

90 Ennodius, *Ep.* 7.21 = *Mon.Germ.Hist.* VII, 246; Palladius, *Hist.Laus.* 2 = *PL* LXXIV.347; cf. Devisse, op. cit., 22.

91 Epiphanius, *Adv. haeret.* 64.2; *Pistis sophia* 140; *PL* LXXIII.879; *Actus Petri cum Simone* (in R.A. Lipsius and M. Bonnet, eds, *Acta apostolorum apocrypha*) 22.

92 *PG* LXVII. 1376–1381; LXV. 281–290; XXXIV. 1065–1068; *PL* XLIX. 563–564; V. Latyshev, *Menologii anon. Byz. saec. X*, 330–334; J. Devisse, in *Image* II.1, 62, 225 nn. 258, 261; Snowden,*Before Color Prejudice*, 102.

93 Cited by P.D. Curtin, *The Image of Africa*, 46.

94 Cf. J.J. Hecht, *Continental and Colored Servants in Eighteenth-Century England* (Northampton, Mass. 1954), 33f., 45f.; Curtin, op. cit., 35, 46; J. Walvin, *Black and White*, 52f.

95 Pet., *Sat.* 110–112; Juv. VI 591; Mart., VI 39.6–9, VII 30; Plut., *De sera num. vind.* 21.563a; Pliny, *HN* VII 51.

96 G.W. Allport, *The Nature of Prejudice*, 181–2; K.J. Gergen, in J.H. Franklin (ed.), *Color and Race*, 117–23; D.B. Davis, *The Problem of Slavery in Western Culture*, 447–52; Jordan, *White over Black*, 4–20; C.N. Degler, *Neither Black nor White: Slavery and Race Relations in Brazil and the United States* (New York 1971) 207–11; M. Banton, *The Idea of Race*, 14, H. Levin, *The Power of Blackness* (New York 1959) 35–38; Cohen, *Français et Africains*, 38f., 307; D. Zanan, 'White, red, and black: color symbolism in black Africa', in A. Portmann and A. Ritsema (eds.), *The Realms of Colour* (Eranos-Jahrbuch, 41, Leiden 1974) 365–96.

97 Cf. Hor., *Sat.* I 4.85: *hic niger est; hunc tu, Romane, caveto* ('This man is black-hearted; Roman, beware of him'); Ovid, *Am.* I 13.33–6, *Pont.*, IV 14.45–6; Tib., III 5.5; Prop., II 11.3–4, 24b.33–4, 27.10; Virg., *Aen.* IV 514, *Georg.* II 130; Claud., *Cons. Stil.* I 278–9; *CLE* 608.3, 682.7, 813.2; Plut., *De lib. educand.* 17; Marcus Aurel., *Med.* IV 18, 18; André, *Étude* 43f., 57; F.J. Dölger, *Die Sonne der Gerechtigkeit und der Schwarze*, 53; Cracco Ruggini 1979, 114; Snowden, *Before Color Prejudice*, 83. The Latin verb *denigrare* ('to blacken', 'denigrate') is perhaps the most apposite example of all, but the fact that its usage is not attested to until the fourth century AD is perhaps significant of a more pronounced tendency towards this sort of metaphorical usage in Christian times.

98 Snowden, *Before Color Prejudice*, 83; cf. G.K. Hunter, *Proc.Brit.Ac.* 53

(1967) 140–2; R. Bastide, in J.H. Franklin (ed.), *Color and Race*, 37; K.J. Gergen. ibid., 121; J. Devisse, in *Image*, II.1, 37–8, 58–60, 80.

99 Suet., *Calig.* 57.4; *Anth.Lat.* 183, 182; cf. André, *Étude* 57, 362–4; Dölger, op. cit. (n. 97), 57–64; Bastide, op. cit. (n. 98), 35–7; Courtès, in *Image*, II.1, 32; Devisse, ibid., 37–8, 59, 80; U.E. Paoli, *Rome: Its People, Life and Customs* 281–2. 'Spooks', malignant spirits, demons and the deities of the Underworld were indeed imagined as black in colour: cf. Lucian, *Philops.* 16, 31, *Charon* 1; Hor., *Odes* II 13.21; Prop., IV 11.1–2; Sen., *Herc. Oet.*, 1704–5; Paus., VI 6.11; Pliny, *HN* II 17; Stat., *Theb.*, II 49, III 538, IV 71; Sil. Ital., *Pun.*, VIII 17; *CLE* 346.4; Ovid, *Met.*, IV 436–8; Virg., *Aen.* VI 128, 134–5, 298–9. Charon, the grim ferryman of the world of the dead, was, in similar spirit, depicted in iconography as black, snub-nosed and thick-lipped (cf. O. Waser, *Charon, Charun, Charos*, Berlin 1898, 133 fig. 12a; Dölger, op.cit., 64–75). Cf. *Anth.Lat.* 189 (where the mythical *Aethiops* Memnon is a black presage of doom for the Trojans).

100 Juv. XV 49f. Wiesen (*Cl. et. Med.*, 31, 1970, 147–8), like J.E.B. Mayor (*Thirteen Satires of Juvenal*, London 1901, II, 372), wrongly supposed that the satirical intention here is to indicate the black's 'inferior' musical skills and 'lowly' status *qua* black.

101 Claud., *Bell. Gild.*, 188–95.

102 Cf. Allport, *The Nature of Prejudice*, 181–3.

103 Cf. Ter., *Phorm.* 705; Sen., *Apocol.*, 13; Plut., *Brut.*, 48; Appian, *BC* IV 17; Florus II 17.7–8; HA, *Sev.* 22.4–5; Pet., *Sat.*, 74; Apul., *Met.* VI 26; Ps.-Lucian, *Lucius*, 22.

104 Cat., 93; cf. Cic., *Phil.* II 41 (*qui albus aterne fuerit ignoras*); Apul., *Apol.* 16 (*libenter te nuper usque albus an ater esses ignoravi*); Quintilian, XI 1.37; C.J. Fordyce (ed.), *Catullus*, 382; cf. Suet., *Calig.* 57.4; *TLL* I, 963 (*dies Aegyptius, dies Aegyptiacus*, synonymous with *dies nefastus*); Dölger, op. cit. (n. 97), 45–57; Snowden, *Before Color Prejudice*, 100–1; Cracco Ruggini 1979, 113f.

105 J.M. Courtès, in *Image* II, 19–32; J. Devisse, ibid., 35–80; Bastide, op. cit. (n. 98) 35–7; Dölger, op. cit. (n. 97), 49–75; Cracco Ruggini 1979, 113f.; Snowden, *Before Color Prejudice*, 100.

106 *PG* XXXIV. 407c; cf. *II Cor.* 11, 14; Origen, *De oratione* 27.12; Dölger, op. cit. (n. 97), 62.

107 J. Devisse, in *Image* II.1, 59; cf. *PG* LXIX.1188, XXV.1367–9, XXXVI.938; Cracco Ruggini 1979, 122–5; R. Bastide, op. cit. (n. 98), 35–37; Dölger, op. cit. (n. 97), 56.

108 *PG* LXIX.1188 (Cyril of Alexandria); cf. Snowden, *Before Color Prejudice*, 104; Cracco Ruggini 1979, 113f.; Courtès, in *Image* II.1, 10.

109 *PG* XLIV. 792.

110 G.R. Dunstan and R.F. Hobson, *Race* 6 (1965) 335; cf. Cracco Ruggini 1979, 125f.; Snowden, *Before Color Prejudice*, 100–1.

111 Dunstan and Hobson, op. cit., 336–7; cf. A.J. Festugière, *Les Moines d'Orient* I (Paris 1960) 23–29; Cracco Ruggini 1979, 127.

112 *Passio Perpetuae* (in J.A. Robinson, *Texts and Studies* I.2, 76) 10; *Actus Petri cum Simone* 22 (in Lipsius and Bonnet, eds., *Acta apostolorum*

apocrypha); *Passio Bartholomaei* (in Lipsius and Bonnet, op. cit.) 7; *Acta Xanthippae et Polyxenae* 17 (in M.R. James, *Apocrypha anecdota: Texts and Studies* II, Cambridge 1893); Dölger, op. cit. (n. 97) 54f.; Cracco Ruggini 1979, 126, 131–2.

113 *Actus Petri cum Simone*, 22 (Lipsius and Bonnet).

114 For this usage, cf. *Anth.Lat.* 182, 183, 293, 353, 354; *Passio Perpetuae* 10 (Robinson, *Texts and studies*, I.2, 76); Dölger, op. cit. (n. 97) 52–3; Tert., *De bapt.* 9 (*CSEL* XX.208). Significantly, the Greek translation of the original Armenian *Passio Bartholomaei* speaks of a demon as '*Aethiops* in appearance, black as soot' (*hōs Aithiopa mauron hōs hē asbolē*), while the Latin translation (a work of the Roman west) reads '*ingentem Aegyptium nigriorem fuligine*': 'a huge Egyptian blacker than soot' (*Pass. Barth*, 7, in *Acta apost. apocrypha*, ed. Lipsius and Bonnet).

115 Dölger, op. cit. (n. 97) 52–57; cf. L. Bugner, in *Image* I, 14; Snowden, *Before Color Prejudice*, 101–2; Cracco Ruggini 1979, 131–3.

116 Cf. R. MacMullen, *Roman Social Relations*, 88f.; T. Reekmans, *Anc.Soc.* 2 (1971) 144–5.

117 *GGM* I, 118 (Agatharchides). Centuries ago Francis Bacon also penetrated to the heart of this problem in his observation that a child's fear of the dark is as natural as an adult's fear of death, and that in either case the fear of the unfamiliar or the unknown is heightened by tales. Cf. Philostr., *Imag.* II 7; Lucretius IV 1283; Ovid, *Ars Am.* 653–4. For an instance of fear of black soldiers (on the part of men unfamiliar with blacks) in more recent European history, see W.B. Cohen, *Français et Africains*, 40. But, on the importance of personal contact as a promoter of attitudinal change in societies where blackness is disliked because it is strange and disturbing, and where no fixed patterns are imposed on black–white relations, see K.J. Gergen, in J.H. Franklin (ed.), *Color and Race*, 118–21 (citing a number of investigations by social psychologists); cf. F. Heider, *The Psychology of Interpersonal Relations*, 184f.; H.E.O. James and Cora Tenen, *Brit.J.Psych.*, 41 (1951) 145f.; eid., *The Teacher Was Black*, 71–114.

118 Allport, *The Nature of Prejudice*, 297–304.

119 Cohen, op. cit. 24, 31–2, 62, 104, 158; cf. J. Walvin, *The Black Presence*, 74f., 86–92 (Olaudah Equiano).

120 Cf. M. Malaise, *Les conditions de pénétration et de diffusion des cultes Égyptiens en Italie*, 71–5, 328–9; Snowden, *Before Color Prejudice*, 97–9; G. La Piana, 'Foreign groups in Rome during the first centuries of the empire', *HTR* 20 (1927) 203f.; J.P.V.D. Balsdon, *Romans and Aliens*, 12f.

121 La Piana, op. cit., 203f.; E.C. Polomé, 'The linguistic situation in the western provinces of the Roman empire', *ANRW* II.29.2 (1983), 510–515; J.P. Waltzing, *Étude sur les corporations professionnelles*, I, 415f.; R. MacMullen, *Enemies of the Roman Order*, 173f. Ancient comments on the psychology of the stranger include Ps.-Lucian's observation that the most delightful blessing for a stranger in a foreign land is an encounter with an old acquaintance (*Amores* 9). Similarly Lucian

pictures his Anacharsis, 'a stranger and a barbarian' in Athens, as having 'experienced no modest confusion of mind' in an atmosphere which he found wholly strange and where even sounds frightened him, while onlookers mocked his alien dress (*Scytha* 3). It was very important for the stranger to establish some local connections as soon as possible (ibid. 8–9).

122 See above, chapter 2, (84). On the question of *collegia*, Malaise (op. cit. 75f.) notes that, in Italian communities with large numbers of foreign residents, slaves and ex-slaves accounted for the majority of devotees of Isis.

123 G.W. Allport, *The Nature of Prejudice*, 129f., 165f., 181f., 261f., 300f.; K.J. Gergen, in J.H. Franklin (ed.), *Color and Race*, 113–23; id., 'Interaction goals and personalistic feedback as factors affecting the presentation of self', *J. of Personality and Soc. Psych.*, 1 (1965) 413–24; K.J. Gergen and E.E. Jones, 'Mental illness, predictability and affective consequences as stimulus factors in person perception', *J. of Abnormal and Soc. Psych.*, 67 (1963) 95–104; F. Heider, *The Psychology of Interpersonal Relations*. 22f., 188f., 192–4; J.W. Brehm and A.R. Cohen, *Explorations in Cognitive Dissonance* (New York 1962) 273; H.E.O. James and Cora Tenen, *Brit.J.Psych.* 41 (1951) 145–72; eid., *The Teacher was Black*, 71–114.

124 James and Tenen, opera cit.; cf. Hiroshi Wagatsuma, in J.H. Franklin (ed.), *Color and Race*, 150.

125 Lucretius IV 1283 (*consuetudo concinnat amorem*); cf. 1149–207; Ovid, *Ars am.* II 653–4 (*eximit ipsa dies omnis e corpore mendas/ quodque fuit vitium, desinit esse mora*); cf. *Rem. am.* 315–45, *Am.* III 3.3–9, III 7.7–8; Hor., *Sat.* I 3.38–40 (*amatorem quod amicae /turpia decipiunt caecum vitia, aut etiam ipsa haec / delectant, veluti Balbinum polypus Hagnae*). Cf. Allport, *The Nature of Prejudice*, 178f.

126 *Moretum* 31–35; HA *Sev.* 22.4–5, *Heliog.* 32.5; Philostr., *Vita Apoll.* III 11, *Vitae sophist,* II 558; *PL* XXI. 415; *Hist. monach.* (ed. E. Preuschen) VIII 35; Luxorius 7, 38, 67, 68.

127 Pliny, *HN* X 121–122; cf. Tac., *Ann.* II 85.5; Suet., *Tib.* 36.1–2; Jos., *AJ* XVIII 65–80; Juv. XII 26–8; Tib., I 3.27–28; M. Malaise, op. cit. (n. 120), 308, 390–5, 447.

128 Cf. V. Latyshev, *Menologii anon. Byz. saec. X,* 330–4; *PG* LXV.281–5; *PL* XLIX. 563–4; Cracco Ruggini 1979, 124; ead. 1974, 148.

129 HA *Sev.* 22.4–5.

130 Suet., *Calig.* 57.4; cf. Malaise, op. cit. (n. 120) 398–400, 75, 228.

131 *PG* LXIV.1279–82 (Meletius); XXVIII.54 (Athanasius); *PL* LXIV.30 (Boethius); Aug., *Civ.dei* XVI 8, *CSEL* XXVIII 1.78 (Aug., *De Genes. ad litt.*); cf. J.M. Courtès, in *Image* II.1, 11–14. For a modern restatement of the ancient argument, cf. Allport, *The Nature of Prejudice*, 171–81.

132 Courtès, in *Image* II.1, 32.

133 Devisse, in *Image* II.1, 35.

134 Cf. *Mon.Germ.Hist.*, III 246.

135 Cited by W.B. Cohen, *Français et Africains*, 39: 'les habitants sont

presque aussi noirs d'âme que de corps et leurs corps sont aussi noirs que l'on nous peint les Demons'.

136 Cf. Devisse, in *Image* II.1, 225 n. 258; L. Bugner, ibid. I, 14.

137 Courtès, in *Image* II.1, 21.

138 Snowden, *Before Color Prejudice*, 107, 101. In fact, Snowden also implies that *some* blacks were probably regarded as diabolical, in so far as he avers that 'it is highly unlikely that *large numbers* of whites', under the influence of this negative colour symbolism, 'would have regarded Ethiopians themselves as demoniacal, diabolical or evil' (ibid. 107: my italics).

139 Cf. Jerome, *Ep.* 107 = *CSEL* LV.192 (AD 403); Palladius, *Hist.Laus.* 52 = *PG* XXXIV.1145c; *PL* XXI.415 (black and virtuous monks) =*Hist. monach.* VIII 35 (in E. Preuschen, ed., *Palladius und Rufinus: ein Beitrag zur Quellenkunde des ältesten Mönchtums, Texte und Untersuchungen*, Giessen 1897); *PG* LXV.284 (antipathy and apprehension).

140 L. Bugner, in *Image*, I, 19.

141 Cf. E.J.B. Rose, *Colour and Citizenship*, 15; Allport, *The Nature of Prejudice*, 165f., 178f.

142 Cf. M. Banton, *White and Coloured*, 73; id., *Race* 1 (1959) 9–12; M. Gluckman, *Race* 4 (1962) 201; Allport, op. cit. 129f.; J. Glissen, *Rec.Bodin* 9 (1958) 5–57.

143 Lucian, *Dial. mort.* 3.337; Mart., *Spect.* 3. Lucian also speaks contemptuously of poor freeborn men working in menial jobs 'like some Indian or Scythian slave' (*Parasita* 52) and here, despite the convention of contrasting Scythian with *Aethiops* (northern with southern), 'Indian' means not *Aethiops*, but either literally Indian, or barbarian from the region of the Red Sea and Indian Ocean (cf. J. Desanges, *Annales d'Éthiopie* 7 (1967) 141–53).

144 Cf. M. Banton, *Race* 1 (1959) 13.

145 J. Devisse, in *Image* II.1, 57 (my italics).

146 K.L. Little, *Negroes in Britain*, 201–2; cf. W.D. Jordan, *White over Black*, 26f.

147 Cic., *De fato* 7, *De nat. deorum* II 42, *De div.* II 84, 89, *De leg. agr.* II 95, *Att.* IV 16.7, *De leg.* I 30, *De off.* I 50; cf. Tac., *Agric.* 11; Dauge, *Le barbare* 58; Thompson, *Platon* 31 (1979) 213–19; Sherwin-White, *Racial Prejudice in Imperial Rome*, 4f., 12–13, 57f.; Jordan, op. cit., 26f.

148 C. Lévi-Strauss, 'Race and history', in Leo Kuper (ed.), *Race, Science and Society* (Paris-London 1975) 100, 103; cf. P.D. Curtin, *The Image of Africa*, 61f.; Thompson, *Platon* 31 (1979) 213f.

149 Cf. Sherwin-White, op. cit. (n. 147), 4f.; Thompson, op. cit. (n. 148), 214f.; id., *Klio* 64 (1982) 389f.; Dauge, *Le barbare* 479f.; B.D. Shaw, *Anc.Soc.* 13/14 (1982–1983) 5–31; K.E. Müller, *Geschichte der antiken Ethnographie*, II, 78f., 97f., 135.

150 Lévi-Strauss, op. cit. 102; cf. Dauge, op. cit., 383f.

151 Colette Guillaumin, *L'idéologie raciste*, 44; cf. M. Gluckman, *Race* 4 (1962) 20.

152 Cf. Allport, *The Nature of Prejudice*, 51–7; W.W. Daniel, *Racial Discrimination in England* (Harmondsworth 1968) 211–223; E.J.B. Rose,

Colour and Citizenship, 15–33, 590. The instinctive Roman response would have matched the sentiment expressed by J.B. Duroselle (*L'idée d'Europe dans l'histoire*, 318), who admits to 'feeling more at home' in the company of a Hungarian or Spaniard than in that of an American of the Middle West, in that of a Harvard academic than in that of a European peasant, in that of the Senegalese Léopold Senghor than in that of a Dutchman or Englishman.

153 Cf. T.R.S. Broughton, *The Romanization of Africa Proconsularis* (Baltimore 1929), 226; P. Garnsey, 'Rome's African Empire under the Principate', in P. Garnsey and C.R. Whittaker (eds), *Imperialism in the Ancient World* (Cambridge 1978), 252–4; Saddington, *ANRW* II.1, 132f.

154 The attitude is clearly indicated in Virgil's (*Aen.* VI 852) vision of Rome's 'mission' as *pacis imponere morem* ('imposition' of the ways of peaceful development on other peoples). Cf. Tac., *Agric.* 21; Pliny, *HN* III 39; Mela I 66 ('the skills associated with peaceful development': *pacis artes*); F.W. Walbank, *HSCP* 76 (1972) 155–6 (Roman policy of 'rewarding conformism'), 167; G. Walser, *Rom, das Reich und die fremden Völker*, 67f.; A.N. Sherwin-White, *The Roman Citizenship* (2nd edn.), 116f.; F. De Visscher, *Rec. Bodin* 9 (1958) 195–208; J. Gaudemet, *Studii Clasice* 7 (1965) 37–47; Dauge, *Le barbare* 57–8, 381–6; Müller, op. cit. (n. 149), II, 14–16.

155 John Rex (*Race Relations in Sociological Theory*, 52) observes that 'The British in particular were ambivalent about the extent to which they wished to see natives in colonial territories socialized into roles appropriate to the new society' created by their colonial enterprise. Others have explained that the imperial 'English' ideological system did not even admit of any viable concept of Anglicization with regard to non-white colonial subjects, for the reason either that, in that ideology, the essence of 'Englishness' was not culture (something that can be absorbed by osmosis), but character (which is inherent and not absorbable), or that the individual's integrity was ideologically perceived as consisting in 'being true to his own culture' (P. Mason, *Patterns of Dominance*, 24, 31; M. Banton, *White and Coloured*, 77–8). Cf. Allport, *The Nature of Prejudice*, 368; Cohen, *Français et Africains*, 292–302; Curtin, *The Image of Africa*, 415f, 425f., 473f.; Little, *Negroes in Britain*, 203f.; Christine Bolt, *Victorian Attitudes to Race*, 190; G.D. Killam, *Africa in English Fiction* (Ibadan 1968), 71f., 159–66. On the contrasting Roman position in terms of imperial needs and interests, cf. M.I. Finley, *The Listener* 79 (1968) 146–7; P.A. Brunt, *Comparative Studies in Society and History* 7 (1965) 267–88; M. Benabou, in L. Poliakov (ed.), *Hommes et bêtes*, 143–52; Dauge, *Le barbare* 57f., 381f.; Müller op. cit. (n. 149), II, 14f., 78–9, 103f., 120–35, 194.

156 Cf. Winkes, *ANRW* I.4, 899f.; A. Calo Levi, *Barbarians on Roman Imperial Coins and Sculpture*; L. Storoni Mazzolani, *The Idea of the City in Roman Thought* (Bloomington/ London 1970), 185.

157 Pliny, *Ep.* IV 22.2; Statius, *Silv.* IV 5.45–46; Mart. XI 53; Pliny, *HN* XVI 4; cf. Walbank, *HSCP* 76 (1972) 155; Allport, *The Nature of Prejudice*, 24–7.

158 L. White, (ed.), *The Transformation of the Roman World: Gibbon's Problem after Two Centuries* (Berkeley and Los Angeles 1966), 294, 310; cf. Allport, op. cit., 24–7, 31–9.

159 Allport, op. cit., 51–57; cf. Banton, *White and Coloured*, 73–78; P. Mason, *Patterns of Dominance*, 24, 31; Little, *Negroes in Britain*, 203f.; W.W. Daniel, *Racial Discrimination in England*,. 211–23; E.J.B. Rose, *Colour and Citizenship*, 15–33, 590; J. Rex, *Race Relations in Sociological Theory*, 52; J.A. Rogers, *Sex and Race* I (9th edn), 207.

160 Cf. Jordan, *White over Black*, 12–20, 40f.; Cohen, *Français et Africains*, 32–8.

161 Cf. Lucian, *Adv. indoct.* 28; *Corpus paroem. Graec.* I 18, 146, 187, II 184, 258 (*Aithiopa smēchein*). For the suggestion of an expected somatic modification in consequence of a change of geographical milieu, cf. Strabo I 2.34, VII 3.2f., XVI 4.27; Paus., IX 21.6, VIII 29.4 ('man, like the other creatures, takes a different shape with a change of atmosphere and land'); Müller, *Geschichte der antiken Ethnographie*, I, 319–20, 331–2, II, 179–80. But, just as they accepted the impossibility of *Aethiops* blanching, Romans of the first and second centuries AD accepted as a natural fact of biology the persistence of darkness of complexion and curly hair among the British Silures (a people believed to have migrated from Spain to the 'cold north' many centuries earlier); Tac., *Agric.* 11.

162 Origen, *Comm. in cant. canticorum*, II 377 (*sol infuscare et denigrare solet. . .gentem Aethiopum. . .cui iam naturalis quaedam inest ex seminis carnalis successione nigredo, quod in illis locis sol radiis acrioribus ferveat et adusta iam semel atque infuscata corpora genuini. . .vitii successione permaneant*). Cf. E. Bernand, *Inscriptions métriques de l'Égypte gréco-romaine*, no. 26.5–6; Lucretius IV 1208–32; Pliny, *HN* VII 51; Plut., *De sera num. vind.* 21.563a; Galen, *De temperamentis* II 6; Pliny, *Ep.* I 12.4 (*nam plerumque morbi quoque per successiones, ut alia, traduntur*, on gout as a hereditary ailment); Erna Lesky, *Die Zeugungs- und Vererbungslehren der Antike*, 92f., 103f.; Cracco Ruggini 1979, 123.

163 H. Hoetink, *The Two Variants in Caribbean Race Relations*. But the concept is not, as Hoetink attempted to make it, an adequate explanation of a race relations situation (the emergence of racist structures); see M.G. Smith, *Race* 10 (1968) 133–6; N.D. Deakin, *Brit.J.Soc.* 19 (1968), 222–4; S.W. Mintz, 'Groups, group-boundaries and the perception of "race"', *Comparative Studies in Society and History*, 13 (1971), 437–50; J. Rex, *Race, Colonialism and the City*, 200–1.

164 Cf. H.J. Perkin, 'Social history', in H.P.R. Finberg (ed.), *Approaches to History: A Symposium* (London 1962), 73.

165 Hiroshi Wagatsuma, in J.H. Franklin (ed.), *Color and Race*, 129–65 (reprinted in Melvin M. Tumin, ed., *Comparative Perspectives on Race Relations*, Boston Mass. 1967, 124–139). A similar idealization of Chinese whiteness as an essential constituent of feminine beauty has been noted in Chinese literature dating from the fourth century BC, in which ladies are lauded for their 'black-painted eyebrows and white-powdered cheeks' or their 'dazzling white' or 'snow-white', untanned

skins. Cf. H.R. Isaacs, in J.H. Franklin (ed.), *Color and Race*, 91–2.
166 Pliny, *Pan.* 48.4 (*femineus pallor*); Plaut., *Capt.* 648, *Pseud.* 1218, *Asin.*
400, *Merc.* 308, *Poen.* 1113 (*specie venusta, ore atque oculis pernigris*: 'an
attractive-looking girl with very dark complexion and eyes'); Ter.,
Heaut. 1061–2, *Phorm.* 51, *Hec.* 440, *Adelphi* 849; Lucian, *Gallus* 17 (the
leukē complexion fundamental to feminine beauty); André, *Étude* 140f.,
306.
167 Tac., *Ann.* XI 16 (Italicus); Apul., *Met.* II 2, 17; Suet., *Vita Ter.*, 5;
Mart. X 12; Lucian, *Paras.* 41, *Catap.* 16, *Timon* 54, *Merc. cond.* 35
(long noses ugly in both sexes), *Navig.* 45 (ugly flat noses in
Mediterranean whites); ibid. 2 (dark skin and thick lips disfavoured),
Dionys. 2, *Gallus* 14; Anon., *De physiog.* (ed. André), 14, 79, 90, 92;
Pet., *Sat.*, 43; Ps.-Lucian, *Amores* 40; Foerster (ed.), *Scriptores physiog.
Graeci et Latini*: Adamantius II 36, 46, Polemo 39–41. The
physiognomonic literature, even when dating later than the third
century AD, for the most part faithfully repeats earlier tracts of the
same genre.
168 Wagatsuma, op. cit. (n. 165), 137.
169 Cf. Hor., *Odes* III 9.2–3; Mart., I 72.5–6, 115, II 41.11–12, IV 62,
VII 13, VIII 33; Pet., *Sat.* 131; André, *Étude* 324f.
170 Sen., *De ira* III 26.3; Vitruv. VI 1.11; Juv. XIII 162–5; Hor., *Odes* I
5.4–5, III 9.3; Mart. V 37.7–8, 68, VI 12, IX 37.2, XII 23, XIV 26;
Pet., *Sat.* 110; Lucian, *Dial. meretr.* 5.290, 11.308, 12.314; Ps.-Lucian,
Amores 40; Tert., *De cultu fem.* II 6.1–3, 7.1; Prop., II 18c.26 (*turpis
Romano Belgicas ore color*) cf. Mart. VIII 33.20 (*et mutat Latias spuma
Batava crines*); Pliny, *HN* XXVIII 191; André, *Étude* 324f.
171 Cf. Ovid, *Am.* 1.14, 3.3.2–9, *Ars. Am.* III 303, *Fasti* II 761–4, 773–4; –
Prop., II 2.3.5f., II 3.9.13–14, 32–34; Luxorius 71, 78 = *Anth.Lat.* 357,
364; Dracontius, *De raptu Helenae* 516–21; Mart., II 33, I 72.5, III
34.2, IV 62, V 47.7, VI 12, 64.3, 68, VIII 33.20, 55.18, IX 37, XII
23, XIV 26; Pliny, *HN* XXVIII 191; Hor., *Odes* I 5.4; Apul., *Met.* II
8, III 14, 19; Tert., *De cultu fem.* II 6; Lucian, *Dial. mort.* 1.333–4;
Dial. marin. 1.289–90, *Gallus* 17; Ps.-Lucian, *Amores* 41; André, *Étude*
320–7.
172 Tert., *De cultu fem.* II6.1–3; Mart., IV 29, 42, V 37.7–9, VI 12, IX
37.2, XII 23, V 68. It is noteworthy that C.C. Rogler (*Social Forces* 22,
1944, 448f.) found a similar attitude in Puerto Rico, where, despite
the generally adverse attitude to pale whiteness, the blond and fair
look in women was often seen as a highly desirable fashionable
variant. Christine Bolt (*Victorian Attitudes to Race*, 131), without quite
understanding the phenomenon, cites a Victorian English writer
whose historical survey of Near Eastern, Greek, Italian, and English
art induced him to comment, 'It is odd how persistently the supreme
ideal of female beauty is fair.'
173 G. Freyre, *The Masters and the Slaves* (New York 1946) 13–14.
174 Cf. Ovid, *Ars am.* II 653f., *Rem. am.* 315–45, *Am.*III 3.2–9, II 4.39–40;
Lucretius IV 1149–207; Mart., V 37.7, I 72, 115, IV 62, III 34, VII
13, XI 60; Hor., *Odes* I 5.4; Cat., 41.3, 43, 86.1–4; Prop., II 12.23–4,

II 25.41–2; Lucian, *Dial. mort.* 1.333–4, *Pro imag.* 5, *Gallus* 17; Ps.-Lucian, *Amores* 14, 26, 40; Apul., *Met.* II 8. But see Apul., *Met.* II 9; Prop., II 2.5; Hor., *Odes* I 33.11, *Epist.* II 3.37; Lucian, *Pro imag.* 5; Ps.-Lucian, *Amores* 26, 40 (all on the theme of beauty without blondness); on dark complexioned beauty, cf. also *Anth.Gr.* V 121, 210; Virg., *Ecl.* 10.37–9, 2.16–18.

175 Lucretius IV 1149–207; Ovid, *Rem. am.* 315–45, *Ars am.* II 653f., *Am.* III 3.2–9, 7.7–8.

176 Lucretius IV 1283 and Ovid, *Ars am.* II 653–654, on the positive effects of habituation; cf. James and Tenen, *Brit.J.Psych.* 41 (1951) 145f.; Hiroshi Wagatsuma, in J.H. Franklin (ed.), *Color and Race*, 150.

177 Cf. Sextus Emp., *Adv. math.* XI 43; Vitruv. VI 1.10–11.

178 Cf. Evans, *Physiognomics in the Ancient World*, 38–40; Luxorius 67 = *Anth.Lat.* 353; Virg., *Ecl.* 2.16–18, 10.37–9; *Anth.Gr.* V 121,210.

179 Origen, *Hom. in cant. canticorum*, I 6; *CCL* LXIX.176 (Greg. Elv.). For apologetic references to 'black' beauty in other contexts, cf. Luxorius 67 = *Anth.Lat.* 353; Virg., *Ecl.* 2.16–18, 10.37–9; *Anth.Gr.* V 121, 210.

180 Cf. Lucian, *Gallus* 17 (whiteness an essential constituent of feminine beauty); Luxorius 67.6–14.

181 Cf. Strabo IV 2.1 (*opsis*), III 4.17, VII 1.2; Ovid. *Ars am.* I 614; Apul., *Met.* V 16; Luxorius 67.6 = *Anth.Lat.* 353.6 (*forma*); Nepos, *Eumen.* 11.5 (*figura*); Pliny. *HN* XXXVI 95; Suet., *Claud.* 4; Juv. XI 140; Sen., *De ira* III 26.3; Mart., III 42, V 49, VII 87, VIII 60, XII 54, 70; Sherwin-White, *Racial Prejudice in Imperial Rome*, 6–7; W.J. Watts, *Acta Cl.* 19 (1976) 83f.

182 Cf. Snowden, *Blacks* figs 70, 72–3, 75.

183 Ovid, *Her.* 15.35–38; cf. Virg., *Ecl.* 10.37–39, 2.16–18; *Anth.Gr.* V 210; Theocr., X 26–9; Sen., *De ira* III 26.3; Juv. II 23, XIII 162f.; VIII 34f.; *Anth.Lat.* 296, 301, 310, 315, 361; J.P. Cèbe, *La caricature et la parodie*, 353–54; U.E. Paoli, *Rome: Its People, Life and Customs*, 273f.

184 HA *Heliog.* 32.5; Luxorius 43 = *Anth.Lat.* 329.

185 *CIL* IV 6892, cf. 1520.

186 *Moretum* 31–35.

187 M. Rosenblum, *Luxorius*, 195; cf. Luxorius 10, 15, 24, 29, 75.

188 Cf. Lucian, *Charon* 1, *Zeus trag.* 6, 27, *Bis acc.* 17, 27, *Lexiphanes* 23, *Litt. Prom*, 4–5, *Demonax* 54, *Anach.* 16; Ps.-Lucian, *Cynicus* 5, 19; Sen., *De ira* III 26.3; Mart. I 3, 104.10, II 32, 58, IV 55, V 49, VI 77.8, XIV 176; Juv. II 23, III 164–6, V 129–31; Apul., *Met.* II 20, 30; *Anth.Lat.* 296, 301, 310, 315, 361; Cèbe, op. cit. (n. 183) 129–40, 345–54; Paoli, op. cit. (n. 183), 272–6.

189 Mart., XIV 176; Philostr., *Vita Apoll.* III 3; Lucian, *Litt. Prom.* 4–5.

190 Quintil., VI 3.28; Pet., *Sat.* 46.1–2, 61.4; cf. Cèbe, op. cit. (n. 183); Paoli, op. cit. (n. 183), 267f.; Desanges, *REL* 48 (1970) 93.

191 Pet., *Sat.* 57; Juv. III 156–57 (*nil habet infelix paupertas durius in se/quam quod ridiculos homines facit*: 'The hardest thing to bear about the unfortunate lack of a gentleman's income is that this condition makes one an object of ridicule.')

192 Mart. VI 77.8; Lucian, *Anach.* 16; cf. Pet., *Sat.* 43 (*tollere mentum*);

Lucian, *Catap*. 16, *Gallus* 12 (*exhyptiazein*).

193 Pet., *Sat*. 61.

194 Cf. Apul., *Met*. III 11 (*lusus*), III 12 (*rubor* or shame caused by mockery), II 20, 30, III 10, 12 (derision with finger-pointing at the victim, in public places); Mart. VII 12; Pet., *Sat*. 61; Lucian, *Prom*. 8–9; Cèbe, *La caricature et la parodie*, 140, 224f.

195 Lucian, *Prom*. 8–9.

196 Cf. Pet., *Sat*. 57 (*homo inter homines* – strictly, 'a *human being* among human beings'); Apul., *Met*. III 10–12, VIII 22–5, II 20, 30; Luxorius 67.6 = *Anth.Lat*. 353.6; *Anth.Lat*. 182–183; *PG* LXV. 184, LXXIII. 970–1; Sen., *De ira* III 26.3. Rosenblum (*Luxorius*, 195) appropriately draws attention to 'the psychology of men and women striving to act as if they had attained what nature has denied to them', in the face of regular mockery of their physical defects. Cf. Allport, *The Nature of Prejudice*, 142–61.

197 Sen., *De ben*. III 28.6; Pet., *Sat*. 77 (*assem habeas, assem valeas*); cf. Lucian, *Timon* 27, *Gallus* 13, *Sat*. 35; Juv. III 86–91; Apul., *Met*. V 10; Allport, *The Nature of Prejudice*, 142–61.

198 Luxorius 29 = *Anth.Lat*. 315.

199 HA *Sev*. 22.4–5.

200 For that unacceptable view, cf. P. Mayerson, *HTR* 71 (1978) 307; W. Den Boer, *Mnem*. 24 (1971) 439; J.M. Courtès, in *Image* II.1, 20; J. Devisse, ibid., 50–51.

201 Cf. P. Mason, *Patterns of Dominance*, 1f., 11–12.

202 Translations of Arabic texts, cited by B. Lewis, *Race and Color in Islam*, 12 (my italics); cf. ibid. 13, 33–36; *PG* LXV.284; *Anth.Lat*., 183, 182.

203 *P. Oxy.* 1681.5f.; cf. H.I. Bell, '*Philanthropia* in the papyri of the Roman period', in *Hommages à Joseph Bidez et à Franz Cumont* (Collection Latomus 2, Brussels 1949). 32–3; H. Braunert, *Die Binnenwanderung: Studien zur Sozialgeschichte Aegyptens in der Ptolemäer- und Kaiserzeit* (Bonn 1964), 213 n. 59; R. MacMullen, 'Nationalism in Roman Egypt', *Aegyptus* 44 (1964) 183f.; Cracco Ruggini 1979, 116–118; L. Troiani, *Commento storico al 'Contro Apione' di Giuseppe* (Pisa 1977), 49, 146.

204 Cf. Cic., *De off*. I 129–30.

205 *P. Giess.* 40, II; C.C. Edgar and A.S. Hunt (eds.), *Select Papyri* (Loeb), 90–93 no. 215; N. Lewis and M. Reinhold, *Roman Civilization* II (New York 1955) 438f. The Greek text speaks of 'the appearance and dress of others' (*allōn opseis te kai schema*), by 'others' evidently meaning 'other social categories'. Cf. *P. Yale* 46, col. i. 13 (complaint of a victim of the contemptuous treatment that *Aigyptioi* were apt to suffer); *P. Zen*. II 66 (victimization suffered owing to inability to 'play the Hellene' – *hellēnizein*); R. MacMullen, *Roman Social Relations*, 46, 163 n. 54; *Corpus pap. Iud.* 156c (the Jewish population in Egypt represented as an almost 'Egyptian' socio-cultural category possessing an un-Hellenic mentality); *P. Oxy.* 480 (document of AD 180: a registrant at the census office divides the population of Egypt into the categories 'stranger, Roman, Alexandrian, Egyptian, freedman'); cf. MacMullen, *Aegyptus* 44 (1964) 184. For similar categorization, cf.

Eusebius, *Praep. evang.* I 9.29; Julian, *Ep.* 111. For derogation of 'rustic' manners, cf. Juv. III 67f.; Dio Chrys., XXXI 162, XXXV 11; Plut., *Moral.* 57a; Mart., VII 58.8; Cic., *Phil.* X 22, *De fin.* III 14; Apul., *Apol.*, 16.10, 9.1, 10.6, 23.5, 70.3; Philo, *In Flacc.* 78; Amm., XXI 10.8, XXX 4.2, XXXI 14.5.

206 MacMullen, *Aegyptus* 44 (1964) 190.
207 C.C. Rogler, *Social Forces* 22 (1944) 448–53; J. Walvin, *The Black Presence*, 74f., 86–92.
208 MacMullen, *Aegyptus* 44 (1964) 188–9; L. Troiani, op. cit. (n. 203), 49, 146; Jos., *Contra Apionem*, II 3–4; on Moses and other monks who were *Aethiopes*, *PG* XXIV.1065–8, 1145c, LXV. 281–90, LXVII. 1376–81; Jerome, *Ep.* 107 = *CSEL* LV. 192; cf. Snowden, *Before Color Prejudice*, 106; Cracco Ruggini 1979, 115–16.
209 Cf. W.D. Jordan, *White over Black*, 7–10; I. Sachs, *The Discovery of the Third World*, 3; id., *Annales* 24 (1968) 883–93; J. Walvin, *Black and White*, 16–43.
210 Cf. Juv. III 288–301; J. Devisse, in *Image* II.1, 57; M. Bloch, *Feudal Society*, 241–79; G.A.J. Hodgett, *A Social and Economic History of Medieval Europe*, 88f., 173–5; Betty Behrens, in *Cambridge Economic History of Europe*, (2nd edn.)V, 549–620; K.L. Little, *Negroes in Britain*, 171f., 179f.; W.D. Jordan, *White over Black*, 216f, 257; P. Mason, *Patterns of Dominance*, 1–13; I. Sachs, *Annales* 24 (1968) 883f.; Guillaumin, *L'idéologie raciste*, 28f; Cohen, *Français et Africains*, 26f.
211 J. Walvin, *Black and White: the Negro in English Society*, 9–10.
212 E. Shils, in J.A. Jackson (ed.), *Social Stratification*, 104–6.
213 Lucian, *Paras.*, 8; cf. *Bis acc.*, 34.
214 Shils, op. cit., 106; W.G. Runciman, in J.A. Jackson, ed., *Social Stratifications*, 33.
215 E. Bernand, *Inscriptions métriques de l'Egypte gréco-romaine*, no. 26. Cf. Lucian, *Bis acc.* 34, 17, *Paras.* 8, *Dionys.* 2, *Nigrin.* 24, *Dial. marin.* 1.289–90, *Menipp.* 11, *Demonax* 63, *Pro imag.* 4, *Timon* 27, *Catap.* 15, *Dial. mort.* 1.333–4, *Merc. cond.* 42, *Imag.* 11; Apul., *Met.*, II 2; J.E. Ifie and L.A. Thompson, *Museum Africum* 6 (1977–1978), 27–8; Shils, op. cit. (n. 209), 112.
216 Cf. MacMullen, *Roman Social Relations*, 6–8, 105–12; T. Reekmans, *Anc.Soc.* 2 (1971) 144f.; P. Garnsey, *Social Status and Legal Privilege in the Roman Empire*, 228–47, 258; Ifie and Thompson, op. cit., 23–9; Shils, op. cit. (n. 212), 104–13.
217 Luxorius, 67–8, 7; MacMullen, op. cit., 112, 92. Petronius' fictional character Trimalchio is perhaps the most obvious example of status inconsistency in Roman literature but see also Juv. I 24–5, 103–8, III 34–40, 132–4, VII 14–16. Tertullian (*De spect.* 22) points to the status inconsistency of jockeys (*aurigae*), who were popular heroes but at the same time men of low rank who had often begun their careers as racing charioteers in slavery; cf. Balsdon, *Life and Leisure in Ancient Rome*, 321–2.
218 Claud., *Bell. Gild*, 188–95; Apul., *Met.* V 30, VI 23; cf. MacMullen, op. cit., 92, 112.

219 *CIL* XI 600; cf. MacMullen, op. cit., 44.

220 Formal use of the terms *honestiores* and *humiliores* for these social categories is not attested to until the second century AD, and the first appearance of *clarissimus* and *egregius* as official designations is later still, but the basic pattern of stratification here indicated was operative throughout the period of four centuries on which the present work concentrates. On the whole question of legal privilege in relation to status, see Garnsey, op. cit. (n. 216), 17–100, 103–52, 182–228. The ideological imperative of *reverentia* for respectable people is bluntly expressed by a character in the novel of Petronius (*Sat.* 107–8).

221 MacMullen, op. cit. (n. 216), 105–6, 193 n. 53; H.G. Pflaum, 'Titulature et rang social durant le Haut-Empire', in C. Nicolet *et al.*, *Recherches sur les structures sociales dans l'antiquité classique* (Paris 1970), 159–85; Garnsey, op. cit. (n. 216), 103–52, 182–208; M.I. Finley, *The Ancient Economy*, 51; F. Millar, 'Condemnation to hard labour in the Roman empire', *PBSR* 39 (1984) 124–47.

222 HA *Sev*, 22.4–5; cf. Cic., *Planc.* 15; Pliny, *Ep.*, IX 5, Libanius, *Or.* 48.31, Garnsey, op. cit. (n. 216), 221f., 245f.; MacMullen, op. cit. (n. 216), 100–8, 195 n. 64; id., *Soldier and Civilian in the Later Roman Empire* (Cambridge, Mass. 1963), 91f., 103–11.

223 Cic., *De invent.*, II 56 (*potentia est ad sua conservanda et alterius adtenuanda idonearum rerum facultas*); cf. Garnsey, op. cit. (n. 216), 208; Pet., *Sat.* 14 (*sola pecunia regnat*), 77 (*assem habeas, assem valeas*).

224 Cf. Finley, *The Ancient Economy*, 44.

225 Apul., *Met.* I 21, II 2, 4f., X 18, V 10 (*nec sunt beati quorum divitias nemo novit*), *Apol.* 17; Lucian, *Nigrin.* 23, *Sat.* 35, *Paras.* 58; Plut., *Cato maior* 18.4.

226 Lucian, *Gallus*, 13–14, *Timon* 23, 27, *Paras.* 58; Juv. III 86–91.

227 Cf. MacMullen, *Roman Social Relations*, 94f.

228 Lucian, *Charon* 13, *Dial. meretr.* 19.362; Pet., *Sat.* 75; Apul., *Met.* X 27; Sen., *Controv.* 10.1.

229 Pet., *Sat.* 43, 75, 110; Lucian, *Dial. meretr.* 19.362, *Timon* 21–3, *Sat.* 29, *Gallus* 14, 17; Mart., VI 39, VII 87; Juv. I 24–5, 103–8, III 34–40, 132–4, VI 599–601, VII 14–16; cf. Reekmans, *Anc.Soc.* 2 (1971) 141–3. MacMullen ('Social history in astrology', *Anc.Soc.* 2, 1971, 106) draws attention to astrologers' predictions about wealth and prominence to be acquired through 'connections' with wealthy and distinguished acquaintances.

230 Cf. Apul., *Met* I 5; MacMullen, *Roman Social Relations*, 92–9, 6–13; id., *Enemies of the Roman Order*, 166.

231 Cf. Snowden, *Blacks*, 176–92; id., in *Image*, I, 184, 220, 224, 232, 238; Bugner, ibid., 18; Desanges, ibid., 257–65; Leclant, ibid., 278–85; Winkes, *ANRW* I.4, 909f.

232 W.V. Harris, 'Literacy and epigraphy, I', *ZPE* 52 (1983), 95–105; Harris notes the advantage enjoyed in this respect by slaves in wealthy households. The evidence on blacks relates mostly to slaves (grooms and personal attendants) in grand households.

233 Snowden, *Blacks*, 176f.

234 Winkes, op. cit., 909f.
235 This, of course, did not apply only to blacks. The social atmosphere is indicated by several texts; cf. Mart., I 72, 107, 115, II 30, III 34, 38, IV 62, V 16, 20, 56, VI 8, 39, VII 13, 30, 57, 64, 87, IX 73, X 47, 74, 76, XI 60; Pet., *Sat.* 45.7, 57.11, 61.4, 69.2–3, 74–6, 126.5–7; Juv. III 147–155, VI 82–113, VII 112–14, 124f., 138–145, 175–7, 241–3; Apul., *Met.* VIII 22; Lucian, *Gallus* 32, *Sat.* 29, *Timon* 21; Balsdon, *Roman Women*, 278–81.
236 Cf. Pet., *Sat.* 83; Mart., X 50, 53, 74.6, V 56, VI 8, VII 57, 64, IX 73; Juv. I 24–5, III 34–40, 147–55, VII 14–16, 34–5, 69–73, 82–8, 112–14, 124–8, 138–45, 175–7, 242–3; *Anth.Lat.* 384; *ILS* 5285. 5287–8; *CIL* XIV.2884; Balsdon, *Life and Leisure in Ancient Rome*, 302–24.
237 Cf. Lucian, *Nigrin.* 29, *Paras* 1; Luxorius 7, 67–8; *Anth.Lat.* 283, 353–4; M. Rosenblum, *Luxorius*, 230; Balsdon, *Life and Leisure in Ancient Rome*, 321–2; Snowden, *Blacks*, 163f. 186–7, fig. 50; id., in *Image*, I, figs 291–2.
238 Snowden, *Blacks*, 163f., 187, figs 50, 5ab; id., in *Image*, I, figs 291–2, 317, 383–4; Desanges, ibid., fig. 346; Leclant, ibid., 285; Pliny, *HN* VIII 131; Luxorius 67–8; *Anth.Lat.* 353–4; Sen., *Ep.* 85.41; Mart., I 104.9–10, VI 77.8; Ach. Tat., IV 4.6. This material relates to blacks in the occupation roles of *auriga*, gladiator, musician, and *venator*.
239 Cf. Pet., *Sat.* 46, 61; Lucian, *Somnium* 1f.; Cic., *De off.* I 150.
240 Cf. Tert., *De spect.* 22.
241 Cic., *De off.* I 150–1; cf. Sen., *Ep.* 88.21; Lucian, *Paras.* 52, *Somnium* 9; Apul., *Met.* I 7; Pet., *Sat.* 38; Pliny, *HN* XXIX 17; Dio Chrys. 7.110; Finley, *The Ancient Economy*, 44; S. Treggiari, in P. Garnsey (ed.), *Non-slave Labour in the Greco-Roman World*, 48f.
242 W.V. Harris, *ZPE* 52 (1983) 92.
243 Cf. Harris, op. cit., 91–110.
244 Philostratus, *Vita Apoll.*, III 11, *Vita sophist.*, II 588; cf. Snowden, in *Image*, I, 204, 229, figs. 265, 293–4.
245 Cf. Pet., *Sat.* 46, 57–8, 61; Lucian, *Timon* 23; Apul., *Flor.* 16, 18, 20.4, *Apol.* 4, 6, 23, 66–73, 76, 78, 87, 94, 98, *Met.* III 15, IX 35, X 1, XI 27–8; Origen, *Contra Celsum*, 3.55; MacMullen, *Roman Social Relations*, 107; T. Kotula, '*Utraque lingua eruditi*: une page relative à l'histoire d'éducation dans l'Afrique romaine', in *Hommages à Marcel Renard* (Coll. Latomus, 101–3, Brussels 1969), II, 386f.; Ifie and Thompson, *Museum Africum* 6 (1977–1978) 30–1.
246 Cf. Juv., III 182–189, 81–83; Lucian, *Timon* 23, *Navig.* 22; Pliny, *Ep.* III 14; Sen., *De ben.* III 28.6; Reekmans, *Anc.Soc.* 2 (1971) 146f.
247 Lucian, *Merc. cond.* 7, 9.
248 Cf. Juv., III 147f.; Pliny, *Ep*, IX 6; Mart., VI 82; Apul., *Met.* I 5; Lucian, *Catap.* 20, *Dial. mort.* 19.362, *Merc. cond.* 24, *Scytha* 3, *Bis acc.* 27, *Lexiphanes* 23; Ps.-Lucian, *Cynicus* 5, 19; Claud., *In Ruf.* I 325–6, II 78f.; Reekmans, op. cit.,·126, 145; MacMullen, *Roman Social Relations*, 30–1, 156 nn. 3–6. For contrasting symbols of high status, cf. Apul., *Met.* I 23, II 2, IV 23, V 10; Pet., *Sat.* 57; Mart., X 13, XII 46; Sen., *Ep.* 123.7, *De ben.* III 28.5; Lucian, *Timon* 54, *Sat.*, 29, 35, *Gallus*

11–12, *Catap.* 16, *Bis acc.* 11, *Navig.* 22, *Nigrin.* 23–4, *Merc. cond.* 3, *Somnium* 14; Epictetus, IV 6.4; Amm. XIV 6.8–10.

249 Cf. Pet., *Sat.* 107–8, 117, 124–6, 77.5; Mart., V 35, X 27, XI 59, V 81, VIII 19; Juv. III 282–5, 137–46, VII 134; Reekmans, op. cit., 131–2.

250 Apul., *Met.* VIII 25.

251 Ibid., X 39–40; cf. Ps.-Lucian, *Lucius* 44.

252 Cf. Juv. XVI 13f.; *P. Lond.* III 1171; *PSI* V 446; F.F. Abbot and A.C. Johnson, *Municipal Administration in the Roman Empire* (Princeton 1926) 467 no. 139, 476 no. 141; P. Herrmann, *Neue Inschriften zur historischen Landeskunde von Lydien und angrenzenden Gebieten* (Oest. Akad. der Wiss., Phil.-Hist. Klasse, Vienna 1965), 11–12; Garnsey, *Social Status and Legal Privilege in the Roman Empire*, 247f.

253 Pet., *Sat.* 14 (*quid faciunt leges, ubi sola pecunia regnat/ aut ubi paupertas vincere nulla potest?*).

254 Cf. Pet., *Sat.* 14; Lucian, *Scytha* 8–9; Ps.-Lucian, *Lucius* 4; Apul., *Met.* II 18; Reekmans, *Anc.Soc.* 2 (1971) 136, 153.

255 Lucian, *Catap.* 15; cf. *Gallus* 14; Juv. VI 413–18.

256 Juv. III 282–8; cf. 278–81, 289–301.

257 Luxorius, 67.6 (=*Anth.Lat.* 353.6).

258 Pet., *Sat.* 32; cf. Lucian, *Prom.* 57–8; Juv. III 278–99; Ps.-Lucian, *Nero* 7.

259 Lucian, *Menipp.* 11, *Navig.* 45, *Charon* 1, *Prom.* 8, *Timon,* 23, 27, *Catap.* 16, *Zeus trag.* 14; cf. Pet., *Sat.* 37–8; Mart., VI 39.6–9.

260 Apul., *Met.* I 21; cf. II 2, 4f,. 18, V 10 (*nec sunt beati quorum divitias nemo novit*), X 18, *Apol.* 17; Ps.-Lucian, *Lucius* 4; Lucian, *Paras.* 58, *Sat.* 35, *Scytha* 8–9, *Nigrin.* 23; Pet., *Sat.* 13–14.

261 Cf. Juv. V 51–6; Sen., *De ben.* III 28.6.

262 Reekmans, op. cit., 127–53. One traditional pattern of behaviour which seems to have persisted is the politeness with which people of high status addressed elderly strangers of humble status when making requests of them: use of the polite terms *mater, parens optima, parens,* and the like (which parallel the modern West African usage of 'Mummy' and 'Daddy' in similar situations); cf. Apul., *Met.* I 21, II 3, IV 26; Pet., *Sat.* 7.

263 Cf. Juv. VI 278, 365f., 421–3, 511–21, 532–59, 599–601, VII 112–14, 175–77, 242–3, VIII 146–50, 185–88, 198–9, XI 5–8; Pet., *Sat.* 45, 110; Mart., VI 39, VIII 30, X 95; Ovid, *Her.* 4.34; Lucian, *Gallus* 17, *Sat.,* 29; Reekmans, op. cit., 122, 127–33, 143–57.

264 Origen, *Contra Celsum,* 3.55; cf. 6.15; Apul., *Met.* IV 14; Lucian, *Dial. mort.* 3.337, *Nigrin.* 21–2, *Somnium* 9; Juv. V 157–58; VIII 40–6; cf. MacMullen, *Roman Social Relations,* 6–8.

265 Ibid. 6f., 34f., 44f., 94f.; Garnsey, *Social Status and Legal Privilege in the Roman Empire,* 100, 141f., 211f., 246f.

266 *P. Oxy.* 2554; Pet., *Sat.* 44.2–3; cf. MacMullen, *Anc.Soc.* 2 (1971) 110; R. Marache, 'La revendication sociale chez Martial et Juvénal', *Rivista di Cultura Classica e Medioevale,* 3 (1961) 30–67; E.J. Kenney, 'Juvenal: satirist or rhetorician?', *Latomus* 22 (1963) 704–20. For other hints of resentment in the minds of humble people, cf. Cic., *De off.* II

85; Lucian, *Bis acc.* 4, *Gallus* 22, *Sat.* 31, *Navig.* 27; Plut., *Mor.* 822c;
Herodian, VII 3.5; Augustine, *Serm.* 345.1.

267 Cf. MacMullen, *Enemies of the Roman Order*, 192f. Significantly, riots
and demonstrations (and the associated violence, looting, and killing)
did not fall into a pattern of poor *versus* rich, even in times of famine
(ibid., 164–85).

268 Ibid., 164–85; cf. A.H.M. Jones, *The Later Roman Empire*, III, 1059f.

269 Apul., *Met.* III 10–12; cf. Pliny, *Ep.* III 14; Tac., *Ann.* XIV 42–5;
Sen., *Controv.*, 10.1; MacMullen, *Roman Social Relations*, 52–66, 4, 119;
id., *Anc.Soc.* 2 (1971), 116; Thompson, *Klio* 64 (1982), 390–1.

270 Allport, *The Nature of Prejudice*, 371.

CONCLUSION

1 Hor., *Ars poetica*, 139: 'Mountains will go into labour only to give birth
to a ridiculous little mouse.'

2 Cited by M. Banton, *White and Coloured*, 63–4, cf. 84.

3 E.J.B. Rose, *Colour and Citizenship*, 14 (with reference to Britain in the
1960s).

4 *Acts* 8.27f.; cf. J.M. Cook, *CR* 22 (1972) 254.

5 Cf. W.W. Daniel, *Racial Discrimination in England*, 219.

6 Cf. Martial, VI 39; Pet., *Sat.* 102; *Anth.Lat.* 183, 182, 189; Claud., *Bell.
Gild.*, 188–95; Juv. VI 599–601; *PL* LXXIII.879, XXI. 454; *Passio
Perpetuae* 10 (Robinson, *Texts and Studies*, I.2, 76); *Actus Petri cum Simone*
22 (Lipsius and Bonnet, *Acta apostolorum apocrypha*, 70).

7 *Moretum* 31–5.

8 Cf. J.M. Courtès, in *Image* II.1, 9–10.

9 *Anth.Lat.*, 182–3; Claud., *Bell.Gild.*, 188f.

10 *SEG* IV 192; cf. Cook, op. cit. 254; E. Bernand, *Inscriptions métriques de
l'Égypte gréco-romaine*, no. 26.

11 Cf. Pliny, *HN* VII 51; Lucretius IV 1208–32.

12 Cf. *CIL* IV 6892; HA *Heliog.* 32.5; Juv. VI 599–601; Mart., VI 39,
VII 87; Luxorius 43.

13 Luxorius 7, 67, 68.

14 Cf. M. Rosenblum, *Luxorius*, 40f., 52f.

15 Cf. *Image* I, figs. 291–2; Snowden, *Blacks*, fig. 50; Lucian, *Nigrin.* 29;
Balsdon, *Life and Leisure in Ancient Rome*, 321–2.

16 Mart., VI 39.9.

17 Cf. Alison Burford, *Craftsmen in Greek and Roman Society*, 11f.; Susan
Treggiari, in Garnsey (ed.), *Non-slave Labour in the Greco-Roman World*,
48f.; Winkes, *ANRW* I4., 908f.

18 L. Bugner, in *Image* I, 12.

19 Cf. Snowden, *Blacks*, figs 70, 72.

20 Luxorius 67.13.

BIBLIOGRAPHY

Abbott, F.F. and Johnson, A.C., *Municipal Administration in the Roman Empire* (Princeton 1926).

Adams, W.Y., 'Post-pharaonic Nubia in the light of archaeology (part 2)', *JEA* 51 (1965) 160–78.

Adams, W.Y., 'Continuity and change in Nubian cultural history', *Sudan Notes and Records* 48 (1967) 1–32.

Adams, W.Y., *Nubia: Corridor to Africa* (London 1977).

Allport, G.W., *The Nature of Prejudice* (Boston, Mass. 1954).

André, J., *Étude sur les termes de couleur dans la langue latine* (Paris 1949).

André, J., 'Virgile et les Indiens', *REL* 27 (1949) 157–63.

Andreev, M.N., 'La lex Julia de adulteriis', *Studii Clasice* 5 (1963) 165–80.

Arkell, A.J., *A History of the Sudan to 1821*, 2nd ed. (London 1961).

Aujac, Germaine, *Strabon et la science de son temps* (Paris 1966).

Bailey, C. (ed.), *T. Lucreti Cari De rerum natura libri sex* (Oxford 1947).

Bairoch, P., *Révolution industrielle et sous-développement* (Paris 1967).

Bairoch, P., 'Écarts internationaux des niveaux de vie avant la révolution industrielle', *Annales* 34 (1979) 145–71.

Baldry, H.C., *The Unity of Mankind in Greek Thought* (Cambridge 1965).

Balsdon, J.P.V.D., *Roman Women: Their History and Habits* (London 1962).

Balsdon, J.P.V.D., *Life and Leisure in Ancient Rome* (London 1969).

Balsdon, J.P.V.D., *Romans and Aliens* (London 1979).

Bang, M., 'Die Herkunft der römischen Sklaven', *RM* 25 (1910) 223–51.

Banton, M., *White and Coloured: The Behaviour of British People towards Coloured Immigrants* (London 1959).

Banton, M., 'Sociology and race relations', *Race* 1 (1959) 3–14.

Banton, M., *Race Relations* (London 1967).

Banton, M., 'What do we mean by racism?', *New Society* 341 (1969) 551–4.

Banton, M., *The Idea of Race* (London 1977).

Bardon, H., *La génie latine* (Brussels 1963).

Barron, S.W., *A Social and Religious History of the Jews* (2nd edn) (New York 1952).

Bastide, R., 'Color, racism and Christianity', in J.H. Franklin (ed.), *Color and Race* (Boston, Mass. 1968) 34–49.

Bates, O., *The Eastern Libyans* (London 1914).

Baudet, H., *Paradise on Earth: Some Thoughts on European Images of no-European Man* (London 1965).

Baynes, N.H., 'The Decline of Roman Power in Western Europe: Some Modern Explanations', *JRS* 33 (1943) 29–35.

Beardsley, Grace H., *The Negro in Greek and Roman Civilization: a Study of the Ethiopian Type* (Baltimore 1929).

Becatti, G., 'Caricatura', in *EAA* II (1959) 342–8.

Becatti, G., 'Negro', in *EAA* V (1963) 393–400.

Becatti, G., *The Art of Ancient Greece and Rome* (New York 1967).

Behrens, Betty, 'Government and society', in *Cambridge Economic History of Europe* (2nd edn), V (Cambridge 1967) 549–620.

Bell, H.I., '*Philanthropia* in the papyri of the Roman period', in *Hommages à Joseph Bidez et à Franz Cumont* (Coll. Latomus 2, Brussels 1949) 31–7.

Belloni, G.G., '*Aeternitas* e anientamento dei barbari sulle monete', in Marta Sordi (ed.), *I canali della propaganda nel mondo antico* (Milan 1976) 220–8.

Benabou, M., 'Monstres hybrides chez Lucrèce et Pline l'Ancien', in L. Poliakov (ed.), *Hommes et bêtes: entretiens sur le racisme* (Paris 1975) 143–152.

Bernand, E., *Inscriptions métriques de l'Égypte gréco-romaine* (Paris 1969).

Berreman, G.D., 'Race, caste and other invidious distinctions in social stratification', *Race* 13 (1972) 385–414.

Biddis, M.D., Review of Sherwin-White, *Racial Prejudice in Imperial Rome*, in *Race* 9 (1968) 402–3.

Bienkowski, P., *De simulacris barbarorum gentium apud Romanos* (Cracow 1900).

Bloch, M., *Feudal Society* (trans. L.A. Manyon, London 1961).

Bolt, Christine, *Victorian Attitudes to Race* (London/Toronto 1971).

Bonacasa, N., *Ritratti greci e romani della Sicilia* (Palermo 1964).

Boquet, G., 'L'image des Africains dans le théâtre élizabéthain', *Annales* 24 (1969) 893–4.

Boucher-Colozier, E., 'Quelques marbres de Cherchel au Musée du Louvre', *Libyca* (Archéologie-Epigraphie) 1 (1953) 23–38.

Bourgeois, A., *La Grèce devant la négritude* (Paris 1971).

Bradley, K.R., *Slaves and Masters in the Roman Empire: A Study in Social Control* (Coll. Latomus 185, Brussels 1984).

Bradley, K.R., 'On the Roman Slave Supply and Slavebreeding', in M.I. Finley (ed.), *Classical Slavery* (London 1987) 42–64.

Braunert, H., *Die Binnenwanderung: Studien zur Sozialgeschichte Aegyptens in der Ptolemäer- und Kaiserzeit* (Bonn 1964).

Brilliant, R., *The Arch of Septimius Severus in the Roman Forum* (Rome 1967 = *Mem.Am.Ac.* 29).

Broughton, T.R.S., *The Romanization of Africa Proconsularis* (Baltimore 1929).

Brown, L.C., 'Color in northern Africa', in J.H. Franklin (ed.), *Color and Race* (Boston, Mass. 1968) 186–204.

Brunt, P.A., 'Reflections on British and Roman imperialism', *Comparative*

Studies in Society and History 7 (1965) 267–88.

Brunt, P.A., *Italian Manpower: 225 BC-AD 14* (Oxford 1971).

Bugner, L. 'Introduction', in *The Image of the Black in Western Art* I (New York 1976) 9–32.

Burford, A., *Craftsmen in Greek and Roman Society* (London 1972).

Calo Levi, A., *Barbarians on Roman Imperial Coins and Sculpture* (Numismatic Notes and Monographs 123, New York 1952).

Cameron, A., *Claudian: Poetry and Propaganda at the Court of Honorius* (Oxford 1970).

Camps, G., 'Recherches sur les origines des cultivateurs noirs du Sahara', *Revue de l'Occident Musulman et Méditerranéen* 7 (1970) 33–45.

Carcopino, J., *Daily Life in Ancient Rome* (2nd edn) (ed. H.T. Rowell, trans. E.O. Lorimer, Harmondsworth 1962).

Cèbe, J.P., *La caricature et la parodie dans le monde romain antique des origines à Juvénal* (Paris 1966).

Chabod, F., *Storia dell' idea d'Europa* (Bari 1962).

Chirst, K., 'Römer und Barbaren in der hohen Kaiserzeit', *Saeculum* 10 (1959) 273–288.

Cipolla, C., *Literacy and Development in the West* (Harmondsworth 1969).

Cipolla, C., *European Culture and Overseas Expansion* (Harmondsworth 1970).

Cogrossi, C., 'Preoccupazioni etniche nelle leggi di Augusto sulla *manumissio servorum?*', in Marta Sordi (ed.), *Conoscenze etniche e rapporti di convivenza nell'antichità* (Milan 1979) 158–77.

Cohen, W.B., *Français et Africains: les noirs dans le regard des blancs, 1530–1880* (trans. C. Garnier, Paris 1981).

Collignon, R., 'Étude sur l'ethnographie générale de la Tunisie', *Bulletin de Géographie Historique et Descriptive* 1 (1886) 309–15.

Cook, J.M., Review of Snowden, *Blacks* in *CR* 22 (1972) 253–5.

Courtès, J.M. 'The theme of "Ethiopia" and "Ethiopians" in patristic literature', in *The Image of the Black in Western Art*, II.1 (Cambridge, Mass. 1979) 9–32.

Courtney, E., *A Commentary on the Satires of Juvenal* (London 1980).

Cox, O.C., *Caste, Class and Race: A Study in Social Dynamics* (2nd edn) (New York 1959).

Cracco Ruggini, L., 'Pregiudizi razziali, ostilità politica e culturale, intoleranza religiosa nell' impero romano', *Athenaeum* 46 (1968) 139–52.

Cracco Ruggini, L., 'Leggenda e realtà degli Etiopi nella cultura tardoimperiale', in *Atti del IVᵒ congresso internazionale di studi etiopici*, I (Rome 1974) 141–93.

Cracco Ruggini, L., 'Il negro buono e il negro malvagio nel mondo antico', in Marta Sordi (ed.), *Conoscenze etniche e rapporti di convivenza nell'antichità* (Milan 1979) 108–33.

Crook, J.A., *Law and Life of Rome* (London 1967).

Cumont, F., 'Tête de marbre figurant la Libye', *Mon.Piot* 30 (1932) 41–50.

Curtin, P.D., *The Image of Africa: British Ideas and Action, 1780–1850* (London 1965).

Daniel, W.W., *Racial Discrimination in England* (Harmondsworth 1968).

Dauge, Y.A., *Le barbare: recherches sur la conception romaine de la barbarie et de la civilisation* (Collection Latomus 176, Brussels 1981).

Davis, D.B., *The Problem of Slavery in Western Culture* (New York 1966).

Davis, S., *Race Relations in Ancient Egypt* (London 1951).

Deakin, N.D., Review of Hoetink, *The Two Variants in Caribbean Race Relations*, in *Brit.J.Soc.* 19 (1968) 222–4.

De Francisci, P., *Spirito della civiltà romana* (Rome 1952).

Degler, C.N., *Neither Black nor White: Slavery and Race Relations in Brazil and the United States* (New York 1971).

Deighton, H.S., 'History and the study of race relations', *Man* 57 (1957) art. no. 147, 123–4.

Demicheli, A.M., *Rapporti di pace e di guerra dell' Egitto romano con le populazioni dei deserti africani* (Milan 1976).

Demougeot, E., 'L'idéalisation de Rome face aux barbares à travers trois ouvrages récents' *REA* 70 (1968) 392–408.

Den Boer, W., 'The native country of Lusius Quietus', *Mnem.* 1 (1948) 327)37.

Den Boer, W., 'Lusius Quietus, an Ethiopian', *Mnem.* 3 (1950) 263–7.

Den Boer, W., 'Lusius Quietus', *Mnem.* 3 (1950) 329–43.

Den Boer, W., Review of Snowden, *Blacks*, in *Mnem.* 24 (1971) 437–9.

Desanges, J., *Catalogue des tribus africaines de l'antiquité classique à l'ouest du Nil* (Dakar 1962).

Desanges, J., 'Un mention altérée d'Axoum dans l'*Expositio totius mundi et gentium* ', *Annales d'Ethiopie* 7 (1967) 141–55.

Desanges, J., 'L'antiquité gréco-romaine et l'homme noir', *REL* 48 (1970 87–95.

Desanges, J., L'Afrique noire et le monde méditerranéen dans l'antiquité: Éthiopiens et Gréco-romains', *RFHOM* 62 (1975) 391–414.

Desanges, J., 'The iconography of the black in ancient north Africa', in *The Image of the Black in Western Art*, I (New York 1976) 246–68, 308–12.

Desanges, J., *Recherches sur l'activité des méditerranéens aux confins de l'Afrique: VIe siècle avant J.-C. - IVe siècle après J.-C.* (Paris 1978).

Deschamps, H., Review of Snowden, *Blacks*, in *Africa: Journal of the International African Institute* 41 (1971) 68.

de Visscher, F., 'La condition des pérégrins à Rome jusqu'à la constitution antonine de l'an 212', *Rec. Bodin* 9 (1958) 195–208.

Devisse, J., 'From the demoniac threat to the incarnation of sainthood: Christians and black', in *The Image of the Black in Western Art*, II.1, (Cambridge, Mass. 1979) 35–80.

de Vries, G.J., 'Maiorem infante mamillam', *Mnem.* ser. 3, 12 (1945) 160.

Diesner, H.J., *Der Untergang der römischen Herrschaft in Nordafrika* (Weimar 1964).

Diesner, H.J., Review of Snowden, *Before Color Prejudice*, in *Gnomon* 56 (1984) 373–4.

Dihle, A., 'Zur hellenistischen Ethnographie', in *Grecs et barbares* (Fondation Hardt, Entretiens sur l'Antiquité Classique 8, Geneva 1962) 205–32.

Dölger, F.J., *Die Sonne der Gerechtigkeit und der Schwarze: ein religions-geschichtliche Studie zum Taufgelöbnis* (Liturgiegeschichtliche Forschungen 2, Münster 1918).

Dowd, J., *The Negro in American Life* (New York 1926).

Drews, R., 'Aethiopian Memnon: African or Asiatic?', *Rh.M.* 112 (1969) 191–2.

Duff, J.D., (ed.), *Juvenal: Satires* (Cambridge 1962).

Dunstan, G.R. and Hobson, R.F., 'A note on an early ingredient of racial prejudice', *Race* 6 (1965) 334–9.

Duroselle, J.B., *L'idée d'Europe dans l'histoire* (Paris 1965).

Earl, D.C., *The Moral and Political Tradition of Rome* (London 1967).

Evans, E. C., *Physiognomics in the Ancient World* (Philadelphia 1969).

Eyben, E., 'Family planning in antiquity', *Anc.Soc.* 11–12 (1980–1981) 5–82.

Febvre, L., *Combats pour l'histoire* (2nd edn) (Paris 1965).

Ferguson, J., (ed.), *Juvenal: The Satires* (New York 1979).

Festugière, A.J., *Les moines d'Orient*, I (Paris 1960).

Feuillâtre, E., *Étude sur les Éthiopiques d'Héliodore* (Paris 1966).

Finley, M.I., 'Race prejudice in the ancient world', *The Listener* 79 (1968) 146–7.

Finley, M.I., *The ancient economy* (London 1973).

Finley, M.I., *Aspects of Antiquity* (Harmondsworth 1972).

Finley, M.I., *The Use and Abuse of History* (London 1975).

Fleischhacker, H. von, 'Zur Rassen- und Bevölkerungsgeschichte Nordafrikas unter besonderer Berücksichtigung der Aethiopiden, der Libyen und der Garamanten', *Paideuma* 15 (1969) 12–53.

Fordyce, C.J., (ed.), *Catullus* (Oxford 1961).

Foucher, L., *Hadrumetum* (Paris 1964).

Freyre, G., *The Masters and the Slaves* (New York 1946).

Furet, F. and Ozouf, J., *Lire et écrire: l'alphabétisation des Français de Calvin à Jules Ferry* (Paris 1977).

Gagé, J., *Les classes sociales dans l'empire romain* (2nd edn) (Paris 1964).

Gardner, J.F., *Women in Roman Law and Society* (London 1986).

Garnsey, P., *Social Status and Legal Privilege in the Roman Empire* (Oxford 1970).

Garnsey, P. and Whittaker, C.R., (eds), *Imperialism in the Ancient World* (Cambridge 1978).

Garson, R.W., 'Observations on the epigrams of Luxorius', *Museum Africum* 6 (1977–1978) 9–14.

Gartner, L.P., *The Jewish Immigrant in England: 1870–1914* (London 1973).

Gaudemet, J., 'L'étranger dans le monde romain', *Studii Clasice* 7 (1965) 37–47.

Gaudemet, J., 'L'étranger au Bas-Empire', *Rec.Bodin* 9 (1958) 209–35.

Gérard, J., *Juvénal et la réalité contemporaine* (Paris 1976).

Gergen, K.J., 'The significance of skin color in human relations', in J.H. Franklin (ed.), *Color and Race* (Boston, Mass. 1968) 112–25.

Gergen, K.J., 'Interaction goals and personalistic feedback as factors affecting the presentation of self', *Journal of Personality and Social Psychology* 1 (1965) 413–24.

Gergen, K.J. and Jones, E.E., 'Mental illness, predictability and affective consequences as stimulus factors in person perception', *Journal of Abnormal and Social Psychology* 67 (1963) 95–104.

Glissen, J., 'Le statut des étrangers à la lumière de l'histoire comparative', *Rec. Bodin* 9 (1958) 27–37.

Gluckman, M., 'How foreign are you?', *Race* 4 (1962) 12–21.

Grant, M., *The Jews in the Roman World* (London 1973).

Green, P., *Juvenal: The Sixteen Satires* (Harmondsworth 1967).

Griffin, J.H., *Black Like Me* (New York 1977).

Grueber, H.A., *Coins of the Roman Republic in the British Museum* (London 1910).

Gsell, S., *Histoire ancienne de l'Afrique du Nord*, I (Paris 1920), V (Paris 1927).

Guillaumin, C., *L'idéologie raciste: genèse et langage actuel* (Paris 1972).

Guillaumin, C., 'Les ambiguités de la notion de "race"', in L. Poliakov (ed.), *Hommes et bêtes: entretiens sur le racisme* (Paris 1975) 201–11.

Haarhoff, T.J., *The Stranger at the Gate: Aspects of Exclusiveness and Cooperation in Ancient Greece and Rome* (London 1948).

Hall, J., 'A black note in Juvenal: satire V. 52–55', *PACA* 17 (1983) 108–13.

Hallet, R., *The Penetration of Africa to 1815* (London 1965).

Han Suyin, 'Race relations and the third world', *Race* 13 (1971) 1–20.

Harris, W.V., 'Towards a study of the Roman slave trade', *Mem. Am. Ac.* 36 (1980) 117–40.

Harris, W.V., 'Literacy and epigraphy (part 1)', *ZPE* 52 (1983) 87–111.

Hay, D., *Europe: The Emergence of an Idea* (2nd edn.) (Edinburgh 1968).

Haynes, D.E.L., *Fifty Masterpieces of Classical Art in the British Museum* (London 1970).

Hecht, J.J., *Continental and Coloured Servants in Eighteenth-century England* (Northampton, Mass. 1954).

Heider, F., *The Psychology of Interpersonal Relations* (New York 1958).

Heinemann, I., 'Antisemitismus', *RE* Supplementband V (1931) 3–43.

Hermann, P., *Neue Inschriften zur historischen Landeskunde von Lydien und angrenzenden Gebieten* (Oest, Akad. der Wiss., Phil.-Hist. Klasse, Vienna 1965).

Hill, D.K., *Catalogue of Classical Bronze Sculpture in the Walters Art Gallery* (Baltimore 1949).

Hodgett, G.A.J., *A Social and Economic History of Medieval Europe* (London 1972).

Hoetink, H., *The Two Variants in Caribbean Race Relations* (London 1967).

Hoetink, H., *Slavery and Race Relations in the Americas: Comparative Notes on their Nature and Nexus* (London 1975).

Howell, P., *A Commentary on Book One of the Epigrams of Martial* (London 1980).

Hughes, E.C., 'Race relations and the sociological imagination', *Race* 5 (1964) 3–19.

Hunter, G.K., 'Elizabethans and foreigners', in A. Nicoll (ed.), *Shakespeare in his Own Age* (Shakespeare Survey 17, Cambridge 1964) 37–52.

Hunter, G.K., 'Shakespeare and colour prejudice', *Proc.Brit.Ac.* 53 (1967) 139–63.

Ifie, J.E. and Thompson L.A., 'Rank, social status and esteem in

Apuleius', *Museum Africum* 6 (1977–1978) 21–36.

Isaacs, H.R., 'Blackness and whiteness', *Encounter* 21.2 (1963) 8–21.

Isaacs, H.R., 'Group identity and political change: the role of color and physical characteristics', in J.H. Franklin (ed.), *Color and Race* (Boston, Mass. 1968) 75–97.

James, H.E.O. and Tenen C., 'How adolescents think of peoples', *Brit.J.Psych.* 41 (1951) 145–72.

James, H.E.O., and Tenen C., *The Teacher was Black* (London 1953).

Jones, A.H.M., *The Later Roman Empire, 284–602: A Social, Economic and Administrative Survey* (Oxford 1964).

Jordan, W.D., *White over Black: American Attitudes toward the Negro, 1550–1812* (Chapel Hill 1968).

Jüthner, J., *Hellenen und Barbaren* (Leipzig 1923).

Kenney, E.J., 'Juvenal: satirist or rhetorician?', *Latomus* 22 (1963) 704–20.

Killam, G.D., *Africa in English Fiction* (Ibadan 1968).

Knoche, U., *Vom Selbstverständnis der Romer* (Heidelberg 1962).

Kotula, T., 'Utraque lingua eruditi: une page relative à l'histoire d'èducation dans l'Afrique romaine', in *Hommages à Marcel Renard* (Collection Latomus 101–103, Brussels 1969) II, 386–92.

Lacoste, Y., *Géographie du sous-développement* (Paris 1967).

La Piana, G., 'Foreign groups in Rome during the first centuries of the empire', *HTR* 29 (1927) 183–403.

Last, H.M., 'The social policy of Augustus', in *Cambridge Ancient History* X (Cambridge 1952), 425–64.

Lawrence, A.W., *Later Greek Sculpture and its Influence on East and West* (New York 1969).

Leclant, J., 'Egypt, land of Africa, in the Graeco-Roman world', in *The Image of the Black in Western Art*, I (New York 1976) 269–85 and 313–15.

Leiris, M., 'Race and culture', in Leo Kuper (ed,), *Race, Science and Society* (Paris/London 1975) 135–72.

Lesky, A., 'Aithiopika', *Hermes* 87 (1959) 27–38.

Lesky, E., *Die Zeugungs- und Vererbungslehren der Antike und ihr Nachwirken* (Akad. der Wiss. und der Lit., Mainz 1950).

Lévi-Strauss, C., 'Race and history', in Leo Kuper (ed.), *Race, Science and Society* (Paris/London 1975) 95–134.

Levy, C., 'L'antijudaisme paien: essai de synthèse', in V. Nikiprowetsky (ed.), *De l'antijudaisme antique à l'antisémitisme contemporaine* (Lille 1979) 51–86.

Lévy, E., 'Les origines du mirage scythe', *Ktema* 6 (1981) 57–68.

Lewis, B., *Race and Color in Islam* (New York 1971).

Lewis, N. and Reinhold, M., *Roman Civilization* (New York 1955).

Lindsay, J., *Daily Life in Roman Egypt* (London 1963).

Little, K.L., *Negroes in Britain: A Study of Racial Relations in English Society* (London 1948).

Lloyd, G.E.R., *Science, folklore and ideology: studies in the life sciences in ancient Greece* (Cambridge 1983).

Lonis, R., 'Les trois approches de l'Éthiopien par l'opinion gréco-romaine', *Ktema* 6 (1981) 69–87.

MacKendrick, P., Review of Snowden, *Blacks* in *AJP* 94 (1973) 212–14.

MacMullen, R., *Soldier and Civilian in the Later Roman Empire* (Cambridge, Mass. 1963).

MacMullen, R., 'Nationalism in Roman Egypt', *Aegyptus* 44 (1964) 179–99.

MacMullen, R., *Enemies of the Roman Order: Treason, Unrest and Alienation in the Empire* (Cambridge, Mass. 1967).

MacMullen, R., 'Social history in astrology', *Anc.Soc.* 2 (1971) 105–16.

MacMullen, R., *Roman Social Relations: 50 BC - AD 284* (New Haven/London 1974).

Malaise, M., *Les conditions de pénétration et de diffusion des cultes Égyptiens en Italie* (Leiden 1972).

Marache, R. (ed.), *Juvénal: saturae III, IV, V* (Paris 1965).

Marache, R., 'La revendication sociale chez Martial et Juvénal', *Rivista di Cultura Classica e Medioevale* 3 (1961) 30–67.

Mason, P., 'An approach to race relations', *Race* 1 (1959) 41–52.

Mason, P., *Prospero's Magic: Some Thoughts on Class and Race* (London 1962).

Mason, P., *Patterns of Dominance* (London 1970).

Mason, P., *Race Relations* (Oxford 1970).

Mauny, R., Review of Snowden, *Blacks*, in *Gnomon* 43 (1971) 829–32.

Mauny, R., Review of Snowden, *Blacks*, in *J.Afr.H.* 12 (1971) 157–9.

Mauny, R., 'Trans-Saharan contacts and the iron age in West Africa', in *Cambridge History of Africa* II (Cambridge 1978) 272–341.

Mayerson, P., 'Anti-black sentiment in the *Vitae patrum*', *HTR* 71 (1978) 304–11.

Mayor, J.E.B., (ed.), *Thirteen Satires of Juvenal* (London 1900–1901).

Mazard, J. and Leglay, M., *Les portraits antiques du Musée Stéphane Gsell* (Alger 1958).

Mélèze-Modrzejewski, J., 'Sur l'antisémitisme paien', in M. Olender (ed.), *Pour Léon Poliakov: le racisme. Mythes et sciences* (Paris 1981) 411–39.

Millar, F., 'The world of *The Golden Ass*', *JRS* 71 (1981) 63–75.

Millar, F., 'Condemnation to hard labour in the Roman empire', *PBSR* 39 (1984) 124–47.

Mintz, S.W., 'Groups, group-boundaries and the perception of "race"', *Comparative Studies in Society and History* 13 (1971) 437–50.

Montagu, A., *Man's Most Dangerous Myth: The Fallacy of Race* (5th edn) (London 1974).

Mörner, M., *Race Mixture in the History of Latin America* (Boston 1967).

Müller, K.E., *Geschichte der antiken Ethnographie und ethnologischen Theoriebildung von den Anfängen bis auf die byzantinischen Historiographen* I (Wiesbaden 1972), II (Wiesbaden 1980).

Mykle, A., *The Song of the Red Ruby* (London 1963).

Nadeau, J.Y.N., 'Ethiopians', *CQ* 20 (1970) 338–49.

Nadeau, J.Y.N., 'Ethiopians again and again', *Mnem.* 30 (1977) 75–8.

Nicolet, C. *et al.*, *Recherches sur les structures sociales dans l'antiquité classique* (Paris 1970).

Oost, S.I., *Galla Placidia Augusta: A Biographic Essay* (London/Chicago 1968).

Paoli, U.E., *Rome: Its People, Life and Customs* (London 1963).

Paschoud, F., *Roma aeterna: études sur le patriotisme romain dans l'Occident latin à l'époque des grandes invasions* (Rome 1967).

Perdrizet, P., *Bronzes grecques d'Égypte de la collection Fouquet* (Paris 1911).

Perkin, H.J., 'Social history', in H.P.R. Finberg (ed.), *Approaches to History: A Symposium* (London 1962) 51–82.

Petersen, L., 'Der mauretanische Reitergeneral Lusius Quietus', *Das Altertum* 14 (1968) 211–17.

Pettigrew, T.F., Allport, G.W., and Barnett, E.O., 'Binocular resolution and perception of race in South Africa', *Brit.J.Psych.* 49 (1958) 265–78.

Pflaum, H.G., 'Titulature et rang social durant le Haut-Empire', in C. Nicolet *et al.*, *Recherches sur les structures sociales dans l'antiquité classique* (Paris 1970) 159–85.

Picard, G. and Picard, C., *Daily Life in Carthage* (London 1961).

Pittard, E., *Les races et l'histoire* (Paris 1924).

Pitt-Rivers, J., Review of Mörner, *Race Mixture in the History of Latin America*, in *Race* 9 (1968) 400–1.

Poliakov, L., *The History of Antisemitism* (London 1974).

Polomé, E.C., 'The linguistic situation in the western provinces of the Roman empire', *ANRW* II.29.2 (1983) 509–53.

Poulsen, F., 'Tête de prêtre d'Isis trouvée à Athènes', in *Mélanges M. Holleaux* (Paris 1913) 217–23.

Poulsen, F., *Catalogue of Ancient Sculpture in the Ny Carlsberg Glyptotek* (Copenhagen 1951).

Radin, M., *The Jews among the Greeks and Romans* (Philadelphia 1915).

Raveau, F., 'An outline of the role of color in adaptation phenomena', in J.H. Franklin (ed), *Color and Race* (Boston, Mass. 1968) 98–111.

Reekmans, T., 'Juvenal's views on social change', *Anc.Soc.* 2 (1971) 117–61.

Reinach, S., *Répertoire de la statuaire grecque et romaine* (Paris 1897).

Rex, J., *Race Relations in Sociological Theory* (London 1970).

Rex, J., 'The concept of race in sociological theory', in S. Zubaida (ed.), *Race and Racialism* (London 1970) 35–55.

Rex, J., *Race, Colonialism and the City* (London 1973).

Richmond, A.H., 'Theoretical orientations in studies of ethnic group relations in Britain', *Man* 57 (1957) art. no. 145, 120–1.

Richmond, A.H., (ed.), *Readings in Race and Ethnic Relations* (Oxford 1972).

Richter, G.M.A., *A Handbook of Greek Art* (6th edn) (London 1969).

Robinson, E.S.G., *Catalogue of the Greek Coins of Cyrenaica* (Bologna 1965).

Rogers, J.A., *Sex and Race: Negro-Caucasian Mixing in All Ages and All Lands*, I (9th edn New York 1967), II (New York 1942).

Rogler, C.C., 'The role of semantics in the study of race distance in Puerto Rico', *Social Forces* 22 (1944) 448–53.

Romanelli, P., *Storia delle province romane dell'Africa* (Rome 1959).

Roos, A.G., 'Lusius Quietus again', *Mnem.* 3 (1950) 158–65.

Roos, A.G., 'Lusius Quietus: a reply', *Mnem.* 3 (1950) 336–8.

Rose, E.J.B., *Colour and Citizenship: A Report on British Race Relations* (Oxford 1969).

Rosenblum, M., *Luxorius: a Latin Poet among the Vandals* (New York/London 1961).

Runciman, W.G., 'Class, status and power?', in J.A. Jackson (ed.) *Social Stratification* (Cambridge 1968) 25–61.

Runciman, W.G., 'Race and social stratification', *Race* 13 (1972) 497–509.

Sachs, I., 'Le noir dans l'art européen', *Annales* 24 (1969) 883–93.

Sachs, I., *The Discovery of the Third World* (Cambridge, Mass. 1976).

Saddington, D.B., 'Roman attitudes to the *externae gentes* of the north', *Acta Cl.* 4 (1961) 90–102.

Saddington, D.B., Review of Snowden, *Blacks*, in *PACA* 12 (1971) 57–8.

Saddington, D.B., 'Race relations in the early Roman empire', *ANRW* II.3 (1975) 112–37.

Schmidt, J., 'Physiognomik', *RE* XX.1 (1941) 1064–74.

Schulz, F., 'Roman registers of birth and birth certificates' (part 1), *JRS* 32 (1942) 78–91; (part 2), *JRS* 33 (1943) 55–64.

Seel, O., *Römertum und Latinität* (Stuttgart 1964).

Seltman, C.T., 'Two heads of negresses', *AJA* 24 (1920) 14–26.

Seltman, C.T., *Greek Coins: A History of Metallic Currency and Coinage down to the Fall of the Hellenistic Kingdoms* (2nd edn.) (London 1955).

Sevenster, J.N., *The Roots of Pagan Antisemitism in the Ancient World* (Leiden 1975).

Shaw, B.D., ' "Eaters of flesh and drinkers of milk": the ancient Mediterranean ideology of the pastoral nomad', *Anc.Soc.*.13–14 (1982–1983) 5–31.

Sherwin-White, A.N., *The Letters of Pliny: A Historical and Social Commentary* (Oxford 1966).

Sherwin-White, A.N., *The Roman Citizenship* (2nd edn) (Oxford 1973).

Shils, E., 'Color, the universal intellectual community and the Afro-Asian intellectual', in J.H. Franklin (ed.), *Color and Race* (Boston, Mass. 1968) 1–17.

Shils, E., 'Deference', in J.A. Jackson (ed.), *Social Stratification* (Cambridge 1968) 104–32.

Shinnie, P.L., Review of Snowden, *Before Color Prejudice*, in *AHR* 89 (1984) 103.

Shyllon, F.O., *Black People in Britain: 1555–1833* (London 1977).

Smith, M., Review of Snowden, *Blacks*, in *AHR* 76 (1971) 139–40.

Smith, M.G., Review of Hoetink, *The Two Variants in Caribbean Race Relations*, in *Race* 10 (1968) 133–6.

Snowden, F.M., 'The negro in classical Italy', *AJP* 68 (1947) 266–92.

Snowden, F.M., 'Ethiopians and the Isiac worship', *Ant.Cl.* 25 (1956) 112–16.

Snowden, F.M., 'Some Greek and Roman observations on the Ethiopian', *Traditio* 16 (1960) 19–30.

Snowden, F.M., *Blacks in Antiquity: Ethiopians in the Greco-Roman Experience* (Cambridge, Mass. 1970).

Snowden, F.M., 'Iconographical evidence on the black populations in Graeco-Roman antiquity', in *The Image of the Black in Western Art*, I (New York 1976) 133–245 and 298–307.

Snowden, F.M., *Before Color Prejudice: the Ancient view of Blacks* (Cambridge, Mass. 1983).

Solin, H., 'Juden und Syrer im weslichen Teil der römischen Welt', *ANRW* II.29.2 (1983) 587–789.

Speyer, W. and Opelt, I, 'Barbar', *JbAC* 10 (1967) 251–90.

Stone, J., 'James Brice and the comparative sociology of race relations', *Race* 13 (1972) 315–28.

Stone, L., 'Literacy and education in England: 1640–1900', *Past and Present* 42 (1969) 69–139.

Storoni Mazzolani, Lidia, *The Idea of the City in Roman Thought: From Walled City to Spiritual Commonwealth* (Bloomington/London 1970).

Sullivan, J.P., 'Martial's sexual attitudes', *Philologus* 123 (1979) 285–302.

Sullivan, J.P., 'Synchronic and diachronic aspects of some related poems of Martial', in S. Kreisic (ed.), *Comparative Literary Hermeneutics and Interpretation of Classical Texts* (Ottawa 1981) 215–25.

Sumner, W.G., *Folkways: A Study of the Sociological Importance of Usages, Manners, Customs, Mores and Morals* (Boston, Mass. 1906).

Tajfel, H., 'Social and cultural factors in perception', in G. Lindzey and E. Aronson (eds), *The Handbook of Social Psychology* (2nd edn), III (Reading, Mass. 1969) 315–94.

Thompson, L.A., 'Strabo on civilization', *Platon* 31 (1979) 213–30.

Thompson, L.A., 'The concept of purity of blood in Suetonius' *Life of Augustus*', *Museum Africum* 7 (1981) 35–46.

Thompson, L.A., 'Domitian and the Jewish tax', *Historia* 31 (1982) 329–42.

Thompson, L.A., 'On "development" and "underdevelopment" in the early Roman empire', *Klio* 64 (1982) 383–401.

Thompson, L.A., 'Observations on the perception of "race" in imperial Rome', *PACA* 17 (1983) 1–21.

Thompson, L.A., and Ferguson, J., (eds.), *Africa in Classical Antiquity* (Ibadan 1969).

Toynbee, A.J., *A Study of History*, I (London 1935).

Toynbee, J.M.C., *The Art of the Romans* (London 1965).

Treggiari, Susan, 'Urban labour in Rome: *mercenarii* and *tabernarii*' in P. Garnsey (ed.), *Non-slave Labour in the Greco-Roman World* (Cambridge Philological Society, Suppl. vol. 6, Cambridge 1980) 48–64.

Trigger, B.G., 'Nubian, negro, black, Nilotic?', in S. Hochfield and E. Riefstahl (eds), *Africa in Antiquity: The Arts of Ancient Nubia and the Sudan* (New York 1978) I, 26–35.

Troiani, L., *Commento storico al 'Contro Apione' di Giuseppe* (Pisa 1977).

Trüdinger, K., *Studien zur Geschichte der griechisch-römischen Ethnographie* (Basel 1918).

van den Berghe, P.L., *Race and Racism: A Comparative Perspective* (New York/London 1967).

Vermeule, C.C., 'Greek, Etruscan and Roman sculptures in the Museum of Fine Arts, Boston', *AJA* 68 (1964) 323–41.

Veyne, P., 'Vie de Trimalcion', *Annales* 16 (1961) 213–47.

Visscher, F. de, 'La condition des pérégrins à Rome jusqu'à la constitution antonine de l'an 212', *Rec.Bodin* 9 (1958) 195–208.

Vogt, J., *Kulturwelt und Barbaren: zum Menschheitsbild der spätantiken Gesellschaft* (Wiesbaden 1967).

Vries, G.J. de, 'Maiorem infante mamillam', *Mnem.* ser. 3, 12 (1945) 160.

von Bissing, F.W., 'Mitteilungen aus meiner Sammlung, III: Kopf einer Libyers', *AM* 34 (1909) 27–32.

von Stern, E., 'Bronzegefass in Bustenform', *JOAI* 7 (1904) 197–203.

Wace, A.J.B., 'Grotesques and the evil eye', *ABSA* 10 (1903–1904) 103–14.

Waddell, W.G., *Selections from Menander* (Oxford 1927).

Wagatsuma, Hiroshi, 'The social perception of skin color in Japan', in J.H. Franklin (ed.), *Color and Race* (Boston, Mass. 1968) 129–65; reprinted in M.M. Tumin (ed.), *Comparative Perspectives on Race Relations* (Boston, Mass. 1969) 124–39.

Walbank, F.W., 'Nationality as a factor in Roman history', *HSCP* 76 (1972) 145–68.

Walser, G., *Rom, das Reich und die fremden Völker in der Geschichtschreibung der frühen Kaiserzeit: Studien zur Glaubwürdigkeit des Tacitus* (Basel 1951).

Walters, H.B., *Select bronzes, Greek, Roman and Etruscan, in the Department of Antiquities, British Museum* (London 1915).

Waltzing, J.P., *Étude sur les corporations professionnelles chez les Romains depuis les origines jusqu'à la chute de l'empire d'Occident* (1885–1900).

Walvin, J., *The Black Presence: A Documentary History of the Negro in England: 1555–1860* (London 1971).

Walvin, J., *Black and White: the Negro in English Society, 1555–1945* (London 1973)

Warmington, B.H., Review of Snowden, *Blacks*, in *Afr.Hist.St.* 4 (1971) 383–6.

Watts, W.J., 'Race prejudice in the satires of Juvenal', *Acta Cl.* 19 (1976) 83–104.

West, R., *Back to Africa* (London 1970).

Westermann, W.L., *The Slave Systems of Greek and Roman Antiquity* (Philadelphia 1955).

White, L. (ed.), *The Transformation of the Roman World: Gibbon's Problem after Two Centuries* (Berkeley/Los Angeles 1966).

Whittaker, C.R., Review of Snowden, *Blacks*, in *Phoenix* 25 (1971) 186–8.

Wiesen, D.S., 'Juvenal and the blacks', *Cl. et Med.* 31 (1970) 132–50.

Winkes, R., 'Physiognomonia: Probleme der Characterinterpretation römischer Porträts', *ANRW* I.4 (1973) 899–944.

Youtie, H.C., '*Hypographeus*: the social impact of illiteracy in Graeco-Roman Egypt', *ZPE* 17 (1975) 201–21.

Youtie, H.C., '*Agrammatos*: an aspect of society in Egypt', *HSCP* 75 (1971) 161–76.

Zanan, D., 'White, red and black: colour symbolism in black Africa', in A. Portmann and R. Ritsema (eds), *The Realms of Colour* (Eranos Jahrbuch 41, Leiden 1972) 365–96.

Zschietzschmann, W., *Hellas and Rome* (London 1959).

INDEX